Maximilian, 1  in the Interior of North America, 1832-1834, part 3 and appendix

Prinz von Maximilian Wied

(Editor: Reuben Gold Thwaites)

(Translator: Hannibal Evans Lloyd)

Alpha Editions

This edition published in 2022

ISBN : 9789356897779

Design and Setting By
Alpha Editions
www.alphaedis.com
Email - info@alphaedis.com

As per information held with us this book is in Public Domain.
This book is a reproduction of an important historical work. Alpha Editions uses the
best technology to reproduce historical work in the same manner it was first
published to preserve its original nature. Any marks or number seen are left
intentionally to preserve its true form.

Contents

CHAPTER XXVIII[1]
WINTER SOJOURN AT FORT CLARKE, FROM NOVEMBER 8TH TO THE END OF 1833

Present State of Fort Clarke—Mr. Mc Kenzie's Journey—Peace between the Mandans and the Yanktonans—Ravages of the Cholera on the Lower Missouri—Mato-Topé—Sih-Chida—Return of my People to Fort Union—Sih-Sa—Narrative of Dipauch—Completion of our New Dwelling—Visit to a Winter Village of the Manitaries—The Great Buffalo Medicine Fête—Juggleries of the Manitari Women—Visit to the Winter Village of the Mandans—Festivity on the Sale of the Dance of the Half-shorn Head—Hunting Excursion—Cold Snow-storms—Accounts from St. Louis—Dance of the Ascho-Ochata—Violation of the Peace by the Sioux—Christmas Festivals—Dance of the Women of the White Buffalo Cow—News from Fort Union—Scarcity of Provisions—Employment of the Dogs for drawing Sledges—Dance of the Half-shorn Head in the Fort—Departure of Mr. Kipp to Fort Union—Increase of the Cold.

No important change had taken place at Fort Clarke during our absence. We found there, besides Mr. Kipp the director,[2] and his family, two interpreters, Belhumeur for the Mandan language, and Ortubize for the Sioux; the former was a half-breed Chippeway, and did not speak the Mandan language as well as Mr. Kipp.[3] Besides these men and their families there were in the fort only six white *engagés*, one of whom was a smith: some of them were married to Indian women. We unfortunately missed Mr. Mc Kenzie, who had left only four days before to return to Fort Union.[4] We had received, through him, a very welcome packet of letters from Germany, which I found here. As I had written to Mr. Mc Kenzie, requesting him to provide us with a winter residence at Fort Clarke, in order more closely to study the Indian tribes in the neighbourhood, instead of accepting his invitation to pass that season with him at Fort Union, where we should have been accommodated in a far more comfortable and agreeable manner, he had had the kindness to give orders for completing a new building at Fort Clarke, in which we were to reside. This order unfortunately came too late, and it was necessary to finish the work in a hurry in the month of November, when the frost was very severe, particularly during the nights, so that our dwelling, being very slightly built, afforded us, in the sequel, but little protection from the cold. The large crevices in the wood which formed the walls, were plastered up with clay, but the frost soon cracked it, so that the bleak wind penetrated on all sides. Our new house, which was one story high, consisted of two light, spacious apartments, with large glass windows; we inhabited one of these rooms, while the other served for a workshop for the carpenter and the joiner. Each room had a brick chimney, in which we burnt large blocks of green poplar, because, for want of hands, no stock of dry wood had been laid in for the winter. The consequence was, that we were obliged to send men every morning, with small carts or sledges, for some miles into the forest, to fetch wood for the daily consumption, which in the intense cold was a truly laborious task. An *engagé* who was employed in our service brought the wood covered with ice and snow into our room, which considerably increased the cold which we already experienced.

As our lodging was not habitable for some time after our arrival, and there was no other room in the fort, Mr. Kipp received us in the small apartment which he himself inhabited with his family, and, though our beds were removed in the morning, yet our presence made it more difficult and troublesome to find accommodation for the numerous Indian visitors who came every day. The stores of the fort were at this time well filled; there were goods to the value of 15,000 dollars, and, in the loft, from 600 to 800 bushels of maize, which a great number of Norway rats assiduously laboured to reduce. Some changes had taken place among the Indians in the vicinity of the fort. At the time of my first visit, in the summer of 1833, the Yanktonans[5] had expressed a wish to make peace with the Mandans and the Manitaries, in which they did not succeed at that time, but accomplished it in September. Two hundred tents of those Sioux had then been pitched in the prairie behind the village; they remained there three or four days, and some traces of their camp still remained. There had been feasting and dances, and Fort Clarke was crowded the whole day with Indians of the three tribes. At this time the prairie in the neighbourhood of the fort was desolate and deserted; part of the Indians had already gone to their winter villages in the forest; many, however, remained in the summer villages, and we had plenty of Indian visitors during the whole winter.

Unpleasant news was received from the United States. The cholera had again broken out at St. Louis, and carried off a great number of persons. It had been brought, by the steam-boats, to the trading-posts on the lower Missouri; at Bellevue, Major Dougherty's post, seven of the ten white inhabitants had died in a few days.[6] The major himself had been very ill, but had happily recovered. Several persons were likewise carried off at the post of Major Pilcher, formerly that of Mr. Cabanné.[7] This dangerous disease had not penetrated to that part of the country where we were; but, as there was too much reason to apprehend that it might extend so far, Mr. Mc Kenzie had taken a young physician with him to Fort Union.

Our first employment was to go on hunting excursions into the prairies round the fort, which afforded us an opportunity of collecting the seeds of the dried plants of the prairie. On one of these excursions, when Mr. Bodmer and Mr. Kipp had gone out together, they happened to separate, when a couple of Indians approached the former with their bows bent, and uttering the war-whoop; he cocked his double-barrelled gun and prepared to defend himself, when Mr. Kipp came up, and relieved him from these unwelcome visitors, the Indians taking flight as soon as they perceived him. Fresh scaffoldings for the dead were erected in the vicinity of Mih-Tutta-Hang-Kush, several Indians having died of the hooping-cough, which was very prevalent. Every day we saw inhabitants of the summer villages removing, with much baggage, laden horses and dogs, to the winter villages. Among other things they carried the strange dresses belonging to the several bands, such as the buffalo heads of the band, Berock-Ochata, and a live owl, which they keep as a fortune-teller. Other Indians dragged dead dogs by a strap, probably as a bait to catch wolves or foxes. We heard, in the village, loud lamentations, and saw the women working at the erection of a scaffold for a woman who had just died.[8]

On the 13th of November, early in the morning, several Indians arrived, who related, with much gravity, that in the preceding night they had observed an extraordinary number of falling stars, all moving in a westerly direction, which they said was a sign of war, or of a great mortality, and asked Mr. Kipp what he thought of it. Many other Indians visited us, of whom several were in mourning, that is, rubbed over with white clay, and all of them spoke of the ominous phenomenon. They were much pleased with Mr. Bodmer's Indian drawings, and asked us many questions about their enemies, the Blackfeet. Among our most constant visitors were the distinguished chief, Mato-Topé, and Sih-Chida (the yellow feather). The former came with his wife and a pretty little boy, to whom he had given the name of Mato-Berocka (the male bear). He brought his medicine drum, painted red and black,[9] which he hung up in our room, and so afforded Mr. Bodmer an opportunity of making a drawing of it. Sih-Chida, a tall, stout young man, the son of a celebrated chief now dead, was an Indian who might be depended on, who became one of our best friends, and visited us almost daily. He was very polished in his manners, and possessed more delicacy of feeling than most of his countrymen. He never importuned us by asking for anything; as soon as dinner was served he withdrew, though he was not rich, and did not even possess a horse. He came almost every evening, when his favourite employment was drawing, for which he had some talent, though his figures were no better than those drawn by our little children. Ortubize, the interpreter, had moved, with his family, to the post of Picotte, a trader among the Yanktonans, where he was to pass the winter.[10] The people who had been sent thither returned, on the 14th of November, with the information that the Sioux were dispersed in the prairie, and that they had made capital bargains with them for beavers' skins. At our post we had to encounter the mercantile opposition of Messrs. Soublette and Campbell, whereby the price of the buffalo skins was very much raised.[11] As our armed men now consisted of seventeen *engagés*, Mr. Kipp went to work and had my Mackinaw boat drawn to land, and secured from the ice, a task which the people had much difficulty in accomplishing. The 15th of November was the first day we saw ice in the Missouri; the sand banks were covered with a wide, thick sheet of ice and the river was still open, no aquatic birds had been seen for a long time; while, on the other hand, small flights of *Fringilla linaria*, which travels southward in the winter appeared in the prairie.

On the 16th November Mr. Kipp sent the men who had come down with me back, on foot, to Fort Union. They took with them two dogs, which drew well-laden *travails* (sledges), and hoped to arrive there in about nine days. We had a visit from the wolf chief, Charata-Numakshi, accompanied by half-a-dozen Manitaries,[12] among whom was a tall, stout fellow, named Tichinga; his hair was tied in a thick knot on his forehead; to this was attached a piece of leather, so ornamented with fringes that his eyes were almost concealed, and he could hardly see. At midday, I saw the first flight of the snow bunting (*Emberiza nivalis*), on the Missouri. They pass the winter here in the prairie bushes, and live upon such seeds as they can pick up. Sih-Sa (the red feather), the young Mandan Indian who, during the day, takes charge of the horses belonging to the fort in the prairie, came back to-day, having painted his whole body with spots of white clay. I asked him why he had done this? to which he replied, that he was thereby enabled to run faster. We likewise received a visit from a Mandan of half French extraction, named Kipsan-Nüka (the little tortoise), whose father was a French Canadian. He affirmed that he had formerly spoken both French and English, but he had entirely forgotten both. Neither his features nor his colour differed materially from the other Indians, whose manners, customs, and dress he closely followed. Every evening brought me a visit from Dipauch, who came to tell me all the legends and traditions, as well as the religious views of his people—conversations which interested me much, and which frequently lasted till late at night. Among his auditors were several young people, who sat listening with the most riveted attention to the disjointed sentences of our narrator; while Mr. Kipp, with great patience, performed the office of interpreter.

On the 17th of November we were visited by an old chief, Ahda-Miga (the man without arms), who, however, has no longer any influence among them. The bowl of his tobacco-pipe was made of an old iron gun-barrel. Mr. Kipp had many similar bowls made by the smith, which he sold to the Indians for six dollars. Dipauch and his friend, Berock-Itainu (the bull's neck), who was his inseparable companion, were presented with bowls of this kind, made in the form usual among the Indians. In the evening a white wolf approached so closely to the fort, that he was fired at from the gate, and attacked by our dogs.

On the 22nd of November we took possession of our new apartment, which was now completed, except that the whitewashed walls were still damp, and the constant wind generally filled it with smoke. We were, however, thankful to have space to carry on our labours, to which we now applied with great assiduity, to make up for the time we had lost. The large windows afforded a good light for drawing, and we had a couple of small tables and some benches of poplar wood, and three shelves against the walls, on which we spread our blankets and buffaloes' skins, and reposed during the night. The room was floored; the door was furnished with bolts on the inside, and the fire-wood, covered with frozen snow, was piled up close to the chimney. We all felt indisposed soon after we took up our abode in this lodging, and were obliged to have recourse to medicine, but this was, probably, to be ascribed principally to the way of living and the state of the weather; for Sih-Sa and other Indians had bowel complaints, catarrh, and violent coughs, for which Mr. Kipp gave them medicines. I examined all the medical stock of the fort, and found neither peppermint nor other herbs, which would have been serviceable at this time; only a handful of elder flowers, and rather more of American camomile, which has a different taste to the European. There were some common remedies, but unfortunately we were without a medical man. Snow-storms, with a high west wind, had set in, and on the 23rd the country was covered with snow, and the Missouri froze for the first time on that day, below the village of Mih-Tutta-Hang-Kush, and it is remarkable that it was frozen on the very same day in the preceding year. We saw the Indian women, as soon as the river was covered with ice, break holes in it, to wash their heads and the upper part of their bodies. The Indians had brought many beaver skins for sale, of which Mr. Kipp purchased eleven large ones, in exchange for a horse and some red cloth; the remainder, for which they demanded another horse, they took back with them. We had a visit from a young Mandan who had a bag made of the skin of the prairie dog, containing some pieces of a transparent selenite from which these Indians extract a white colour by burning it in the fire. Mato-Topé had passed the evening with us, and, when we went to bed, laid himself down before the fire, where he soon fell asleep. On the following morning he rose early, washed himself, but left his two buffalo skins lying carelessly on the floor, for us to gather them up, these Indians taking every opportunity to be waited on by the Whites. As we were molested during the night by numerous rats, we put my little tame prairie fox into the loft above us, where some maize was kept, and here he did excellent service. This pretty little fox afforded us much amusement during the long winter evenings. He was nearly a year old, but still liked to be caressed and played all kinds of antics to attract notice.

Several wolves, which the Indians had brought to me, were laid down near the fort, after they had been stripped of their skins, but we did not succeed in alluring one of their species by this bait. Dreidoppel, on his excursion, had killed a couple of wolves, which he allured by imitating the voice of a hare, and then shot with his fowling piece. The hares had now put on their white winter coats, and could scarcely be distinguished from the surrounding snow. They were seen sitting singly on the hills, and we took them for buffaloes' skulls when there was no snow on the prairie.

On the evening of the 25th of November we were alarmed by information that some hostile Indians were near the fort. Dipauch and Berock-Itainu, who were called the soldiers of the fort, immediately took their arms, cautiously opened the gate, and discovered a Manitari, who was concealed near one of the block-houses, from which he was soon driven rather roughly. At this time, Charbonneau came to invite us to a great medicine feast among the Manitaries, an invitation which I gladly accepted.[13]

On the morning of the 26th we had fine weather and a clear sky, very favourable for our expedition. At nine o'clock, Bodmer, Charbonneau and myself set out, on foot, with our double-barrelled guns and the requisite ammunition, accompanied by a young Manitari warrior. We proceeded up the Missouri in a direction parallel with the river, leaving Mih-Tutta-Hang-Kush on our right hand, and taking the way to Ruhptare which runs along the edge of the high Plateau, below which there is a valley extending to the Missouri, covered with the maize plantations of the Mandans, with some willow thickets and high reeds. On the left hand the prairie extended to the hills: it was covered with low, withered, yellowish grass, and presented a barren, desolate appearance. After proceeding about an hour, we came to a stone, undoubtedly one of those isolated blocks of granite which are scattered over the whole prairie, and which the Indians, from some superstitious notion, paint with vermilion, and surround with little sticks, or rods, to which were attached some feathers. This stone, and many similar ones in the prairie, are considered, by many Indians, as medicine; but I was not able to learn what ideas they entertain concerning the one here described. A little farther on, in a small ravine which crosses the path, there was an elm, the trunk of which was painted in many places with vermilion; rags, stained with vermilion, were suspended from it, together with a little bag containing some of the same colour, as a sign that the tree was sacred or medicine. A covey of prairie hens rose, with loud cries, from this ravine. At this spot 1000 or 1200 Sioux had attacked the united Mandans and Manitaries thirty years before, but lost 100 of their people. One of those Indians was afraid to proceed on this path, because he suspected that a wolf-pit, or trap, might be in the way; but the partisan, or chief, wishing to shame him, went before, and actually fell into such a pit, with sharpened sticks at the bottom, by which he was killed. From this place we came, in about half an hour, to the Mandan village, Ruhptare, which is now totally abandoned. The construction of the huts and medicines, the stages for the dead, everything, in short, is just the same as at Mih-Tutta-Hang-Kush, only a much greater number of the stages stood near the huts, and flocks of ravens sat upon them. To the left of the village there is a little hill, which was quite covered with these strange erections, and poles with offerings suspended from them.

We went through the village, in the centre of which there is a circular space, with the representation of the ark of the first man, and the figure of Ochkih-Hadda on a pole before the medicine lodge. We soon came to the bank of the river, and saw three Indians attempting to cross the ice of the Missouri, which had scarcely been frozen over twenty-four hours. Charbonneau went first, and we followed him on the path marked out by some poles stuck in the ice. While we were proceeding, carefully examining the ice with the butt-end of our guns, we were overtaken by the old Mandan chief, Kahka-Chamahan (the little raven), who wore a round hat, with a plume of feathers, and who now led the way.[14] After we had passed the Missouri we met, on the beach, some elegantly dressed Mandans, with whom we did not stop to converse. We turned to the close willow thicket which skirted an extensive forest on the north bank of the river: the path led through it, in many windings, till we reached the winter village, Ruhptare, which is closely surrounded by a thicket of willow, poplar, ash, cornus, and elm. Here the chief took leave of us, as we could not accept his invitation to his hut. We saw the women everywhere busy in tanning skins, and carrying wood. Most of the high trees in the forest had been cut down; but there was a shrub-like symphoria, with rounded elliptical leaves, and small bunches of whitish-green berries, which, when quite ripe, are of a bluish-black colour. This plant grows in great abundance as underwood in all the forests in these parts. Vitis, celastrus, and clematis, were entwined about some of the trees, but the wild vine was nowhere thicker than a little finger. There are many open spots in the wood, covered with thin grass and other kinds of plants, and also reeds.

We followed the winding path through this intricate wilderness, to the hills, which bound the prairie, at the foot of which we proceeded parallel to the Missouri: they are partly clay hills, of angular forms, from which marshy springs issue in many places, all which were at this time frozen over. Several of these places were covered with extensive thickets of reeds, and at the foot of the hills there were some bushes, among which the Indians had set fox-traps, which they endeavour to conceal with brushwood and buffaloes' skulls laid on it. We here saw some Indians, and heard the report of their guns. At the foot of the hills we saw the foot steps of the Virginian deer, but we observed only a few birds, chiefly crows, ravens, snow buntings, and the coal titmouse. When we had gone about half an hour, the hills receded from the river, and as soon as the wood terminates, the wide prairie extends along the Missouri, where we lately visited, on our arrival, Ita-Widahki-Hischa (the red shield). We proceeded for several hours through the desolate plain, which was covered with yellow, withered grass, now and then broken by gentle eminences, where bleached buffaloes' bones, especially skulls, are scattered about. We met with a couple of Indians, heavily laden with skins, resting themselves, who immediately asked us for tobacco. We had here an opportunity of seeing the wolf pits, in which the Indians fix sharp stakes, and the whole is so covered with brushwood, hay, and dry grass, that it cannot be perceived. As our feet began to be very painful, we sat down to rest near a stream, now almost dry, bordered with high grass, which at this time was lying on the ground. As I was no longer accustomed to such long journeys on foot, I had asked Mr. Kipp for horses for this journey, but there were none in the fort at that time. Our European boots and shoes had wounded our feet, and it was with much pain that we ascended the pretty steep hills which now again came nearer to the river. I obtained from Charbonneau a pair of Indian shoes, in which I found it easier to walk, but the thorns of the cactus, which grew on the hills, pierced through them, and caused me pain in another way.

Towards evening, when we descended from the hills to the river, we again came to an extensive wood on the banks, in which one of the winter villages of the Manitaries is situated. We had, however, to walk several miles along a very winding path before we reached it. Being extremely tired, and our feet sore and wounded, it cost us some exertion to get over fallen trunks of trees, sharp stones, &c., in the way. The scenes which are inseparable from the dwellings of the Indians soon appeared; slender young men, galloping without saddle, who were driving their horses home from the pasture; women cutting or carrying wood, and the like. A young Indian joined us, who immediately offered, out of civility, to carry my gun, which I did not accept. He was an Arikkara, who had been captured, when a child, by the Manitaries—a good-tempered, well-behaved young man. He was tall and slender, with a pleasing countenance, long, narrow eyes, and a slightly curved nose.

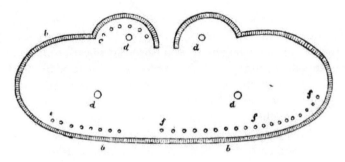

Plan of Minitaree medicine feast

Club, with carved head

It was nearly nightfall when we reached the Manitari village, the large huts of which were built so close to each other that it was sometimes difficult to pass between them. We heard loud lamentations as we approached, and learnt that a child had just died, and that a corpse had been deposited, a few days before, on poles placed in the boughs of a tree. At the farther end of the village was the residence of Mr. Dougherty[15] a long, low, log-house, divided into three apartments, of which that in the centre was used for a storehouse, the northern apartment being assigned to the family, and the southern to the *engagés*. We were received with much kindness, and, being thoroughly tired by a fatiguing journey of, at least, nine leagues, we were truly glad to rest our weary limbs before a blazing fire. A number of Manitari Indians were assembled, who, however, gradually retired whilst we took some refreshment, not having tasted anything since we breakfasted at Fort Clarke. It being reported that herds of buffaloes were at no great distance, a party of Indians resolved to give them chase on the following day, and to implore the blessing of heaven upon their undertaking by a great medicine feast. Notwithstanding the pain I suffered in walking, the prospect of witnessing so novel a scene was so exciting that I immediately set out about seven o'clock in the evening, accompanied by Dougherty and Charbonneau, to see the Indian ceremony, which was instituted by the women. Between the huts, in the centre of the village, an elliptical space, forty paces or more in length, was enclosed in a fence, ten or twelve feet high, consisting of reeds and willow twigs inclining inwards.[16] An entrance was left at *a; b* represents the fence; *d* are the four fires, burning in the medicine lodge, which were kept up the whole time. At *e* the elder and principal men had taken their seats; to the right sat the old chief, Lachpitzi-Sihrisch (the yellow bear); some parts of his face were painted red, and a bandage of yellow skin encircled his head. Places were assigned to us on the right hand of the yellow bear. At *f*, close to the fence, the spectators, especially the women, were seated: the men walked about, some of them handsomely dressed, others quite simply; children were seated around the fires, which they kept alive by throwing twigs of willow trees into them. Soon after Charbonneau had introduced us to this company, six elderly men advanced in a row from the opposite hut, and stopped for a moment at the entrance of the great medicine lodge.

They had been chosen, by the young men, to represent buffalo bulls, for which they afterwards received presents. Each of them carried a long stick, at the top of which three or four black feathers were fastened; then, at regular intervals, the whole length of the stick was ornamented with small bunches of the hoofs of buffalo calves, and at the lower end of the stick were some bells. In their left hand they carried a battle-axe, or war club, and two of them had a stuffed skin which they called a badger, and used as a drum. They stood at the entrance, rattled their sticks incessantly, sang alternately, and imitated, with great perfection, the hoarse voice of the buffalo bull. They were followed by a tall man, whose physiognomy strikingly resembled that of a Botocudo. He wore a cap, trimmed with fur, because he had been formerly scalped in a battle. He represented the director of the ceremony and the leader of the old bulls, behind whom he made his appearance. The bulls now entered the medicine lodge and took their seats at *c*, near the fence, behind one of the fires. In front of them they laid the badger, which is equivalent to what is called the tortoise in the Okippe of the Mandans.[17] Each of the bulls fixed his weapon in the ground before him; two of them had clubs, with a head, on which a human face was carved.[18] Several young men were now employed in carrying round dishes of boiled maize and beans, which they placed before the guests. These dishes were handed to each person successively, who passed them on after tasting a small quantity. Empty wooden dishes were frequently brought and placed at our feet, the reason of which I could not, at first, comprehend, but soon learned from my neighbour, the Yellow Bear. As soon as the provision bearer—a tall, handsome, very robust, and broad-shouldered man, wearing only his breechcloth, ornamented at the back with long tufts of hair—came to take away one of these empty dishes, the old chief held his hands before his face, sang, and made a long speech, which seemed to me to be a prayer uttered in a low tone of voice, and then gave him the dish. These speeches contained good wishes for success in hunting the buffalo, and in war. They invoke the heavenly powers to favour the hunters and the warriors. In this manner two dishes were sometimes placed before us, and we also exerted ourselves in uttering good wishes in the English and German languages, which the Indians guessed from our motions, though they could not understand our words. If the speech was lengthy, they were specially gratified; the provision bearer stopped, listening very attentively, nodded his satisfaction, and passed his hand over our right arm from the shoulder to the wrist, and sometimes over both arms, and then again spoke a few words expressive of his thanks. In this manner the ceremony of the repast lasted above an hour; every person present partook of it, and offered up their good wishes for a successful buffalo chase. Meantime, the young men, in the centre of the space, prepared the tobacco pipes, which they brought first to the old men and the visitors; they presented the mouth-piece of the pipe to us in succession, going from right to left: we each took a few whiffs, uttered, as before, a wish or prayer, and passed the pipe to our next neighbours. Among those who carried the dishes and pipes, there was another young man who had been scalped, and who also wore a cap; he had received many wounds in the attack made by the Sioux on the Manitari villages, and had been left on the field as dead. The pipe bearers often turned their pipes towards the cardinal points, and performed various superstitious manœuvres with them. The six buffalo bulls, meantime, sitting behind the fire, sang, and rattled the medicine sticks, while one of them constantly beat the badger skin. After a while they all stood up, bent forward, and danced; that is, they leaped as high as they could with both their feet together, continuing to sing and rattle their sticks, one of them beating time on the badger. Their song was invariably the same, consisting of loud, broken notes and exclamations. When they had danced for some time, they resumed their seats.

The whole was extremely interesting. The great number of red men, in a variety of costumes, the singing, dancing, beating the drum, &c., while the lofty trees of the forest, illumined by the fires, spread their branches against the dark sky, formed a *tout ensemble* so striking and original, that I much regretted the impracticability of taking a sketch of it on the spot. When the ceremony had continued a couple of hours, the women began to act their part. A woman approached her husband, gave him her girdle and under garment, so that she had nothing on under her robe; she then went up to one of the most distinguished men, passed her hand over his arm, from the shoulder downwards, and then withdrew slowly from the lodge. The person so summoned follows her to a solitary place in the forest; he may then buy himself off by presents, which, however, few Indians do. This honour was offered to us, but we returned to the lodge, after having made a present, on which pipes were again handed to us. The fires already burnt dim, many Indians had retired, and we asked the old chief, whether we might be permitted to do the same? At first he refused, but, on our repeating the question, he gave us leave. On other occasions, when circumstances allow all the inhabitants of the village to unite, many additional ceremonies take place; more dances are performed, and each of the bands dances that which is peculiar to itself, which could not be done to-day. The dance of the old buffalo bulls, with entire buffalo skulls, is said to be very interesting. This festival always continues for four successive nights, and, even on this occasion, the rioting and noise continued uninterruptedly throughout the night.

On the following morning, the 27th of November, the weather continued bright and clear. I observed in the thickets near the dwelling of Dougherty, large numbers of the little coal titmouse, but no other bird except the *Picus pubescens*. A number of Indians congregated very early around our fire, one of them having even ventured to take up his night's quarters with us. The Yellow Bear and the man who was scalped came early, the former to beg for some coffee; he looked miserable and faint, as if he were in want of food, and had a black silk handkerchief tied round his head. The scene outside was very animated: we observed many very handsome young men, in fine new dresses, some of whom were playing the game called billiards, and on the river, which was now quite frozen over, many children and young people were amusing themselves with sliding and other gambols. Some women were bringing wood from the forest, others cutting holes in the ice to procure water, and some playing with a leathern-ball, which they flung upon the ice, caught it, and then threw it into the air, catching it as it fell. At noon the thermometer was at 47°, but a high wind arose, and we were obliged to pass the whole day under shelter of Mr. Dougherty's roof, where we witnessed many very interesting scenes, the apartments being visited by a succession of Indians throughout the day.

The following day was spent in the same manner. The younger people, half naked, again played upon the ice, and I paid a visit, accompanied by Charbonneau, to the Yellow Bear. Mr. Dougherty had formerly resided in the hut which he now inhabited, and for which he had to pay 80 or 100 dollars. The beds, consisting of square leathern cases, were placed along the sides of this spacious hut, and the inmates sat round the fire variously occupied. The Yellow Bear, wearing only his breechcloth, sat upon a bench made of willow boughs, covered with skin, and was painting a new buffalo robe with figures in vermilion and black, having his colours standing by him, ready mixed, in old potsherds. In lieu of a pencil he was using the more inartificial substitute of a sharp pointed piece of wood. The robe was ornamented with the symbols of valuable presents which he had made, and which had gained the Yellow Bear much reputation, and made him a man of distinction.

About twenty Manitaries had gone to hunt buffaloes, and as we had no meat, we waited with no small degree of impatience for their return. Our fast was of longer duration than we liked, for it was late before a few of our hunters arrived, and the scalped man brought us some meat, so that we did not get our meal till evening. At nightfall, a handsome young man came to us, accompanied by two girls, it being the custom of the Indian youths to stroll about in this manner. They had not been long in our room, when somebody knocked at the door, on which the two girls crept into Charbonneau's bed to hide themselves, as they suspected it was some of their friends come to look after them; but it proved to be only a messenger from Charbonneau, who, wishing to procure us a pleasant diversion for the evening, let us know that the women in a certain hut were about to perform a medicine dance; and, availing ourselves of the intimation, we hastened to the spot without loss of time.

On the left hand of the wooden screen at the door of the hut a fire was burning, and before it were spread out skins upon some hay, on which five or six men were seated in a row, one of whom beat the drum, and the other rattled the schischikué. They were more than usually vehement in the performance of this music; the drummer especially exerted himself to the utmost, and all the rest accompanied him with singing. Some elderly women were seated near the wall; a tall, robust woman, however, especially attracted our attention; she was standing in the centre of the hut; her dress consisted of a long yellow leather robe, trimmed with a quantity of fringes, and ornamented with pieces of red and blue cloth. We took our places to the right of the musicians, just in front of a number of spectators, consisting of women and children, who were prevented from pressing forward by a young man, who made use of the official dignity of a stick, with which he was invested for the occasion. The woman standing in the centre pretended that she had a head of maize in her stomach, which she would conjure up, and again cause to disappear. We had come rather too late, for the ear of maize had already disappeared; but Charbonneau spoke to the people, to whom we gave ten carrots of tobacco, and the trick was repeated. Our tobacco was thrown on a heap of roasted buffalo ribs, which were piled up on willow boughs, and there it remained till the end of the ceremony, the object of which was to procure a good crop of maize in the succeeding year. The din of the music now recommenced with renewed vehemence, and four women began to move. They waddled like ducks, making short steps, with their feet turned inwards, and keeping time to the quick beat of the drum; while their arms hung down motionless by their sides. The medicine woman danced alone near the fire, to which she sometimes put her hands, and then laid them upon her face. At length she began to totter, to move her arms backwards and forwards, and to use convulsive motions, which became more and more violent. Now, as she threw her head backwards, we saw the top of a white head of maize fill her mouth, and gradually came more forward, while her contortions greatly increased. When the head of maize was half out of her mouth, the dancer seemed ready to sink down, when another woman advanced, laid hold of her and seated her on the ground. Here, supported by her companion, she fell into convulsions, and the music became overpoweringly violent. Other women brushed the arm and breast of the performers with bunches of wormwood, and the head of maize gradually disappeared; on which the juggleress rose, danced twice round the hut, and was succeeded by another female. After this second woman had danced in the same manner, a stream of blood suddenly rushed from her mouth over her chin, which, however, she extracted from a piece of leather that she held in her mouth. She, too, was cured of her convulsions as she lay on the ground, and then danced around the fire. Other women came forward and danced behind one another, which concluded the ceremony.

Almost all these people pretended that they had some animal in their stomach; some a buffalo calf, others a deer, &c. The scalped man told us that he had a buffalo calf in his left shoulder, and often felt it kick. Another, who pretended that he had three live lizards in his inside, complained to Charbonneau that these animals gave him pain, on which Charbonneau gave him a cup of coffee, but as this remedy did not relieve him, a cup of tea was given him, and this produced the desired effect. Notions of this kind are so common among the Indians, and they are said to have so firm a hold on the faith of the people, that it would be labour lost to attempt to convince them of their folly.

On the 29th of November, during which we continued in the Manitari village, the whole forest was covered with hoar frost; all the woods on the banks were clothed in white, and the red youths were sporting on the ice; the whole forming an interesting and animated scene. Mr. Bodmer painted several animals and birds for the Indians, such as cocks, eagles &c., which they pretended would make them proof against musket balls. In the evening Mr. Bodmer and Dougherty again went to the medicine feast, but the women did not, on this occasion, make their appearance, for which nobody, not even Charbonneau, who was so well acquainted with the Indians, could assign any reason. After dark our house-door was twice forced open, and we again observed how much more rude and savage the Manitaries are than the Mandans. Dougherty, who did not yet possess a fort, and was obliged to live among the former, suffered greatly from their importunity and rudeness; he was afraid even to give them a refusal, lest he might thereby bring upon himself greater inconveniences, for a continued and close intercourse with these people is always attended with danger. We had not been able to borrow horses to return to Fort Clarke; but, on the 30th, Mr. Dougherty succeeded in obtaining one, and Durand, a clerk of Messrs. Soublette and Campbell, who had arrived on horseback, returned with us, and allowed Mr. Bodmer to ride with him.

At nine o'clock we took leave of our kind hosts, Dougherty and Charbonneau, and set out on our return. In the forest-village belonging to the inhabitants of Ruhptare, we stopped at a hut, in which Garreau, an old trader of Messrs. Soublette and Campbell, resided.[19] There was an abundance of meat hanging up in this hut, as they had had a very successful buffalo hunt. From this place I sent back my horse; but Durand, though with great difficulty, got his across the frozen river; the poor beast was nearly exhausted, it often slipped, and sometimes fell down. At twilight we reached Fort Clarke, where, during our absence, good news had been received of the cessation of the cholera in St. Louis and the neighbourhood.

During November the weather had, on the whole, been tolerably pleasant: a few days were stormy, with some snow and slight frost; and this kind of weather continued at the beginning of December. A high stage of strong posts was erected in our court-yard, where a part of the stock of maize was deposited, thereby to protect it from the voracity of the rats. It was defended from the rain by the leather covering of Indian tents.

The Mandan village near the fort was now entirely forsaken by the inhabitants. The entrances to the huts were blocked with bundles of thorns; a couple of families only still remained, one of which was that of Dipauch, whom Mr. Bodmer visited every day, in order to make a drawing of the interior of the hut.[20] Instead of the numerous inhabitants, magpies were flying about, and flocks of snow buntings were seen in the neighbourhood about the dry plants of the prairie, where the Indian children set long rows of snares, made of horsehair, to catch them alive.

Belhumeur had been sent several times to the prairie, and had brought back buffaloes' flesh; but the animals were so far off that we could not always be supplied, and were forced to live on hard dried meat and boiled maize; our beverage consisted of coffee and the water of the Missouri. Dreidoppel had killed several wolves, prairie dogs, and prairie hens; the Indians had brought me some white hares and other smaller animals. One of our dogs was shot in the foot by an Indian, with an arrow. Neither the motive nor the perpetrator of this hostile act could be discovered.

Heads of sledge dogs

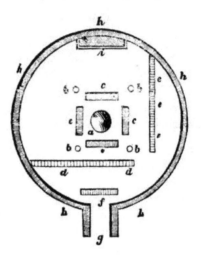

Plan of Mandan hut

Mandan, in bull-dance costume

Having been invited by the Indians to the winter village, to be present at a great medicine feast, we proceeded thither, on the 3rd of December, in the afternoon. Mr. Kipp took his family with him, and Mato-Topé and several other Indians accompanied us. We were all well armed, because it was asserted that a band of hostile Indians had been seen among the prairie hills on the preceding day. Our beds, blankets, and buffalo skins were laid on a horse, on which Mr. Kipp's wife, a Mandan Indian, rode. Thus we passed, at a rapid pace, through the prairie, along the Missouri, then below the hills, which are pretty high; and I cannot deny that, in the valleys and ravines, through which some small streams that we had to pass flowed, our whole company looked anxiously to the right and left to see whether any enemies would issue from their ambush. We had to pass a narrow gorge behind a little thick copse, where many Indians had been killed by their enemies. After proceeding about an hour and a half we reached the village in the wood, which is the winter residence of the inhabitants of Mih-Tutta-Hang-Kush. We stopped at the hut of Mr. Kipp's father-in-law, Mandeek-Suck-Choppenik (the medicine bird), who accommodated us with a night's lodging. The description of this hut may serve for all the winter huts of these

Indians.[21] It was about twenty paces in diameter, and circular: *h* is the fence or wall of the hut, supported inside by strong, low posts, on which rests the vaulted roof, which has a square hole to let the smoke escape; *g* is the entrance, protected by two projecting walls covered above. At *f* is the door, consisting of a piece of leather stretched on a frame. At *d d* there is a cross wall of considerable height, made of reeds and osier twigs woven together, to keep off the draught of air. At *e e e* there is another cross wall, only three feet high, behind which the horses stand; *a* is the fireplace, round which, at *c c c c*, are the seats of the inmates, consisting of benches formed of basket-work, covered with skins; *b b b b* are four strong pillars which bear the roof, and are very well united above by cross beams. At *i* there was a large leather case for the beds in which the family slept. A chain, with a large kettle, was suspended from the roof over the fire, to cook our supper, consisting of very pleasant flavoured sweet maize. The master of the hut was absent, but his wife, daughter, and son-in-law, received us very kindly. We had still a little time before the commencement of the medicine feast, which consisted of the dance of the half-shorn head, which the soldiers sold to the raven band. This feast was to last forty nights, and the son-in-law of our host was among the sellers. We sat around the fire and smoked, while the drum was beat in the village to call the two parties together. After seven o'clock we repaired to the medicine lodge; it was entirely cleared, except that some women sat along the walls; the fire burned in the centre, before which we took our seats, near the partition *d d*, with several distinguished men of the band of the soldiers. At our left hand, the other soldiers, about twenty-five in number, were seated in a row; some of them were handsomely dressed, though the majority were in plain clothes. They had their arms in their hands, and in the centre were three men, who beat the drum. On the right side of the fire stood the young men of the raven band, who were the purchasers; they were obliged to satisfy the soldiers, who were the sellers, by making them valuable presents, such as horses, guns, powder and ball, blankets of different colours, kettles, &c.; to continue the feast forty nights; to regale them, for that time, with provisions and tobacco, and offer their wives to them every evening. The soldiers had consented to these terms, and the festival took place every evening in the following manner:—

We had all taken our seats before the band of the sellers arrived; but we soon heard them singing, accompanied by the drum, and they entered with their insignia; these consisted of four poles, or lances, seven or eight feet long, the iron points of which resembled sword blades, and were held downwards; the rest of the instrument was wrapped round with broad bands of otter-skin, like that of the Blackfeet,[22] and decorated at the point and other places with strips of skin: two of these poles are curved at the top. The others were a club with an iron point, painted red and ornamented with feathers; then three lances, decorated alternately with black and white feathers;[23] and, lastly, a very beautifully ornamented bow and quiver. These nine insignia were brought in, the soldiers, however, stopping, at first, near the door behind the cross wall. When they had remained for some time in this position, singing and beating the drum with great violence, they entered, placed the lances against the wall, and fixed the club in the ground near one of the pillars that supported the hut; after which they all took their seats near the wall. While the singing and dancing were continued alternately for some time, the purchasers filled their pipes and presented them to all of us in succession. We took one or two whiffs; they did the same, and carried the pipe round to the left hand, but offered it only to the visitors and to the sellers. This smoking continued a long time, during which each of the guests received a small cake of sweet corn baked in fat. In about half an hour two of the soldiers rose and danced opposite each other. One of them was a tall, powerful man, with a weak, effeminate voice. He wore nothing but his robe and leggins, but without any ornaments; he took the club and held it firmly in his left hand; his right hand hung straight down; he bent his body forwards and danced, that is, he leaped with his feet close together, keeping time with the music. The head and legs of the other dancer were very handsomely ornamented, but the breast and shoulders were bare. He took one of the first four lances, which he held in both hands, and the two men then danced, or leaped, opposite each other. In a few minutes the first dancer put the lance aside and sat down, while all the other members of this band uttered the war-whoop, accompanied by the quick beating of the drum, now and then shouting aloud. Silence then ensued; the man with the club addressed the purchasers, called them his sons, and enumerated some of his exploits; after which he presented to them the war club. One of the purchasers called him his father, passed his hand along his arm, took the weapon from his hand, and put it in its place again. The other dancer again came forward, did the same, spoke of his exploits, and presented the lance to a man or son of the other band, who received it with the same ceremony, and put it also in its place again. There were singing and dancing in the intervals, but no schischikué was heard. Two other soldiers then rose, related their deeds, how they had stolen horses, taken a medicine from the enemy, and the like, and presented two of the insignia to the purchasers. When this had been done four or five times, the women of the raven band rose; four of them threw aside their robes, snatched up the lances, carried them successively out of the hut, and, some time after, brought them in again. They hastened to pass by us, and some of them appeared to feel ashamed. This ceremony was repeated twice: these women then came, passed their hands down the arms of the strangers and of the fathers, took up their robes and went out, in the same manner as has been related in the medicine feast of the Manitaries. When they returned the second time, Mr. Kipp rose to go away, and I followed him.

Some of the women were fat and corpulent, others very young, and one but little past childhood.

This feast was continued in the same manner forty nights. During the purchase of the dance of the half-shorn head, the buffalo medicine feast, which continues four nights, was celebrated in another hut. We retired to the hut of the Medicine Bird, smoked our cigars, and lay down in our clothes to sleep on buffalo skins spread on the floor. The weather was frosty, and it was very cold even in the hut; the Indians set a watch, during the night, that they might not be surprised by their enemies.

On the 4th of December, early in the morning, we left the village; we did not keep along the hills, but took another path through the thickets, which led in some places over frozen marshes, which were partly covered with reeds. The wood, which was spangled with hoar frost, is very much cleared, and contains but few large trees. A high, cold southeast wind blew in the prairie, and afterwards became violent. At eight o'clock we reached the fort, where we much enjoyed a hot breakfast. Several Mandans came to see us, among whom was the strongest man of this nation, named Beracha-Iruckcha (the broken pot), whom no one had yet been able to overcome in wrestling, though he had been matched with white men, negroes, and Indians, remarkable for their strength. Sih-Chida and Maksick-Karehde (the flying eagle), also visited us; the latter was the tallest man among the Mandans, and belonged to the band of the soldiers.[24]

Snow had already set in, yet still the buffaloes did not come nearer, and we were in want of fresh meat, and of tallow to make candles; and all the meat we could get was obtained from individual Indians returning from the chase. In the environs of the fort there were, at this time, wolves, foxes, and a few hares, and during the night we heard the barking of the prairie wolves (*Canis latrans*, Say), which prowled about, looking for any remnants of provisions. In our excursions we everywhere met with wolves, foxes, hares, weasels, and mice, especially on the banks of the streams, and set snares of iron wire, in order to learn what species of mice could bear this winter weather. Our snares were often carried away by the wolves and foxes, but we frequently caught the *Mus leucopus*, which is especially the prey of the weasel. If any one imitate the voice of the hare, in order to attract the wolves, a number of magpies immediately come and settle in the neighbourhood. Scarcely any kinds of birds were found in the forest but *Pica hudsonica, Picus pubescens, Parus atracapillus, Fringilla linaria,* and *Tetrao phasianellus,* of which several were shot.

On the 10th of December, Charbonneau returned to the service of the American Fur Company, and took up his quarters in the fort, which gave me an opportunity to have much conversation with him respecting the Manitaries, with whom he was well acquainted. On the 11th, Dreidoppel, with his rifle, shot a prairie wolf (*Canis latrans*) on the ice of the Missouri, which crept into a burrow, where he could not get at it. He was returning to the fort, when a couple of Indians called after him, who had dragged the animal alive from its retreat, and brought it to our lodging, when Mr. Bodmer made a sketch of the head.[25] On the 13th of December, when Fahrenheit's thermometer was at 17°, several birds of the species *Bombycilla garrula* were brought to us: they are found in these parts during the summer also, and are said to breed here, which I think is doubtful. I obtained many wolves from the quite white to the perfectly grey, common variety, which the Indians sold for two rolls of tobacco a-piece. They also often caught ermines in horsehair snares, which they sell dear. As we continued to be in want of fresh meat and tallow, we had to send people for these necessaries to the Indian villages, and Mr. Kipp likewise went thither in his sledge, in order to trade. On one occasion his horse broke through the ice, so that it remained for an hour in the water, and was quite benumbed. An extremely cold storm from the north had blown away the wooden screen from our chimney. On the 15th of December, and on the preceding evening, we had a heavy fall of snow, which ceased when the wind veered a little to the north. At eight o'clock the mercury in Fahrenheit's thermometer was at 14°. The appearance of the prairie at this time was very remarkable, resembling the sea agitated by a terrible storm. The extensive surface of the snow was carried by the wind in a cloud; it was scarcely possible for the eye to bear the cold blast which drove the snow before it, and enveloped us in a dense cloud, above which the sky was clear, and the tops of the prairie hills were visible. We were, therefore, the more sensible of the enjoyment of our bright fire, seated about which we passed our time agreeably in various occupations. About this time the enemy had stolen six horses from the Manitaries. We had been for some time without meat, when the Indians, hunting at a considerable distance, at the forks of Teton River,[26] killed fifty-five buffaloes. On this occasion, Mr. Kipp's horse was lost, which, bridled and saddled as it was, had joined a herd of buffaloes; and two foals had perished in the cold.

On the 16th the mercury was at 2°, Fahrenheit, below zero. For some time past the water in our room was frozen every day, notwithstanding the large fire which we kept up. Towards the 19th of December, the weather was again fine; in a few days there was snow, and the Missouri rose so high that it partly overflowed the ice that covered it. Some of Mr. Soublette's people arrived from St. Louis, which they had left on the 14th of October, and confirmed the accounts which we had already received of the cessation of the cholera. They told us that, in October, the snow was fifteen inches deep on the banks of the Konzas River, and that the party escorting the caravan from Santa Fé had been so closely hemmed in by the Indians (probably Arikkaras), that they had been compelled, by want of provisions, to slaughter fourteen of their horses.[27]

On the 22nd of December, a number of white maggots were found under a piece of poplar bark, which were completely enclosed in ice, but all came to life when they were warmed at the fire. On the 23rd, the mercury was at 10° Fahrenheit, above zero; the sky was bright and clear, the wind blew from the east, the icy covering of the river smoked and the woods were covered with hoar frost. The ravens came near to the fort to pick up food; the wolves, in consequence of our frequent excursions, had retired to a greater distance.

On this day, at noon, we heard the drums of the Indians, and a crowd of their people filled the fort. At their head were fourteen men of the band of the bulls, from Ruhptare, distinguished by their strange costume.[28]

The whole head was covered with a wig, consisting of long plaits of hair, which hung down on every side, so that even the face was completely concealed. The appearance of these men was very singular in the cold weather, for their breath issued from between the plaits of hair like a dense vapour. They wore in their heads feathers of owls, ravens, and birds of prey, each of which had at the tip a large white down feather. One of them had a very handsome fan of white feathers on his head, doubtless the entire tail of a swan, each of the feathers having at the tip a tuft of dyed horsehair. They were closely enveloped in their robes, and had bow-lances ornamented with feathers, coloured cloth, beads, &c., and most of them had foxes' tails at their heels. Some of these men beat the drum, while they all formed a circle, and imitated the bellowing of the buffalo bulls. After they had danced awhile, some tobacco was thrown to them, and they proceeded to the village in the forest further down the river, taking off their wigs. The frozen Missouri was covered with Indians on this occasion, and presented an interesting scene. At this time the Sioux stole from the prairie thirty-seven horses belonging to the Mandans. On this day Dreidoppel had dragged the entrails of a hare about the prairie, and then concealed himself; he soon saw six wolves follow the scent and approach him; but it was so cold that he could not wait for them. Our cook, a negro, had a violent dispute with an Indian from Ruhptare, who had taken a piece of meat out of his pot, and the affair might have led to unpleasant consequences. The Indians of that village are the worst of the Mandans. Several articles had been stolen, which was nothing uncommon among our worthy neighbours, for even the wife of Mato-Topé had pilfered something in our room.

On the 24th of December, and on the preceding night, there was a very strong cold wind from the northwest (Fahrenheit's thermometer +12½°), which blew all the hoar frost from the trees. Many Indians knocked violently at our door, and attempted to force it, as we did not open it immediately. About four o'clock Papin and three other *engagés*, with seven horses, arrived from Picotte's post among the Yanktonans, which they had left two days before, and told us that they had there found 200 tents of the Yanktonans. At midnight the *engagés* of the fort fired a volley to welcome Christmas day, which was repeated in the morning: the 25th of December was a day of bustle in the fort. Mr. Kipp had given the *engagés* an allowance of better provisions, and they were extremely noisy in their Canadian jargon. The poor fellows had had no meat for some time, and had lived on maize, boiled in water, without any fat. Pehriska-Ruhpa, a robust Manitari, who had long lived among the Mandans, visited us, and soon afterwards Mato-Topé, but they took no notice of each other, as they were not on good terms, and the former immediately withdrew. He promised to have his portrait taken in his handsome dress.[29]

At noon there was a concourse of Indians in the fort: the woman's band of the white buffalo cow came to perform their dance.[30] The company consisted of seventeen, mostly old women, and two men, with the drum and schischikué; the first of these two men carried a gun in his hand. A stout elderly woman went first; she was wrapped in the hide of a white buffalo cow, and held, in her right arm, a bundle of twigs in the form of a cornucopia, with down feathers at the top, and at the lower end an eagle's wing, and a tin drinking vessel. Another woman carried a similar bundle. All these women wore round their heads a piece of buffalo's skin in the form of a hussar's cap, with a plume of owl's or raven's feathers in front, some of which were dyed red; only two of them wore the skin of a polecat; all the men were bare-headed. The women were uniformly painted; the left cheek and eye were vermilion, and they had two blue spots on the temple near the right eye.[31] All except the first wore painted robes, and two of them only had the hairy side outwards. When they had formed a circle the music began in quick time; the men sung, and the women who were dancing responded in a loud shrill voice. In their dances they rock from side to side, always remaining on the same spot. After they had been dancing for some time there was a pause, when the dance recommenced. Only the oldest of these women, most of whom were exceedingly plain, had the tattooed stripes on the chin which are peculiar to this band.

They had scarcely left us, after receiving a present, when three *engagés* arrived with letters from Fort Union. They informed us that Mr. Mc Kenzie had built a new fort at the mouth of the Rivière aux Trembles, which he had called Fort Jackson, and appointed Mr. Chardon director.[32] Up to the 15th, when these messengers left Fort Union, the weather had been very mild; the river was quite free from ice, and no snow had fallen. Mr. Mc Kenzie invited me to visit him at Fort Union, but the inclemency of the weather rendered such a journey extremely unpleasant. The wind had blown down all the pickets at Fort Union, and some Indians, probably Gros Ventres des Prairies, had shot a white man on the Yellow Stone. Information had been brought by some Indians that Doucette, when on a journey from Fort Mc Kenzie to the Kutanas, had been shot by the Blood Indians.[33]

On the 26th of December the wind blew the snow into the air and obscured the sky. With a temperature of 12°, Fahrenheit, early in the morning we observed a rainbow among the clouds of snow, with a parhelion in the centre. We dispatched a number of letters, which were forwarded on the 27th by *engagés*, from station to station, down the river. Four men, with two sledges, and a number of horses, were sent from the fort, two of whom were to receive a supply of fresh meat for use at the trading post of the Yanktonans, from which they were expected to return in four days. Sih-Chida brought us the paper which his father, at that time the first chief of the Mandans, had received from General Atkinson and Major O'Fallon, several years before, when a treaty of friendship and commerce was concluded with the Indians.[34] This document was written on large paper in the English and Manitari languages. Most of the Indian names, which were doubtless given by Charbonneau, were incorrectly written. As we had now no meat, our breakfast consisted of coffee and maize bread, and our dinner of maize bread and bean soup. Our people caught an Indian dog in the fort, intending to put him in a sledge, but he was so wild and unruly, bit and howled so furiously, that it was long before they could obtain the mastery. An *engagé* then knelt upon him to put on the harness, but when this was done he discovered that he had killed the poor dog. These dogs, if they are not broken in, are quite unfit for the sledge; when, however, they are accustomed to the work, they draw a sledge over the snow more easily than the best horse. If the snow is frozen, they run over it, where the horse sinks in, and they can hold out much longer. They can perform a journey of thirty miles in one day; and if they have rested an hour on the snow, and had some food, they are ready to set out again. A horse must have sufficient food, frequent rest, and a good watering place, and when it is once tired it cannot be induced to proceed. I have been assured by some persons that they had made long journeys, for eight successive days, with dogs, during which time the animals did not taste any food. In the winter, when the Indians go to hunt the buffalo, they drive, in light sledges, over the frozen snow, into the midst of the herd; the Indian, with his bow and arrows, sits or kneels down in the sledge; and dogs that have been trained, cannot be held back when they perceive the buffalo herd. In the north three good dogs are seldom to be purchased for less than 100 dollars. A single dog, when it is very good and strong, costs sixty or seventy dollars; on the Missouri, however, they are by no means so dear.

On the 28th December, about noon, we again heard the Indian drums: several soldiers announced the band which had lately purchased the dance of the half-shorn head. The whole company, very gaily and handsomely dressed, soon afterwards entered the fort, followed by a crowd of spectators. About twenty vigorous young men, with the upper part of the body naked (having thrown off their robes which they wore at their entrance), painted and ornamented in the most gaudy manner, formed a circle in the court-yard of the fort. Their long plaits of hair were covered with reddish clay. One eagle's feather, or several other feathers, were fixed transversely in the hair; others had a long plait hanging down, with five or six brass rosettes, in the manner of the Sioux; several had a bunch of owl's feathers hanging down, necklaces of bears' claws and otters' tails, wolves' tails at their heels, red cloth or leather leggins, often painted, or with bells fixed to them; they had a looking-glass suspended from the wrist, or the waist, and carried the several insignia of the dance, such as the long hooked sticks, or rods, adorned with otter's skin and feathers, the straight rod, covered with red cloth[35] &c., and had guns or bow-lances in their hands. One of them wore a long feather cap, with horns and strips of ermine on his head; another sat on horseback, and was daubed with yellow clay, and bleeding wounds were painted on his body: he carried a bow and arrows, without a quiver; his leggins were of red cloth, trimmed with a row of bells. His horse was likewise painted, and the bridle ornamented with red and black cloth. The three musicians belonged to the band of the soldiers. They were dressed in shabby blanket robes. As soon as the drum was beat, the dancers bent their bodies forward, leaped up with both feet together, holding their guns in their hands, and the finger on the trigger, as if going to fire. In this manner they danced for about a minute in a circle, then gave a loud shout, and, having rested a little, began the dance again, and so on alternately. Some tobacco was thrown on the ground before them, after which they soon broke up, took up their robes and went to Ruhptare, where they danced and passed the night, and then exhibited their performances among the Manitaries.[36]

Mr. Kipp had received orders from Mr. Mc Kenzie to go to Fort Union, and he accordingly made the necessary preparations for this winter's journey. He purchased, from the Indians, eighteen dogs; and the getting sledges in readiness caused some bustle in the fort.

On the 29th of December, the thermometer, at eight o'clock in the morning, was at 19° Fahrenheit, and the high northwest wind was so cutting that we could not hold it out long in the prairie. Notwithstanding this, the dogs were collected, and harnessed with considerable difficulty, as they made much resistance. Mr. Kipp travelled with five Indian sledges, with a sufficient number of well-armed *engagés*. Charbonneau accompanied him on what is called a cariole (a convenient wooden sledge, drawn by one horse), in order to purchase meat for us of the Indians. The appearance of the caravan was very amusing, for many of the dogs, not trained to this service, jumped from one side to the other and could not be brought into order but by the use of the whip. The three dogs which drew the principal sledge had, on their collars, a large double bow, covered and ornamented with red, yellow, blue, and white fringe, to which a bell was suspended.[37]

About noon the snow storm increased, and it was so cold in our apartment that, notwithstanding a good fire, we were unable to work. The high wind drove the snow through the crevices in the walls and the doors, and the whole place was filled with smoke. The thermometer at noon was 14° Fahrenheit. The night, too, was stormy, and on the 30th the hurricane from the west roared exactly as at sea; a great deal of snow lay in our room, and the water was frozen. In the prairie we could not keep our eyes open on account of the excessive glare: exposure to the weather was painful both to man and beast. It was hoped, however, that it would soon cause the herds of buffaloes to come nearer to us; but this expectation was not realized though it was said that there were many at the post of the Yanktonans. Our horses were obliged, during this dreadful weather, to walk about the whole night in the court-yard of the fort, with a mass of ice and snow on their backs. As Gautier, an old *engagé*, was bringing wood into the room, and the door remained open a short time, Mr. Bodmer's colours and pencils froze, so that he could not use them without hot water. Writing, too, was very difficult, because our ink was congealed; and, while the side of our bodies which was turned to the fire was half roasted, the other was quite benumbed, and we were often forced to rise in order to warm ourselves. The cook had his ears frostbitten in going to the river to fetch water.

To add to our chapter of misfortunes, news was received that the Yanktonans had stolen some horses from the Mandans, and killed several. This was the fourth time that these Indians had broken the peace concluded in the preceding September, and the Mandans were so incensed at their treachery that they were disposed to recommence the war.

This day Mr. Kipp got no further on his journey than the Manitari village, because some of his dogs had broken loose and run away, and several of his people had their faces frostbitten. The last day of the year was clear and cold: at eight o'clock in the morning the mercury was at 16½°, by Reaumur's thermometer, below freezing point: a vapour rose from the river. Towards noon the wind again blew high, the frozen snow crackled, and no animals, not even wolves or ravens, were to be seen. Before this weather set in, the Indians had ridden fifteen miles into the prairie, where many of them were almost frozen to death, but were recovered by being wrapped up in blankets, and laid before the fire.

FOOTNOTES:

[1] Part III of our reprint of Maximilian's *Travels* begins with chapter xxviii of the original London edition (1843).—ED.

[2] For Fort Clark and its custodian, James Kipp, see our volume xxii, p. 344, note 317, and p. 345, note 319.—ED.

[3] Simon Bellehumeur, probably this interpreter's father, was in 1804 a North West Company's voyageur on upper Red River. One of the same name also acted as express and scout in the time of General Alfred Sully's campaign (1864) through the Little Missouri Bad Lands. See Montana Historical Society *Contributions*, ii, pp. 314-330; and *Larpenteur's Journal*, ii, p. 362.—ED.

[4] For Kenneth Mc Kenzie, see Wyeth's *Oregon*, in our volume xxi, p. 45, note 25. Fort Union is noticed in our volume xxii, p. 373, note 349.—ED.

[5] See our volume xxii, p. 305, note 263, for account of the Sioux bands, of which the Yanktonai was one of the largest. They were inclined toward peace with the United States although tradition relates that one of these bands participated in the sieges of Forts Meigs and Stephenson in the War of 1812-15. Their habitat was the Upper James River, above the Yankton. They are divided into two bands, Upper and Lower Yanktonai, the former being now located on Standing Rock reservation, North Dakota, the latter near Crow Creek agency, South Dakota.—ED.

[6] For Major Dougherty, see our volume xiv, p. 126, note 92; for Bellevue, xxii, p. 267, note 221.—ED.

[7] Pilcher is noted in our volume xiv, p. 269, note 193; Cabanné, in volume xxii, p. 271, note 226.—ED.

[8] For burial customs, see our volume xxiii, p. 360, note 329.—ED.

[9] See Plate 81, figure 17, in the accompanying atlas, our volume xxv.—ED.

[10] Honoré Picotte was a French-Canadian who came to the Missouri about 1820, and entered the Columbia Fur Company. Afterwards (1827-30) he was a member of the French Fur Company; and when that was merged in the American Company he became a partner in the Upper Missouri Outfit. He had much influence with the Sioux, among whom he married, and for many years was stationed at Fort Pierre (see our volume xxii, p. 315, note 277). Audubon met him at this post in 1843; and in later years he had charge of the annual voyage of the trading steamer to the upper river. In 1846 Father De Smet was his guest at Fort Pierre. About two years later Picotte retired from the active business of the company, and removed to St. Louis. In the early days of the trade, he had a brother associated with him; and his half-

breed son, Charles F. Picotte, was a noted figure in early Dakota history. See South Dakota Department of History *Collections*, ii, pp. 246-248.—ED.

[11] For Sublette and Campbell, and the rivalry of their company with that of the American Fur Company, see our volume xxiii, p. 198, notes 154, 155.—ED.

[12] For this chief, see our volume xxii, p. 345, note 318.—ED.

[13] A sketch of Charbonneau is found in our volume vi, p. 32, note 3; consult also *Original Journals of the Lewis and Clark Expedition*, vii, pp. 329, 330; see also index to that work.—ED.

[14] Lewis and Clark made (1804) this Mandan second chief of the village of Ruhptare. Upon the return voyage of the explorers, two years later, he agreed at first to accompany them to the United States, but later, through jealousy of another Mandan chief, refused. See *Original Journals*, i, pp. 212, 216; v, pp. 341, 343.—ED.

[15] Joseph Dougherty, for whom see our volume xxiii, p. 218, note 167.—ED.

[16] See p. 25, for plan of Minitaree medicine feast. See also our volume xxiii, p. 334.—ED.

[17] For this instrument, see our volume xxiii, p. 325, note 293.—ED.

[18] See p. 25, for illustration of club with carved head.—ED.

[19] Garreau settled among the Arikara Indians at an early day (about 1785), being probably the first white settler in South Dakota. Lewis and Clark found him in the Arikara villages on both their outward and return journey—*Original Journals*, i, pp. 7, 272; v, p. 355. His son Pierre was a noted interpreter, being for many years located at Fort Berthold. See *Larpenteur's Journal*, i, p. 124, for his portrait; see also Boller, *Among the Indians*, pp. 181, 182, 245-248.—ED.

[20] See Plate 52, in the accompanying atlas, our volume xxv.—ED.

[21] See accompanying ground-plan of Mandan hut.—ED.

[22] See our volume xxiii, p. 113, for Blackfeet badge of Prairie-dog band.—ED.

[23] See our volume xxiii, p. 113, for badge of Raven band.—ED.

[24] See Plate 53, in the accompanying atlas, our volume xxv; the figure in the background represents Maksick-Karehde (the Flying Eagle); that in the foreground, Sih-Chida (the Yellow Feather).—ED.

[25] See our volume xxiii, p. 247, for head of this animal.—ED.

[26] Teton River, so named by Lewis and Clark from that tribe of Sioux Indians, was originally called by the Dakota Watpa Chicha, a term translated into the modern Bad River. It is a South Dakota prairie stream, between White and Cheyenne rivers. Its forks were probably at the entrance of Frozenman's Creek, its largest northern tributary.—ED.

[27] For the Santa Fé trade, see preface to our volume xix; the caravan for 1833 went out under the leadership of Charles Bent, and brought back large returns. See *Niles' Register*, xliv, p. 374.—ED.

[28] See p. 37, for portrait of a Mandan, in bull-dance costume. For an account of this band or company, see our volume xxiii, pp. 294, 295.—ED.

[29] See Plate 56, in the accompanying atlas, our volume xxv.—ED.

[30] See previous mention of this union in our volume xxiii, p. 297.—ED.

[31] For a representation of this costume, see Plate 28, in the accompanying atlas, our volume xxv.—ED.

[32] Fort Jackson was built by Chardon (for whom see our volume xxiii, p. 188, note 144) in December, 1833. It was sought thereby to intercept the Assiniboin and Cree tribesmen who came from the Saskatchewan Valley, thus getting possession of their furs before they reached the rival traders of Sublette and Campbell's opposition. Chardon took twenty men with him from Fort Union, and built a post fifty feet square, naming it in honor of the president of the United States. The post was not long maintained. In 1845 Larpenteur made a camp on Poplar River, but does not mention any preceding fur-trade station thereon.—ED.

[33] For this expedition, see volume xxiii, pp. 153, 154.—ED.

[34] For a brief account of this expedition of 1825, see our volume xxiii, p. 227, note 182. The treaty is given in *Treaties between the United States and the Several Indian Tribes 1778 to 1837* (Washington, 1837), pp. 356-359. Sih-Chida was son of the chief known commonly as Four Men.—ED.

[35] See badges of Prairie-Dog and Raven bands in our volume xxiii, p 113.—ED.

[36] For the dance of this band, see Plate 25, in the accompanying atlas, our volume xxv.—ED.

[37] See illustration, p. 37, for heads of sledge dogs.—ED.

CHAPTER XXIX
CONTINUATION OF OUR WINTER RESIDENCE AT FORT CLARKE, TILL OUR DEPARTURE, FROM JANUARY 1ST TO APRIL 18TH, 1834

Increase of the Cold in the beginning of January—The Arrival of our People from Picotte—Parhelia—Changes of Temperature—Sih-Chida's Prayer—My Thermometer stolen—Reconciliation of Mato-Topé and Pehriska-Ruhpa—Consecration of a Medicine Son at Ruphtare—Visit of some Yanktonans—Hunting of the Indians in the severe Cold—Dance of the Women of the White Buffalo Cow at Ruphtare—Mr. Kipp's Return—Scarcity of Provisions—Enemies in the Indian Village—Rapid Thaw—The Mandans kill an Assiniboin—Cunning and Boldness of the latter—The Scalp Dance of the Manitaries—Superstition of the Indians—They remove to their Summer Village—The Arikkara, Pachtuwa-Chta—Dance of the Meniss-Ochata—Blindness caused by the Snow—Commencement of my Illness—Arrival of the Spring Birds—The Mad Dogs' Dance in the Fort—Dance of the Ischoha-Kakoschochata in the Fort—Breaking-up of the Ice in the Missouri—Dance of the Berock-Ochata—Arrival of the People entered for my Service—My Recovery by the use of Green Herbs—Preparations for our Departure.

January set in with increasing cold, which at eight in the morning was 18° Reaumur, and on the 2nd, at the same hour, 25°, Reaumur, below freezing point. On the 3rd the mercury sank into the ball, and was frozen; it remained there on the 4th, but on the 5th it rose, and at eight in the morning was 9° below zero. During these cold days, some of our woodcutters had their noses and cheeks frostbitten. The horizon was hazy; the river smoked; neither man nor animal was to be seen; yet a party of Mandans, with their wives, were in the prairie hunting buffaloes, of which they killed forty. At night the cold was so intense, that we could not venture to put our hands from our bodies, lest they should be frozen. In the morning we could scarcely endure the severity of the weather, till we had a blazing fire, for the bleak northwest wind penetrated through all the seams of the building. We received information that Mr. Kipp had remained with the Manitaries till the 2nd of January, and had not proceeded on his journey till the cold had somewhat abated. Almost all his people had some part of their body frostbitten, and eight of his dogs had run away. Some Indians who visited us presented rather a novel appearance, having their hair, and even their eyelashes, covered with hoar frost and icicles. In our own room, the boots and shoes were frozen so hard in the morning, that we could scarcely put them on; ink, colours, and pencils were perfectly useless. During this cold we were visited by a deaf and dumb Mandan, who had no covering on the upper part of his body under his robe. On the 3rd of January, at noon, when the sunbeams, shining on the frozen snow, were extremely dazzling, the thermometer being at 24° below zero, I saw no living creatures in the neighbourhood of the Indian village, except flocks of the snow-bunting, and a few ravens, two species of birds which are capable of enduring the severest cold. The Yanktonans, and the people whom we had sent to Picotte, returned, on the 4th of January, with dried meat, as well as tallow for candles: they said that, during the two coldest days, they had halted in the forest, but that, in the night, the wolves had carried off part of their meat. On the 5th of January the air was misty, and at one o'clock there were two parhelia at a considerable distance from the sun; they were, however, faint and rather irregular. It was scarcely possible to obtain water from the river, and the water-casks in our room were frozen to the bottom. Unfortunately, too, our woodcutters brought us only driftwood, which had lain so long in the water that it would not burn. Picotte had sent a small cask of wine by our people, as a present from Mr. Mc Kenzie for the Mandans, which was delivered to the chiefs for distribution.

At eight o'clock in the morning of the 6th, there was a fall of snow; the temperature in the open air was 29° Fahrenheit, in our room only 25°. The wind blew from the west, and at noon the snow was mixed with rain, so that the water dripped on our books and papers from the loft, which was covered with snow. The robes and hair of the Indians were wet, and they very unceremoniously, therefore, came to dry themselves before our fire; this was not very agreeable, nevertheless we were glad that we could resume our usual occupations. At noon the temperature was 39½° Fahrenheit, and in the evening it became considerably warmer, so that we could leave our hands at liberty during the night, without their being affected by the cold. The night, however, was very stormy, and Sih-Chida laid himself down to sleep on the ground before our fire. These changes of temperature were very remarkable. On the 7th we again had cold, with a tempestuous west wind; at noon, the thermometer stood at 12°, and in the afternoon it again snowed. Sih-Chida once more passed the night with us, and, when all was silent, made a long address to the lord of life, in which he besought him to send buffaloes, that they might not starve. He spoke in a rapid half-suppressed tone of reproach, and without any gesticulation.[38] On the following day, Dreidoppel went into the forest in quest of game, but could not proceed on account of the drifted snow; he only saw some flocks of prairie hens. At noon, when I went to look at the thermometer, I found that it had been stolen by the Indians. Our friend Sih-Chida immediately ran out, and discovered the instrument concealed by a woman under her robe, and, to my great joy, brought it back to me. Bidda-Chohki (generally called La Chevelure levée, the scalped man), visited us, and gave me some words of the Manitari language, but he was not in a very good humour, because he could not get any brandy. The next day this man dressed himself very handsomely in order to have his portrait taken, but the mercury was again 20° below zero, and it was too cold in our room to paint, for colours and pencils were frozen, though standing close to the fire, and had to be thawed in hot water. We calculated that we should burn in our chimney at least six cords of wood in a month if this cold continued. Mato-Topé had become reconciled to Pehriska-Ruhpa, and purchased a green blanket, which he showed to us, as a present for him. We heard that a wolf had attacked three Indian women in the forest, who had been obliged to defend themselves with their hatchets.

On the 14th of January, the cold was only 8° below zero, but there was such a high, piercing wind, that our woodcutters complained more than when the cold was more severe. In these prairies it is, for the most part, the wind which makes the cold intolerable; and though persons who ventured out wore woollen caps which left only the eyes exposed, yet their faces were frostbitten. Our provisions were very bad, for Picotte had sent us only tough, hard, stale meat, besides which we had nothing but maize and beans, and the water of the river. Mato-Topé, in his finest dress, accompanied by many Indians, visited us. He wore a large hood of red cloth, adorned with forty long eagles' feathers, and was going to Ruhptare, where a medicine son was to be adopted.

Double rainbow

Little Soldier (Tukan Haton), a Sioux chief

In the night of the 14th, the wind blew with such violence, that it scattered the heap of ashes from the fire place all over the room, so that our beds, benches, and clothes were completely covered with them. Mato-Topé returned on this day from Ruhptare, and told us, with great satisfaction and self-complacency, that he had enumerated all his exploits, and that no one had been able to surpass him. Old Garreau, who was constantly with our *engagés* in the fort, complained to me, that, for a long time, he had lived on nothing but maize boiled in water; and this was really the case with many persons at this place, as game became more and more scarce. When Garreau first came to these parts, game abounded, and beavers were heard in all the streams, striking with their tails; now, however, even the Indians are often reduced to want of food. On the 21st of January, while the Indians passed the night without fire, in the prairie, in order to hunt, the thermometer was at 30° below 0 (27½° Reaumur); the wind was easterly, and pretty high. The land and the river were covered by a dense mist, through which the sun penetrated when just above the horizon; on either side was a large crescent, which rose as high as the upper surface of the mist, the eastern one extending to the frozen surface of the river. They were at some distance from the sun, and, like it, appeared of a light yellowish-white through the misty vapour.[39] Sometimes we observed, in the light misty clouds on the horizon, two short, beautifully coloured rainbows, at some distance from the sun, which, being interrupted by the upper stratum of clouds, did not rise to any great height. The snow was now frozen so hard, that it could be broken into large pieces, which emitted a clear sound when struck with the foot. In the sunshine the atmosphere sparkled with innumerable particles of floating ice. The Indians had cut some holes in the ice on the Missouri, to procure water, and fenced them round with poles and brushwood covered with buffalo hides, as a protection against the cold wind. At noon the weather was rather milder, the temperature being 10½° below zero. Three Yanktonans came to the fort with a view to persuade the Mandans to join in an expedition against another tribe.

Mr. Bodmer took a very excellent likeness of Psihdje-Sahpa, one of the three Yanktonans.[40]

On the 23rd of January information was brought that a herd of buffaloes was only six miles from the fort; accordingly, three *engagés*, with the Arikkara, were sent in pursuit of them, and returned at night with two cows and a young bull, two of which were given to the fort. The Mandans had killed about fifty of this herd: our hunters had almost all their fingers frozen, but they knew well how to restore circulation by rubbing the limbs with snow. The Indians did not visit us so frequently at this time, because they were well supplied with meat: the Arikkara, however, came to us to attend a feast in Belhumeur's apartment, where we were to be regaled with buffalo flesh. On the 29th, the women of the band of the white buffalo cow, from Ruhptare, came to the fort to perform their dance, on which occasion they were dressed in the same manner as the women from Mih-Tutta-Hang-Kush, only they had not the bundles of brushwood. The musicians were three men, who wore caps of white buffalo skin. Knives, tobacco, and glass beads were laid on the ground as presents for them, after which they proceeded to the lower Mandan village, from which they came back, the following day, in grand procession, over the frozen river. Mr. Kipp soon afterwards arrived from Fort Union, with three or four dog sledges, and six men: they were completely covered with ice, their noses and cheeks were livid, and they appeared quite frostbitten. Besides staying four days with the Manitaries, Mr. Kipp and his party had been twelve days on their journey to Fort Union. At the beginning they had nothing to eat; and the poor dogs had been so completely starved for nine days, that they could scarcely crawl along, so that no burden could be laid upon them, and the party were obliged to travel the greater part of the way on foot, in deep snow. They encountered a war party of nine Assiniboins, some of whom ran away, but the others were sent by Mr. Kipp to hunt, by which means he procured meat, and the *engagés*, too, succeeded in killing a few elks and deer. It was affirmed that the mercury of Fahrenheit's thermometer had been for a whole fortnight at 45° below zero (77° below freezing point), at Fort Union. No buffaloes had appeared in the vicinity, nor any Indians, who remained farther down the river. The hunters of Fort Union had been absent nearly a month, in which time they killed only two bulls, two cows, and a calf. Except in some few places, provisions were extremely scarce this winter on the whole of the Missouri, from Fort Clarke upwards. No accounts had been received from Fort Mc Kenzie. I had wished to receive several articles from Fort Union; but Mr. Hamilton was not able to send them, the sledge being too heavily laden; he, however, promised to forward them without fail, in the spring, with the people who were to be sent to conduct us down the Missouri to Fort Pièrre. Mr. Kipp had been eleven days on his journey back, and had again been obliged to perform a considerable part of it on foot. The dogs had had nothing to eat for three days, and now the poor beasts were fed with hides cut in pieces, for we had no meat. Numbers of the fowls in the forest perished in the cold. On the last day of January there was a change in the weather; at eight in the morning, with a west wind, the mercury was at 22° Fahrenheit, and we could scarcely bear the warmth of the fire in our apartment. Towards noon a complete thaw set in, and the mild weather immediately brought us a number of Indian visitors.

On the 1st of February, Mr. Kipp sent three *engagés*, with two dog sledges, down the river, to the post among the Yanktonans, which was under the superintendence of Picotte, to procure meat, for we subsisted entirely on maize broth and maize bread, and were without tallow for candles; the dogs that were sent with the *engagés* howled most piteously when they were harnessed, their feet being still sore and bleeding from the effects of their late journey. On this day news was received from Mih-Tutta-Hang-Kush, that three hostile Indians (Assiniboins), had been in the village during the night, for the purpose of shooting somebody, for in the morning the place where they had concealed themselves was discovered, from one of the party having left his knee-band behind. They had not been able to fire through the wall of the hut, and had retired at daybreak without attaining their object; traces were also found of some hostile Indians, who had come over the river.

On the 2nd of February, one of the sledges sent to Picotte came back, having been broken on the way. The man who came with it fell in with the Mandans, who were going to hunt buffaloes, and detained him, lest he should frighten the animals away. In the preceding night, the Assiniboins had stolen three horses from the Manitaries, 150 of whom immediately mounted their horses to pursue and kill them.

At eight o'clock on the morning of the 3rd, the thermometer stood at 39°; the face of the country had assumed quite a different aspect; large tracts of land were wholly free from the snow, which was fast melting away, and only the hills were partially covered; yet, with this rapid thaw, the ground had not become wet, for it was immediately dried by the continual wind; but there was a considerable quantity of water on the ice which covered the river. The ravens and magpies again flew about in the prairie in quest of food.

In the afternoon news was received that the Manitaries, who had gone in pursuit of the Assiniboins, had overtaken a small party, and killed a young man, whom they had found asleep, cruelly awakened with whips, and then murdered in cold blood. These Assiniboins are very daring, and often approach the villages of the Mandans and Manitaries, either singly or in small parties, and sometimes surprise individuals and shoot them. Thus an Assiniboin suddenly fired at a number of young people who were standing near the palisades of the village, and killed one of them. The others raised an alarm, while the murderer took the scalp of the youth he had killed, fled down the steep bank of the river, where many persons were bathing, and made his escape through the very midst of all these people. Other Assiniboins stole eleven horses from a Manitari hut, and were not even perceived till they were in the act of leading off the last of the animals. They stole four horses from a hut in which Charbonneau was sleeping, and made their escape with their booty, without being seen by any one. To-day arrows were found sticking in the huts and posts of the village, which they had discharged at random during the night in the hope of killing one of their foes.

On the 4th and 5th, the weather was mild; the horses were again sent out to graze in the prairie, our waggons went to fetch grass, and, towards noon, the day was really quite warm. We were still without meat, none of the parties whom we sent out having been able to procure any. Our stock of tallow, too, was exhausted, and we were obliged to content ourselves with the light of the fire. For several succeeding days, the weather being still mild, we were much interested in watching the activity of the Indians on the river; among them a number of women brought heavy burdens, especially of wood, from the lower forest village, to Mih-Tutta-Hang-Kush. They had to pass, opposite the fort, a channel formed through the midst of the frozen river, which was covered with a thin coat of ice; this they broke very deliberately with their long poles, and then waded through. Some carried their small leathern boats to the channel, in this they deposited the wood, and then pushed it along. The manner in which they took up the heavy burdens was remarkable. A woman lay down on her back, upon the bundle of wood, while another raised her with the burden till she was able to bend forward, and then stand upright with her load. A great many women were thus occupied, for the Indians were desirous of going to their summer village, because they were now too much scattered to be safe while the enemy was so near at hand.

On the 9th of February the inhabitants of Ruhptare had all removed from their winter to their summer quarters; they were evidently afraid that the ice would break up early, and the water of the Missouri rise considerably.

On the 10th, two of our people came from Picotte, with a sledge drawn by two dogs, and informed us that there were many buffaloes in the neighbourhood, consequently our fear of want of provisions was dispelled. At Fort Pièrre, on the River Teton, the cold had been more intense than had been known for many years, the mercury having remained for a considerable time between 30° and 40° below zero. Three of Mr. Laidlow's people,[41] who were travelling at the time, had suffered so severely from the frost, that their lives were despaired of. The ice of the Missouri had, for a few days, been very unfavourable for travelling, as it was covered to some depth with water, and our people, consequently, had suffered much. In the afternoon of that day, the Manitari chief, Lachpitzi-Sirish (the yellow bear), arrived, bringing on his horse a small supply of meat, and a young buffalo calf, which he presented to us, this disgusting little black animal being reckoned a great dainty by them. His robe was painted with suns, and on his back he carried his bow, with a beautifully ornamented quiver of panther's skin. Charbonneau immediately accommodated him in his bed room. On the following day we sent a couple of our hunters to Fort Union, with letters to Mr. Mc Kenzie. The fort was crowded with Manitaries who wished to perform before us the scalp dance, in commemoration of having slain an enemy on the preceding day. A number of tall, handsomely dressed men, having their faces blackened, soon filled every apartment. Itsichaika (the monkey-face), and the other chiefs, had arrived, and these Indians, who are not nearly so well behaved as the Mandans, very deliberately took possession of all our seats and fireplaces. We bolted the door of our own apartment, where we quietly remained, permitting only a very few of the Indians to enter.

At two o'clock the Manitari women arrived in procession, accompanied by many children and some Mandans. Eighteen women, marching two and two in a close column, entered the court-yard of the fort, with a short-measured, slow pace. Seven men of the band of the dogs, having their faces painted black, or black striped with red, acted as musicians, three of them having drums, and four the schischikué. They were wrapped in their buffalo robes, and their heads were uncovered, and ornamented with the feathers of owls and other birds. The faces of some of the women were painted black, others red, while some were striped black and red. They wore buffalo dresses, or blankets, and the two principal were enveloped in the white buffalo robe. The greater part of them had the feather of a war eagle standing upright, and one only wore the large handsome feather cap. In their arms they carried battle-axes or guns, ornamented with red cloth and short black feathers, which, during the dance, they placed with the butt-end on the ground; in short, while performing this dance, the women are accoutred in the military dress and weapons of the warriors. The right wing was headed by the wife of the chief, Itsichaika, who carried in her hand a long elastic rod, from the point of which was suspended the scalp of the young man slain on the preceding day, surmounted by a stuffed magpie with outspread wings;[42] lower down on the same rod hung a second scalp, a lynx skin, and a bunch of feathers. Another woman bore a third scalp on a similar rod. The women filed off in a semicircle; the musicians, taking their stand on the left wing, now commenced a heterogeneous noise, beating the drum, rattling the schischikué, and yelling with all their might. The women began to dance, waddling in short steps, like ducks; the two wings, or horns of the crescent, advanced towards each other, and then receded, at the same time singing in a shrill tone of voice. It was a complete caterwaul concert. After awhile they rested, and then recommenced, and continued dancing about twenty minutes. The director of the fort now caused tobacco, looking-glasses, and knives, from the Company's stores, to be thrown on the ground in the middle of the circle. Hereupon the women once more danced in quick time, the musicians forming themselves into a close body, and holding their instruments towards the centre. This concluded the festivity, and the whole band retired to the Mandan forest village.

There was a heavy fall of snow during the night, and the morning of the 12th again presented the landscape clothed with its white covering. Mr. Bodmer had taken an excellent portrait of Machsi-Nika, the deaf and dumb Mandan, in his war dress. He came to our residence to-day with angry gestures, and evidently greatly enraged against us, so that I was afraid that this half-witted, uncivilized man would attack the artist. Mr. Kipp was requested to clear up the matter, and it appeared that his anger had been caused by a malignant insinuation of the perfidious old Garreau, who had pointed out to him that Bodmer had drawn him only in a mean dress, while all the other Indians were represented in their handsomest robes. This ill-natured insinuation completely exasperated the poor man, and we in vain endeavoured to pacify him, by assuring him that we intended to make him known to the world in a truly warlike costume. Mr. Bodmer then thought of an expedient: he quickly and secretly made a copy of his drawing, which he brought in, tore in half, and threw into the fire, in the presence of the Indian. This had the desired effect, and he went away perfectly satisfied.

In the afternoon the Manitaries returned from the Mandan village, and again took deliberate possession of the various apartments of the fort. The Monkey-face, a cunning, perfidious Indian, who wore a new red felt hat, is the chief who now takes the lead among the Manitaries. Accordingly, as soon as he took leave, all the Indians followed him. One of the chiefs, with his family, sat a long time in our room, and were much interested with Mr. Bodmer's drawings, and astonished and delighted with our musical box. A Mandan who was present thought that a little white man, who was making this pretty music, must be concealed in it. All of them asked for presents, and they would certainly have pilfered many things if we had not kept close watch over them. At length our door was opened, and a tall, heavy man, with a blackened face, entered, and, like all the rest assembled there, demanded something to eat. We, however, gave him to understand that we had nothing to give them, as we were supplied by Mr. Kipp, and with this answer they were obliged to be satisfied. Towards evening our provision store was replenished by three sledges, laden with meat, sent by Picotte, which arrived in the fort.

On the following day, a very high, cold wind arose, which blew the snow off from the ice that covered the river, and the Indian women, carrying their burdens, frequently fell down on the slippery surface. The Mandans had found a dead buffalo cow in the prairie, and, although it was in part decayed, they greedily devoured it.

On the 17th, at eight in the morning, with a temperature of 1° below 0, the woods were covered with hoar frost; the wind blew from the south, and veered to the southwest; the river had risen considerably, and, in some places, overflowed its banks. The sledges had much difficulty in crossing the river without getting into the water, and the ice broke under one of them. At noon, the temperature was 10°, and afterwards there was a fall of snow. Dreidoppel shot a beautiful red fox in the prairie, but had no success against the wolves. The Mandans told us, that they had gone, some days before, to hunt buffaloes, and had driven a herd of them towards the mountains, where there is a good opportunity to use the bow and arrows; they had, therefore, pursued the animals rapidly, but, on reaching them, they found but a very few buffaloes, the others, as they affirmed, having sunk into the ground: they had, doubtless, taken refuge in the nearest ravines. They assigned, as the cause of this sudden disappearance of the buffaloes, that their party was headed by a man who, in the preceding year, had caused five Assiniboins, who had come to them as messengers of peace, to be killed, and that, on account of this unjust act, he was now always unsuccessful in hunting.

The mercury remained now a little above or below zero, but at noon the sun had much power, and the reflection from the snow was very dazzling, which induced our hunters to make for themselves wooden snow spectacles, in the manner of the Esquimaux. The dumb Mandans had been successful in hunting, and brought several horse-loads of meat, which we bought of them. In the afternoon, when the temperature was 8° or 9°, I heard an Indian child crying at the door of our room; it had touched a piece of iron with its tongue, and the skin immediately came off.

At daybreak, on the 27th, in the morning, the mercury was at 26°, Fahrenheit, below zero, or 59° below freezing point; and at 8 o'clock, when the sun shone brightly, at 11° below zero, with a west wind. During the night, the horses had broken a window in Mr. Kipp's room, so that we had a very cold breakfast there. In our apartments everything fluid was frozen, and the quilts on the beds were covered with hoar frost. We had now some fresh meat, but our stock of sugar was at an end, and we had to sweeten our coffee with treacle. We were visited by the three deaf and dumb Mandans, whose fourth brother, Berock-Itainu, whom we have before mentioned, is not so afflicted: there is, likewise, a deaf and dumb child in the village. Kiasax, the Blackfoot, who had accompanied us to Fort Union, visited us to-day for the first time, and we showed him the portraits of his countrymen, with which he was much pleased. The Indians were busy in conveying many things to the summer village, though the prairies were covered with snow; and numerous horses were seeking a scanty subsistence by scraping it away with their hoofs to get at the dry grass.

On the 27th of February, Mr. Kipp had pieces of ice hewn on the river to fill his ice cellar. A high west wind increased the cold, but the snow melted away because the thermometer was at 38° at noon. We saw the Indian boys pursue and catch the snow-buntings, of which there were large flocks in the neighbourhood of the villages; and the prairie wolves now prowled about in couples: in the evening there was a heavy fall of snow. The Indians removed to their village: all their horses, even the foals, were loaded: they likewise cut blocks of ice from the river, which the women carried home on their backs, in leather baskets, in order to melt them to obtain water. The Indian children amused themselves with ascending the heaps of snow, and gliding down on a board, or a piece of the back-bone of a buffalo, with some of the ribs attached to it. Mato-Topé paid us a visit in a very strange costume; his head-dress was much more suitable for an old woman than for a warrior. His head was bound round with a strip of wolf's skin, the long hairs of which stood on end, and which hung down behind. Some feathers, standing upright, were placed among the hair, which, except at the tip, were stripped, and painted red. This chief, indeed, had on a different dress almost every time he came to see us. Sometimes he wore a blue uniform, with red facings, which he had obtained from the merchants. Mr. Bodmer took the portrait of a handsome Manitari partisan to-day.[43] He was not pleased that we intended to keep his portrait, as he was going on a military expedition, and said that Mr. Bodmer ought, at least, to give him a copy of the drawing. This being refused, he drew a portrait of the artist, and his performance showed that he possessed some talent for the art.

On the evening of the 28th of February, Picotte sent up the letter-bag from St. Louis, and I had the pleasure of receiving despatches from Germany, with very agreeable intelligence. This post was forwarded, on the 2nd of March, to Fort Union, by two of the *engagés* in dog-sledges. Bodmer drew the portrait of an old Manitari, whose proper name was Birohka (the robe with the beautiful hair), but the Mandans called him "Long Nose," on account of the prominence of that feature. He wore a cap of white buffalo skin, and an ample brown robe painted with wreaths of feathers; before he would suffer his portrait to be taken, he demanded a black silk neckerchief as a recompense, which was given him.[44] As all the Indians had now removed to their summer village, Mr. Kipp took the usual complement of soldiers into the fort, four of whom served as a guard against the importunities of the women and children; they were Mato-Topé, Dipauch, Berock-Itainu, and another whose name I do not know. The first never smoked his pipe in another person's room, if anybody stirred from his place or looked at him. We had some interesting conversations with several sensible and inquiring Indians, especially with the soldiers of the fort.

On the morning of the 5th of March, the mercury being at 29°, we had a very severe snow storm from the north, which continued till near ten o'clock. On the following day, Mato-Topé introduced to us a tall, robust Arikkara, named Pachtuwa-Chta, who lived peaceably among the Mandans. He was a handsome man, but not to be depended upon, and was said to have killed many white men.[45] Another tall man of the same nation frequently visited us, generally observing that he was not like Pachtuwa, as he had never killed a white man. Mato-Topé, after repeated solicitations, prevailed on Mr. Bodmer to paint for him a white-headed eagle, holding in his claws a bloody scalp, to which he, doubtless, attached some superstitious notion, but I could not see exactly what it might be. Mato-Topé gave me very accurate information respecting his own language, and that of the neighbouring Indian nations, and took great pleasure in communicating to me some words of the Mandan and Arikkara languages, the latter of which he spoke fluently.

On the 7th of March, the band of the Meniss-Ochata (dog band), from Ruhptare, danced in the medicine lodge at Mih-Tutta-Hang-Kush. Mr. Bodmer went to see the dance, and met Mato-Topé, who, however, puffed up by his high dignity as a dog, would not notice him. Sih-Chida, who also belonged to this band, went into the lodge, where he discharged his gun. In the afternoon the band approached the fort, and we heard the sound of their war pipes at the gates. A crowd of spectators accompanied the seven or eight and twenty dogs, who were all dressed in their handsomest clothes. Some of them wore beautiful robes, or shirts of bighorn leather; others had shirts of red cloth; and some blue and red uniforms. Others, again, had the upper part of their body naked, with their martial deeds painted on the skin with reddish-brown colour. The four principal dogs wore an immense cap hanging down upon the shoulders, composed of raven's or magpie's feathers, finished at the tips with small white down feathers. In the middle of this mass of feathers, the outspread tail of a wild turkey, or of a war eagle, was fixed. These four principal dogs wore round their neck a long slip of red cloth, which hung down over the shoulders, and, reaching the calf of the leg, was tied in a knot in the middle of the back. These are the true dogs, who, when a piece of meat is thrown into the fire, are bound immediately to snatch it out and devour it raw.[46] Two other men wore similar colossal caps of yellow owl's feathers, with dark transverse stripes, and the rest had on their heads a thick tuft of raven's, magpie's, or owl's feathers, which is the badge of the band. All of them had the long war pipe suspended from their necks. In their left hand they carried their weapons—a gun, bow and arrows, or war club; and in their right hand the schischikué peculiar to their band. It is a stick adorned with blue and white glass beads, with buffalo or other hoofs suspended to it, the point ornamented with an eagle's feather, and the handle with slips of leather embroidered with beads.[47]

The warriors formed a circle round a large drum, which was beaten by five ill-dressed men, who were seated on the ground. Besides these, there were two men, each beating a small drum like a tambourine. The dogs accompanied the rapid and violent beat of the drum by the whistle of their war pipes, in short, monotonous notes, and then suddenly began to dance. They dropped their robes on the ground, some dancing within the circle, with their bodies bent forward and leaping up and down with both feet placed close together. The other Indians danced without any order, with their faces turned to the outer circle, generally crowded together; while the war pipe, drum, and schischikué made a frightful din.

On the 10th of March, two *engagés*, sent by Picotte, arrived, with letters and a sledge laden with dried meat. One of these men was blinded by the snow, a circumstance very usual in this month, from the dazzling reflection of the sun from an expansive surface of snow. He was obliged to get his companion to lead him by taking hold of the end of his stick.

On the 11th of March I felt the first symptoms of an indisposition, which daily increased, and soon obliged me to take to my bed. It began with a swelling in one knee, and soon extended to the whole leg, which assumed the colour of dark, extravasated blood. A violent fever succeeded, with great weakness, and, having neither medical advice nor suitable remedies, my situation became daily more helpless and distressing, as there was nobody who had any knowledge of this disorder. The other inhabitants of the fort were likewise indisposed, and our provisions were very bad and scanty. To economize our stock of coffee we were forced to make it wretchedly weak, and, for want of sugar or treacle, to sweeten it with honey, of which we had about twenty pounds. Our beverage was, generally speaking, the water from the river; and, as our supply of beans was very low our diet consisted almost exclusively of maize boiled in water, which greatly weakened our digestion.

The man blinded by the snow was so far recovered on the 13th, that he was able to return to Picotte. The first wild ducks were seen on this day, flying up the Missouri, and Mr. Kipp immediately set about making shot, to go in pursuit of these birds, which we had been most anxiously expecting. On the 14th, a store (*cache*) of maize was opened in the fort, the contents of which were perfectly dry, and in good preservation. Pehriska-Ruhpa spent several days with us, in order to have his portrait taken in his dress of one of the chiefs of the dog band. When the sitting was over, he always took off his ponderous feather cap, and rubbed it twice on each side of his head, a charm or precaution which he never neglected. He then seated himself with his friend, Mato-Topé, by the fire-side, when both took their pipes, the latter, however, always turning round first, and making everybody in the room sit down. During the tedium of my confinement to bed, I was enlivened by the frequent visits of the Indians, and I never neglected to continue my journal, which, from fever and consequent weakness, was often very fatiguing. Mr. Kipp kindly sent me some new-laid eggs every day, as well as rice, which he had reserved for me, and from which I derived great benefit. The inmates of the fort had nothing to eat but doughy maize bread and maize boiled in water; but Mr. Kipp, who did not like the latter, was obliged to fast.

On the 16th of March, the first wild swans were seen flying towards the northwest. Ducks were in the pools of water in the maize plantations of the Mandans; and Dreidoppel had observed the *Fringilla Canadensis*, as a harbinger of spring. Violent storms from the northwest had prevailed for some days; the Missouri was much swollen, but the breaking-up of the ice could not yet be expected, and we had repeated falls of snow. Mato-Topé and Pehriska-Ruhpa, who had gone out to hunt, succeeded in killing five buffaloes, and from them we obtained some meat; for, to show their liberality, they gave away a great deal of it, together with several coloured blankets. The first white-headed eagle (*Aquila leucocephala*) was seen to-day; and I received the first prairie dog, which was also a sign of the approach of spring, as these animals leave their burrows at this season. On the 27th of March, the band of the mad dogs danced in the fort; and, towards evening, an Indian from Ruhptare, who had had a dispute with Mr. Kipp about a beaver skin, revenged himself by breaking a pane of glass in our room. Our people pursued, but could not overtake him. As it was feared that he might commit greater acts of violence, the soldiers of the fort were sent to Ruhptare on the 28th, to protect a fur trader who resided there.

On the 30th, the first flock of fifteen or twenty wild geese passed over: the wind was high, and, on the following day, a good deal of ice broke up in the river. On the 1st of April the wind blew stormy, with a thermometer of 33° at noon. On the 2nd, the women at Mih-Tutta-Hang-Kush celebrated the spring corn feast, of which Mr. Bodmer made a sketch. This feast is always observed on the return of the wild geese, which are the messengers of the old woman who never dies. The Indians had already killed some of these birds. The festival was over at eleven o'clock in the forenoon, but some of the women remained the whole day, reclining near the offerings hung up in the prairie. Great numbers of young men were running races, and all was animation about the village.

On the 3rd of April, the band of the Ischoha-Kakoschochata, eighteen in number, danced in the fort, led by Mato-Topé, on horseback, in full dress, wearing his splendid feather cap. The ice broke up so rapidly in the river, that it was necessary to set a watch over our boats during the night, lest the rising water should carry them away. On the following day the icy covering of the river gave way, but soon froze again, only leaving a channel across the middle. Many ducks and geese, as well as a plover, appeared on the ice. On the 5th of April, the weather being stormy in the morning, and the temperature 59½° Fahrenheit, the river had risen about a foot, and towards noon it suddenly rose between three and four feet more, so that, at twelve o'clock, the ice on the surface began to move, the temperature being 68°. But in the night the river again fell a foot, and there was a slight frost. At nine in the evening the temperature was 55°, and we had a storm of thunder and lightning.

On the 7th of April there was but little floating ice on the river, which had fallen during the night. We saw several swans. On the 8th the Manitaries danced the scalp dance in the fort, and the Indians amused themselves in the prairie with races and various games. At one o'clock in the afternoon, the ice in the upper Missouri suddenly broke up, and brought down many trunks of trees, which endangered our boats. The Indians immediately availed themselves of this opportunity to land a good deal of the wood; they also brought ashore a drowned elk, which, though already in a state of decomposition, they actually ate, and the smith of the fort, a Canadian, did not disdain to partake of it with them. Some dead buffaloes likewise floated by, and the Indians followed them, for the same purpose. In the evening, though the quantity of ice was considerably diminished, yet some people who were to have gone down the river were obliged to defer their voyage.

The morning of the 9th of April being fine and serene, and the ice having almost entirely disappeared from the river, seven men were sent down to Picotte in Indian leather boats. The grass began to sprout, and some young plants appeared in the prairie, even a pulsatilla, with purple blossoms, apparently the same as the *P. vulgaris* of Europe; the Indians call this plant the red calf-flower. At noon the thermometer stood at 65°, with a northeast wind, and the river was free from ice. Towards evening, nine men of the band of the buffalo bulls came to the fort to perform their dance, discharging their guns immediately on entering. Only one of them wore the entire buffalo head;[48] the others had pieces of the skin of the forehead, a couple of fillets of red cloth, their shields decorated with the same material, and an appendage of feathers, intended to represent the bull's tail, hanging down their backs. They likewise carried long, elegantly ornamented banners in their hands. After dancing for a short time before us, they demanded presents. Besides the strange figures of this dance, Mr. Bodmer painted the chief, Mato-Topé, at full length, in his grandest dress. The vanity which is characteristic of the Indians induced this chief to stand stock-still for several days, so that his portrait succeeded admirably.[49] He wore on this occasion a handsome new shirt of bighorn leather, the large feather cap, and, in his hand, a long lance with scalps and feathers. He has been so often mentioned in my narrative, that I must here subjoin a few words respecting this eminent man, for he was fully entitled to this appellation, being not only a distinguished warrior, but possessing many fine and noble traits of character. In war he had always maintained a distinguished reputation; and on one occasion, with great personal danger, he conducted to Fort Clarke a numerous deputation of the Assiniboins, who had come to Mih-Tutta-Hang-Kush to conclude peace, while his countrymen, disregarding the proposals, kept firing upon the deputies. Mato-Topé, after having in vain exerted himself to the utmost to prevent these hostilities, led his enemies, with slow steps, amidst the whistling balls and the arrows of his countrymen, while he endeavoured to find excuses for their culpable conduct. He had killed many enemies, among whom were five chiefs. He gives a facsimile of a representation of one of his exploits, painted by himself, of which he frequently gave me an account.[50] He was, on that occasion, on foot, on a military expedition, with a few Mandans, when they encountered four Chayennes, their most virulent foes, on horseback. The chief of the latter, seeing that their enemies were on foot, and that the combat would thereby be unequal, dismounted, and the two parties attacked each other. The two chiefs fired, missed, threw away their guns, and seized their naked weapons; the Chayenne, a tall, powerful man, drew his knife, while Mato-Topé, who was lighter and more agile, took his battle-axe. The former attempted to stab Mato-Topé, who laid hold of the blade of the knife, by which he, indeed, wounded his hand, but wrested the weapon from his enemy, and stabbed him with it, on which the Chayennes took to flight. Mato-Topé's drawing of the scene in the above-named plate, shows the guns which they had discharged and thrown aside, the blood flowing from the wounded hand of the Mandan chief, the footsteps of the two warriors, and the wolf's tail at their heels—the Chayenne being distinguished by the fillet of otter skin on his forehead. The buffalo robe, painted by Mato-Topé himself, and which I have fortunately brought to Europe, represents several exploits of this chief, and, among others, in the lower figure on the left hand, the above-mentioned adventure with the Chayenne chief.[51]

The 10th of April was warm and fine, the thermometer at noon at 80°, the wind south, and the river had fallen three feet. Several of our Indian friends, among whom was Sih-Chida, had taken leave, intending to assist a large party of Manitaries and Mandans in a military expedition. They set out on their march about this time, and we afterwards learnt that a war party of the Manitaries had completely plundered a couple of beaver hunters, white men; and that their partisan, whose name was Pierce Iron, had acted the principal part on this occasion. On the other hand, the Assiniboins had stolen thirty-four horses from the Manitaries, who shot one of the thieves.

On the afternoon of the 14th of April, the people whom Mr. Mac Kenzie had promised to send to accompany me down the river to Saint Louis, at length arrived from Fort Union. There were, however, many others with them, and the whole party amounted to twenty men, among whom were Belhumeur and Mr. Chardon as leader. The violent storm on the preceding days had hindered them from travelling, and they were obliged to halt. They brought us letters from Fort Union, and news from Fort Mc Kenzie. As my people could now be spared, I looked daily for the arrival of Picotte, who, with many men, was to go up to Fort Union, as, without the help of his men, my Mackinaw boat could not be caulked. A main point now was my recovery, which was singularly rapid. At the beginning of April I was still in a hopeless condition, and so very ill, that the people who visited me did not think that my life would be prolonged beyond three or, at the most, four days. The cook of the fort, a negro from St. Louis, one day expressed his opinion that my illness must be the scurvy, for he had once witnessed the great mortality among the garrison of the fort at Council Bluffs, when several hundred soldiers were carried off in a short time; of this there is an account in Major Long's expedition to the Rocky Mountains.[52] He said that the symptoms were in both cases nearly similar; that, on that occasion, at the beginning of spring, they had gathered the green herbs in the prairie, especially the small white flowering *Allium reticulatum*, with which they had soon cured the sick. I was advised to make trial of this, recipe, and the Indian children accordingly furnished me with an abundance of this plant and its bulbs: these were cut up small, like spinage, and I ate a quantity of them. On the fourth day the swelling of my leg had considerably subsided, and I gained strength daily. The evident prospect of speedy recovery quite reanimated me, and we carried on with pleasure the preparations for our departure, though I was not yet able to leave my bed.

On the 15th of April, Picotte arrived with about twenty men, and had his boat laden with maize, which he was to carry to Fort Union. They immediately set about preparing the Mackinaw boat for our voyage down the river, and Picotte set out on the 16th, notwithstanding a heavy rain. Every preparation was completed on the following day; the boat was brought to the landing-place, furnished on the deck with a spacious Indian tent covering, and all was made ready for our voyage, Mr. Chardon resolving to accompany me to Fort Pièrre on the Teton River.

On the 18th of April, at noon, the boat was loaded; and, after we had partaken of our last frugal dinner at Fort Clarke, we took a cordial farewell of Mr. Kipp, with whom we had passed so long a time in this remote place, and who had done everything for me that was possible in his circumscribed condition. Accompanied by the inhabitants of the fort, and many of our Indian friends, among whom was Mato-Topé and Pehriska-Ruhpa, all of whom shook hands at parting, we went on board our boat. The weather was favourable, though there was a strong wind from the southwest. Some cannon-shot were fired by the fort as a farewell salute, and we glided rapidly down the beautiful stream of the Missouri.

FOOTNOTES:

[38] Compare with this the invocations of the Omaha, given in Dorsey, "Siouan Cults," U. S. Bureau of Ethnology *Report*, 1889-90, p. 373.—ED.

[39] See p. 59, for illustration of a double rainbow.—ED.

[40] See Plate 45, in the accompanying atlas, our volume xxv.—ED.

[41] For sketch of this trader, see our volume xxii, p. 316, note 279.—ED.

[42] See Plate 50, in the accompanying atlas, our volume xxv.—ED.

[43] The second figure from the left, in Plate 50, in the accompanying atlas, our volume xxv.—ED.

[44] This portrait is in Plate 50, the third figure from the left, atlas, our volume xxv.—ED.

[45] See Plate 27, in the accompanying atlas, our volume xxv.—ED.

[46] A "very admirable likeness of Pehriska-Ruhpa in this strange costume" is represented in Plate 56, in the accompanying atlas, our volume xxv.—ED.

[47] For a description of this dance among the Minitaree, see our volume xxiii, pp. 314, 315.—ED.

[48] See Plate 51, in the accompanying atlas, our volume xxv.—ED.

[49] See Plate 46, in the accompanying atlas, our volume xxv.—ED.

[50] See Plate 55, in the accompanying atlas, our volume xxv.—ED.

[51] See Plate 54, figure 1, in the accompanying atlas, our volume xxv.—ED.

[52] See our volume xiv, pp. 282, 283.—ED.

CHAPTER XXX
RETURN FROM FORT CLARKE TO THE CANTONMENT OF LEAVENWORTH, FROM APRIL 18TH TO MAY 18TH

Violent Storms and Bad Weather—Arikkara Villages—Meeting with two Fur Boats—Fort Pièrre, and our Stay there—The Mauvaises Terres—Sioux Agency—Cedar Island—Punca Island—Melone's Insubordination—Meeting with Punca Indians—L'Eau qui Court—Meeting with the Assiniboin Steamer—Melone's Mutiny and Punishment—Gardner as Pilot—Council Bluffs—Visit to Major Pilcher's Trading House—Belle Vue—Beauty of the Environs—Caterpillars—Nishnebotteneh—Roubedoux House on the Black Snake Hills—The Otos and Missouris—Village of the Kickapoos—The Cantonment of Leavenworth—Stay there—Dr. Fellowes.

Spring had but partially clothed the surrounding prairies with new verdure, even the willow bushes, which are generally the most forward, had scarcely assumed a slight tint of green; and, though some solitary ducks appeared as heralds of the fine season, the chilly temperature reminded us that winter was still lingering. On the 18th, we lay to on the right bank, on the other side of Goose-egg Lake,[53] and, on the following morning, encountered a very violent storm, and I discovered that my pretty prairie fox had escaped during the night, a loss which I the more regretted, as this rare animal has, probably, never been brought alive to Europe, whither I had fondly hoped to carry it. We had now made all our arrangements for the voyage, and my people had taken their respective posts. Our steersman, Fecteau, was very unskilful, and our three rowers, Melone, an American from the lower Missouri (whose real character we did not learn till some time after), Bourgua, a Canadian, and an old Pole, who had roamed half the world over, but was still the most industrious of the whole, all proved very indifferent workmen. Having partaken of our breakfast which was prepared on the shore, we passed the Butte Carrée[54] at seven o'clock; here we saw a troop of twelve elks, and many white cranes, swans, wild geese, and ducks of various species. At twelve o'clock we reached Heart River, where we found great numbers of wild geese. Our thermometer stood at 61°. At three o'clock we stopped at Picotte's winter post among the Yanktonans, to which we had so often sent from Fort Clarke for supplies of meat, &c., but the house was now deserted.[55] In the neighbourhood is a pond, to which our hunters immediately bent their steps, to shoot water-fowl. In the vicinity they saw prairie hens, woodpeckers, thrushes, turkey-buzzards, and birds of prey, also a couple of swans, one of which they wounded, but did not succeed in securing, and brought back only a few ducks. In the evening twilight, when we were about to lay-to, a troop of ten or twelve elks came down to the river to drink, but one of my people, firing his piece prematurely, frightened them away, and we thus lost our chance of taking one of these large animals. During the night a tremendous storm of rain came from the north; on the 20th of April the whole country was covered with snow, and at nine in the morning the thermometer had fallen to 35°. The storm obliged us to remain at the spot where we had passed the night, and my people, who always lighted a fire on shore, found but slight protection from the storm among the willow bushes. The thermometer, at noon, was at 41°. The hunters had seen some game, but shot only a prairie hen, which had a strong taste of garlic, the chief food of this, bird. The snow ceased to fall at about four o'clock; the night was cold, and the men who slept near the fire were aroused by some wild animal, which made them conjecture that Indians were near, on which Chardon, who had lived many years among the Osages, set a watch for the rest of the night.

On the 21st we passed the mouth of Cannonball River.[56] The hills were sprinkled with snow, and not a vestige of verdure was to be seen, though, the preceding day, the willows and rose-bushes had a tinge of green. Our hunters again set out on an excursion towards a neighbouring lake, where they saw many cranes and water-fowl, but shot only a few ducks. Some cabris crossed the river right in front of us, but, in spite of the exertions of our rowers, we could not overtake them. We were equally unsuccessful with a herd of buffalo cows and some bulls. The following day was again so stormy that we were not able to proceed on our voyage, and the wind threatened to rend our leathern tent on deck; the country was covered with snow: towards evening the wind abated, the night was pleasant, and the next morning opened upon us calm and cheerful. The poplar and other thickets were beginning to bud, and some of the willow bushes were quite green. Cabris were seen in the prairie, vultures in the air, and pigeons on the bank.

At noon we reached the abandoned Arikkara villages, and landed a little further down.[57] While our dinner was preparing, Mr. Bodmer and Chardon, well armed, made an excursion to the forsaken Indian huts, in order to procure for me some skulls and prairie bulbs. They found the graves partly turned up by the wolves, and the bodies pulled out, wrapped in their blankets and robes. They brought two well preserved male skulls, which I added to my collection; one of these is now in the anatomical museum of the university of Bonn, and the other in the collection of Mr. Blumenbach at Göttingen.[58] At half-past four o'clock, when we had proceeded about ten miles from the villages, and were opposite the mouth of the Grand River,[59] we were again visited by so heavy a storm, that we were compelled to lay-to, and light a fire for our people to warm themselves. While here, a couple of flocks of more than 160 pelicans passed over us in their way up the river, but we did not succeed in obtaining any of these fine birds. Towards evening the storm and rain, mingled with snow, were so extremely violent, that our boat was driven by the waves against the stones on the bank, and became leaky. Our people on shore found no protection under their blankets; they were kept awake throughout the night, and were frequently obliged to bale the water out of the boat. Towards midnight there was a frost, and on the morning of the 24th the country was again covered with snow. Our effects, which had, in the first instance, been completely soaked by the water, were frozen quite stiff. At eight o'clock the thermometer was at 33°, with a northwest wind. We saw a good deal of game, and Dreidoppel wounded, at a great distance, a cabri, in the midst of a troop of eighteen or twenty of those animals, but unfortunately brought us back nothing but a prairie dog. In the evening we lay-to at a steep bank opposite the mouth of Little Chayenne River.[60]

Early in the morning of the 25th we perceived a couple of fires burning on the bank, which must have been just left by some persons, and shortly afterwards we saw, in our van, two leather boats, which we succeeded in overtaking in about an hour's time. The people had halted to make a fire, and I therefore stopped to hold some conversation with them. They were Picotte's men, among whom were Ortubize, with his family, and Papin the hunter, returning to Fort Pièrre from the winter post, with the furs which had been obtained during that season. While we were conversing with them, Dreidoppel collected prairie bulbs. Papin gave me a part of a cabri; and the clerk who directed the boat, and whose name was likewise Papin, gave me a beautiful swan, but the large wing feathers were unhappily pulled out. The weather being very warm and fine, we rested here till eleven o'clock, and I then received into my boat a couple of women and a man named Crenier, who had been severely wounded. We passed the mouth of Big Chayenne River, and halted in the evening fifteen or twenty miles above Fort Pièrre. The heavily laden leathern boats having likewise come up, and set up their tents on the bank, we bivouacked together, and supped magnificently upon our roasted swan.

About two o'clock of the afternoon of the following day (the 26th), after our boat had several times run aground, we reached the landing-place at Fort Pièrre. Here there was still snow in the ravines of the mountains, and the bushes were but just beginning to bud. Several Sioux Indians, who were on the bank, shook hands with us. Mr. Laidlow, with some clerks of the Company, came to meet us, and conducted us to the fort, amidst a salute of several cannon-shot.

Fort Pièrre was in excellent condition.[61] The whole surrounding plain was covered with scattered tents of the Sioux, mostly of the Teton branch, and a few Yanktonans. Mr. Laidlow very kindly accommodated us, and assigned to us a spacious dwelling: I caused my boat to be unladen, as it was hinted that the vicinity of the half-starved Indians might prove dangerous to my bears. We found Fort Pièrre in great want of fresh provisions, no buffaloes having been seen during the whole winter, and the inmates of the fort, as well as the Indians, being very numerous. I could easily have taken on board, at Fort Clarke, a considerable cargo of maize for Fort Pièrre, but we had not been informed that there was any scarcity existing here. For his own table, consisting of ten or twelve persons, Mr. Laidlow had generally bought dogs of the Indians, but these were now scarce, and consequently very dear: twelve dollars were paid for the dog destined for our repast to-day. There were, however, many superior provisions in the fort, which we enjoyed at Mr. Laidlow's table, after having long been deprived of them: one of these luxuries was new wheaten bread, and there were also potatoes, cabbages, carrots, several kinds of preserves and pickles, as well as coffee, sugar, tea, &c. I found here, also, a part of my stock of provisions which I had brought from St. Louis last year, such as coffee, sugar, brandy, candles, &c., which would have been invaluable to me at Fort Clarke. The brandy had, however, been almost exhausted, and the cask filled up with water.

We were soon invited, with Messrs. Laidlow, Chardon, Papin, and the old interpreter, Dorion,[62] to the tent of one of the Sioux. After we had taken our seats on a new blanket ornamented with porcupine quills, the flesh of a dog was taken from the kettle, and handed to the company. It was very fat, about the colour of mutton, but the taste was really so excellent, that we speedily surmounted our prejudice and antipathy. Other Indians continued coming in, and, ranging themselves in a circle, commenced smoking, but they suddenly started up, and left the tent. Mr. Laidlow received as a present the robe upon which he had sat. Before we commenced our meal, the host made a formal address to his visitors, in which he spoke of his attachment to the Whites, for which Mr. Laidlow returned thanks through the interpreter. We went back to Mr. Laidlow, where another fat roasted dog was served up. Mr. Laidlow's spacious sitting apartment was filled the whole day with a large party of Indians, whose chief motive for coming was to see us. Among them was our old acquaintance, Wah-Menitu,[63] who was rejoiced to see us again. Generally speaking, it was not Mr. Laidlow's custom to admit the Indians into his own room.

A high wind prevailed throughout the day, and my people slept on board the boat. The two bears, which were brought into the fort, attracted great attention from the Indians, many of whom were constantly assembled about the animals to look at them. The prairie in the environs of the fort was already green, and several small early plants were in flower. I much regretted that I could not remain long enough to visit the interesting tract of the Mauvaises Terres, which is some days' journey from hence. Mr. Laidlow, who had been there in the winter, gave me a description of it. It is two days' journey, he said, southwest of Fort Pièrre, and forms, in the level prairie, an accumulation of hills of most remarkable forms, looking like fortresses, churches, villages and ruins, and doubtless consisting of the same sand-stone as the conformations near the Stone Walls. He further stated that the bighorn abounds in that tract.[64]

On the 27th of April I visited the stores of the Fur Company, which contained goods to the amount of 80,000 dollars. In the afternoon some hunters arrived, with twenty horses, who had been absent about three weeks on a buffalo chase, but returned with only one horse-load of meat. From their appearance I should certainly have taken them for savages. In the afternoon I took a walk in the prairie, though my strength was not fully restored, and the sight of the verdant plain was most refreshing to my mind. No birds were to be seen except the starling (*Sturnella ludoviciana*), which enlivened me with its short whistling note. Below the ridge which bounds the low bank of the river, the wild plum was covered with its snowy blossoms, which appear at the same time with the leaves; the scent is exactly like that of the flowers of our blackthorn. A small pink flower of the class *Tetra dynamia* covered the prairie. The beautiful yellow blossom of the *Hyerochloa fragrans* was likewise open. The Indian horses, which graze here, had now abundance of food, and quickly recovered from the effects of their fast in the severe winter. I visited the tents of the Indians, of whom, at least, fifty had gone away this morning on account of the scarceness of provisions. I was much struck with the difference of the physiognomy of the Sioux, after living so long among other tribes. Their features are much less agreeable, the cheek-bones more prominent, and their stature is lower and less vigorous than that of the Mandans, Manitaries, Arikkaras, and Crows. On the other hand, the expression of their countenances is more frank and good-tempered than that of those tribes. By way of comparison, I subjoin a woodcut of the Little Soldier, our former travelling companion, who, at this time, was absent on an expedition.[65]

Mr. Bodmer took several views of the country, and also made a sketch of the stage of a distinguished Sioux warrior, whose remains had been brought from a great distance with much pomp, and were covered with red cloth. Groups of Sioux were in the vicinity.[66] My people erected a new awning with large tent coverings for our voyage down the river; and I received, by the kind care of Mr. Laidlow, many fresh provisions of different kinds, which greatly contributed to the perfect re-establishment of my health. On the 29th Mr. Laidlow sent some men with pack-horses, under the direction of La Chapelle the interpreter, to Fort Clarke, in order to obtain a supply of maize from Mr. Kipp.

A heavy storm, accompanied with rain, retarded our departure for some hours, but towards evening the weather improved, and about six o'clock I was able to take leave of Mr. Laidlow and the inmates of the fort. The crew of my Mackinaw boat now consisted of ten persons, for I had obtained an able rower, named Dauphin, from Carondelet, near St. Louis, who was, at the same time, a better steersman than Fecteau. A man named Descoteaux,[67] who intended to sell his beaver skins, of which he possessed about 200, in the United States, requested me to give him a passage, in return for which he promised to work. I likewise took on board a sickly young man, who was too weak for the service of the Fur Company.

We glided rapidly down the Missouri, and soon passed the mouth of Teton River, which is about two miles and three quarters distant from Fort Pièrre in a south-easterly direction. At this place, Messrs. Soublette and Campbell, the opponents of the American Fur Company, had built a fort, at which I was not able to stop.[68] We lay-to, at night, about six miles from Fort Pièrre.

On the 30th of April we had a heavy rain throughout the day, so that the poor men at the oars were wet through. Descoteaux, who had remained behind, and had run along the banks through the whole night in order to overtake us, made his appearance at eight o'clock, thoroughly soaked. The weather was so very unfavourable on this day that we found it necessary to stop repeatedly and kindle a fire, that the people might dry and warm themselves. We therefore lay-to a good deal earlier than usual in the evening, near a very fine wild forest of old red cedars a foot and a half in diameter. In the evening the rain ceased, and the night was calm. On the morning of the 1st of May the weather was very cool: at about six o'clock we reached the Big Bend, where Dreidoppel and Dauphin landed to seek for game, while the boat made the great *détour* on the river.[69] They found a number of impressions of shells on the burnt hills, and saw a large village of prairie dogs, one of which they shot; in the dry bed of a stream they found several tents of the Sioux, the inmates of which met them on horseback, and had some amicable conversation with them. At noon the weather was warm, the thermometer being at 64°, and at three o'clock we arrived at Sioux Agency, the post of Major Bean.[70] Here we found Cephir, the interpreter, and three white men, who were suffering greatly from want of provisions. No buffalo herds had been seen here during the winter, and the men had lived on salt pork and the flesh of the cabri. The Sioux constantly pursue this animal, and on our arrival sent one to the fort. They were impatiently expecting the Company's steam-boat, with which Major Bean was to return. Thirteen Sioux tents were at this time near the fort; others had been here waiting for the steamer, but the want of provisions had forced them to disperse. It was not long before we received a visit in our boat from Wahktageli, whose portrait Mr. Bodmer had before taken, and who now repeated the assurance of his great attachment to the white men. We took advantage of the fine evening to prosecute our voyage, and then lay-to on the north bank. Dreidoppel had shot a duck, and several good-sized catfish were caught. The croaking of the frogs and howling of the wolves were our vesper song.

The following morning (2nd of May) was very cool, and a thick fog hung over the river. We soon passed the mouth of White River, but the wind becoming too high compelled us to lay-to on the south bank, where the waves drove the boat with such violence against the rocky bank, that it sprung a leak, and let in much water. We found it necessary to cut down a couple of trees, and fasten the boat to them, in order to make it more steady. Meantime we made an excursion to the ravines and hills. Cactus and yucca grew here in abundance, and some plants of the prairie were already in flower; and on the banks of the stream the young foliage was partly eaten away, which was said to have been done by the porcupines. We found prints of the footsteps of some game, and, in the dry bed of a brook, traces of the musk-rat, one of which Mr. Bodmer had killed. We likewise saw some black-tailed deer, and small hares (*Lepus Americanus*), the beautiful yellow-headed oriole, the sparrow-hawk, the turkey-buzzard, and several other kinds of birds. We left this place about noon on the 3rd of May, but made little progress on account of the storm and rain, and lay-to in the evening on the north bank, not quite a mile beyond Bijoux Hills.[71] The storm became very violent during the night; most of the people slept on land, as they were afraid that a tree which was standing very obliquely might give way to the storm and fall on our boat: nothing but the state of weakness, caused by my illness, could have made me so indifferent to this danger that I did not attempt to avoid it. The tree, however, did not fall. The wind abated towards the morning, and was succeeded by such torrents of rain, that on the following day (the 4th) we saw the water pour down from the left bank like cascades, the greater part of the neighbouring prairie being overflowed. Opposite to Bijoux Hills we were for a long time aground on a sand bank. Here we saw the first swallows returning to the north for the summer. In the afternoon we reached Cedar Island, and, proceeding a little further, lay-to for the night on the north bank.[72] Vegetation was pretty forward; but no birds had yet come; only the woodpecker and titmouse, which brave the winter, were to be seen. On the 5th, the wind being favourable, a sail was hoisted, but at eight o'clock the wind increased so much that we were obliged to stop at a large and beautiful island (Punca Island), where, having secured the boat, we dispersed in search of game. When I returned to the boat I learned that Dauphin had killed an elk calf, and most of my people had gone with him to the place where the animal lay, in order to secure the prize. We waited an hour and a half by the fire till they returned, when I wished immediately to proceed on our voyage; but Melone, one of my rowers, stepped forward, and positively declared that he would not go on board till he had had his fill of the venison, though he had taken a sufficient portion of meat in the morning. A violent altercation ensued; the obstinate fellow was compelled to go on board; but I was now aware of the character of this troublesome American, who was so much addicted to drinking that it was necessary to keep a watchful eye over him. We proceeded through the channel near the island, but at the further end the wind suddenly caught the vessel, so that it was quite unmanageable, and the sail was rent. We crossed over to the south bank, and lay-to near an extensive thicket of willow. It was so full of climbing plants and trees, that we could scarcely penetrate into it, and tracks of wild animals were everywhere to be seen. All the birds had sought refuge from the storm in the thickest recesses of the wood, and scarcely a living creature was visible. We here found, as on our first visit, the beautiful *Sylvia coronata* (Latham), and shot a turkey-buzzard, the crop of which Fecteau took out, affirming that it was an effectual remedy for the bite of venomous serpents. Towards five o'clock, as the storm abated, we proceeded on our voyage, passed the mouth of Punca River, and soon after sunset came to three tents of the Punca Indians on the south bank, where the trader, Dixon, with several *engagés* from Fort Pièrre, was at that time residing. Primeau, the Punca interpreter, who, in the preceding year, when on board the steam-boat, had communicated to me some words of the Punca language, was also with these people.[73]

We were informed that the Fur Company's steamer was near at hand, on its way up the river, intelligence which was very agreeable to me. The Punca Indians whom we saw here had a miserable, dirty appearance, and they, too, had suffered from want of provisions. They had their hair cut short in the nape of the neck and across the forehead. Their leather tents, some of which were painted, stood on a narrow green plain at the foot of steep hills, where the wood had been felled and burnt. I here procured the skin of a skunk, which differed from all the animals of this kind that I had hitherto seen. It was all over of a blackish-brown colour, with only a small white stripe on the upper part of the neck. From this place I crossed the river, and we kindled our fire in the willow thicket before the steep rocky hills. This place was directly opposite the mouth of L'Eau qui Court. At daybreak on the following morning (the 6th of May) we heard the note of the wild turkey, but did not stop. A large flock of pelicans flew up the Missouri, and numbers of blackbirds were on the banks. We passed Rivière à Manuel,[74] and towards eleven o'clock saw the Assiniboin steamer, which lay still on the north bank for want of water. We were hindered by the sand banks and the high wind from getting up to the Assiniboin, and therefore lay-to on the south bank, directly opposite. At this place there was a dense thicket of willows, and behind it an extensive forest. The woodcutters of the steam-boat happened to be engaged in felling wood, under the direction of a clerk, about a mile higher up, and, having observed our fire, came to us towards noon. A boat was afterwards sent to fetch them, which brought me a note from Captain Bennet, commander of the Assiniboin, in which he invited me to make haste to come on board, as they were impatient to see me again, after so long an absence. Captain Bennet also sent a number of men to row my boat across the stormy river, and with their aid we reached the Assiniboin at noon. We were received with much joy by our former travelling companions, Messrs. Sanford, Bean, Bennet, &c., and our accounts and news from the upper Missouri filled up a good part of the day. We also found on board our Indian friend, Schudegacheh, the Punca chief, who was extremely glad to see me again. There was likewise another chief, and several Indians. Schudegacheh's dress was remarkably handsome. His shirt was of beautiful otter skin, with a red cloth collar: he wore a cap of otter skin, and a tobacco pouch of the same material. This dress was extremely becoming to this fine man. The other chief wore a robe painted with red figures. They had a long conference with their agent, Major Bean, after which they took off all their clothes, and laid them on the ground before him, as a present, so that they sat quite naked, except the breechcloth. Major Bean at first declined accepting these things, but Schudegacheh would not take back his otter garment. The village of these Indians, consisting of nearly 100 tents, was about four days' journey up L'Eau qui Court.[75]

After spending the afternoon and evening on board the steamer, we took leave of our friends, and returned to our boat, intending to proceed early on the following morning; but, to my no small vexation, I found my people in a very excited state, and partly drunk; Dauphin alone seemed to know what he was about.

On the following morning (the 7th of May), Fecteau, Descoteaux, and Melone were still intoxicated, so that our departure was delayed, and I had to bear the noise and disorderly conduct of these men. We got over a dangerous place, where there were many snags; passed, at eleven o'clock, the mouth of the Rivière à Jacques, and then, the wind being very high, lay-to on the right bank.[76] My hunters went to a lake, about a mile off, in the hope of shooting some water-fowl, but did not succeed. I made my way, through the willow thicket, to the extensive verdant prairie, where a red fox sprang up before me. I saw many birds of various kinds—swallows, woodpeckers, finches, sylvias, and a couple of falcons (*Falco cyaneus*, Cuiv.); likewise butterflies, among which, *Papilio plexippus*, and many *Libellalœ*, in very warm places, sheltered from the wind. When I returned to the fire, I found my people asleep on the grass, in consequence of their excesses on the preceding day: Melone, however, was busy in bringing his trunk and other things from the boat to the land; after which he stepped forward and declared that "he would not go any further with us, and that his comrades, the other rowers, had agreed with him to leave us;" so that we Europeans would have been left alone in this wilderness. The news of this plot, arranged by the men in their drunken fit, during my absence yesterday, surprised me not a little. I called the other people, and asked them if this was really their intention; but they had now thought better of it, and protested that they would not leave us. Melone, enraged at their want of resolution, broke out into violent abuse; so I told him that, conformably to his wish, he might remain here by himself. On this he suddenly changed his tone, spoke civilly, and at length begged for a passage to his native place, Liberty; but I kept him to his word: we went on board, and left him alone in this wilderness. This evil-disposed man, who had formerly been a soldier in the service of the United States, and was much addicted to drinking, had exchanged his rifle, on board the Assiniboin, for a considerable quantity of provisions, a hatchet, brandy, &c., and thus sufficiently proved his intention of leaving me in this shameful manner. As he was skilful in the use of the hatchet, and had a sufficient stock of provisions, it would be easy for him to make a boat of large poplar stems, and reach the neighbouring post of Le Roi.

On this day we proceeded twelve or fifteen miles. The country was flat, and the banks, in some parts, clothed with fine forests. At sunset we lay-to at a convenient place on the right bank, where a narrow strip of lofty, verdant wood filled the space between the river and the steep white hills: there was an undergrowth of the red willow (*Cornus sericea*), which was just coming into flower. The *Fringilla Pennsylvanica* was numerous, and fresh tracks of wild animals appeared in all directions. At twilight a great many of the whip-poor-wills flew round the fire within three paces of it, and quite stunned our ears by their cries. A couple of them were shot, the first of these birds that I had seen.

On the following morning (the 8th of May), we passed some extensive sand banks, on which we observed the avoset, and many wild geese. Towards ten o'clock we reached the mouth of Vermilion River,[77] where many Sioux Indians were at that time assembled: here commence the lofty forests, which are peculiar to the banks of the lower Missouri, and in which the note of the whip-poor-will resounds in the evening.

I had been informed, on board the steamer, that a man named Gardner, one of the best pilots on the whole course of the Missouri, and, at the same time, thoroughly acquainted with the Indian wilderness from his having been long engaged in hunting beavers, had gone down the river a short time before me, and I was advised to overtake him, and, if possible, to engage him as pilot, as our steersman was unskilful, and the snags in many parts of the river very dangerous.[78] We soon perceived Gardner's miserable flat leather boat, with a cargo of skins, before us, and presently overtook it. I immediately offered to take his furs into my boat, which was more secure, if he would act as steersman, to which he most readily agreed. His boat was very unsafe and bad, and at the same time was so heavily laden, that its edge was scarcely above the water, and it proceeded very slowly. He was on his return from hunting beavers on the Upper Yellow Stone, and had two men with him. We lay-to, and, while the people were transferring the cargo of Gardner's boat to ours, we made an excursion into the interesting country. The chain of hills was clothed with young verdure, and covered and surrounded with tall trees and forests; beautiful thickets, mixed with cedars, grew on the banks; all appeared in the fresh loveliness of spring. In the hollow upper boughs of the lofty, colossal trees, numbers of the purple swallow (*Hirundo purpurea*) had built their nests; flocks of blackbirds were among the high grass, between the trunks of the trees, where the little wren (*Troglodytes aedon*) poured forth its cheerful song; the sparrow-hawk was sitting at the end of a high branch; and on the ground, among the roots of the trees, we descried what we thought was a mouse running along, which, however, proved to be a little bird; it was too near to be fired at, and we could not make it rise on its wing. At length, however, we killed it, and found it to be the pretty little finch called, by Wilson, *Fringilla candacuta*. The ash-grey finch (*Fringilla hyemalis*), the snow-bird of Wilson, who represents this bird larger than it is in nature, built its nest here.

Towards one o'clock in the afternoon we reached Le Roi's plantation, and lay-to at the sand bank opposite to it, the wind being very high. We dispersed in order to try our fortune with our fowling-pieces, but found on the bank an intricate thicket full of burs, so that we could scarcely penetrate it. Numbers of birds animated this thicket, the cormorant (*Carbo*) sat on the tall trees on the bank, the whip-poor-will uttered its plaintive note, and bats hovered over the river. We passed the evening sitting round our fire, when Gardner told us anecdotes of his many adventures and combats with the Indians. He gave me a particular account of the death of Glass, the old beaver-hunter whom I have already mentioned, and which particularly interested me, because I possessed the scalp of one of the two Arikkara Indians who were killed by Gardner on account of that murder. The following were the circumstances of that event. Old Glass, with two companions, had gone from Fort Cass to hunt beavers on the Yellow Stone, and, as they were crossing the river on the ice further down, they were all three shot, scalped, and plundered by a war party of thirty Arikkaras who were concealed on the opposite bank. These Indians, who are most dangerous enemies to the Whites, went then to the sources of Powder River, and it happened that Gardner, with about twenty men, and thirty horses, was in the neighbourhood.[79] As it was dark when they were seated about several fires, the Indians suddenly appeared, addressed them in the Manitari language, surrounded the fire, and dried their shoes. Gardner, being well acquainted with the character of the Indians, immediately took some precautions, which was the more necessary, as a Manitari woman, who was with his party, told him that the strangers were Arikkaras. He gradually collected his people round one of their fires, with their arms in readiness to act. He was also afraid for his horses, which were scattered in the prairie, and some of which were actually missing, and he had already sent some of his men to erect in the neighbourhood what is called a fort, of trunks of trees, for the night. The Indians are accustomed, when they intend to steal horses, suddenly to give a signal, on which they all jump up, scatter the horses, and drive them away with them. Gardner, aware of this, watched the enemy closely, and when, on the signal being given, they all withdrew, three of them were seized, thrown down and bound. When the Arikkaras perceived this, several of them came back, pretended to be innocent of the stealing of the horses, and begged for their captive comrades; but Gardner declared to them that, if they did not immediately deliver up all the horses, the prisoners must die; one of whom, however, had cut the cords with which he was bound, and escaped. The Indians entreated for a long time, but were refused. The others seeing that they must die, commenced their death-song, related their exploits, and affirmed that they were distinguished warriors. One of them had old Glass's knife, and his rifle also had been seen in the possession of these Indians. The horses, however, were not brought, and the prisoners, alleging a pressing necessity, were taken aside; but in the thick copse they attempted to escape, on which one of them was stabbed, and several shots fired at the other, who was then killed with the knife. They were both scalped, and I received one of the scalps as a present, which was unfortunately lost in the fire on board the steamer. Gardner, by way of precaution, had all the fires put out, and passed the night in the fort, which was now completed. They were not disturbed during the night, and found, in the morning, that the Indians had retired with their booty, leaving the prisoners to their fate. The Arikkaras had begged for one of them in particular, who was a celebrated warrior, and had even brought back three horses, which they tied up near at hand, to exchange them for the prisoners; but Gardner did not attend to their request.

On the 9th of May we reached the mouth of Joway River, and at three in the afternoon that of Big Sioux.[80] The heat was pretty considerable; and we saw the great heron (*Ardea herodias*), and a flock of pelicans, some of which were grey, go up the river. We then came to Floyd's Grave, and at a bend in the river reached a spot, to the northwest of which there was a village of the Omahas, of about fifty huts. I wished much to visit these people, but we could not well stop, because our provisions were getting low, and we had already lost too much time through the continued storms. In the evening we stopped for the night on the left bank opposite the mouth of Omai Creek.[81]

On the following morning the weather was fine and warm, the thermometer at eight o'clock being at 72°. Wood-ducks in pairs, and flocks of wild geese and pelicans, attracted our attention, till we reached, about ten o'clock, the beautiful green hills of Waschinga-Saba's grave,[82] where we saw some deer and wolves, and found the tracks of these animals in all directions. The rising wind afterwards obliged us to lay-to, because there was a very dangerous place, with many snags, just before us; but when the wind abated Gardner steered my boat very skilfully between the snags. About sunset we passed the mouth of Little Sioux River, and lay-to three miles below it, on the opposite bank. On the 11th we were very frequently obliged to stop, and meanwhile amused ourselves with looking at the beautiful birds in the thickets. At six o'clock we reached Soldier's River, and lay-to in a safe bay on the left bank. The weather was cool on the 12th. When we set out, one of my hunters shot a cormorant with his rifle. At ten o'clock we passed the ruins of the old fort of Council Bluffs, and in the afternoon reached Boyer's Creek, just before which we saw the first plane tree on the Missouri.[83] From this spot this species of tree becomes more and more common as you descend the river, which is very winding. We landed, between one and two o'clock, at Major Pilcher's trading house, formerly belonging to Mr. Cabanné.[84]

Mr. Pilcher gave us a very cordial reception after so long an absence, and we passed the whole day with him. A lawyer, of the name of Randolph, was at this time here to investigate a criminal case which had lately occurred; an *engagé* had shot his comrade, as was supposed in cold blood. There were not many Indians at the trading house at this time; however, there were some Otos, Missouris, Omahas and a couple of Joways, and Ongpa or Onpa-Tanga (the big elk), the principal chief of the Omahas, was daily expected;[85] I would gladly have waited to see him, had time permitted my doing so. Mr. Bodmer took the portraits of an Omaha and an Oto Indian. These two tribes do not differ in their manners, dress, and personal appearance. They wear their hair short, nay, sometimes the head is completely shorn, except a tuft behind, and in front; the upper part of the body naked, and strings of wampum in their ears.

At this time there was more order and cleanliness in Mr. Pilcher's house than during our former visit, and the store had been removed into the upper floor. It contained a large quantity of skins, among which were 24,000 musk-rats, which are sold at twenty-five cents a piece. The packs of these latter were very regularly piled up in a square. There was also a good stock of buffalo and beaver skins. Mr. Pilcher presented me with a very beautiful skin of a large dark brown wolf, which had been killed on the upper part of Boyer's Creek; it is, however, not a species, only a variety.

After dinner I took an excursion to the neighbouring finely wooded hills, which were now flourishing in the greatest luxuriance. Birds of various kinds were very numerous in a beautiful gently sloping valley, through which the Omahas pass when they go to their villages. Among the many kinds of trees and shrubs, I observed cratægus, or pyrus, twenty feet in height, covered with white blossoms, oaks, elms, &c. Near the house very fine cattle were grazing, and numbers of swine, all of which roamed at liberty in the woods. There are extensive plantations of maize and fields of potatoes, and Mr. Pilcher was so good as to furnish me with a supply of provisions from his store. This place had likewise been visited by the cholera in the preceding summer, but it had not carried off so many persons as at Dougherty's agency at Belle Vue, because Mr. Pilcher had a better stock of medicines. At nightfall we took leave of Mr. Pilcher, and went on board our boat, intending to proceed early the next morning, the 13th of May. During the night a dog stole a part of our stock of meat, the door of the cabin not having been very well secured. Towards eight o'clock we lay-to on the right bank of the river, at a lovely verdant prairie covered with thickets and tall insulated trees. There we found many beautiful birds; among them were numbers of the red-breasted *Fringilla ludoviciana*; we shot a good many of them, but they were so fat that we had considerable difficulty in preserving the skins. We had a fruitless chase after some wild turkeys. Towards noon we arrived at Belle Vue, Major Dougherty's agency,[86] which is about thirty-four miles from Pilcher's trading house, and lies at the foot of the wooded chain of hills on which Mr. Pilcher's residence is situated. We landed, but unfortunately found only a few *engagés*, for Major Dougherty was absent at St. Louis, and was not expected to return till the middle of July. The majority of the persons whom we had seen here on our first visit had died of cholera, during the preceding summer, seven of ten persons having been carried off in the short space of twenty-four hours. They had all been buried by one man, who was now here, and who himself was ill when he was obliged to perform this last office for the dead. The disease had, however, quite passed away, and the fort was now healthy. The environs of Belle Vue presented great attractions to the naturalist at this season. The richly wooded hills, with their deep shady ravines and wild glens, were animated by the cuckoo, and a number of splendid birds, while innumerable bright winged butterflies fluttered about over the strawberry blossoms, the magnificent azure phlox, and a variety of other beautiful flowers.

After we had luxuriated in this romantic spot, we returned to take in a stock of provisions, and, being refreshed by that great rarity, a glass of new milk, we continued our journey. Towards noon we reached the mouth of the river La Platte, which is about six miles distant from Belle Vue. At sunset we passed Fife-Barrel Creek, and stopped opposite an island of the same name on the right bank of the Missouri. As soon as we landed I set out with my gun in my hand, and, passing through a lofty avenue of willows, came to a narrow marsh, quite overgrown with typha. The ground was swampy, but the raccoons had trod a regular footpath. The morass was bounded by hills covered with trees and bushes of the loveliest verdure, enlivened by the baltimore and the green icteria. The latter incessantly poured forth its song, which contains a strophe similar to that of the nightingale. It is remarkable that the cheerfulness and activity of these birds increase greatly towards evening. The whip-poor-wills were very numerous in the willow copse on the bank, and in the evening twilight their notes resounded on every side.

The morning of the 14th opened brightly upon us, and we set out early and passed Weeping-water River, landing several times to pursue the wild turkeys, whose note attracted us to their retreats.[87] We often saw these proud birds in the lofty trees, perched up beyond the reach of small shot. The most beautiful birds of this country select for their resort the airy summits of the woods, especially of the fine primeval forest on the bank, where we lay-to at ten o'clock. This noble forest comprises all the varied trees of this climate, with an undergrowth of prickly ash, hazel-bushes, cornus, &c., entwined with *Vitis hederacea* and other parasitic plants. The stems are tall, straight, and closely crowded together; many were lying on the ground decayed, covered with moss and lichens, which frequently impeded our progress. Here we soon shot a variety of birds, and saw some parrots, which Gardner had already observed on Weeping-water River. In short we might have found here ample employment for a long time. A particular species of caterpillar abounded to such a degree in these forests, that all the branches of the trees, especially the willows and poplars, were thickly loaded with them. As soon as we entered the copses our clothes were covered with these caterpillars and their webs. We lay-to for the night about a mile below Little Nemawha Creek, where Dauphin caught a catfish weighing 15 lbs.

On the 15th we were about five miles from our night's quarters to the mouth of the Nishnebottoneh, which we reached at eight o'clock. In the fine forest at this spot our hunters shot only one rabbit, and wounded a deer, which we did not obtain. At noon we lay-to on the right bank, Gardner having promised to look for some wild honey. I may remark by the way, that though the bee was not known in America till it was introduced by the Europeans, it is now spread over the whole continent. The Indians are said to call it "the white man's fly." It is now common far up the Missouri, where the honey is eagerly sought for by both Whites and Indians, who cut it out of the hollow trunks of the trees. The spot where we rested and prepared our dinner was below the beautiful verdant wooded hills, and was shaded by high trees, inhabited by the most brilliant birds, which afforded much sport to our hunters. Along the bank and distant hills extended a splendid forest, through which winded a solitary Indian path, where the grey squirrels were very numerous. We found much recreation in this solitary wilderness, but here, too, the caterpillars annoyed us greatly; they were of a bluish-green colour, with a double row of green and yellow spots. We afterwards passed the Grand Nemawha, and lay-to, for the night, opposite Solomon's Island, six miles above Wolf River.[88]

On the 16th of May the river was covered with a thick fog, which prevented our proceeding on our voyage as early as usual. At half-past seven o'clock we were opposite the mouth of Wolf River, where we saw a herd of six or seven deer, and lay-to at nine o'clock on the right bank. The lofty forest here had a thick undergrowth of box-alder and cornus, which was completely covered with caterpillars and their webs. At noon we reached Nodaway River, and were charmed with the prospect of the sublime forest scenery of the banks, and the picturesque islands in this river.[89] Luxuriant woods appeared on every side, covered to the summits of their highest branches with graceful light green climbing plants, so that the trunks looked like verdant columns.

Their foliage was shining and juicy, like the whole of the luxuriant vegetation that surrounded them. Even from our boat we could see, in the dark forest, the scarlet plumage of the beautiful red tanagra, which the French on the Mississippi call the pope, the splendid cardinal, and the bright red baltimore. The meridian sun shed a glorious effulgence over this magnificent scene; where, however, the red-bud, and the other early blossoming trees, had already lost their flowers. Most of the trees of these forests on the lower Missouri have not the beautiful large flowers common to those of Brazil, but, with a few exceptions, have only catkins. For the first time after a long interval we saw the kingfisher on the bank. Towards four o'clock in the afternoon we reached the beautiful chain of the Black Snake Hills, and, not long after, Roubedoux's trading house in the neighbourhood of the Joways and Saukies, or Sacs.[90] The forest-covered hills, as well as the prairie stretched at their foot, were now adorned with the most lovely verdure. The two houses at this spot were painted white, which, when seen from the river, gave them a very picturesque appearance amid the surrounding green. Behind the dwelling houses were extensive fields of maize, protected by fences, and very fine cattle were grazing in the plain. Mr. Roubedoux, the owner of the house, and his son, were from home, and some ignorant *engagés* could not comply with my desire to obtain fresh provisions, and to pay a visit to the Indians in the vicinity, to accomplish which I requested them to provide me with horses. About thirty Oto and Missouri Indians had been here a couple of days, and had just gone to the neighbouring Indians to purchase brandy. About six miles from hence lies a village of the Joway Indians, and at about the same distance down the Missouri, one of the Saukies. These Indians are able to obtain as much brandy as they please at the extreme settlements of the Americans, about fifteen miles from this place, who, at their own risk, pass the limit of the Indian country, fixed by the government in the latitude of the Cantonment of Leavenworth. This great facility of procuring cheap and bad spirits is extremely ruinous to the Indians, and accelerates the destruction of their race. We were dissuaded from visiting these two Indian tribes, because they had, for several days, been indulging in the immoderate use of whisky, and were in a dangerous state of excitement. A great number of Oto Indians gradually assembled near Roubedoux's house: many of them were quite intoxicated, and nearly all had four or five casks of this fatal draught fastened to their horses.

The Oto, Missouri, and Joway Indians, at least the young people, had their hair shorn in the manner of the Saukies and Foxes: several, however, especially the elder men, wore their hair short in the neck. I saw one of the Missouris with his hair hanging half-way down his back. Their dress and customs are said not to differ from the Saukies. They had holes in their ears, in which they wore bunches of wampum: some young men had red cloth tied round their heads, and one of them wore a cap made of the entire skin of a bear's head, with the ears, which gave him a very grotesque appearance. All these Indians were weaker, and of lower stature, than those of the upper Missouri, especially the Manitaries, Mandans, and Crows. The Otos and Missouris intended to go to-day with their stock of whisky to their villages on the other side of the river, and wished us to set them over, to which, however, I was not disposed to accede. Mr. Bodmer took the portrait of an athletic Missouri youth. This tribe was formerly numerous and powerful, but, being defeated by the Foxes, Saukies, and Osages, it lost its independence, and the few that remain have intermingled with the Otos.

We made some little excursions in the neighbourhood, and found in the prairie and the lofty trees many beautiful plants and fine birds; the day was hot, and the evening remarkably pleasant; a numerous company of Indians, who were not a little troublesome, visited us in our boat, and stopped till ten o'clock. We left our night's quarters early on the following day, the 17th, and proceeded down the river, the banks of which were clothed with tall forests. The thermometer at noon was at 75°, but the wind was high, and compelled us to lay-to; we therefore took advantage of the delay to go ashore, and make some addition to our collection of plants and birds. About four in the afternoon, though the wind was still high, we were enabled to pursue our course. We were not long in making Cow Island, about nine miles from Leavenworth, where a good deal of cattle belonging to the military post were grazing. A little before sunset we came to the isolated dwelling of a white man, and saw several Indians, there being a settlement of the Kickapoos, who were removed from the eastern provinces, at a short distance from the river. We lay-to for the night on the right bank, and several of my people went on before us to Leavenworth. On the 18th, during a heavy rain, we made the three miles to the post; we heard some musket-shot, a signal that the guard was relieved, and soon reached the landing-place of the Cantonment. The sentinel informed us that we must immediately appear before the commanding officer, and compelled us, in an imperious manner, to keep close and march before him. We arrived like prisoners at the house of the commander, where Major Ryley received us with tolerable politeness, and supplied me with the provisions, meat, bread, &c., which I required, taking care, however, to be well paid for them.[91]

The Cantonment of Leavenworth is pleasantly situated; ten or twelve neat and spacious buildings, surrounded with a gallery or verandah, are occupied by two companies of the 6th regiment, not more than eighty men, with ten officers, who were detached from Jefferson Barracks, near St. Louis. Dr. Fellowes, the military physician, who in the preceding year travelled with us to this place, received me with much cordiality, and gave me a good deal of information respecting this interesting country. He had been very successful with his cholera patients, for, out of a great number, one only had died, because he always attacked the disorder at its very commencement.

The heavy rain had converted the surrounding country into a swamp, so that we could not conveniently visit the environs of the Cantonment. The soil is very fruitful, and the whole country clothed in rich verdure. About four miles from this place, down the river, the Indian line meets the Missouri at right angles; this is the frontier of the Indian territory, which the Cantonment is destined to protect. Near this post is the village of the Kickapoos, inhabited by a poor and rather degenerated race. Major Morgan,[92] who kept a large store of provisions and other necessaries, had a share in Gardner's fur trade; the latter accordingly quitted me at this place. To celebrate his happy return the people drank rather too freely, and were endeavouring to make Descoteaux do the same, in order to induce him to sell his beaver skins below their value, but I would not suffer this, and took him with me. The people here have a sufficient number of cattle and swine, as well as plenty of milk, butter, and cheese. My collections were here enriched with many interesting specimens. Dr. Fellowes had the kindness to give me a goffer (a large field-mouse), undoubtedly *Diplostoma bulbivorum*. Unfortunately the specimen was not complete.

FOOTNOTES:

[53] Not the lake of that name noted in our volume xxii, p. 368, note 344, but one between Knife and Heart River, North Dakota.—ED.

[54] For the location of Butte Carré (Square Butte), see our volume xxii, p. 340, note 312.—ED.

[55] This post was probably at or near Apple Creek, which by its connection with the lakes east of the Missouri furnishes communication with the upper James, the usual habitat of the Yanktonai.—ED.

[56] See our volume xxii, p. 338, note 306.—ED.

[57] For the site of these villages, see our volume xxii, p. 335, note 299.—ED.

[58] See our volume xxii, p. 173, note 87.—ED.

[59] Grand River, the Weterhoo of Lewis and Clark (*Original Journals*, i, p. 183; vi, p. 49), rises near the sources of the Little Missouri in northwestern South Dakota, and flows east into the Missouri in Boreman County. It is a prairie stream paralleling Cannonball and Cheyenne rivers, and largely destitute of timber.—ED.

[60] For this stream, see our volume xxii, p. 334, note 295.—ED.

[61] For Fort Pierre, see our volume xxii, p. 315, note 277.—ED.

[62] See, for this man, Bradbury's *Travels*, our volume v, p. 38, note 7.—ED.

[63] For the visit of this Teton Sioux, see our volume xxii, p. 329.—ED.

[64] This tract was the area later famous as the Bad Lands of White River. Had Maximilian been able to visit this region, he might have antedated the discoveries made by J. V. Hayden and F. B. Meek, which awakened much interest in the scientific world. This area, extending nearly five hundred miles in each direction, lies between Cheyenne and White rivers east of the Black Hills. It is a tertiary formation of indurated sands, clays, and marl, cut up into ravines and cañons by streams and climatic action. In certain places it takes on the form of a gigantic city in ruins. To the scientist, however, the chief interest is its fossils, immense numbers of which are imbedded in the formation. The first descriptive account was that of Dr. H. A. Prout, who visited the region in 1847, given in the *American Journal of Science*, iii, 2d series, pp. 248-250. Two years later, Dr. John Evans went through this district, and the next year it was visited by Thaddeus A. Culbertson in the interest of the Smithsonian Institution. A thorough examination was made in 1853 by J. V. Hayden and F. B. Meek; the former passed through again in 1857, the results

being embodied in American Philosophical Society *Transactions*, xii, new series (Phila., 1863). The fossil remains were described by Professor Joseph Leidy in *Contributions to Extinct Vertebræ Fauna* (Washington, 1873). Hayden made still another visit to this region in 1866, the results of which were published in his *Geographical and Geological Survey of the Territories*. The White River Bad Lands are still difficult of access, and not as yet visited by tourists.—ED.

[65] See p. 59, for portrait of Little Soldier (Tukan Haton), a Sioux chief. Consult also our volume xxii, pp. 311-313, for Maximilian's relation of this chieftain's visit.—ED.

[66] See Plate 44, in the accompanying atlas, our volume xxv.—ED.

[67] In the early part of the nineteenth century there was a free-trader of this name on Minnesota River, where he was later murdered by his Indian wife. See *Henry-Thompson Journals*, p. 941.—ED.

[68] The opposition post had been built since our author ascended the river. It was begun October 17, 1833, a "little below old Fort Tecumseh." According to Maximilian it was directly at the mouth of Teton River, probably in the northern angle. It was occupied only about a year, then being sold with all its effects to the American Fur Company. See Chittenden, *Fur-Trade*, iii, p. 956.—ED.

[69] See our volume xxii, p. 313, note 272.—ED.

[70] For the agency and agent, see our volume xxii, p. 235, note 171, and p. 304, note 261.—ED.

[71] For Bijoux Hills and White River, see our volume xxii, pp. 301, 302, notes 258, 259, respectively.—ED.

[72] For Little Cedar Island, see our volume xxii, p. 296, note 257. Maximilian here intends the present island of that name.—ED.

[73] For Primeau and Ponca River, see our volume xxii, p. 286, note 248, and p. 291, note 253. The trader was William, half-breed son of Colonel Robert Dickson, who had been agent for the British government among the Northwestern Indians during the War of 1812-15. William's mother was a Sioux, and he assisted his father during that war, being still in the pay of that government in 1817; see *Wisconsin Historical Collections*, xi, p. 350. By 1821 he was established in trade on Lake Traverse, whence one of his letters (written in French) shows traces of considerable education; *ibid.*, x, p. 140. He accompanied a delegation to Washington in 1824 as interpreter for the United States (consult *Minnesota Historical Collections*, vi, p. 205), and two years later was licensed as a trader. Some time before 1832, he crossed to the Missouri River and entered the employ of the American Fur Company, for

whom he had a post called by his name, near the mouth of Petit Arc Creek in South Dakota. There Larpenteur met him in 1838, and states that he shortly after committed suicide. Compare also E. D. Neill, *History of Minnesota* (Minneapolis, 1882), p. 452.—ED.

[74] For Niobrara River (l'eau qui court), see our volume v, p. 90, note 54. Emanuel Creek (Rivière à Manuel) is noted in volume xxii, p. 290, note 251.—ED.

[75] For the Ponca Indians, see our volume v, p. 96, note 63. When Lewis and Clark ascended the river (1804) the village of this tribe was on the stream called by their name, not on the Niobrara. The name of the chief Schudegacheh signified Smoke, and Catlin speaks (*North American Indians*, i, p. 212) of him as "a noble specimen of native dignity and philosophy."—ED.

[76] For James River (à Jacques), see our volume xxii, p. 282, note 238.—ED.

[77] See our volume vi, p. 87, note 31.—ED.

[78] For this trapper, see our volume xxiii, p. 197, note 153.—ED.

[79] For the earlier adventures of Hugh Glass, see our volume xxii, p. 294, note 255. Powder River, called Red Stone by Lewis and Clark, is the most easterly of the great southern affluents of the Yellowstone. It rises in Central Wyoming, on the eastern slopes of the Big Horn Mountains and south thereof, near the sources of the Big Cheyenne and North Fork of Platte. The valley of Powder River was a favorite rendezvous of trappers, for it afforded both game and pasturage in abundance.—ED.

[80] For these streams, see our volumes xxii, p. 280, note 236; and vi, p. 85, note 30, respectively.—ED.

[81] For Floyd's grave, see our volume v, p. 91, note 56. Omai is now Omadi Creek, in Dakota County, Nebraska.—ED.

[82] See Plate 12, in the accompanying atlas, our volume xxv. For this noted chief, known in English as Blackbird, see Bradbury's *Travels*, our volume v, pp. 84-86.—ED.

[83] These are all three Iowa streams, the last two entering the Missouri in Harrison County, and Boyer's in Pottawattamie County. See our volume xxii, p. 275, note 231, for the fort at Council Bluffs.—ED.

[84] For Cabanné and his post, see our volume xxii, p. 271, note 226. Cabanné had been obliged to return to St. Louis to defend himself against the legal action of Le Clerc. See Chittenden, *Fur-Trade*, i, pp. 346-350. A brief sketch of Joshua Pilcher is in our volume xiv, p. 269, note 193.—ED.

[85] For this chieftain, see our volume v, p. 90, note 52; also, our volume xiv, pp. 258-262, where Big Elk holds council with the officers of Long's expedition.—ED.

[86] For a brief history of Bellevue, see our volume xxii, p. 267, note 221.—ED.

[87] For the geographical places mentioned in this paragraph, see our volume xxii, p. 264, note 217.—ED.

[88] For the rivers mentioned, see our volume vi, pp. 72, 73, notes 23, 24. Both Solomon's Island and Wolf Creek are mentioned by Lewis and Clark (*Original Journals*, i, pp. 72, 73); the former has been swept away by the river. For Wolf Creek, see our volume xiv, p. 181, note 150.—ED.

[89] Nodaway River is described in our volume v, p. 37, note 5.—ED.

[90] For this trader and his post, see our volume xxii, p. 257, note 210.—ED.

[91] See our volume xxii, p. 253, note 204, for the persons and places mentioned in this paragraph.—ED.

[92] The eastern boundary of the Indian country, which was also the western boundary of Missouri, consisted of a line running directly north and south through the middle of the channel of the mouth of Kansas River. In 1824 commissioners were appointed to survey the western and southern line of Missouri, and in 1830 this was adopted as the boundary of the Western Territory (see our volume xxi (Wyeth), p. 50, note 31). This boundary is, however, nearly thirty miles (by the river) below Fort Leavenworth. Probably Maximilian confused this with the boundary of Fort Leavenworth military reservation.

The treaty of 1832 with the Kickapoo tribe arranged for their removal to a tract southwest of the Missouri, situated about Fort Leavenworth; see *Indian Treaties* (Washington, 1837), pp. 532-535.

Major Morgan was not the military officer who accompanied Long's expedition, referred to by Maximilian, *ante* (our volume xxii, p. 260). The one here mentioned was a trader and early settler near Fort Leavenworth—probably Alexander G. Morgan, who in 1831 was postmaster at the fort.—ED.

CHAPTER XXXI
VOYAGE FROM THE CANTONMENT OF LEAVENWORTH TO PORTSMOUTH, ON THE MOUTH OF THE OHIO RIVER, FROM MAY 18TH TO JUNE 20TH

Little Platte River—William's Ferry—The Mormons, a Religious Sect—St. Charles—Land Journey to St. Louis—Residence there—The Indian Barrows—Mouth of the Ohio—New Harmony—Journey to Vincennes and Louisville on the Ohio—Cincinnati—Portsmouth.

On the afternoon of the 18th of May, I left the Cantonment of Leavenworth amid a very heavy rain, which continuing on the 19th I lay-to, and made my people light a fire on shore, to warm themselves, and dry their clothes. As soon as we had left Little Platte River, I observed numerous isolated settlements, from which others had taken their rise. At Portage l'Independence, I saw Mr. Soublette, who had been ill for some time.[93] As I had very recently visited his trading post on the upper Missouri, I was enabled to give him the most recent intelligence respecting it. He has always been engaged in the fur trade; in the first instance, in opposition to the American Fur Company; subsequently, however, in connection with it; he was now waiting for the steam-boat, Oto,[94] intending to go by it to St. Louis.

About five o'clock we reached the landing-place of Liberty, but I did not make any stay there. Descoteaux here fell in with one of his acquaintances, a Canadian beaver hunter, and begged permission to leave me; I did not wish to detain the man, and accordingly set him on shore with all his furs and skins. At nightfall we came to a settlement called William's Ferry, or Charaton-Scatty; here, on the northern bank, we lay-to for the night, under shelter of a lofty umbrageous forest.[95] We passed the 20th on the same spot, our boat having received some injury, and we accordingly had it repaired; at the same time we caused our effects to be dried, as they had been thoroughly drenched by the rain.

We met with a friendly reception in a house near the landing-place, where the mistress sold us poultry, buttermilk, &c., for which she at first declined accepting any payment. The whole country in the valleys, as well as on the mountains, was covered with a lofty shady forest of magnificent trees, of every variety common to this climate, which, being refreshed by the late rains, were clad in the most brilliant verdure. The splendid plumage of the bright red baltimore, and the vermilion tanagra (*Tanagra rubra*) was very striking, amidst the dark foliage of the forest; the latter is here called the flax-bird, from its feeding on the buds of that plant. We listened with pleasure to the note of the cuckoo, which much resembles that of the European bird. We heard frogs and tree-frogs in the vicinity, and the whistle of some animal exactly like that of our yellow-striped salamander, and doubtless one of that family,[96] under the fallen trunks of the trees. I was much surprised, during these travels in North America, to meet with so few animals of the lizard kind, whereas tortoises were very numerous.

There was only a single path along the bank from one plantation to another; all else was covered with a thick forest. There were wild, lonely valleys, with colossal tulip trees, and an undergrowth of papaw, which was now in flower; a carpet of ferns was spread on the ground in the dark shade, where a small clear stream meandered among the grasses and other plants. The dwellings of a few planters were scattered on the hills. In this wild and romantic valley I saw but few birds; and, in general, I remarked, in these woods on the Missouri, that far more birds lived in the vicinity of the plantations than in the recesses of the forest, an observation which is confirmed by McKenney,[97] and of which I have spoken in my travels in Brazil. We saw no mammalia in these woods, though there are many squirrels; the number of which, however, must have greatly decreased if what Bradbury says is true, that 2,000 of them had been shot in one hunting excursion.[98] I unwillingly left a spot so interesting to the naturalist, especially as I had no agreeable conversation to expect on board the boat. My live bears attracted all the inhabitants in the neighbourhood; nay, the people here were more eager to see the much-dreaded grizzly bears than even in Europe.

Our vessel was crowded with curious persons, and, besides these, an unwelcome intruder had intoxicated the greater part of my people. Among our inquisitive visitors there were several men belonging to a religious sect known here by the name of Mormons. They complained bitterly of the unjust treatment which they had lately experienced. They had lived on the other side of the Missouri, and, as they asserted, had been expelled, on account of their doctrines, by the neighbouring planters, their dwellings demolished and burnt, their plantations destroyed, and some of them killed, on which they settled on the north bank of the river. I was not able to learn whether all this was true, or why, after an interval of one or two years, they have not obtained redress from the government. So much, however, is certain, that, if these people spoke the truth, it would be a great disgrace to the administration of justice in this country, which calls itself the only free country in the world.[99]

According to their account, an angel appeared in 1821 to the founder of their doctrine, and brought him golden tables of law, on which the contents of a certain chapter of the Bible were engraved, and which is the substance of the doctrine. The inscription was translated, and the angel took the tables away.

They spoke also of a prophet Mormon, but I was not able clearly to comprehend the mystical meaning of their words.[100] A sensible old man gave me some notion of their doctrine, to which he seemed to be much devoted. He affirmed that their sect was perfectly harmless, and never molested others, a point respecting which their neighbours might, perhaps, give a different testimony.

These backwoodsmen were much interested by all our effects, and were particularly struck with our percussion guns and rifles. In those parts where the woods have been cleared, the country which they inhabit is extremely fertile. Deer and wild turkeys are still met with; but bears are not numerous, and the panther is only now and then seen. The elk (*Cervus Canadensis*) has been long since extirpated. The wood-rat (*Neotoma?*) is not uncommon; it does mischief to the fruits, and gets into the so-called smoke-houses, where meat is smoked and dried. The common grey wolf is said to be very numerous: the black race is seldom seen here, and the white never, which is a proof that it is a distinct species.

On the 21st of May we passed Fire Prairie and the mouth of Fishing Creek,[101] and again saw magnificent forests, the trees of which were so lofty that our guns were unable to reach the birds perched on the upper branches. The ground was covered with flowers, among which was a beautiful sky-blue iris, and with an undergrowth of papaw trees, above which arose the tall forest trees, such as the *Gleditschia triacanthos*, sassafras, tulip trees, &c., entwined with the *Vitis hederacea*. The red tanagra shone like a glowing coal amid the dark forest.

On the following day, the 22nd of May, we met the Joway steamer, which could with difficulty proceed up the shallow river. Old Roubedoux, who was on board, brought news from St. Louis. He had purchased from the Fur Company, for 500 dollars, the trading house on the Black Snake Hills, from which we had just come.[102] Having halted near the steam-boat at noon, with a temperature of 89°, we made a short excursion into the wood, where I procured the beautiful red adder, *Coluber coccineus*. The colour of its exquisitely marked body is a brownish vermilion, and, therefore, not so purely vermilion as the splendid coral adder of Brazil. The forest was so full of the caterpillars which have been already mentioned, that walking through it was most disagreeable. At five in the afternoon we passed Grand River,[103] and lay-to for the night six miles further down, on the south bank, at a plantation, the friendly inmates of which, though very well disposed, could give us only a small supply of provisions.

On the 23rd, in the neighbourhood of Little Arrow Rock,[104] we saw some persons catching an immensely large white catfish, the weight of which must have been very great, but I was not able to stop and examine it. At this place we heard a strange noise under the boat, which my people affirmed was produced by the prickly fins of the fish called by them casburgot, or malacigan (*Catastomus carpio*, Les.), and by the Americans, buffalo-fish. It weighs from five to six pounds. Towards evening we passed Franklin, and stopped at Boonville.[105] Two negro slaves, who were returning from the plantations, were very much astonished at the sight of my bears: one of them had a long tin speaking-trumpet, with which these men, when working in the forest, are called together. It may not be irrelevant to remark that all the negroes of these parts are slaves. Fine tall trees covered the hills on the bank, which my people ascended in order to purchase provisions in the scattered dwellings of the planters.

On the 24th we passed the small town of Columbia, below the mouth of the Manitu stream, where a quantity of logs of wood, for the use of the steam-boats, was piled up on the bank. At noon the thermometer was at 90°. An uninterrupted forest, with beautiful scenery, adorned the canal during the entire extent of this day's voyage. Having passed the village of Maryanne, on the northern side, we reached Jefferson City at six in the afternoon.[106] This place is still in its infancy and most of the habitations are scattered, while the ground between them is not yet levelled. It is covered with heaps of stones and high weeds; and cows and pigs were roaming about at liberty. We could not obtain any provisions except salt pork, biscuits, and whisky. In the bookseller's shop, as it is termed, we only found a few school books. In the evening I proceeded to the plantation of a person named Ramsay,[107] where a number of negroes congregated about our boat, from whom I was fortunate enough to purchase some poultry. These people were dressed in all sorts of left-off clothes, and forcibly reminded me of similar scenes in Brazil.

At eight o'clock in the morning of the 25th, we passed Côte sans Dessein; and at noon, when the thermometer was at 88°, reached the little town of Portland, which was founded about two years since. Near the mouth of Gasconade River we met the Oto steam-boat.[108] We stopped for the night below the Rivière à Berger, and on the morning of the 26th lay-to at the settlement of a man named Porter, to which the name of Washington has been given, though at present it consists of only a few isolated dwellings: the inhabitants were very courteous and obliging.[109] The adjacent forest was animated by many interesting birds; and I here purchased a live young bear. Opposite to this place, four or five miles up the country, a Mr. Von Mertels, of Hanover, has settled; and here, a few years since, Dr. Duden resided, who has written on North America, and who is still much talked of in this country.[110] In the evening we reached St. Charles, to which great numbers of German emigrants now resort,[111] and lay-to at the settlement of Mr. Chauvin, who keeps an inn, and has set up a stage between this and St. Louis. Here we passed the night, but the rain was so heavy, that we were prevented leaving the house. The people spoke to us a great deal of the many persons who had fallen victims to the cholera the year before. There is a ferry at this place over the Missouri, in which the large wheel is set in motion by six horses.

On the 27th, after the rain had ceased, we went by land to St. Louis: the weather was warm and damp, and the brilliant humming-birds fluttered about the plants in the court-yard of the house. As the stage did not run to-day, I hired a long, open, farmer's wagon, with three horses, in order to reach the Mississippi as speedily as possible, while Dreidoppel was to go by water, with my collections, &c. We immediately entered the forest, where colossal trees, especially the sugar maple, oak, elm, &c., covered a hilly ground, overgrown with many interesting plants, about which the most beautiful butterflies peculiar to this country were hovering. From time to time we saw planters' dwellings all built of wood, covered with planks, and roofed with shingles, the chimneys being of brick. Among the many species of trees is the black oak, which is used for dyeing and tanning. A great quantity of the bark is sent to England. The forest extends many miles, and, becoming gradually thinner, is succeeded by the open prairie, which does not differ from the prairies of the west, especially of the upper Missouri. We stopped at an isolated inn to refresh our horses, and were still six or seven miles from St. Louis. The last part of the road lay through a wood of dark green oaks, in which I saw many circular pools of water, which undoubtedly owed their origin to the sinking of the earth, of which Mr. Say speaks, in the account of Major Long's expedition.[112] These pools are fifty or sixty paces in diameter, and are inhabited by numerous frogs, whose croaking is heard at a great distance. At noon we alighted at the Union Hotel in St. Louis, after an absence of above a year.

St. Louis was now healthy, and not suffering from the cholera, as we had expected; there had, however, been a couple of cases in a steamer from New Orleans. No change of consequence had taken place since our last visit. At the factory of the American Fur Company I found very agreeable letters from Europe. Here I saw Mr. Lamont, to whose amiable family we were introduced, but I greatly regretted the absence of General Clarke.[113] We received much kindness in the house of Major O'Fallan, who is perfectly acquainted with the Missouri, and the aboriginal inhabitants. Here we saw a collection of Indian portraits and scenery by Mr. Catlin, a painter from New York, of which we were able to form an opinion after our recent travels in the country.[114] Major Dougherty, our friend and travelling companion, had the goodness to give us a night's lodging, and we were highly gratified by his conversation about the countries which we had just left, and with which he is well acquainted.

Among the remarkable objects in the vicinity of St. Louis are the ancient Indian barrows, the traces of which I had hitherto in vain attempted to find on the whole course of the Missouri. In order to take a view of them, we crossed the Missouri in a steam-ferry, where there is room for the horses and carriage, and in the upper story of its pavilion, a light, airy chamber. On the opposite bank are a good many houses, inns, and shops, under the shade of lofty old trees. Fish, turtles, vegetables, and other provisions, are daily sent from this place to the market in the town. The surrounding country is level, sandy, and, in part, marshy; the road passes alternately through open meadows and copses to the skirts of an extensive verdant plain, or prairie, after we had crossed a wooden bridge thrown over the pretty stream called Kahokia Creek, the banks of which are picturesquely bordered with fine trees.[115] The colour of the water is dark brown, like many forest streams in Brazil, and forms a beautiful camera obscura. The open plain, which we now reached, was everywhere clothed with young grass, and in several spots with low bushes. As soon as we had passed the skirts of the forest on the Mississippi, a long row of very flat ancient Indian barrows came in sight, extending parallel with the river, and a second row, forming an angle with the first, in which some of the barrows are higher than others. Right in front of the angle formed by the two rows is the most considerable barrow of all, which does not appear at first sight, though it is at least sixty feet high. It is called Trappist's or Monk's Hill, because some French monks of the order of La Trappe formerly lived here.[116] I may remark by the way, that many settlers of French origin live in this part of the country.

We proceeded in the direction of the above hill, which is about six miles from the river; it is covered with greensward and a few old trees, and some new wooden buildings are erected on it. In the prairie stood a group of very tall poplars, under which a herd of cattle was reposing. Here we left our wagon, but the bull, who seemed to be lord and master, was at first much inclined to oppose our passage. Numerous birds of many species and beautiful butterflies were fluttering about in the ardent noontide sun. The Indian hills, or barrows, of which Say counted seventy-five, have a very striking appearance; they stand in a row, generally isolated, but sometimes two are side by side. Some of them still retain their conical form, while others are very much flattened. There are similar barrows near St. Louis on the other side of the Mississippi, most of which have, however, been destroyed by cultivation and building. The destination and the origin of these remarkable barrows and walls, which have been the subject of so much discussion, are still involved in obscurity; while the government of the United States alone might have collected the necessary materials on the subject, if it had employed competent persons to excavate, carefully to examine, survey, and describe all the monuments of this kind that are scattered over the states of the Union.[117] Even at this time, it is not wholly too late to do much towards the accomplishment of so interesting an inquiry; not a moment should, however, be lost. Baron Alexander Von Humboldt has given an interesting essay on the subject in his valuable works; and several American writers have collected and published many particulars respecting these remains. Of some of them Warden has given ground plans and sketches, but no favourable result can be expected till the excavation is prosecuted in earnest.[118] Perhaps the flint knives resembling those of Mexico[119] might be found near St. Louis. These barrows have a close resemblance to the ancient German barrows which are everywhere found in our forests. A late traveller (Dr. De Wette) conjectures that the American barrows are not produced by art, but by nature, because there is no fosse round them from which the earth was taken; this notion is, however, very easily refuted, as the barrows and walls are arranged in regular figures and lines, and in like manner no fosse or excavation is to be seen round the barrows in the German forests. The earth was taken from the surface in the neighbourhood, but it was by no means necessary on that account to excavate a fosse. With regard to the regular position of the barrows of St. Louis, they have in this respect a close resemblance to the kurghans of the Russian steppes, which also lie in long regular lines. The very form, too, of both seems to be quite similar, if we except the stone images which are often seen on the kurghans. Pallas, in his "Tour through Southern Russia" (Vol. I. Vig. 1), gives a sketch of a row of barrows which perfectly resemble those of St. Louis.[120]

A pleasant westerly breeze which sprung up, was a great relief to us in the sultry heat, and continued till we returned to the shady forests on Kahokia Creek, which we reached at two o'clock. Numerous tortoises live in this stream. The banks of the Mississippi, near St. Louis, are likewise remarkable for various impressions of shells and zoophytes in the limestone; among them are the beautiful crinoides, which are found in great perfection close to the buildings of the town. Mr. Lesueur has collected and sent to France specimens of all these fossil remains, and every information on the subject is contained in his and other similar works. I neglected, while I was at St. Louis, to see the tame buffaloes which Mr. Pièrre Chouteau kept on his estate near the town, though I should have been very glad, for many reasons, to have seen these animals in a domestic state. I have been frequently told, in America, of hybrids of the buffalo (bison) and the tame race, but never saw any; and several naturalists, especially Mr. Thomas Say,[121] have always affirmed that no instance ever occurred of hybrids, capable of propagating their kind, of that animal and the tame species. He declares that every case into which he examined turned out to be unproved. Mr. Gallatin has, indeed, lately spoken on the subject, and pronounced against Mr. Say's opinion. He calls the bison a mere variety of the common ox; but this may be easily refuted.[122] The bison is quite a different species from the ox, as is clear, not only from its outward form, high withers, short tail, the formation of the head, and the peculiarity of its long hair, but likewise from the osteology, the number of the ribs and vertebræ being different in the two animals.

There is another point on which I differ from Mr. Gallatin, namely, his denial of the great decrease in the number of buffaloes in general. For when we consider how far these animals have been driven up the country, and that, in these very parts, they are even less numerous than formerly, we have a fact which at once proves a great decrease, of which nobody in the interior of the country can entertain a doubt.

After staying about a week we took leave of our friends at St. Louis, and embarked on board the Metamore steam-boat, which left on the 3rd of June. Messrs. Chouteau, Lamont, General Pratte, and Ortley, accompanied me on board, where we bade each other farewell.[123] We glided rapidly down the Mississippi, and passed Chester before evening, but were soon obliged to lay-to, because we were apprehensive that the night would be dark.

Our voyage on the 4th of June was extremely pleasant; the forests on the Mississippi were clothed in the brightest verdure, climbing plants interlaced the tall trees, and the papaw was in greater luxuriance than I have anywhere seen; but here, too, the caterpillars had partly stripped the bushes. Towards nine in the morning, after the early vapours were dispelled, we reached the mouth of the Ohio, the clear green water of which contrasted strongly with the grey and muddy stream of the Mississippi. We stopped at the landing-place at the junction of the two rivers, to wait for the steamer expected from New Orleans, and to take on board some of its passengers. The Ohio is at this time too shallow for the large Mississippi steam-boats to ascend it, and they, therefore, transfer their passengers to the smaller boats from St. Louis, Cincinnati, Louisville, and Pittsburg, which, in the present instance, occasioned us a most unpleasant delay. The Boonslick, a large boat from New Orleans, lay aground in the Mississippi, waiting to be relieved.[124] We therefore proceeded to her with a flat boat, by the aid of which she was lightened of a part of her cargo, consisting of lead. This business detained our Metamore a considerable time, after which we returned to the landing-place: we made use of this delay to undertake an excursion into the forest which borders upon the town. *Papilio Ajax* and *Turnus* were very numerous, and we caught a great many, especially of the former. In the shade of the forest we found the red Mississippi tanagra, which I had not before seen on my whole journey; and, likewise, observed its nest, which did not seem to annoy the birds. The beautiful baltimore and many other interesting birds were likewise frequent. At three o'clock the boat's bell summoned the scattered party to return. Two large New Orleans steam-boats, the Mediterranean and the Chester, now arrived. The former, which is the largest on the Mississippi, and about the size of a frigate, only much higher, came along side our vessel.[125] It had several cholera patients on board, and two persons had died of that disorder during the voyage. It was by no means pleasant to us to be obliged to receive passengers from this boat; nevertheless we took a good number of them on board higher up the river, at Smithland, whither this large boat was able to accompany us. In the evening we arrived at the village of Paduca, where we passed the night; and at noon the following day (the 5th of June) reached Smithland at the mouth of Cumberland River, where we stopped no longer than was necessary to receive the passengers from the Mediterranean; after which we proceeded on our voyage, in calm, hot weather, up the Ohio, which appeared in all its beauty, passed Cave-in-Rock,[126] continued our voyage during the night, and early in the morning of the 6th of June reached Mount Vernon, where we quitted the steamer. We then procured a carriage (dearborn), and pursued our journey to Harmony by land.[127]

This road, which I have already described, was extremely pleasant, on account of the luxuriant foliage of the lofty forest, though the trees, especially the beeches, had in many places suffered from the frost. The finest tulip, storax, and sassafras, with many other kinds, spread a cool shade, while innumerable butterflies afforded us much entertainment. The ajax, the blue and black philenor, the yellow and black turnus, &c., were countless. Our driver frequently alighted from his seat to shoot with his rifle some grey squirrels, which are here very common, for dinner. About noon we had the pleasure of meeting Mr. Say and our other friends at Harmony, in good health. I here became acquainted with Mr. Robert Dale Owen,[128] a very well informed man, and derived much instruction and gratification from my conversation with Messrs. Say, Lesueur, Owen, Macklure, Twigg, &c., by whom we were most kindly received.

On the 9th of June, after taking leave of our friends, I left New Harmony, with Mr. Lesueur, to continue our journey by way of Vincennes, to which place Mr. Twigg accompanied us on horseback.[129]

The whole country through which we passed, except near Vincennes, close to the Wabash, is an uninterrupted forest, in which the dwellings of the settlers or backwoodsmen lie scattered on both sides of the wood. They are, as I have already described them, for the chief part, block-houses, &c. and only here and there is a brick building to be seen. The fields are everywhere surrounded with fences. The country soon becomes hilly, and the soil in the vicinity of the Wabash is very fertile. The heat and dust were excessively annoying in this dry season; however, fresh, cool water was everywhere to be found, each dwelling-house being usually supplied with a well. A stranger is much struck with the dress of the women, living in small, wretched cottages, where he not unfrequently sees, if not a lady in fashionable attire, yet in a style of dress which, in Europe, he would neither look for nor see in habitations far superior. In these little cages there are immense four-post bedsteads, which occupy nearly the whole of the small chamber, which, like the cobbler's stall, "serves for bedroom, parlour, kitchen, and all." The door and windows of these hovels are generally open. Though the weather was particularly dry this spring, the corn looked very well; the soil of the forest is everywhere a very rich black mould, except in one place, where, for a couple of miles, sand suddenly appears. Mr. Lesueur, who has often visited and examined this part of the country, directed my attention to the entire change of vegetation. Instead of the many kinds of lofty trees in the forests of Indiana, we find, in this sandy tract, the low, black oak, which is not above thirty or forty feet high; as soon as that is passed the tall trees again appear. Here the fallen trunks give a wild and romantic appearance to the forest, where great numbers of cattle and swine were feeding. We here saw a place where the inhabitants of the neighbourhood assemble for religious exercises, which are called camp meetings. These singular assemblies have been described by many travellers, and Mrs. Trollope does not appear to have exaggerated in her account of them.[130] We observed vestiges of huts, fireplaces, and the eminences fenced round, which serve as pulpits, from which their spiritual teachers preach. We stopped, at noon, at a small village in the wood, consisting of only five or six houses, which is called Owensville.[131] Close to the cottage where we dined was a large clover field, in which innumerable butterflies, especially ajax and philenor, were fluttering. Volney observes, that he travelled through the extensive forest, from Louisville to Vincennes, in the month of July, without seeing a single settlement, or hearing the song of a bird.[132] The first part of this sentence is no longer applicable; but I can confirm the latter, for which many authorities might be quoted.

Before evening we reached Prince Town, which is built with a large square in the centre.[133] We passed the night in a good inn, where, as is common in this country, a sort of punca was suspended over the table in the dining-room; this was drawn backwards and forwards by a negro, and served at once to cool the air, and to chase away the swarms of troublesome flies. On the following day we passed through lofty and more thickly-wooded forests than yesterday, consisting in many places of old beeches which had suffered much from the frost: indeed, both the fruit and mast were destroyed completely by the frost in this part of the country. The catalpa was in full blossom, but, though the ground was covered with a luxuriant growth of plants, none of them were yet in flower. We saw numbers of the grey squirrel, which was served up to us in the inn as a delicacy. Beautifully romantic little valleys intersect the tall and gloomy forest, where we now and then met some farmers, whose wives were all on horseback, smoking their pipes. After taking some dinner at an isolated saw-mill in the wood, we reached, three miles further off, the White River, in a fertile valley, where the heat was very oppressive, because the forest completely impeded any circulation of air. The wild vine flourishes here in great luxuriance, the soil being very rich.

The White River is a fine stream, rather narrower at this place than the Wabash, and there is a ferry to cross over to the other side.[134] There the face of the country is considerably changed, for, the soil being sandy, the vegetation of the sand and prairies of St. Louis again recurs. It is worthy of remark, that all the plants in the sandy soil were now in flower, whereas in the rich black mould of the forest none were yet in blossom.

When the rather hilly country on the White River was passed, it became flatter, and we at length issued from the forest into the verdant plain of the Wabash, in which Vincennes is situated, at the distance of twelve miles from the White River. As we approached Vincennes, we observed, on the right hand, a hill covered with oak bushes, called Warrior's Hill, from which the Americans observed the enemy when they took this place from the English.[135]

Vincennes is one of the most ancient settlements of the French, founded in 1736. There was formerly a fort here, belonging to the series of posts by which a communication was kept up in this wilderness. It was subsequently called Old Post, and is said to have received its present name from a Captain Vincennes, who possessed the confidence of the Indians, and to whom they presented a piece of land.[136] It is now a mean-looking, scattered place, consisting of several unpaved streets, on the bank of the Wabash. Many old buildings are still to be seen, remaining from the time in which so many French settlements were founded in the west. Most of the houses built at that time are small, and have only one story; which is likewise the case at Vincennes, but the Americans have, however, erected many new brick buildings. The court-house, standing at the verge of the prairie, is, as usual, a square edifice, covered with white plaster. The descendants of the French, of whom there are many families, do not belong to the better class of the inhabitants, but are low, ignorant, and superstitious. The place is, however, thriving, and promises to possess, in time, a considerable trade. Many Americans have settled in it, and some of them have well furnished shops: but a bookseller who set up a shop there met with no encouragement whatever, and was obliged to leave.

In front of the house of the former governor, which stands in a pleasant open spot near the river, are some ancient shady trees, and a garden, containing many rare and beautiful plants, is attached to it; formerly it was kept in good order, but it is now sadly neglected and suffered to run to ruin.[137]

We put up, in Vincennes, at Clarke's Hotel, where the stages start from; and I intended to proceed on my journey the following day, but the landlord and postmaster declared, rather laconically, that I must wait for the next opportunity, because our baggage was too heavy. This caused a delay of two days, which I endeavoured, in Mr. Lesueur's company, to turn to the best account. Mr. Badolet, of Geneva, who has long resided at this place, and is thoroughly acquainted with the country, was unfortunately indisposed.[138] He takes much interest in the promotion of knowledge, and through his instrumentality a library has been formed, which, though still in its infancy, consists of about 1500 volumes. New books are added every year, and there are already some valuable works. Mr. Badolet likewise purchased the well preserved lower jaw of a mastodon, which was found in the White River. Mr. Lesueur made a drawing of this jawbone, which is deposited in the library. Another interesting character lives here, but forgotten, neglected, and in great poverty—I mean Colonel Vigo, who rendered important services to the Americans at the capture of Vincennes. They, indeed, gave him the rank of colonel, but suffer him to starve.[139]

In our excursions in the vicinity of this place we found many interesting plants. Mr. Bodmer took a view of Vincennes from the top of Warrior's Hill; while Mr. Lesueur visited the Indian barrows, of which there are several in the plain, and which the French settlers call *mamelon*.[140] One of these hills was examined on a former occasion, and an excavation made through a wolf's den on one side of it, but nothing was taken from it but white clay; without doubt the examination must have been superficial.

On the 13th of June we parted from our friend, Mr. Lesueur, and left Vincennes by the stage. We first passed through a tract of alternate meadows and thickets, and then, for a couple of miles, through the unbroken forests which characterize Indiana. After proceeding thirteen miles we came to a solitary post-house in the wood, where breakfast was ready, and of which we partook while they were changing horses. We then crossed in a ferry, an arm of White River, which runs between picturesque wooded banks. The roads were bad; decayed trunks of trees were constantly in the way; the ground broken and uneven; and our stage, drawn by four very spirited horses, sustained many a violent jolt. We came to Washington and Mount Pleasant,[141] where the farmers were cultivating their fields, in which isolated trees were frequently seen, but which afforded no shade from the sultry sun, for they were all destroyed by the fire. They are cut down, from time to time, when the people are in want of timber; and, as a sign that they are to be felled in the next winter, a circular ring is hewn into the bark. It is said to be very difficult to cultivate the land in Indiana, on account of the extremely vigorous vegetation. Except in the vicinity of the Wabash and the White River, it is, however, not so fertile as in Illinois, where, in the environs of Springfield, for instance, it is scarcely necessary to do more than hoe the ground, in order to obtain the finest crops. An acre of land there yields from sixty to eighty bushels of maize, and fifty bushels of wheat. The effects of the frost were everywhere visible on the trees: it had caused much damage, and killed all the fruit for this year. The fruits of the field were about as forward as they would be on the Rhine at this season. In the plantations there were great numbers of oxen, horses, sheep, and swine, the former of which were particularly large and handsome. At Mount Pleasant we found in the inn a good many books lying about; among them were some geographical works. From this place we descended an eminence to the bank of the second arm of the White River, which flows through fine forests. The water was transparent, and the banks steep. Being set over with a ferry, we came to a tall, gloomy forest, consisting almost wholly of large beech trees, which afforded a most refreshing shade. The forest continued without intermission, but the beeches were soon succeeded by other species of trees indigenous to this country. We passed the most elevated part of the road through the picturesque forest scenes, where the lofty crowns of the trees shut out the sky from our view. They were the most splendid forests I had yet seen in North America. In the evening we stopped, twenty-three miles from Mount Pleasant, at a capital inn, called Horsit, surrounded with farm buildings in good condition. We were quite astonished at meeting, in this lone, wild, sequestered spot, with such a respectable house and table; everything was particularly neat and comfortable. Early on the morning of the 14th we set out again. About six miles further on, is the little town of Paoli, in a calcareous spot, where pieces of limestone everywhere stand out. We then proceeded by the side of Litcreek, some miles from whence the stage stopped, and the passengers breakfasted at the house of Chambers, a Quaker.[142] We were told that this part of the country is very salubrious, and the air extremely pure, but it takes strangers some time to get accustomed to the water, which is impregnated with lime. We saw numbers of horses in the forest, but the breed is not so good in Indiana as in other states. At Greenville, a small village, was a large concourse of the neighbouring farmers, whose horses and vehicles were tied to the fences. They had come to take part in the election of some magistrate. The heat was excessive, and the dust very troublesome. Several parties of farmers were in the public-houses, where a rude, noisy crowd were drinking whisky and playing at various games. We soon reached the summit of the calcareous chain of hills, which we had ascended gradually and imperceptibly, and approached the southern declivity, where an extensive and magnificent prospect opened before us. The wide valley, or, rather, the vast plain of the

Ohio, suddenly unfolds itself to the eye of the astonished traveller. As far as the eye can reach, a dense, uninterrupted forest covers the country, and the beauteous river, like a streak of silver, meanders through the landscape. In the distance lie the red masses of the houses of the towns of Louisville and New Albany, which extend on both sides of the Ohio. We soon passed the slope of the chain, and drove rapidly through a highly cultivated country to New Albany, on the banks of the river.[143]

I did not stop at New Albany, where there had lately been several cases of cholera, but proceeded to Louisville, where we soon arrived, and embarked the same evening, on board the Paul Jones steamer. In this town, too, there had been some cases of cholera, but the people did not seem to be afraid of that disorder. After proceeding about thirty miles up the Ohio, some accident happened to our engine, and we were obliged to lay-to. On the following day, the 15th, the forests of the Ohio appeared in the luxuriant verdure of the varied foliage of their lofty trees, among which the colossal planes were especially conspicuous. Near Kentucky River our engine again broke; it was, however, repaired, during the night, at Vevay.[144]

On the 16th we reached Rising Sun, saw Petersburg and Aurora, where the United States mail steam-boat, the Franklin, passed rapidly by us, then came to Lawrenceburg, and arrived about noon at Cincinnati.[145]

Cincinnati is a considerable town, and carries on an extensive trade, and is frequented by numerous steam-boats, of which a considerable number were now lying on the banks of the Ohio. Many travellers have already described everything worthy of notice in this town, and I will, therefore, only mention some establishments connected with natural history, which we were now able to visit at our leisure, as we were no longer apprehensive of the cholera. The Western Museum, belonging to Mr. Dorfeuille, which Mrs. Trollope has described, is the only one worthy of notice. I observed several interesting articles, though all American establishments of this kind are calculated, not for the advantage of science, but for pecuniary gain. This museum is lighted up every evening at eight o'clock, and an indifferent concert is performed, chiefly by Germans. In one of the rooms was a small fountain, round which the visitors sat upon benches, gazing at it with astonishment. The owner has a taste for the sciences, and would pay greater attention to them, if he met with more encouragement to do so; but his museum did not attract many visitors till he introduced, in the upper rooms, an absurd representation of hell. Grottoes, in which a number of frightful skeletons are moving about, and among whom the devil acts a principal part; these, and other hideous scenes, attract the vulgar multitude, and bring considerable profit. Mr. Dorfeuille has, however, several interesting specimens, such as petrifactions, fossil impressions, Indian antiquities, Mexican curiosities, and some fragments of parchment with hieroglyphics painted on them; the best of which, however, was at this time in the hands of Mr. Bullock, an Englishman, who resides some miles from hence, and which I therefore did not see.[146]

On examining the booksellers' shops, I found only some elegantly bound works on the *belles lettres*, a few on the statistics of different countries, but none relating to natural history, nor any portraits or history of the too much neglected Indian nations. I there formed several valuable acquaintances, among others, Dr. Daniel Drake, who is well known as an author, and whose work, "The Picture of Cincinnati," and other essays, prove that he has not neglected the study of nature.[147] I met with many old acquaintances, among others, Mr. Richard Owen, of New Harmony;[148] and in all my excursions saw great numbers of Germans, of whom it is estimated that 10,000 reside here. German is everywhere spoken. German peasants arrived continually, and traversed the streets, but most of them are of the lowest and most uneducated class, and are not calculated to give the Americans a favourable impression of our nation.

Instead of going immediately into the country, and hiring themselves to the farmers, in order to learn the nature of the agriculture of this country, they loiter about the town, where they fall into the hands of abandoned countrymen of their own, squander the little property they have brought with them, and are then despised by the inhabitants. At present, however, there are many respectable and intelligent Germans here, who have already contributed to give the Americans a more favourable opinion of our people. Some of these estimable men have conceived the laudable plan of establishing a society for the protection and settlement of their countrymen, which will certainly prove highly useful.

On the 19th of June I left this town on board the United States mail-boat, Guyandotte, and proceeded up the Ohio. The Lady Scott steamer set out at the same time with us, but our steamer soon left her far behind. As slavery is abolished in the state of Ohio, the crew of our vessel were nearly all white men. There are three such mail-boats, which have to forward the despatches of the government, but they perform this office only occasionally, because they receive only five dollars each time. The most rapid vessels are chosen for this service; they have the words, "United States Mail," painted on their paddle-box.

About noon, on the 20th of June, we lay-to at Portsmouth,[149] above the mouth of the Sciotto River, and I landed at this place, intending to proceed on the Ohio Canal.

FOOTNOTES:

[93] For the Little Platte, see our volume xiv, p. 174, note 141. Independence is noted in our volume xix, p. 189, note 34 (Gregg). As it was situated three miles from the river, both Wayne City and Blue Mills contended for the business of the landing place. Portage l'Independence was at the former, or even higher up the river—possibly cutting off the bend wherein the Kansas River enters, since Maximilian does not speak of passing that stream.

The person whom Maximilian met was Milton G. Sublette (for whom see Wyeth's *Oregon*, in our volume xxi, p. 67, note 44). He went out with the Wyeth expedition in the spring of 1834, but because of illness turned back (May 8) near the Kansas River, and had just arrived at Independence Portage when the prince's vessel came down the Missouri. William L. Sublette, the chief partner of Sublette and Campbell, had led out a party to the mountains which passed Wyeth's about May 12. See Townsend's *Narrative*, in our volume xxi, p. 151; and "Correspondence and Journals of Captain Nathaniel J. Wyeth," in *Sources for the History of Oregon* (Eugene, Oregon, 1899), pp. 132, 221, 224.—ED.

[94] The "Oto" (Otto), built at Jeffersonville, Indiana (1831), was Sublette and Campbell's steamer, which visited the upper Missouri in 1833. Somewhere on the upper river Sublette sent the boat back, and proceeded by keelboat to Fort Union. Probably the steamer had wintered near Council Bluffs.—ED.

[95] For Liberty, see our volume xxii, p. 249, note 197. Williams's Ferry was at the present site of Missouri City; the settlement had been begun by Shrewsbury Williams shortly before Maximilian's visit, and was incorporated as a city in 1859.

"Charaton Scatty" is the phonetic spelling of "Charretins écartés," two creeks separated by a short distance. Lewis and Clark, in *Original Journals*, i, p. 57, give the name as "Sharriton Carta."—ED.

[96] The knowledge of naturalists respecting reptiles or amphibia has been increased in a surprising manner of late years. The work now publishing by Messrs. Duméril and Bibron, promises to be the most complete on the subject. A vast number of species has been found, some of which are hardly capable of being sufficiently defined: thus, the authors of the above-mentioned excellent work seemed to have proceeded, in some cases, rather hastily. I will mention only one or two instances: vol. v., p. 88, I find in the synopsis, "*Tupinambis monitor*, Maxim., Prince of Wied;" whereas I never thought of calling the lizard in question *Tupinambis*. Vol. iii., p. 80, *Alligator sclerops*, and page 86 the same, where I am quoted in reference to two species of crocodile, though it is very certain that I could not observe in Brazil more

than one species. In these two descriptions there is much confusion; and in this respect we must also not follow Spix, who considered the varieties of age as distinct species. I could quote many other instances, if this were a proper place for such discussion.

In the work of Messrs. Duméril and Bibron there are likewise many mistakes with respect to the Brazilian reptiles described by me; and it seems that the authors, like many other French naturalists, quote my descriptions of those animals without having read or even seen them, otherwise they would certainly have preferred my statement of the colour of the animals from the life, to a description of the faded specimens preserved in spirits, which are met with in the museums; or to the equally incorrect statements of Dr. Spix, who, it is well known, forgot to note the colour of the animals when alive, and whose representations of them are likewise from specimens preserved in spirits.—MAXIMILIAN.

[97] For Thomas L. McKenney, see our volume xxii, p. 29, note 3.—ED.

[98] See our volume v, p. 280, note 157.—ED.

[99] For a contemporary description of the troubles with the Mormons in Jackson County, Missouri, see Gregg's *Commerce of the Prairies,* in our volume xx, pp. 93-99. Gregg's point of view is that of a sympathizer with the Missouri backwoodsman; Maximilian's is that of the doctrinaire. For a recent historical description of these events, consult W. A. Linn, *Story of the Mormons* (New York, 1902), pp. 161-207; see also J. H. Kennedy, *Early Days of Mormonism* (New York, 1888); and Thomas Gregg, *Prophet of Palmyra* (New York, 1890), pp. 127-148. The Mormon point of view is presented in B. H. Roberts, *Missouri Persecutions* (Salt Lake City, 1900). A conflict between two such differing classes as the Missouri pioneers and the Mormon emigrants was inevitable, and it was fortunate that there was so little consequent bloodshed.—ED.

[100] On the psychology of the Mormon movement, and the origin of the Book of Mormon, see J. W. Riley, *Founder of Mormonism* (New York, 1902).—ED.

[101] For these geographical place-names, see our volume xxii, pp. 247, 248, notes 192, 194, respectively.—ED.

[102] Robidoux had formerly been in charge of an American Fur Company's post higher up the river. In 1826 he was transferred to the trading house at Blacksnake Hills, where he was a salaried employé until the purchase here narrated by Maximilian. See *History of Buchanan County,* Missouri (St. Joseph, 1881), pp. 391-396.—ED.

[103] For Grand River, see our volume xv, p. 178, note 62.—ED.

[104] See, for this point, our volume xiv, p. 162, note 127.—ED.

[105] Old Franklin and the town of Boonville, on the opposite bank, are noted in our volumes xix, p. 188, note 33 (Gregg), and xxi, p. 89, note 59 (Wyeth), respectively.—ED.

[106] Columbia, the seat of the state university, is described in our volume xxi, p. 133, note 8 (Townsend); Jefferson City, the capital, in volume xxii, p. 242, note 183.

Marion, on the southern (not northern) bank of the Missouri, is a village in Cole County, in a township of the same name. It was platted at Moniteau Rock, below a creek of the same name, and at first was county seat for Cole. Defeated in the contest for the state capital, the town lost also the court-house, which was removed (1826) to Jefferson City. The place was incorporated in 1837, but has never attained prominence.—ED.

[107] Major Josiah Ramsey, Jr., was one of the first two settlers of Jefferson City, of which he was appointed trustee in 1825.—ED.

[108] Côte sans Dessein is noted in our volume v, p. 48, note 20. For Gasconade River, see our volume xiv, pp. 136, 137. Portland, in Auxvusse Township, Callaway County, was laid out in September, 1831. It no longer exists as a separate village.—ED.

[109] Berger Creek is a small Franklin County stream, flowing into the Missouri from the southwest.

Washington (Missouri) was settled some time prior to 1818, and incorporated in 1841. The first brick house was built in 1834. It is the largest town in Franklin County, and originally had a considerable German element among the population.—ED.

[110] Gottfried Duden was a young German physician, who, after a journey to the United States and a residence of several years (1824-27) in Montgomery (now Warren County, Missouri), wrote a book relating his experiences. His work was much read, and as he gave a pleasant picture of life in the interior of North America, it induced a large emigration, especially from southwest Germany and along the upper Rhine. Many of these emigrants were of the educated classes, and have been valuable citizens to Missouri. See Duden, *Bericht über eine Reise nach den westlichen Staaten Nordamerika's und einen mehrjährigen Aufenthalt am Missouri* (Elberfelt, 1829); several later editions followed.—ED.

[111] For St. Charles, see our volume v, p. 39, note 9. This was originally a settlement of French inhabitants, but during the decade of 1830-40 German immigration flowed in so rapidly that both the township and county of St. Charles have a majority of settlers of German descent.—ED.

[112] See our volume xv, p. 173. The theory there advanced is, that the land between the Mississippi and Missouri "would appear rather to have subsided from the waters of a quiet ocean than to have been brought down from above."—ED.

[113] A brief sketch of Daniel Lamont is in our volume xxii, p. 314, note 274. General William Clark made his home in St. Louis after his Western expedition (1804-06), and died there in 1838. See our volume v, p. 254, note 143, for a brief sketch of his career.—ED.

[114] See our volume xxii, p. 32, note 9; also Smithsonian Institution *Report*, 1885, part ii.—ED.

[115] Cahokia Creek is a small stream in St. Clair County, Illinois. It formerly discharged into the Missouri at the French village of the same name; but its channel is now changed, so that its mouth is some miles above. For the tradition that this change was of artificial origin caused by a habitant who attempted to injure the village, see Flagg's *Far West*, in our volume xxvii, chapter xli.—ED.

[116] The Trappist order and monastery are described in much detail by Flagg in his *Far West*, published in volume xxvi of our series, chapter xv. Consult this account, with accompanying notes.—ED.

[117] For recent government work on this subject, consult Lucien Carr, in Smithsonian Institution *Report*, 1891; Cyrus Thomas, in United States Bureau of Ethnology *Report*, 1890-91; and also Flagg, *op. cit.*—ED.

[118] For von Humboldt, consult our volume xviii, p. 345, note 136; Warden is noted in volume xxii, p. 149, note 63.—ED.

[119] See design in Plate 81, in the accompanying atlas, our volume xxv. See also our volume xxii, pp. 174, 175.—ED.

[120] Peter Simon Pallas (1741-1811) was born in Berlin, but early invited to Russia to assume charge of scientific explorations in that empire. His *Bemerkungen auf einer Reise durch die südlichen Statthalterschafter des russischen Reichs* was published in 1799-1801.—ED.

[121] For a brief sketch of this naturalist, whom Maximilian visited at New Harmony, see our volume xiv, p. 40, note 1.—ED.

[122] Albert Gallatin (1761-1849), a Swiss emigrant, whose services as United States statesman in finance and diplomacy were considerable, devoted the latter portion of his career to scientific pursuits, especially to the subject of North American ethnology. Maximilian here refers to his well-known "Synopsis of Indian Tribes of North America," published in American Antiquarian Society *Transactions*, ii (Cambridge, 1836). The reference to the

bison appears on pp. 139, 140, wherein Gallatin claims to have had upon his farm in western Pennsylvania a mixed-breed ox of the domestic cattle and bison stock.—ED.

[123] The "Metamore" steamer was built at Louisville in 1832. For these St. Louisians, see our volume xxii, pp. 235, 282, 314, notes 168, 239, 274, respectively.—ED.

[124] The "Boone's Lick" was built at Pittsburg in 1833; she was when built one of the largest of the river boats, being of two hundred and ninety-five tons displacement.—ED.

[125] The "Mediterranean" and "Chester" were both built at Pittsburg in 1832; the former, of six hundred tons burden, exceeded any other river craft by nearly two hundred tons.—ED.

[126] See Plate 7, in the accompanying atlas, our volume xxv.—ED.

[127] For Maximilian's earlier visit to New Harmony, see our volume xxii, pp. 163-197.—ED.

[128] Robert Dale Owen (1801-77) was the son of the founder of the New Harmony community. Born in Glasgow, he was educated largely in Switzerland, and came to the United States with his father in 1825. After the failure of the community, the younger Owen conducted a journal in New York for some years; but, having married, he returned to New Harmony about the time of Maximilian's visit, to make this his permanent home. He was influential in Indiana politics, serving in the State legislature (1835-41), two terms representing his state in Congress (1843-47), and materially assisting in the revision of the Indiana constitution in 1850. In 1853 he was appointed chargé d'affaires at Naples, being later raised to ministerial rank (1855-58). Owen was a radical in religion and politics, and to spread his opinions wrote many books. His argument for immediate emancipation is said to have had much weight with Lincoln.—ED.

[129] William A. Twigg, son of a clergyman of the Church of England, was one of the original members of the New Harmony community; his descendants still live in the region. See George B. Lockwood, *New Harmony Communities* (Marion, Indiana, 1902).

Alexander Maclure, brother of William, one of the founders of the New Harmony settlement, was the person Maximilian here intends. He lived for many years at this place.—ED.

[130] For Mrs. Trollope and her notes on America, see our volume xxi, p. 44, note 24 (Wyeth).—ED.

[131] Owensville, in Gibson County, was laid out in 1817 and named for Thomas Owens of Kentucky. John C. Warrick was the first merchant and postmaster. By 1900 the town had attained a population of 1,019.—ED.

[132] For Volney, see Flint's *Letters*, in our volume ix, p. 237, note 121.—ED.

[133] For a brief notice of Princeton, Indiana, see Hulme's *Journal*, in our volume x, p. 46, note 16.—ED.

[134] White River rises near the Ohio line, and flows southwest across Indiana into the Wabash, embouching between Knox and Gibson counties. It is the largest stream wholly within the state, and waters a fertile, well-wooded valley of about nine thousand square miles.—ED.

[135] For an historical sketch of Vincennes, see Croghan's *Journals*, in our volume i, p. 141, note 113. Warrior's Hill was called by the Americans under George Rogers Clark (1779), Warrior's Island, since they had, upon the expedition against Vincennes, been wading through a submerged district, and found this grove of oaks the first considerable spot of dry land on which to encamp. It was situated immediately northeast of Grand Morass Pond, in full view of Vincennes. See Thwaites, *How George Rogers Clark won the Northwest*; for a detailed account, consult C. W. Butterfield, *George Rogers Clark's Conquest of the Illinois and the Wabash Towns*, 1778 and 1779 (Columbus, Ohio, 1904), pp. 323-326, 711.—ED.

[136] François Margane, sieur de Vincennes, is frequently confused with his uncle, Jean Baptiste Bissot, also sieur de Vincennes. Both commanded for the French among the Miami Indians, but the younger built (probably in 1727) the fort at the site called by his name. He was born in Canada in 1672, succeeded to his uncle's estate in 1719, and about the same time came to the Wabash. His death occurred during the Chickasaw campaign (1736); while leading the Miami contingent he was captured and burned at the stake. The town of Vincennes was frequently called "O Post," a corruption of the French form "Au poste."—ED.

[137] The residence of General William Henry Harrison, first governor of Indiana Territory, still stands in the northwestern portion of the town, at the intersection of Water and Scott streets. It was the earliest brick mansion in this section of the country, and was begun in 1805 on the plantation that Harrison had bought the previous year, and named "Grouseland." At this place occurred the famous interview between its owner and Tecumseh, the Indian chief who was afterwards vanquished in the battle of Tippecanoe (1811). Upon Harrison's departure for North Bend, Grouseland became the residence of his son, John Cleve Symmes Harrison, whose wife was the only child of General Zebulon M. Pike. The gardens were long noted for their beauty.—ED.

[138] Jean Badollet, born in Geneva, Switzerland, in 1758, was the son of a Protestant minister. He was a college friend of Albert Gallatin, and at his request immigrated in 1785 to the United States. Taking charge of a colonizing project in southwestern Pennsylvania, he for some years acted as Gallatin's business manager. Upon the organization of Indiana Territory, Badollet was appointed register of the land office, removing to Vincennes, which he thereafter made his home. He retained his office until 1836, when his son was appointed in his stead. Badollet served as a member of the constitutional convention of Indiana in 1816 and strongly opposed the introduction of slavery into the new state. His latter years were clouded because of poor health, and he died in 1837.—ED.

[139] For a brief sketch of Vigo, see André Michaux's *Travels*, in our volume iii, p. 31, note 8.—ED.

[140] The highest Indian mounds of the state are found in the vicinity of Vincennes. For a critical discussion, see E. T. Cox, "Archæology," in Indiana Historical Society *Publications*, i, pp. 217-240.—ED.

[141] For Washington, Indiana, see Faux's *Journal*, in our volume xi, p. 203, note 68.

Mount Pleasant was a post village on the Vincennes-New Albany turnpike, thirty-five miles east of the old capital. It was the seat for Martin County until 1846; but being avoided by the railroad, has declined in importance, having now no post-office.—ED.

[142] The turnpike road being followed by the travellers crossed Daviess, Martin and Orange counties, substantially along the line of the present Ohio and Mississippi Railway.

For Paoli, see Welby's *English Settlements*, in our volume xii, p. 230, note 37.

"Litcreek" is Lick Creek, a small westward-flowing affluent of the East Fork of White River, in Orange and Martin counties, Indiana.

For Samuel Chambers, see Hulme's *Journal*, in our volume x, p. 62, note 29.—ED.

[143] Greenville is a small post village in Floyd County, Indiana, twelve miles northwest of New Albany; in 1900 it had a population of three hundred.

For New Albany, consult Hulme's *Journal*, in our volume x, p. 44, note 15.—ED.

[144] For the Swiss settlement of southeastern Indiana, of which Vevay was the capital, see our volume v, p. 316, note 164.—ED.

[145] Rising Sun, of Ohio County, Indiana, thirty-five miles southwest of Cincinnati, was platted (1814) by John James, an emigrant from Maryland. Its population in 1900 was 1,548.

Aurora, in Dearborn County, four miles below Lawrenceburgh, was laid out in 1819, and incorporated three years later. At the time of Maximilian's visit the population was about six hundred; by 1900 it had increased to 3,645.

Petersburg was a small hamlet three miles below Aurora; it never attained commercial prosperity.

For Lawrenceburgh, see our volume xiii, p. 62, note 36.—ED.

[146] See Mrs. Trollope's description in *Domestic Manners of Americans* (London 1832), pp. 68-70.

For William Bullock, whose residence was at Hygeia, near Covington, Kentucky, see our volume xix, preface.—ED.

[147] For a brief sketch of Dr. Drake, see Nuttall's *Journal*, in our volume xiii p. 61, note 35.—ED.

[148] Richard, a younger son of Robert Owen, was born at New Lanark, Scotland, in 1810. He was educated chiefly in Switzerland, and came to New Harmony (1828) fresh from his literary studies. His tastes inclining to scientific pursuits, he was associated with his brother, David Dale, in several geological surveys, among them an exploration (1849) of Lake Superior. He engaged in the Mexican War with the rank of captain, and in the War of Secession held an Indiana colonelcy. Upon the death of his brother (1860), Richard Owen was appointed Indiana state geologist, and for fifteen years thereafter held the chair of natural science in the state university, publishing a *Key to the Geology of the Globe*. Upon retirement from professional duties, Owen returned to New Harmony, where he occupied the Rapp mansion until his death in 1890.—ED.

[149] For a sketch of the history of Portsmouth, see Nuttall's *Journal*, in our volume xiii, p. 59, note 31.—ED.

CHAPTER XXXII
PASSAGE OF THE OHIO CANAL AND LAKE ERIE TO THE FALLS OF NIAGARA, FROM THE 21ST TO THE 30TH OF JUNE

Voyage on the Ohio Canal—Chillicothe—Circleville—Licking Summit, the Highest Part of the Canal—Hebron—Fall of the Canal at Akron—Cleveland—Lake Erie; its Navigation—Buffalo—The Seneca Indians—The Six Nations—Niagara River—The Village of Niagara—The Falls of Niagara—Divine Worship of the Tuscarora Indians.

Portsmouth is rather an inconsiderable town, with low houses, and broad, unpaved streets, built in the angle of the confluence of the Sciotto with the Ohio. Here begins the Ohio Canal, which connects that river with Lake Erie.[150] This fine canal is navigated by numerous boats, which are built in the same style as the keel-boats of the Missouri, but have many convenient small chambers; they are from seventy-seven to eighty feet in length, fourteen in breadth, and are drawn by two horses, on which the driver is seated. These Ohio Canal boats are not so well arranged and fitted up as those on the Erie Canal, where they have distinct boats for passengers and goods, which is not here the case. They are also slower, because fewer horses are employed. In the middle of the boat is the long space for the goods; in front two small cabins; and at the back is the saloon or dining room. At the sides of the cabins are cushioned seats, on which, as well as on the floor, the beds are arranged for the night. In the other cabins are berths for the ladies.

On the afternoon of the day on which we arrived we went on board a canal boat, where I met with an agreeable, well-informed, travelling companion in Dr. Pitcher, an attentive observer of nature, and military physician of Fort Gibson, on the River Orkansa, who was accompanied by his family.[151] We set out at six o'clock in the afternoon, with very fine weather. The banks of the canal were covered with wood, especially sugar maples. Before night we came to some sluices, and a mill with seventy saws for cutting freestone, which is found in the neighbourhood, into blocks for building, tombstones, &c.

On the 21st we passed through very fine forests of sugar maples and beeches, where numerous baltimores were flying about. The country is very fertile; it was formerly clothed with wood; and the detached block-houses of the settlers are constantly met with. On many spots of the surrounding hills the may-apple (*Podophyllum*) grew in abundance; others were covered with an undergrowth of the papaw tree: the kingfisher was frequently seen on the banks of the canal. Near three combined sluices is a feeder, which connects the canal with the Sciotto. There is a weir in the river, in the deep waters of which it is said there are a very great number of soft-shell tortoises. About a league and a half from Chillicothe, after passing Indian Creek, the canal is carried over a stream called Paint Creek. This aqueduct is broad, has three arches, and two stone pillars, over which the water of the canal flows; and on each side of the aqueduct is a floored way, with a railing for the horses and foot passengers. Towards evening we arrived at Chillicothe, a small town, with 2000 or 3000 inhabitants, in the wild and fertile valley, which is evidently in a state of rapid improvement.[152] There are about 150 Germans here, who are in general well spoken of. The breeding of cattle is the chief occupation of the inhabitants of this part of the country, and they export oxen and swine. They have, however, begun likewise to follow agriculture, and now export a small quantity of wheat.

When the first planters settled here, they found two Indian tribes—the Shawnees of the Americans, or Chavenons of the French, and the Wyandots, who had been driven hither from the north.[153] On the spot where the town now stands were formerly several conical Indian barrows, in one of which were found some bones, potsherds, and beads, which were made of hard wood. Another barrow was composed, at the upper part, of stones; it contained bones, and two copper bracelets, which appeared to be beaten or hammered, not cast. A third barrow, overgrown with trees, which still exists, and is situated on a rather lofty wooded eminence, had at the summit a mixture of sand and stones, and then clay, under which were ashes mixed with bones, which crumbled away when exposed to the air.[154]

An extremely violent thunder-storm, with torrents of rain, surprised us when we were leaving Chillicothe, at nine o'clock in the evening, where an obliging German, of the name of Bauman, had given us hospitable entertainment. We proceeded during the night, and early in the morning of the 22nd passed several sluices, and then traversed a low, wooded country on the Sciotto, which is here full of small verdant islands, covered with trees. Fine lofty forest trees adorned the country; the elder bushes were in blossom; and the red-headed woodpecker and the kingfisher everywhere displayed their beautiful plumage. We now came to the considerable town of Circleville, which has many brick buildings, and must have increased greatly since it was visited by Duke Bernhard of Saxe Weimar.[155] The duke gives a detailed description of the remarkable ancient walls, in the interior of which this place was built; but they have been greatly demolished since that time. The court-house stands in the centre of the Indian circle wall, and the greater part of the town still lies within it. This wall enclosed a space of seventeen acres and three quarters, but the greater part of it has now disappeared. Withoutside the western extremity lies a hill, from whose summit an admirable view of the town, &c., is obtained. Here, too, we see another deplorable instance of the love of destruction which animates the Americans; for, instead of preserving these interesting ancient remains with the greatest care, they have erected buildings exactly on the site of the levelled walls, respecting the former state and opening of which nothing now remains, except some scanty, superficial accounts given by Attwater and other American writers.[156]

After we left Circleville we saw, on the canal, a great number of shells (*Unio*), of a greenish colour, with darker stripes, which are very frequent here; most of them were floating without the animal, which was, however, found dead in some of them. The canal traverses a country agreeably diversified with wood and meadows, which was formerly covered with uninterrupted primeval forests. We saw, likewise, some low, marshy land, overgrown with rushes and reeds, upon which the beautiful oriole (*Psaroc phoeniceus*), with its splendid plumage, was sitting. This fine bird lives chiefly in the marshes and by the water-side, where it builds its nest. Sandpipers, and other birds of that kind, animated the low meadows; and among the bushes I saw the rice-bird.

After traversing a wooded country, with remarkably fine sugar maples and walnut trees, we came to Walnut Creek, which flows through a shady forest. Near the little town, Lockbourn, which was founded only three years ago, there are eight sluices close together, where the Columbia feeder issues from the canal, which rises at this place about 100 feet, and then runs along the eminence.[157] The forest is not so lofty on the summit, and the tops of many of the trees are withered. Thus we traversed by water the fine forest of the state of Ohio, and, as it was Sunday, saw the inhabitants in their best dresses. It was a most agreeable journey, during which we sat quite at our ease on the deck. We had left the Sciotto at Lockbourn, passed Waterloo, Winchester, Havensport, New Baltimore, and Millersport, and on the morning of the 23rd reached the highest point over which the canal has to pass.[158] This point is called Licking Summit, because it is in Licking township, in the county of Muskingum, which contains the towns of Irville and Nashport. From Portsmouth to the highest point of the canal there are fifty-one sluices.[159] At sunrise we reached Hebron, a town commenced in November, 1825, in Union township, on the great national road from Zanesville to Columbus, which commences at Hagerstown, comes from Cumberland, on the Potomac, and passes through the states of Ohio, Indiana, and Illinois.[160] Many workmen were employed upon the road, and a quantity of stones was brought, on the canal, in large square flat boats. About nine o'clock we passed the first three sluices downwards, for the canal gradually descends from Licking Summit to Lake Erie. We came to Licking River, and soon after to the little town of Newark, through which the canal passes. In the year 1830 Newark had 1000 inhabitants, but has now considerably increased. This town has broad streets, a large market-place, and several new churches.[161] All the plantations and fields in this part of the country have fences, on which the red-headed woodpecker is frequently seen. Seven miles from Newark the canal joins Licking River, a very pretty little stream, which flows through a picturesque rocky valley, overgrown with pines and other trees. The rocks, which appear to consist of grauwacke, have a singular stratification, with caverns in which the cattle seek the protection of the shade from the sultry sun. The passage of about a mile or a mile and a half through this beautiful wooded chain of hills is very romantic. It is succeeded by open spots with plantations, where the canal leaves the Licking, which it soon afterwards approaches more closely. In the hollow between the two waters many lofty trees were growing, especially planes and poplars, partly entwined with lovely climbers. It is sixteen miles from Newark to Nashport, a small place, where some Indian barrows still exist. The bank of the canal is covered with verbascum in flower, which was introduced from Europe. Ironstone and coal are found in the vicinity. On the banks there is always some wood, but not so tall or luxuriant as on and near the Ohio. Sometimes we came to picturesque spots, then to sluices, and to a great many bridges, under which the boats have to pass: sometimes the canal runs in a straight line through beech forests. About twenty-three miles from Newark it is carried, at a considerable height, over the Tomaha Creek. We then came to the village of Frazeysburg, a place with detached wooden houses, where many witch-hazel bushes grow on the side of the canal, the branches of which were formerly used for divination, like those of the hazel bush in Europe; for this superstition was brought by the emigrants across the Atlantic Ocean.[162]

During the night we passed the little villages of Webbsport and Roscoe, and at daybreak came to Evansburg, and then to New-comers Town, a village which has now only seven or eight houses.[163] The country round is pleasant and diversified. In the canal a yellow-striped snake swam rapidly past us. We had seen the black snake and the water snake the day previous. Near the village of Port Washington, the valley was broad and wooded;[164] having passed which, we came to Gnadenhütten, a village consisting of about seven houses, originally founded by the Moravians, who have, however, abandoned it. The present inhabitants are chiefly of German origin; they speak German, and among them were some newly arrived German settlers.[165] In this country, near Trenton and Newcastle, are considerable coal mines.

At Lockport, a small village in Tuscarora county, there are beautiful prospects from the river; the banks are clothed with forests, the stagnant branches are covered with nymphæa, and other water plants, and immense plains stand in the valleys. At Dover, a neat little town, in an agreeable situation, the canal comes very near the river; over this is a large covered bridge, in the erection, much timber has been needlessly expended.[166] Not far from Dover is Zoar, a pretty settlement of Würtemberg Separatists, at which we arrived in the cool of the evening. A man named Bäumler, who is advanced in years, but said to possess considerable talents, is the chief of this colony; it is in Tuscarora County, on the east bank of the river of the same name.[167] In the year 1833, this colony had sixty very neat buildings, all roofed with new red tiles, which are not common in America, and which looked remarkably well in the green valley. At a distance we observed considerable buildings, and the inn in the form of a church. The Ohio Gazetteer says, that the settlement was originally founded on a piece of land of 4,000 acres, which the company purchased in 1810, and the greater part of which is now well cultivated.[168] The Separatists possess, besides, 1500 or 2000 acres of land in the vicinity, as well as some vineyards, which are said to produce very good wine. The situation of Zoar, at the bottom of the broad level valley, with luxuriant fields and lofty trees, at a short distance from the river, is extremely pleasant. The inhabitants are said to be very industrious, and to have several manufactories, and I regret that I was unable to make myself better acquainted with this interesting place. A long wooden bridge is thrown across the canal and the river: close by is an inn, built by the inhabitants, and called the Zoar Canal Hotel. Just as I was at the spot, the shepherd drove a numerous flock of sheep over the bridge, and answered my questions in genuine Swabian German. His entire dress and equipments were quite in the German fashion: a shepherd's crook, a broad leather bandolier, ornamented with brass figures, a flat broad-brimmed hat, and a large grey coat; a costume very uncommon in America. His dogs, too, were exceedingly careful in keeping the flock together. During the night we passed the villages of Bolivar and Bethlehem, and at daybreak, on the 25th of June, were at Massillon, a picturesque spot, in Stark County, which was founded in 1826, and has now 100 houses and 500 inhabitants.[169]

At eight o'clock we reached Fulton, a village with some neat houses in Stark County. This whole country was manifestly once covered with a primeval forest. The cat-bird was common on the banks; we observed turtles, bull-frogs, and tree-frogs, and often saw snakes swimming rapidly across the canal. There were most charming wood scenes on the Tuscarora, where a dwarf-rose grew in abundance, and had a most pleasing appearance with its large flowers. About noon we reached the town of New Portage, where the traders used formerly to convey the goods which were intended for the trade with the Indians, from one river to the other. Soon afterwards we came to a marshy place, with a forest of larches, which shed their leaves in the winter time: it grows round a small lake, through which the canal passes. A bridge is built over the whole length of the lake, for the horses which tow the canal boats. A little further on, where the canal expands into a kind of small lake, is Akron, a considerable town in a remarkable situation.[170] It was founded in 1825 in Portage County, and has already an extensive trade, many neat wooden houses, stores, manufactories, an iron foundry, and an establishment where, by means of a wheel, bedsteads and other articles of furniture are turned. At Akron the valley begins to decline rapidly: the canal passes through the middle of the town, and, in order to bring the boats down from a considerable, steep, rocky eminence, ten or twelve sluices are erected one above the other. The vicinity is one of the most curious spots on the course of the canal, with scattered buildings, a busy population, much water, and fine forests. On reaching the foot of the eminence, you glide along the beautiful dark brown mirror of the canal, through luxuriant verdure, where wood and meadows alternate, and the tall tulip, walnut, and sassafras trees reflect their graceful forms in the unruffled surface of the water. The sluices, of which we counted twenty-one in a space of two miles and a half, were at greater intervals from each other as we approached the River Cayahoga, which the canal follows to Lake Erie.[171]

The next morning we were still five miles from Lake Erie, a distance which we accomplished at about ten o'clock, when we reached the little town of Cleveland. The sea-like expanse of the large Lake Erie was very striking when emerging from the wooded valleys, and the sight of it reminded me of my approaching voyage to my native country. The dark blue lake stretches to the far horizon, like the ocean; the eye is attracted by the white sails and the smoke of the steam-boats; while the finest weather and the purest atmosphere favoured the illusion.

Cleveland is a large, rapidly improving town, with several thousand inhabitants, full of life, trade, and business.[172] It is situated in Cayahoga or Cuyahoga County, and is built partly on a high ridge, partly on the river below. The outskirts are scattered, but the principal streets are regular. It contains many large buildings, several churches, a school or academy, a prison, good inns, and numerous shops and stores; the trade is very considerable in consequence of the junction of the great lakes with the Ohio and the Mississippi. Numbers of canal boats are assembled here, and also the two-masted schooners which navigate the lake. Several large, commodious steamers, generally full of passengers, come and depart daily. The Cayahoga flows through the lower part of the town; both sides of the mouth of the river are lined with wood; and on the right bank there is a long mole, with a lighthouse at the extremity. A second lighthouse is built a little to the right, upon an eminence; and in the far distance, on the right hand, the coast is lost in the misty horizon, and, on the left, disappears amid thick forests.

We met with many Germans at Cleveland, especially newly-arrived emigrants, and also an obliging young fellow-countryman, whom I had seen at Pittsburg, and who had obtained a good situation in a mercantile house in this place. Several steam-boats arrived and departed, bound to Detroit, and, at length, the Oliver Newbery came in, on its way to Buffalo. I immediately availed myself of the opportunity to visit that town, and set out from Cleveland at noon. On leaving the mouth of the Cayahoga there is an uninterrupted view of the vast expanse of Lake Erie, the splendid bluish-green waters of which, like those of all the great Canadian lakes, are exactly of the same colour as those of Switzerland. The dark brown waters of the Cayahoga are strongly contrasted to a considerable distance with those of the lake.[173] We steered along the south bank, where we had a fine prospect of Cleveland, and we were favoured by the most charming weather, which showed the lake to great advantage: in a storm the waves often run very high, and prove dangerous to navigation. The southern or American shore is not much elevated; the northern forms the boundary of Canada, the English possessions in North America. The south coast has no lofty eminences, and is entirely covered with forests. The steamer touched at Fairport, Ashtabula, and Salem, where great numbers of bats were hovering over the entrance into the port. After leaving Salem our engine got into disorder; and on the following morning, the 27th, we reached Dunkirk, a small place, built in the Dutch fashion, of which there is no mention in the Ohio Gazetteer of 1833.[174] A lighthouse stands on a neighbouring point of land. At eleven o'clock we came in sight of Buffalo, lying at the end of the lake, where we saw a race between two large steam-boats. As we approached the town, where we landed at twelve o'clock, a great number of steamers presented a very animated scene. Buffalo has been rapidly improving of late, and in a few years will be a considerable and important place. It has at present about 1000 houses, and 12,000 inhabitants, and promises to become one of the chief commercial ports of the country. The Erie Canal, which connects the great lakes with the eastern seaports of the Union, commences here. In the summer months, the neighbouring Falls of Niagara attract a great number of strangers, all of whom visit Buffalo. The streets of this town are, for the most part, regular and broad, crossing each other at right angles, and contain many handsome brick buildings, large inns, nine or ten churches and chapels, and good shops and magazines of every kind. In the lower part of the town, the water of the lake and the canal has been conducted into the streets, forming small harbours, where numbers of ships lie in perfect security. The town extends along the slope, and on the ridge of a gentle eminence; and from one of the highest points there is a striking prospect of the bright mirror of Lake Erie, which vanishes in the misty distance, and on the land side, of the Niagara River, and its opposite or Canadian bank. Buffalo was burnt by the English in 1814; it is said that only one house was left standing. The town was not immediately rebuilt, and it is only since the construction of the fine Erie Canal that it has risen so rapidly. When we consider the shortness of the time, the sudden improvement of the town, which is now of so much importance, really seems incredible; and perhaps there is no other country in the world where such a sudden rise would be possible.[175] They are now laying down iron railroads, one of which is to lead to Niagara. There are at present above thirty steam-boats for the communication between Buffalo, Cleveland, Detroit, and Niagara, and the number increases every year. The object, however, which most attracted me was the village of the Seneca Indians, in the vicinity of Buffalo. They possess a piece of land, which begins a mile and a half southeast of the town. Here they live in small, neat, wooden houses, which are surrounded by their fields and plantations, in a wooded country, and the pretty little church is in the centre of this Indian colony. The Indians who are settled here are employed in agriculture, the breeding of cattle and horses; and, like other country people, they go to the town with their wagons. Their dress is nearly the same as that of the Whites. Both the men and women frequently wear round felt hats: the men have, in general, a red girdle under their large blue upper coat, and the women wrap themselves in blankets. I found the physiognomy of most of these people quite genuine and characteristically Indian, as well as the brown colour, and their smooth, coal-black hair; some of them do not much differ in this respect from the Missouri tribes. A good many of them speak English, but some are quite ignorant of it; and, in their communications with each other, all use the old Indian dialect. It is said that there were at first 900 Indians settled here, mostly Senecas, mixed with a few Onondagos and Cayugas; but their numbers have decreased. All these tribes spoke the same language. They received from the government 49,000 acres of very fine fertile land. They have a clergyman and a school. The inn is kept by a half-breed Indian, who, however, did not appear to value himself on his Indian descent, but rather desired to be considered a white man.[176]

The Senecas are one of the six nations who, in former times, were the enemies of the French in Canada, and, with the exception of the Oneidas, assisted the English, in the war of 1775, against the Americans. The works of Charlevoix, Lahontan, and Colden, give information respecting the history of these once powerful, warlike people, who dwelt on the borders of the great lakes. The six allied nations were the Senecas, Cayugas, Onondagos, Tuscaroras, Oneidas, and Mohawks; the latter came from the south, and were admitted at a later period into the union of the five tribes.[177]

We visited some of these families, who showed us their bibles and prayer books in the Indian language; we bought specimens of their work, adorned with porcupine and other dyed quills, and likewise bows and arrows, which they still esteem. Deeply regretting the destruction of the remarkable aboriginal inhabitants of the east of North America, I returned in the evening to Buffalo, where our baggage and the live animals were embarked under the superintendence of Dreidoppel, on board an Erie Canal boat, for Albany, a distance of 363 miles. I myself took a place in the stage for Niagara, and we left Buffalo on the 28th of June. The road lies along the Erie Canal, which is here parallel with the River Niagara, passes through the village of Blackrock, and, near the hamlet of Tonawanta, crosses the creek of that name, which falls, at no great distance, into the river.[178]

The River Niagara issues from the east end of Lake Erie, forming the channel which connects it with Lake Ontario, the level of which is lower. The length of the course of the Niagara, from Lake Erie to Lake Ontario, is 36½ miles, and its fall in this distance amounts to 322 feet. It is the frontier between Canada and the United States, and forms, between the two great lakes, the celebrated waterfall. Its surface is adorned with several islands, the largest of which, called Grand Island, was sold in 1815, by the Seneca Indians, to the state of New York, for 1000 dollars, and an annuity of 500 dollars. This island is said to be twelve miles long, and from two to seven broad: it is in the vicinity of Lake Erie, and the river is afterwards pretty free from islands till you come near the falls, where there are several small ones. The water of the Niagara has the splendid green colour of the Swiss lakes, and is nearly twice as broad as the Rhine; on the opposite bank is the village of Chippeway, where, on the 5th of July, 1814, there was an action, in which the English were defeated.[179]

There is a considerable population along the road from Tonawanta to the falls of Niagara, which are twenty-two miles from Buffalo. Towards noon we came to the village of Niagara, which we entered at the side furthest from the river, and put up at a very good inn. It is a small village close to the falls, forming two irregular unpaved streets, but containing some good houses.[180] The banks present a very picturesque diversity, with pines and other trees, bearing a general resemblance to the scenery of Switzerland. Opposite to our inn was the house of a man named Hooker, who acts as guide to travellers visiting the falls, and has a small collection of natural curiosities, and specimens of Indian manufacture.

The grand, sublime scene, which we now visited, has been described by a vast number of travellers—Larochefaucault-Liancourt, Weld, Volney,[181] and many others since their time;[182] so that all accounts must be in some measure mere repetitions; but, as the diversity of such descriptions can but tend to give a more correct view of the subject, a few remarks may not be considered irrelevant here.

At a short distance from the village of Niagara, the river, which, according to Volney, is 1200 feet in breadth, begins to flow in an uneven rocky bed, with a rapid descent, and its whole surface is, in many places, in violent commotion, covered with white foam, and, as it were, boiling, in consequence of its breaking in high waves against the masses of rock.

Portions of these rocks, the larger of which deserve the name of islands, are covered with pines, some green, others in a decayed state: of these rocky islets there are fifteen above the falls. The pines being frequently broken and snapped, and here and there piled up in the water, greatly contribute to heighten the effect of the savage grandeur and sublimity of the scene. The roaring of the cataract is heard at a considerable distance,[183] and lofty columns of mist and vapour ascend into the air. The stranger is conducted from the village to the above-mentioned rapid, and then proceeds, by a long, strongly-built wooden bridge over the end of the rapid, to Bath Island, where there are warm and cold baths (*a*, in the subjoined woodcut).[184] A considerable paper-mill has been erected here, and a toll for passing the bridge is paid, once for all, for the whole time you may remain here. The toll-keeper sells refreshments and various curiosities of the country, minerals, Indian rarities, and the like.

A second bridge leads from Bath Island to Goat Island,[185] which is about seventy acres in extent, entirely covered with a beautiful forest of sugar maples, beeches, hornbeams, elms, birches, &c., beneath which the asarabaca, may-apple, and various other plants, are growing; none of them were, however, in flower. The shores of this island are shaded by old pines and very large white cedars, such as we should in vain look for in Europe, and many fine shrubs grow on the banks. There were formerly a great number of Virginian deer in this beautiful forest, but they grew so familiar, and became so troublesome by running after strangers, that they were removed. The blueheaded jay and the Hudson's Bay squirrel are numerous. From the bridge which leads to Goat Island there is a convenient path, on the right hand, which goes along the shore through the wood; and, after proceeding a short distance, the stranger suddenly finds himself on the rather steep declivity, immediately above the fall of the right or southern arm of the river, which is called the American branch. The sight is striking, and much grander than all the descriptions I had read of it led me to conceive. The broad expanse of bright green water falls perpendicularly 144 to 150 feet into the abyss below, which is entirely concealed by the vapour, the whole torrent of falling water being completely dissolved into foam and mist in the midway of its descent. Below the fall, and before its surface is quite calm, it recovers its green colour, which is, of course, totally lost in the rapidity of its descent. To make my description more clear, I subjoin a little plan of the cataracts drawn by Mr. George Catlin,[186] and published in Featherstonehaugh's "Essay on the Ancient Drainage of North America, and the Origin of the Cataract of Niagara," in the Monthly American Journal of Geology, Vol. I., July, 1831.

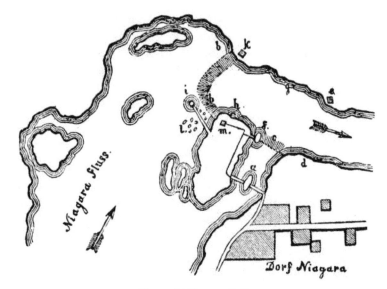

Plan of Niagara Falls

Harpoon for dolphins

The southern or American part of the fall, *c*, is divided above by a narrow rocky island, *f*, to which a bridge has been thrown. This rocky island is closely overgrown with white cedar (*Arbor vitæ*), the tall, thick, whitish trunks of which, with their stiff, extended boughs, scarcely leave space for the shrubs that grow between them, in which the cedar bird (*Bombycilla cedrorum*) builds its nest. The northern chatterer or silk tail, of which the Prince of Musignano[187] has given a plate in his "Supplement to Wilson's Ornithology," is likewise found here in small companies during the winter. After we had admired the lesser, or American part of the fall, we returned to the top of Goat Island, again following the path which now runs along the eastern edge of the island through the dark shade of the forest, and, having gone between 500 and 600 paces, came in sight of the second larger fall, which is called the English or Horse-shoe Fall, *b*, which is formed by the left, or the northern arm of the river. This splendid waterfall occupies the whole breadth of the bed of the river, forming, towards the Canadian shore, a receding angle, where the masses of water from both sides of the Horse-shoe meeting each other, fall, with a thundering noise, in one conjoined body, 150 feet perpendicular height. The clouds of vapour that rise from this cataract are far more considerable than those of the American fall. They cover and veil the neighbouring rocky, wooded banks, by their rising columns, in which the sun forms the most beautiful rainbows. In the angle of the fall, where the waters, pouring from three several sides, meet with a fearful concussion, and, dissolving into snow-white spray, are lost to the eye in vapour, they rage and boil with tremendous fury. This is the focus from whence rise the clouds of steam and vapour which involve the circumjacent country to a great distance in rain and mist, and, according to the direction of the wind, assume manifold and most fantastic forms.

In order to approach nearer to the sublime scene, a staircase has been contrived on the steep bank at the place where we now stood, and where a small house, with seats, *m*, has been built; and below, at *h*, a wooden tower is erected, with a winding stair, from the upper gallery of which, as well as from windows made here and there at the sides, there is a view of the wondrous scene, gradually changing as you ascend. Here we were struck mute at the overwhelming sight of this abyss of waters.

Beautiful plants grow among the boulders, the rocks on the banks of the river, such as the gueldar rose, the white cedar, the *Rubus odoratus*, now flowering in all its loveliness, the lime, maple, and sumach. By proceeding from the waterfall, below the bank of Goat Island, along the river, and round the point of the island, we come to the cauldron of the American fall, and can almost go under the precipitous mass of waters, at the risk of encountering the penetrating rain and wind. In the same manner one may likewise get under the Horse-shoe Fall, and both are points of view indescribably interesting. We now ascended the wooden stair, and came to the small house, from whence, in the gloomy shade of the forest, we enjoyed a view of the surpassing scene from above. The walls are here completely covered with names and initials of visitants from all quarters of the globe. After resting here, the delighted spectator is conducted, by another stair, to the river below, and thence, across a long wooden bridge, to a high stone tower, built on the rock, in the water. This tower is erected immediately over the angle of the Horse-shoe abyss; it is ascended by a stair, and the visitor is suddenly transported into an entirely new scene of stupendous magnificence. The eye is lost in the depth of the foaming whirlpool, the light spray of which envelops the admiring spectator, whose ear is stunned with the roaring sound of the cataract. No language can describe the grandeur and sublime impression of the scene, from which we could with difficulty tear ourselves. We remained long lost in admiration while contemplating the unique phenomenon; and, returning to our inn, made an excursion, some time afterwards, to the other side of the river. For this purpose we descended, by a covered wooden staircase, from the village of Niagara to the south side of the American fall, and came to the bank of the river below the falls. Though not more than 300 or 400 paces beneath them, the water is but very slightly agitated, and we were soon ferried over to the Canadian bank. Here we had the falls directly before us, and enjoyed an excellent view of both. From this spot Mr. Bodmer took his general view of this sublime scene, which is the best that I have yet met with, and is, in every respect, perfectly faithful to nature.[188] On the eminence above there is what is here called a confectionary, in which there are some tolerably good representations of the falls by Megarey. From this place we went to an isolated house, in which an Englishman has placed a zoological cabinet, which contains a fine collection of the birds of Canada. It occupies two stories of the house, and is shown for money. There are many interesting specimens, but I met with only a few that I could purchase. At a short distance from this house is a small projection from the high bank, called Table Rock, from which there is an incomparable view of the Horse-shoe Fall, which has been described by many persons.[189] At a neighbouring dwelling the curious traveller is provided with a covering of oiled silk, or oiled cloth, to enable him, without getting wet, to descend a high flight of steps which leads him under the rushing mass of waters of the Canadian fall.

The next day being Sunday, I took the opportunity to go and see divine service performed among the Tuscarora Indians, who are settled about eight miles from the Falls of Niagara. The road to it leads towards Lake Ontario, along the high banks of the beautiful Niagara River, alternating with woods and fields, where the inhabitants live dispersed in their wooden houses. The forests consist of furs, Weymouth pines, oaks, chestnuts (the latter in full bloom), sassafras, and wild cherry trees, the fruit of which was not yet ripe. The European fruit trees were loaded with fruit, and appeared not to have suffered from the frost, but the Italian poplar does not seem to thrive in this climate. About three miles from Niagara, the view, looking back on the falls, was very striking; the clouds of spray and vapour rose at this time very high, and were most splendidly illumined by the sun's rays. A mile and a half further on we looked down into a wild ravine, 150 or 200 feet, overgrown with pines and other trees, under which the river forms a rapid, covered with white foam. This rapid is called the Devil's Hole; but the descriptions given of it are greatly exaggerated, for in Europe, in Switzerland for instance, there are much grander scenes of this kind. A small English corps here suffered a defeat in the American war, being driven by the Americans and their Indian allies into this ravine.[190]

When I had passed the wood and came again into the fields, where the scattered houses of the Indians, built in the European style, are situated, I saw before me their small white church, and had a near and charming view of the wooded rocky shores of the splendid green Ontario.[191] The scenery about that lake and the Niagara, and that on the banks of the Hudson, is, unquestionably, the finest that I saw in North America. The road leads along the edge of the valley of the Niagara, and affords a wide view into the distant plain beyond Lake Ontario. A gloomy forest extends, without interruption, to the distant horizon, and in the foreground there is a dark inlet, where the end of the lake is hidden by lofty trees. Volney very accurately describes this scene as "Une véritable mer de forêts, parsemées de quelque fermes et villages, et de nappes d'eau des lacs Iroquois."

I drove up to the church, which was crowded with Indians; the clergyman was already in the pulpit. As he did not understand the language of the Tuscaroras, he preached in English, and the schoolmaster at his side interpreted all he said.[192] When the sermon was ended and prayers read, during which all the Indians remained sitting, the interpreter began to sing, and the congregation, in which there were only three or four Whites, joined in a very good tone, the men generally singing a second part. The clergyman, a young man, who had not been long in this parish, gave me some account of his congregation, which consisted of about 300 souls. Another portion of the Tuscaroras is settled, I think, on Grand River.[193] Very few understand English—they are Presbyterians, and live on the whole like the Senecas, whom they resemble in external appearance, and whose language is the same. There is less originality among them than among the Senecas at Buffalo. Their features, colour, and hair seem to be more changed by their intercourse with the Whites; yet I saw, now and then, a characteristic physiognomy, especially among the women. They are of middle stature, and their dress is like that of the Senecas at Buffalo. They were allied with the English in the American war.

After a stay of several days, the greater part of which was passed on the banks of the great falls, lost in admiration of their sublimity, I took the stage to Tonawanta, intending to return to New York by Lake Erie and the River Hudson.[194]

FOOTNOTES:

[150] For the Ohio and Erie Canal, see Bullock's *Sketch*, in our volume xix, p. 151, note 22.—ED.

[151] Dr. Zina Pitcher (1797-1872) was a graduate (1822) of Middlebury College, Vermont. He entered the army (1822) as assistant surgeon, becoming surgeon with rank of major in 1832. In 1836 he resigned from the army, and began practice in Detroit, where he became a prominent citizen. In 1842 and 1844-47 he was mayor of the city, held the office of county (1843) and city physician (1848-51), and served upon the board of health. Dr. Pitcher was interested in education and was one of the first regents of

the University of Michigan (1837-51), giving much time and thought to the establishment of that institution, especially its medical school. Upon retiring from the board of regents, he was made professor emeritus of medicine. Dr. Pitcher's literary interests were considerable; he was librarian of the first Michigan Historical Society, editor of the *Peninsular Journal of Medicine*, and contributor to Schoolcraft's work on Indians, in whose therapeutics he took much interest. His home in Detroit was the seat of widespread hospitality.

For Fort Gibson, on the Arkansas, see Gregg's *Commerce of the Prairies*, in our volume xx, p. 105, note 73.—ED.

[152] Indian Creek is a small, eastward-flowing affluent of the Scioto, in Ross County, Ohio. See, for Paint Creek, our volume ix, p. 118, note 56; Chillicothe is noted on p. 186, note 35, of F. A. Michaux's *Travels*, our volume iii.—ED.

[153] Chillicothe was a Shawnee term for town or village. This tribe had in the Scioto Valley several dwelling-places thus named; compare Thwaites and Kellogg, *Dunmore's War* (Wisconsin Historical Society, 1905), p. 292, note 7; see also Croghan's *Journals*, in our volume i, p. 134, note 102.

For the Wyandot, consult Weiser's *Journal*, our volume i, p. 29, note 26. The habitat of the Wyandot was in northwest Ohio and southeast Michigan, but on their hunting excursions ranged to the Shawnee territory.—ED.

[154] Consult, on the mounds of Ohio, a recent account by Gerard Fowke, *Archæological History of Ohio* (Columbus, 1902); see also Mrs Cyrus Thomas, "Bibliography of Earthworks of Ohio," in *Ohio Archæological and Historical Quarterly*, i (1887-88).—ED.

[155] For the work in which Duke of Saxe-Weimar describes his travels in the United States, see Wyeth's *Oregon*, in our volume xxi, p. 71, note 47.

Circleville was so named from an ancient earthwork found upon the site. Near this place were the chief villages of the Shawnee, also the Pickaway Plains, well known in pioneer history, where Lord Dunmore halted his army and made the treaty of Camp Charlotte (see *Dunmore's War*, cited in note 153 above, pp. 302, 386). Circleville was selected (1810) as the seat of the newly-erected county of Pickaway; in 1814 it was incorporated as a town, and in 1853 became a city. The population in 1900 was about seven thousand.—ED.

[156] Caleb Atwater was Massachusetts born (1778) and in 1816 emigrated to Ohio, where he lived chiefly at Circleville, until his death in 1867. His services to the state were in many lines, political, educational, and legal. During a term in the legislature, he laid the foundation of the public school system of the state, and furthered public improvements, especially canals. He

was much interested in antiquities, and a corresponding member for Ohio of the American Antiquarian Society. Under their auspices he published the work on "Western Antiquities" to which Maximilian here refers. Atwater therein gives a description and ground plan of the Circleville circumvallations; see American Antiquarian Society *Transactions* (Worcester, Massachusetts, 1820), i, pp. 109-267. This article was republished in *Writings of Caleb Atwater* (Columbus, Ohio, 1833).—ED.

[157] Soon after leaving Circleville, the Ohio and Erie Canal crosses Scioto River, and follows its eastern bank as far as Lockbourne, on the southern boundary of Franklin County, passing Walnut Creek—an eastern affluent of the Scioto—in Pickaway County. Lockbourne was laid out in 1831, by Colonel Kilbourne, who compounded its title from the eight canal locks at this site, and the last syllable of his own name. The spur of the canal which runs hence to Columbus (not Columbia) is eleven miles in length. The first canal-boat to make the trip from Chillicothe to Columbus passed over the route in 1831. Its arrival at the state capital was the occasion of a celebration in honor of the completion of the enterprise.

Columbus was laid out (1812) on the east bank of the Scioto, opposite the older town of Franklinton, by four proprietors who offered to the legislature inducements, which were accepted, to make this the state capital. The place was incorporated in 1816, and made a borough in 1834.—ED.

[158] At Lockbourne the canal leaves the valley of the Scioto, and, turning north across Franklin and Fairfield counties, follows the valley of Walnut Creek until near Licking Valley. All the places mentioned by Maximilian were platted about the time of the determination of the canal route.

Canal Winchester, in southeastern Franklin County, was laid out (1826 or 1827) by a family named Dove, from Winchester, Virginia. Waterloo and Millersport are in Fairfield County, and even now are small villages.—ED.

[159] Licking Summit, the highest point on the canal, 413 feet above the level of Portsmouth, is on the watershed between the Scioto and Muskingum systems. At this place excavation for the canal was begun July 4, 1825, when Governor Clinton, of New York, threw out the first spadeful of earth, as one of the features of a celebration in anticipation of the building of the canal. Near this point, also, was constructed the Licking reservoir, with an area of three thousand acres, to supply water for the lower reaches of the canal.—ED.

[160] For the westward extension of the National, or Cumberland Road, see Woods's *English Prairie*, in our volume x, p. 327, note 76.

Hebron, in Union Township, Licking County, when laid out (1827) by John Smith, at the junction of the Ohio Canal and the National Road, appeared destined to a considerable future. With the building of railways, however, its commercial importance declined, the population in 1900 being but 455.—ED.

[161] For Newark, now chief city of Licking County, with a population (1900) of 18,157, see Flint's *Letters*, in our volume ix, p. 305, note 153.—ED.

[162] Nashport and Frazeysburg, both in Muskingum County, are canal towns which have acquired no particular importance.—ED.

[163] These are all canal towns, the first three in Coshocton County, of which the first-named is entirely extinct. Roscoe was first named Caldersburg, and laid out in 1816; when the canal came, the name was changed in honor of the English author.

Evansburg was laid out (1830) by Isaac Evans, a pioneer and veteran of the War of 1812-15.

New Comerstown, in Tuscarawas County, is interesting as the site of an early Delaware Indian town, called by Heckewelder, Gekelemukpechink. When the Delawares, in the middle of the eighteenth century, removed from the Allegheny to the Tuscarawas Valley, their principal chief, Netawatwes (the Newcomer), built his village near this site, which was the centre of tribal activity until the Revolutionary War. The American town was not laid out until the time of the canal building (1827).—ED.

[164] Port Washington, in Salem Township, Tuscarawas County, was originally called Salisbury. It was laid out as a canal town and incorporated in 1827. Abram Garfield, father of the future president, contracted for the work on the canal between New Comerstown and Port Washington.—ED.

[165] The Moravian missions to the Indians were begun about 1745, in eastern Pennsylvania. In 1772, at the special request of their Delaware converts, the mission was removed to the Tuscarawas Valley, and three towns founded therein—Salem, Shoenbrunn, and Gnadenhütten. The latter was the scene of the massacre (1782) of the Christian Indians by a party of backwoods militia. See Theodore Roosevelt, *Winning of the West* (New York, 1889), ii, pp. 142-167; and Thwaites, *Withers's Border Warfare* (Cincinnati, 1895), pp. 313-329. For sixteen years after this atrocity, the village of Gnadenhütten was deserted. About 1798 it was restored by the Moravians, and the following year white settlers began to move in. The first emigrants were Pennsylvania Germans; later, many Germans came direct from Europe to this region, which has still a considerable Teutonic element in its population. The town of Gnadenhütten was incorporated in 1824.—ED.

[166] Lockport, usually called Blake's Mills, was platted (1829) by two German proprietors above Lock No. 13.

Dover was principally settled (1807) by Pennsylvania Germans. When the canal passed through, Canal Dover became the official name of the town. At one time the village aspired to be county seat.—ED.

[167] Because of persecution in their native land, the Würtemberg Separatists left their homes in several parties. One of these, led by George Rapp, founded the New Harmony and Economy settlement; another, under the leadership of Joseph M. Bäumler, came to Philadelphia in 1817, and by December of that year had begun a settlement on the Tuscarawas, which they named Zoar. Not until 1819 was the community system established, and then because of the exigencies of the situation and their position on the frontier, rather than doctrinaire theory. The numbers of the settlement were largely increased in 1832, when a second band arrived from Würtemberg. The leader of the colony, Joseph Bäumler (later spelled Bimeler), was of obscure peasant origin, but a man of ability and enterprise. Under his care the community prospered until his death in 1852. Celibacy was at first imposed as a rule of the community, but later was rescinded. In 1898, by mutual consent of the members, the community dissolved, the majority still living at the village of Zoar, which in 1900 possessed but two hundred and ninety inhabitants. For further details, consult W. A. Hinds, *American Communities* (Chicago, 1902), pp. 91-123; and E. O. Randall, "Separatist Society of Zoar," in *Ohio Archæological and Historical Quarterly*, viii, pp. 1-100.—ED.

[168] *The Ohio Gazetteer, or Topographical Dictionary*, was first compiled by John Kilbourn, of Columbus, Ohio. The edition used by Maximilian was probably the eleventh issue, published at Columbus in 1833. The statement therein is, that the land was purchased in 1818 (not 1810). The details of the purchase in Bäumler's name were arranged in 1817; but the title did not pass until the next year, and it was the spring of 1818 before the main body of the Zoar colonists arrived from Philadelphia, where they had been charitably entertained during the preceding winter by the Society of Friends.—ED.

[169] Bolivar, in the northern portion of Tuscarawas County, owed its existence to the Ohio Canal. The town was laid out in 1825 by two proprietors from Canton, Ohio, who at first christened it Kelleysville, for one of the canal commissioners. He, however, declined the honor, whereupon the name of the South American emancipator was chosen. Between the villages of Zoar and Bolivar, Maximilian passed the site of the former Fort Laurens, erected during the Revolution (1778) as an outpost for the protection of the Western frontiers. In February and March, 1779, the garrison, under command of Colonel John Gibson, sustained a protracted siege by a motley host of Wyandot and Mingo warriors, led by a few British soldiers. After the raising of the siege, Fort Laurens was found too remote

from the frontier to be provisioned without undue risk; whereupon, in the autumn of 1779, the post was abandoned.

The township of Bethlehem, Stark County, was so named for the original home in Pennsylvania of the Moravian missionaries, one of whom, Christian Frederick Post, built (1761) within its precincts the first cabin in the present state of Ohio (see his *Journals*, our volume i). The village of Bethlehem, on the northern boundary of the township, was laid out about 1806 by Jonathan W. Condy, who intended to found there a religious society of Swedenborgians, upon the model of the Moravian settlement in Pennsylvania. The plan failed, and the village only revived upon the building of the canal.

Massillon (a thriving place of about 12,000 inhabitants) was a canal town, platted after the route had been arranged. Upon the opening of the line thence to Akron, a celebration was held at the new town of Massillon, which had been named in honor of a famous French theologian of the seventeenth century.—ED.

[170] Canal Fulton was laid out in 1826 by two residents of Canton, Ohio. Its population in 1900 was 1,172.

New Portage is the southern terminus of the once well-known portage path from the Cuyahoga to the Tuscarawas, which furnished in early Indian history the most practicable route from Lake Erie to the Ohio. The road was about eight miles long, and has recently been retraced; consult A. B. Hulbert, *Red-Men's Roads* (Columbus, 1900), p. 33. This path also furnished a boundary between Indian Territory and that of the United States, as agreed upon by the treaties of Fort McIntosh (1785), Fort Harmar (1789), and Greenville (1795). The American town of New Portage was expected to be the future metropolis of the region, but declined with the growth of Akron.

The marshy place described by Maximilian is Summit Lake, which later, connected with surrounding basins, became the reservoir, partly natural, partly artificial, for the canal upon the watershed between Lake Erie and the Ohio.

Akron (named from a Greek word meaning elevation) was a canal town; when founded it was in Portage County, but later was made the seat of Summit County, erected in 1840. Although founded in 1825, the town was not incorporated until 1836; it was erected into a city in 1865, and by 1900 had attained a population of 42,728.—ED.

[171] The descent from the summit of the portage to Lake Erie is steep, and requires a stairway of forty locks (sluices). This was the first portion of the work to be completed. The first boat from Akron to Cleveland went through July 4, 1827, amid popular rejoicings.

For Cuyahoga River and its early history, see Croghan's *Journals*, in our volume i, p. 107, note 72.—ED.

[172] Cleveland, the metropolis of the Western Reserve, was first surveyed in 1796, when the original log-cabin was built, and the site named in honor of Moses Cleaveland, agent for the Connecticut Land Company, then engaged in exploiting the reserve. During the early years, its growth was extremely slow, the total population in 1800 being but seven. After the War of 1812-15, settlers began to arrive with more frequency, the village being incorporated in 1814. The era of prosperity opened in Cleveland with the period of canal transportation. The inauguration of the Erie Canal (1825) gave impetus to the place, which increased with rapidity when made the terminus of the Erie and Ohio Canal. Cleveland was incorporated as a city in 1836; in 1900 it was the largest borough in Ohio, and the seventh city in size in the United States.—ED.

[173] Lake Erie is 290 miles in length, and sixty-eight miles at its greatest breadth. Its depth is said nowhere to exceed 100 or 120 feet.—MAXIMILIAN.

[174] For the early history of this region, see Croghan's *Journals*, in our volume i, pp. 103-106, with accompanying notes.

Fairport, in Lake County, Ohio, was laid out in 1812 by Samuel Huntington and four partners at the mouth of Grand River, three miles from the earlier city of Painesville. The first villages were platted south of Lake Erie, on higher ground, the lake ports being neglected until commerce increased. Fairport has a good harbor, and had (1900) a population of 2,073.

Ashtabula, on a creek of the same name, gives its title to a county. The town is two miles from the mouth of the creek, and was incorporated in 1827.

Salem Crossroads was the early name for the village of Brocton, in Chautauqua County, New York. The first settlement was made about 1805. The nearest harbor, which is not a good roadstead, lies below Van Buren Point.

Dunkirk would not appear in the Ohio Gazetteer, being a town in New York State, first settled (1805) at the mouth of Canadaway Creek. In 1809 the harbor was known as Chadwick's Bay, from the first permanent settler on the coast. The name Dunkirk was given about 1817, in honor of the famous French port.—ED.

[175] For the early history of Buffalo, see Buttrick's *Voyages*, in our volume viii, p. 42, note 4; upon its destruction in the raid of 1814, see Evans's *Tour*, in our volume viii, p. 182, note 40; also William Dorsheimer, "Buffalo during the War of 1812," in Buffalo Historical Society *Publications*, i, pp. 185-210; and S. C. Becker, *Sketches of Early Buffalo* (Buffalo, 1904), pp. 118-132.—ED.

[176] For another account of this village, see Evans's *Tour*, in our volume viii, p. 183, note 41; on the mission, see H. R. Howland, "Seneca Mission at Buffalo Creek," in Buffalo Historical Society *Publications*, vi, pp. 125-164.— ED.

[177] For the authorities mentioned in this paragraph, consult J. Long's *Voyages*, in our volume ii, p. 28, note 3, and p. 41, note 10; also Nuttall's *Journal*, our volume xiii, p. 116, note 81. The Tuscarora, not the Mohawk, was the tribe migrating from the South. Concerning this migration, see our volume ii, p. 44, note 12.—ED.

[178] For the history of Black Rock, see Buttrick's *Voyages*, in our volume viii, p. 46, note 9.

Tonawanda Creek rises in Wyoming County, New York, flows north through Genesee, and, turning west, forms the boundary between Niagara and Erie counties, entering Niagara River opposite Grand Island. The name in the Seneca language means "rapids," or "riffles." The site of the town of Tonawanda was first settled in 1808; three years later, a block-house was built, in anticipation of an Indian attack, nevertheless, during the War of 1812-15, the hamlet was burned, and little was done to rebuild the place until 1823, when, upon prospect of the near approach of the Erie Canal, the town was platted. The village growth was slow, however, and the place was not incorporated until 1854. It had in 1900 a population of 7,421, and was a manufacturing village of some importance.—ED.

[179] Grand Island, with a cultivable area of 17,381 acres, was in dispute between the United States and Canada until the boundary commission of 1819 decided that the main current of Niagara River lay west of the island. Previously, however (1815), New York had made the purchase from the Seneca, referred to by Maximilian; the price aggregated about $11,000. In 1819 squatters were driven off by order of the state, and in 1824 the island was surveyed and opened for purchase. A contemplated Jewish settlement, to be called Ararat, came to nought. The island was erected into a separate township of Erie County in 1852.

For a brief notice of the battle of Chippewa, see Evans's *Tour*, in our volume viii, p. 175, note 33.—ED.

[180] The first permanent settler on the American side of the falls was Stedman, one of a company of traders whom Sir William Johnson permitted (about 1760) to build a log cabin at the place. This was maintained, chiefly for the portage business, until 1795, when Stedman removed to the Canadian side; after the British evacuation (1796), the land lay unoccupied until 1805, when it was offered for sale, one of the first purchasers being Augustus Porter, a prominent citizen of Niagara village. He removed his family to this

place in 1806, and built a mill and blacksmith's shop, obtaining also the portage lease for several years. After the destruction by the British (1813), settlement began again; the village was incorporated in 1847, and in 1892 the city of Niagara Falls, which now has a population of about 20,000.—ED.

[181] For the American travels of Count Chassebœuf de Volney, consult Flint's *Letters*, in our volume ix, p. 237, note 121.

François Alexandre Frédéric, duc de la Rochefoucault-Liancourt (1747-1827), travelled in America during his exile, which was occasioned by the French Revolution, in whose early stages he had taken a prominent part. He was a friend to republican institutions, and his *Travels* are replete with just and favorable accounts of American life and customs. His work appeared first in French, in 1798; the English edition was entitled, *Travels through the United States, the Country of the Iroquois, and Upper Canada in 1795-97* (London, 1799).

Isaac Weld was an Irishman (1774-1856) whose American travels were undertaken in order to induce the immigration of his people to the United States. His excellent and accurate work, *Travels through the States of North America, and the provinces of Upper and Lower Canada (1795-97)*, (London, 1799), was much quoted and ran through several editions, including a translation into French.—ED.

[182] For other descriptions of Niagara Falls included in our series, see Evans's *Tour*, volume viii, pp. 174-179; Flint's *Letters*, volume ix, pp. 315-321; and Bullock's *Sketch*, volume xix, pp. 142-149.—ED.

[183] Mrs. Trollope, page 203, considers that the reason why the noise of the falls is not very great, is because they are not confined between high rocks, and I agree with her. Though the colossal Falls of Niagara may, doubtless, be called some of the greatest in the known world, yet Captain Back, in his "Journey to the Frozen Ocean," page 451, affirms, that the cataract, called by him "Parry's Fall," surpasses the former, and all others, in "splendour of effect."—MAXIMILIAN.

[184] See p. 169, for plan of Niagara Falls.—ED.

[185] Goat Island was purchased (1816) from the state by Augustus Porter (for whom see Evans's *Tour*, in our volume viii, p. 178, note 35), who pastured a flock of goats thereon. About 1816 the first bridge was built, which was carried away during the succeeding winter. That built in 1818 endured until 1856, when it was replaced by an iron structure.—ED.

[186] For Catlin, see our volume xxii, p. 32, note 9.—ED.

[187] See our volume xxii, p. 39, note 15, for Charles Bonaparte, prince of Musignano and Canino.—ED.

[188] See Plate 72, in the accompanying atlas, our volume xxv.—ED.

[189] For the fall of this interesting eminence, see Bullock's *Sketch*, in our volume xix, p. 145, and note 13.—ED.

[190] The Devil's Hole is a small ravine about two miles below Suspension Bridge, on the American side of Niagara River. The defeat here mentioned did not occur during the Revolution, as Maximilian intimates, but at the time of Pontiac's Conspiracy (1763). A company of traders, crossing by the Lewiston-Fort Schlosser portage, was ambushed by a band of Seneca, and driven over the precipice. Reinforcements of troops from Fort Niagara met with a similar fate, and fell into an ambush, when all but eight were slain. The relics of this massacre were long in evidence in the vicinity.—ED.

[191] Lake Ontario is twice as deep as Lake Erie, and Volney considered it to be the crater of a volcano.—MAXIMILIAN.

[192] After their migration from North Carolina, the Tuscarora lived upon Oneida lands until the period of the American Revolution. When General John Sullivan raided the Iroquois territory (1779) he was ordered to spare the neutral Tuscarora; the British sympathizers among them fled to the English Fort Niagara, and after the war the majority of the tribe settled upon a tract a mile square, given them by the Seneca, two miles east of the fort. Later the Holland Land Company ceded to this tribe two square miles of contiguous territory, and still later the Tuscarora purchased 4,329 acres with the proceeds of a sale of their North Carolina lands. Here the majority of the tribe lives to this day. In 1813, their houses and church were burned by a raid of British Indians, whereupon the Tuscarora retreated to Oneida Castle, to return to their reservation at the close of the war. From 1838-46 there was agitation about removal, first to Wisconsin, later to Indian Territory. Of one band who went out (about 1846), a third died in a year, and many returned to their old homes. The Tuscarora are the most progressive Indians of the state of New York, having good farms and fine orchards; many desire to become citizens, and to have their lands allotted in severalty. See Bullock's *Sketch*, in our volume xix, p. 150, note 20.—ED.

[193] The Tuscarora mission was begun in 1805 by the New York Missionary Society, and for some years conducted by the American Board of Foreign Missions; in 1821 the charge of this mission was transferred to the Presbyterians. At the time of Maximilian's visit Reverend Joel Wood was the missionary, but he remained only one year (October, 1833-October, 1834). The few Tuscarora who had followed Joseph Brant to Canada after the Revolutionary War settled on Grand River, north of Lake Erie, in a township called from their name in the present county of Brant, Ontario.—ED.

[194] Maximilian here intends the Erie Canal, instead of Lake Erie. For a brief sketch of the building of this waterway, see Buttrick's *Voyages*,, in our volume viii, p. 88, note 37.—ED.

CHAPTER XXXIII
RETURN ON THE ERIE CANAL AND THE RIVER HUDSON TO NEW YORK—VOYAGE TO EUROPE

The Erie Canal—Lockport—Rochester—Perinton on the Irondequot—Clyde—Montezuma Marshes—The River Seneca—Syracuse—Saline Tract near Salina—Remains of the Onondago Nation—Onondago Hill—Manlius—Canastote—Oneida—Remains of the Oneida Nation—Verona—New London—Rome—Oriskany—Beautiful Valley of the Mohawk River—White's Town—Utica—German Flats—Amsterdam—Rotterdam—Schenectady—The Iron Railroad to Albany—Hudson River—New York—Voyage to Europe.

Early in the morning of the 1st of July we left the Eagle Hotel, at Niagara, and travelled twelve miles to Tonawanta, where we found a packet boat, towed by three horses, on board which we embarked about noon. The boats on the Erie Canal are much the same as those on the Ohio Canal; but here they are fitted up only for passengers, and take no goods on board, except their baggage; hence they are more convenient, lighter, and more rapid than luggage boats. Our boat had fourteen or sixteen berths, which were very commodiously arranged. The horses drawing these boats are always on the trot, and they perform a distance of 104 miles in twenty-four hours. Twelve hundred such boats navigate this canal, the original cost of which was 700,000 dollars; whereas that of the Ohio Canal was only 400,000. This great work was commenced in 1817, and completed in eight years.

We proceeded first on the Tonawanta River as far as the village of Pentleton, where we entered the canal. About five miles from this place it is cut through a stratum of grauwacke, which rises from four to fifteen feet above the water; but the depth of the ravine soon increases, and the bridges are thrown, at a great height, over the canal. At Lockport, an extensive place, situated on the eminence, the canal is conducted, by means of five sluices, down a slope of at least sixty feet.[195] The prospect from the eminence is very beautiful. The canal descends between two hills, connected at a considerable elevation by a bridge, under which the boats pass. On the following day we came to Rochester, on the River Genessi, which has a large aqueduct eighty feet in length. This river is celebrated for its waterfalls. There are many fine forests, especially of beech; some, however, consist entirely of oaks. I observed in the canal many turtles and water-snakes. Near the village of Perinton is Irondequot or Irondequit Creek, with wooded banks. The forests here were filled with the finest species of trees. Beyond Fairport the *Arbor vitæ* grew vigorously to the height of thirty and forty feet, as well as larches, planes, walnuts, oaks, elms, maples, all entwined by wild vine and ivy.[196] The peculiar smell of the *Arbor vitæ* was powerfully wafted to us by the wind. These forests are wild and magnificent. Dry trunks of pines lay confusedly one over another: in the shade cattle were feeding, whose bells produced an agreeable harmony. We could have fancied ourselves transported to the forests of the Hartz, if the country had been mountainous. The wheat was not yet ripe, nor the potatoes in blossom. The land was still in part covered with the stumps of the trees that had been cut down. All the dwellings are of wood, and the fields are everywhere intersected by wooden fences. The dense beech forests constantly reminded us of the scenery of Germany.

In the afternoon we came to the rising town of Clyde, which lies on Clyde River, and towards evening to the Montezuma Marshes, which are about three miles in extent.[197] They are formed by the overflowing of the lakes of Cayuga and Seneca,[198] and the water in them is said to be from four to eight feet deep. The farmers have cultivated the dry spots in these marshes. At twilight we came to some places where the canal crosses Seneca River; and at eight o'clock were at the mouth of that river, over which a long wooden bridge is built for the horses that tow the boats.

On the following day, the 3rd July, we came to the neighbourhood of Syracuse, in Onondago County, which is traversed by Onondago Creek, and was formerly the abode of the numerous Indian tribe of that name, which was one of the six nations.[199] It is now cultivated; the soil is fruitful, and thriving towns have arisen in various parts. This tract was purchased from the Indians, and part of it settled by them. Syracuse is a place of some importance; it is usually denominated a village, but it certainly looks as if it were entitled to the appellation of town. Twenty years ago there was one solitary dwelling on this spot; now there are 500 houses, among which are some large buildings, several churches, a large inn, a court-house, prison, bank, and many respectable shops.[200] All the environs are strongly impregnated with salt, and there are saline springs, from whence a great quantity of salt is obtained. The salt water is conducted for about a mile from the springs at Salina to the vicinity of Syracuse, where it is evaporated by the sun in shallow vessels, and the salt crystallized. The works are to the north of Syracuse.[201]

As several roads and canals cross at this place, we had to wait for passengers, especially for the packets from Lake Oswego, which is now navigated by steam-boats. During this interval we viewed the traces of the extensive fire which had taken place in the preceding spring. Though many buildings have been rebuilt in a better style than before, the marks of the fire are everywhere to be seen. To the southwest of Syracuse there is an extensive valley, bounded by wooded eminences, in which many neat villages are seen; among them one called Onondago Hill, erected upon a verdant rising, is worthy of notice, the remnants of the Onondago Indians being settled here. It is reckoned to be eight miles from Syracuse to the spot where the chief town, Onondago, lay. Here they had their council fires, and here the powerful and warlike nation deliberated on public affairs, resolved upon war, concluded peace, &c. Onondago Hill is said to be a neat town, and was formerly the seat of the courts of justice, which, however, are now removed to Syracuse. At the latter place we saw several Onondago Indians, who do not much differ from the Senecas and Tuscaroras; their costume is exactly similar, and the women were also wrapped in white blankets.

After some delay, our boat pursued its voyage, and I saw large tracts of land entirely covered with the stumps of woods that had been cleared; others with the remains of stems burnt black, which present a singular, unattractive sight. The dry heights are covered with pine, of which the inhabitants affirm that six different sorts are here found—the hemlock, the spruce, the white, the yellow, the Norway, and the pitch pine, the two latter of which grow on barren grounds.

We took on board a great number of passengers at Syracuse, so that our boat was crowded to excess; yet the arrangements for the accommodation of so many people of every description, and of both sexes, were extremely judicious and well contrived.

Beyond the village of Manlius I observed thickets of *Arbor vitæ*, especially in marshy spots, where pines flourish. After passing Chittenango Creek we came to the village of the same name; and an hour later to Canastote, a large village with new houses, and a couple of churches. The few fields of wheat in the vicinity were not yet ripe. At noon we were in the village of Oneida, which is irregularly built on both sides of the canal.[202] Here we happened to meet with above 100 Oneida Indians, whose lands, assigned to them by the government, lie to the south of this place. The women wore round black felt hats; the men red woollen scarfs over their blue great coats. Their complexion was a yellowish-brown, not dark. They were of low stature, especially the women, as has been observed of all the remnants of the six nations, and have retained more of the national features than the men. We were informed that some of these people were to embark here and proceed to Green Bay, near which they intended to settle.[203] They lived hitherto twelve or fifteen miles from this place, scattered on their plantations, and their settlement is usually called a village, though the dwellings are all isolated. Here stands a building, commonly called Oneida Castle, where they discuss the affairs of their tribe, and the Council Grove, a spot with lofty old trees, under which the Oneidas assemble on important occasions. They now meet every year at Oneida Castle, on the 6th of June, form a circle in Council

Grove, every family by itself, and the agents of the government pay seven dollars to each of them, because they sold their land to the United States. The counties of Oneida and Madison comprise the former abode of the Oneidas, but they now live in this part of the country, having sold a portion of their land to the United States. Of all the tribes of the six nations, they were the only one who remained faithful to the Americans in the early wars.[204]

From Oneida we soon came to Verona, a small village, where there is a manufactory of window glass, to the south of Lake Oneida, to which it was intended to make a canal from this place. At two we arrived at the little village of New London, in a country abounding with hemlock pines. Large quantities of timber, planks, logwood, &c., are sawn here, and shipped in flat-bottomed canal boats.[205] Five miles from New London is Rome, at a small distance from the canal; it is a considerable place, with five churches, which are seen from a distance.[206] The country round is an extensive plain, through which the Mohawk flows, and is bounded by forests in the horizon. The canal then traverses the village of Oriskany, on Oriskany Creek, which was one of the principal abodes of the Oneida nation.[207]

Passing through a rich, verdant country, adorned with pleasant habitations and fine forests, illumined with the most cheerful sunshine, we came, at six o'clock in the afternoon, to White's Town, a neat and thriving place on the left bank of the canal, founded by a person of the name of White, who, as the first settler, gave his name to the town, and whose grandson, Mr. Henry White, was on board our boat.[208] On the right of the canal stands the great cotton manufactory of Mr. Marshall, of New York, which forms an entire village;[209] two similar establishments are in the immediate neighbourhood, and it appears that there are at least twelve cotton manufactories on Sacquit Creek, which falls into the Mohawk. When Mr. White settled here, this large tract of country was inhabited by the Oneida Indians, whose chief, Skenandoah, kept up a very good understanding with the new settlers. This was the scene of the event already recorded by other travellers, when Mr. White entrusted them with his eldest daughter, at that time a child two years old, because they had conceived a particular affection for her. In the sequel, the family were uneasy about the fate of the child, but the Indians brought her back, loaded with presents, and were delighted at this proof of confidence.[210]

The country about White's Town, and, in fact, the whole valley of the Mohawk, is picturesque and beautiful, and is unquestionably the most pleasant that I have yet seen in North America. On every side there are neat, cheerful towns, manufactories, corn, saw, gypsum, and other mills, in the latter of which, the gypsum, which is piled up on the banks of the canal in large grey blocks, is ground to manure the fields. This country was formerly inhabited by the Mohawks, who, being friends to the English, removed, and settled in Canada.[211]

At Utica,[212] a large town with regular streets and good houses, there was a brisk traffic, and the servants of the inns crowded about the boats to receive the passengers; but I proceeded on the voyage, and enjoyed the fine scenery, the Mohawk meandering, between lofty trees, through the extensive verdant valley. During the night we passed German Flats, which was originally cultivated by Germans, whose descendants still live here, and whose language is spoken by many settlers near the canal.[213] We passed through Canajoharie, and on the 4th of July still followed the valley of the Mohawk, which had much increased in breadth. In the river, the navigation of which is now transferred to the canal, there are beautiful islands covered with poplar, willow, and other thickets, and a covered bridge crosses it at Amsterdam, a place consisting of about 100 tolerably good houses, from which it is sixteen miles to Schenectady, where, having passed Rotterdam during dinner, we arrived at three in the afternoon.[214]

Schenectady, where the passengers quit the boats to proceed by the railway to Albany, is a considerable place. Carriages stood ready to convey the passengers to the railway, and we entered them without delay. They are long and roomy, contain many passengers, and run on ten small wheels. One horse drew each carriage for 200 paces towards an eminence, where it was taken off, and the carriages fastened to a rope, and drawn up by a steam-engine. On the eminence, the whole train, with the closed carriages for the luggage of the passengers on the river, is connected with the steam-engine, and in about an hour we arrived at Albany, sixteen miles distant.[215]

It was early in the afternoon when we reached Albany, a large town with 26,000 inhabitants, the capital and seat of government of the state of New York, on the bank of the fine, large River Hudson. I will not repeat what may be found in every American hand-book for travellers, but only observe, that it was the Day of Independence, one of the great festivals in America, which was interesting to us, because it was on that day (the 4th of July) two years before, that I landed on the American coast. We heard some firing, and now and then cannon were discharged in the streets, and sky-rockets and fireworks displayed. Crowds of people thronged every place. An introduction from Dr.

Pitcher, with whom I had travelled on the Erie Canal, procured me the interesting acquaintance of Dr. Edwin James, author of the account of Major Long's "Expedition to the Rocky Mountains," who is well known in the literary world as a botanist and geologist. I found him a singularly amiable, unassuming person, and passed the evening very agreeably in his family circle. He is at present engaged on the Indian languages, especially that of the Chippeways, among which people he resided for a long time.[216] He had the kindness to escort me about the city, which has many handsome buildings, some broad streets, and in the centre a large square, round which the most important public edifices are erected. The capitol is built on a gentle eminence; it cost 120,000 dollars, is 115 feet long, 90 feet wide, and 60 feet high, and is adorned on the east front with four Ionic columns. The academy, which cost 92,000 dollars, and the city hall, built of white marble, likewise stand in this square. The square itself is laid out very tastefully, covered with greensward, and intersected with broad walks, and is a great ornament to the town.

At eight o'clock in the morning of the 5th of July we embarked in the Albany steamer for New York. The Hudson or North River is even here a fine broad stream, with picturesque banks, but soon widens considerably: my navigation of it is unquestionably the most agreeable voyage that I made in America. The distance, which is 144 miles (by land 160 miles), is conveniently performed in one day, though it is often accomplished in twelve or fourteen hours. The steam navigation is very brisk on the river, except in winter, when it is impeded by the ice. The steamers on the Hudson are very large, and no such accidents occur as on the Mississippi and the Ohio, because only low pressure engines are employed.

The Albany was a large vessel, of the size of a frigate, with three decks, of which the upper one was covered by an awning. The middle deck was eighty paces in length; the lower space contained three very elegantly furnished cabins—the two at the back for the ladies, and, in front, the large cabin or dining-room, which was adorned with oil paintings. Our proud vessel glided swiftly down the stream, and the beautiful banks speedily vanished from our view. After proceeding thirty miles, we reached the town of Hudson, opposite the Catskill Mountains, a picturesque range, with fine summits, such as are seldom seen in North America. This range is also called Catsbergs; the highest summit is near Greene, eight or ten miles distant from the river. Along the shore, at the foot of this range, lies the village of Catskill, on Catskill Creek, which runs through the village, and flows into the Hudson. Here we landed, and took in some passengers, who, in token of their having come from those more elevated regions, brought in their hands large bunches of the beautiful kalmia blossoms. The village contains about 350 houses and 5000 inhabitants. I would recommend the view of the Catskill Mountains to every landscape painter.

Lower down, the character of the banks of the river has much similarity with that of Italian Switzerland; bright verdant plains alternate with the loveliest woods; while numerous little vessels, especially schooners, glide swiftly on the bosom of the river, which is double the width of our Rhine; and many steamers (among them the colossal Champlain, with four chimneys), towing large flat boats filled with passengers, added greatly to the animation of the scene. After dinner we lay-to at Newbury. Below this, rounded hills covered with wood appear along the shore, not unlike the Rhenish. The river now runs through a narrow, picturesque gorge, almost shut in by the verdant hills. On the western coast lies West Point, where the military academy of the United States is situated; below this, the country grows more open and flat, and the river becomes very broad and majestic. We passed the large house of correction at Singsing, on the eastern coast, and arrived at New York before evening.

We rejoiced to find the town in a perfectly healthy state, and all our friends well. On the 8th of July I visited Philadelphia, which can now be easily accomplished by means of the railway from Amboy. At Bordentown we went on board the Philadelphia steamer, and reached that town at five in the afternoon. Our two days' stay here was devoted to visiting friends; and I am indebted to Professor Harlan for introducing me to Mr. Duponceau, a learned investigator of the Indian languages, as well as for taking me to several collections of natural history.[217] The museum of the society of natural sciences contains many interesting curiosities, among which I may mention Dr. Morton's collection of skulls.[218] In the museum of Mr. Titian Peale I saw many objects which deserve close investigation.

Early on the 11th of July we re-embarked on board the Burlington for Bordentown; thence by railway to Amboy, and returned to New York by the Swan steamer. Here we found an accumulation of business, consequent upon our approaching voyage to Europe; Messrs. Gebhard and Schuchart, however, very kindly gave us every assistance, and greatly helped to expedite our affairs. I again spent a most pleasant day at the country-house of Mr. Schmid, the Prussian consul, where I had the gratification of seeing Mr. Astor, so justly esteemed in the fur countries.[219] There was a great uproar at this time in the streets of New York; the mob attacked the negroes, and some clergymen, who took their part, had their windows broken and houses demolished. Towards evening, the militia paraded the streets, and occupied different posts, in order to check these riots. Dr. Julius gives an account of this assault upon the negroes in New York, page 369.[220]

We engaged berths on board the packet-boat Havre, Captain Stoddart; it belongs to the Havre Line, whose vessels are from 400 to 600 tons burden, and go every week, in winter as well as in summer. The arrangements are particularly good, the table capital, with abundance of fresh milk and meat every day.

As the packet was to leave on the 16th of July, our collections, &c., were put on board on the 15th, and we bade our friends and acquaintances farewell. At ten o'clock on the day fixed for our departure we went, accompanied by many friends, on board the Rufus King steamer, which received her passengers on the North River Pier, and conveyed them in twenty minutes to the packet, which was lying in the fine harbour near the city. The anchor was already weighed, and the pilot on board. As soon as the baggage of the several passengers was disposed of in the hold, the Havre spread all her sails, but the wind being very faint, it was eleven o'clock before we were opposite the lighthouse of Statenland, which lay on our right hand, and the batteries of Long Island on our left. The wind soon became quite contrary, and we were obliged to cast anchor and take in our sails: several steam-boats passed us, and we wanted them to take us in tow, but, to our great vexation, they refused to stop. Towards evening, however, the wind rose a little, and we tacked slowly towards the sea.

At six in the morning of the 17th of July we lay opposite Sandy Hook, a little above the lighthouse. At half-past twelve we saw, at a distance on the left hand, Fire Island lighthouse, which is forty miles from Sandy Hook; and on the 18th we lost sight of the coast. Our voyage was on the whole favourable: we did not pass over the bank of Newfoundland, but on the 24th and 25th of July were very far to the south of it. We afterwards had a fresh and favourable wind, and followed the track of the Columbia, (as laid down in the charts), which performed the voyage from Portsmouth to New York in fifteen days.

On the 30th of July we made 5° in twenty-four hours. The sight of the numerous vessels which passed us full sail was very striking, and greatly cheered the whole of the ship's company. We proceeded at the rate of nine or ten knots an hour; the wind was favourable, and, though very strong, even our topmost sails were spread, an experiment which other nations do not often venture upon; but the Americans are very bold seamen. On the 2nd of August we were to the north of the Azores, which I had seen in 1817, and on the following day spoke the brig Helen Douglas, from Hamburgh, and communicated reciprocally our longitude and latitude. We overtook several ships, which the Havre soon left far behind her.

Our people endeavoured to harpoon some dolphins, but the handle of the instrument, which was admirably contrived, soon broke.[221]

At *a* there is a joint; *b* is a movable ring; *d* is the sharp edge of the instrument; *f* the back, which is blunt. When the point *e* is forced into the body of the animal, it penetrates so far, that the resistance of the body moves the ring *b*; the whole head springs from the position in which it was held by the ring; the edge *d* continues to act in an horizontal direction, and the point *c* forms a barb by which the instrument remains fixed in the animal.

On the 6th of August we overtook the Congress, a large ship bound from New Orleans to Liverpool, which had come thus far in forty-eight days. We soon got the start of her, and on the following day were already in the channel, having passed Cape Lizard in the night. At three in the afternoon land was descried from the mast-head; it was the Island of Guernsey: we then saw Alderney, and afterwards Cape la Hogue on the French coast, very clearly. The wind became more fresh every moment, and, twilight setting in, we greatly desired to obtain a pilot. At length we saw a boat contending with the waves, which, with considerable exertion, brought us a pilot from Havre. We sailed in the dark, passed the lighthouse at Cherbourg, and afterwards saw that of Harfleur, our ship running seven or eight knots an hour.

Early on the morning of the 8th of August we were off Havre de Grace, with a violent head wind, and waited for the proper time to enter, which, as in many ports in the channel, can only be done at high water. We were the more impatient for this moment, as the wind continued to increase, and threatened to rise to a storm. Large ships from Martinique and Guadaloupe, under French colours, shared the same trial of patience with ourselves. At length, after ten o'clock, the pilot gave the signal—the sails were spread, and the Havre hastened to enter the port. A great crowd of people was assembled on the pier, and breakers raged at the narrow mouth of the harbour; however, we soon felt the effect of the mole which human art has opposed to the fury of the elements, and at half-past eleven o'clock the Havre cast anchor in Europe.

FOOTNOTES:

[195] Pendleton, in Niagara County, was settled before the projection of the canal by Sylvester Pendleton Clark, who built the first log tavern here in 1821. Although a junction on the canal, and later a station on the Erie Railway, the town has not attained much prosperity.

For Lockport, see Bullock's *Sketch*, in our volume xix, p. 151, note 21.—ED.

[196] Rochester, Perinton, and Fairport, all in Monroe County, on the canal, were settled before the route was laid out. The first permanent settlement at Rochester was not until 1803, although saw and grist mills had been built some years earlier, and worked intermittently. The name given to the village

- 126 -

in 1811 was in honor of Nathaniel Rochester, of Maryland, an early purchaser of lands. The village incorporation took place in 1811.

Perinton, named for its first settler, Glover Perrin (about 1790), had little growth until the opening of the canal; the name is now applied to the township in which Fairport is situated. The first settler of the latter town came in 1810; there were but nine houses there, seven of which were log-cabins, at the opening of the canal (1822). It numbered in 1900, 2,439.

Irondequot Creek was an early highway into Iroquois territory. It was the rendezvous (1687) of the expedition led by Denonville, governor of Canada, against the marauding Seneca. See Thwaites, *Lahontan's Voyages in North America* (Chicago, 1904), i, pp. 123-130.—ED.

[197] Clyde, in Wayne County, New York, had its first permanent settlers in 1811. It was at first called Lauraville; later, the river was, by a Scotch settler, named Clyde, and upon incorporation (1836) this was applied to the settlement.

Montezuma marshes, in southwest Cayuga County, were called by the aborigines Tiohero.—ED.

[198] This part of the country is remarkable for the number of fine lakes, all of which have very harmonious names, taken from the old Indian language, such as Canandaigua, Cayuga, Seneca, Onega, Ontario, Oswego, Onondago, &c. From the immense Lake Superior, the area of which is estimated at 30,000 square miles, to the small lakes only a few miles in length, their forms differ entirely, and are in part highly picturesque. These lakes and rivers have been judiciously suffered to retain their ancient harmonious Indian names; whereas the Americans have, in general, transferred the names of European towns and districts to this land, where we often meet with excessively dissonant, inappropriate names, which frequently call forth a smile, as Dr. Julius very justly observes, Vol. I. p. 420.—MAXIMILIAN.

Comment by Ed. Nicolaus Heinrich Julius, author of *Nordamerikas sittliche zustande, nach eigener Enshauungen in den jahren 1834-36* (Leipzig, 1839).

[199] For the Onondaga, see Croghan's *Journals*, in our volume i, p. 60, note 23.—ED.

[200] The site of Syracuse had been that of an Indian village, where Ephraim Webster, coming from New England, built a trading post in 1786. It was included in the salt reservation established in 1797 and offered for sale by the state in 1804. The first purchaser was Abraham Walton, who built a mill upon the site the following year. Walton intended to found a village, but not until the establishment of the canal did Syracuse outgrow its embryonic stage. Meanwhile several names had been in use; Milan was suggested in

1809; South Salina was used for three years (1809-12); Corinth was desired, but a Corinth post-office already existing, Syracuse was suggested, because of a certain resemblance to the site of the famous Sicilian city. Organized as a village in 1825, Syracuse finally became a city in 1847.—ED.

[201] The salt springs of this vicinity were noted by Jesuit missionaries in the seventeenth century. By 1770, salt from this region was an article of barter among Indian tribes. The first made by white men was in 1788; primitive methods were followed, however, until in 1797 the state set apart a reservation of thirteen thousand acres, embracing the saline springs, and the next year manufacture on a large scale was begun. Although much of the land was afterwards sold by the state, control of the salines was maintained by the government for a hundred years; in 1898, however, the state finding participation in this manufacture unprofitable, the springs became private property.—ED.

[202] Manlius was first settled in 1792, when a log-cabin inn was opened upon its site, which was first called Liberty Square. Shortly after 1800 the name was changed to Manlius, and the first postmaster appointed. The town had in 1900 a population of 1,219.

Chittenango and Oneida, in Madison County, were not early settlements, but due to the growth of canals and railroads. Oneida was incorporated in 1848, and had (1900) a population of 6,364.

The site of Canastote (signifying "Cluster of pines") was purchased (1810) by Reuben Perkins; the settlement was, however, due to the canal, and was incorporated in 1835. It has attained a population of about three thousand.—ED.

[203] The Oneida Indians, one of the "five nations" of the Iroquois confederacy, lived east of the Onondaga, in the present Madison and Oneida counties. In 1788 they ceded their land to New York state, retaining a large reservation, which has been gradually disposed of for successive annuities. About 1820 the project of their removal to Wisconsin was broached, and two delegations representing diverse interests among the Oneida, headed respectively by Dr. Jedidiah Morse, and Reverend Eleazer Williams, visited the West, and entered into arrangements with the Menominee and Winnebago tribes for territory contiguous to Green Bay. These treaties were the subjects of much negotiation, but the controversy was finally settled (1831) by the United States government in favor of the New York Indians. With the Oneida were three tribes of New England Indians—the Stockbridge, Munsee, and Brothertown—who had previously been (in the latter part of the eighteenth century) received among the Oneida in New York. The migration of these various tribes began about 1823, and continued at varying intervals until about 1846, a small remnant only remaining in New

York. In Wisconsin they located permanently; the Munsee and Brothertown having assumed citizenship, are for the most part absorbed in the white population of Brown, Outagamie, and Calumet counties, chiefly the last named, although a few are mingled with the Oneida on their reservation near Green Bay. The latter number about two thousand, and are in a fairly prosperous condition, chiefly farmers. On the Stockbridge reservation in Shawano County there are about five hundred engaged in farming and lumbering. Consult *Wisconsin Historical Collections*, ii, pp. 415-449; xv, pp. 25-209; and J. N. Davidson, *Unnamed Wisconsin* (Milwaukee, 1895).—ED.

[204] Oneida Castle was located south of the modern town of that name, in Lenox Township, Madison County, on the borders of Oneida County. At this village Reverend Samuel Kirkland established himself as a missionary in 1766, and it was chiefly due to his influence that the main body of the Oneida remained neutral during the Revolutionary War. After the removal to Wisconsin a few of the tribe clung to their original home, and about a hundred and fifty are still to be found in this vicinity.—ED.

[205] Verona's first settlement was made in 1797 by Captain Ichabod Hand, who kept a tavern on the road from Rome to Oneida Castle.

New London is a small hamlet in Oneida County, erected during the progress of the canal. Its first settler came in 1824, and the following year a post-office was erected.—ED.

[206] The site of Rome was on the Oneida portage between the Mohawk Valley and waters flowing into Lake Ontario. As early as 1756 the English had erected Fort Bull at the western extremity of the portage, but this was promptly captured and destroyed by French troops. Two years later, Fort Stanwix was erected by the British general of that name; the cost was $60,000, and the fort was heavily garrisoned until the close of the French and Indian War. In 1768 the famous treaty with the Iroquois, making a great land cession to the English colonies took place at this outpost. At the outbreak of the Revolution the name of the fort was changed to Schuyler, and the next year (1777) it was besieged by Major Barry St. Leger with a force of Indian allies; the post was finally relieved by General Benedict Arnold. The first settler near the fort was a German, Johann Reuff (or Roof). He fled at the time of the siege, and the place was without inhabitants until 1785-87, when New England colonists began to arrive. The site of Rome was purchased by a New York merchant named Lynch who laid out a town (1796) and called it Lynchburg; this was later changed for the classic cognomen, and the village of Rome incorporated in 1819.—ED.

[207] Oriskany (Indian dialect, signifying "nettles") was the site of the battle of August 6, 1777, when General Nicholas Herkimer, of the American army, repulsed the invading British forces under Major St. Leger. The village was

settled in 1802 by Colonel Garrett Lansing, a Revolutionary soldier, and a post-office opened about 1821.—ED.

[208] Hugh White of Middletown, Connecticut, was one of the four purchasers of a confiscated Tory patent known as Sadequahada, he being the first settler west of German Flats, on the Mohawk. Coming out to his purchase in 1784, with his entire family of sons and sons-in-law, he settled what was for a time known as Whitestown, whither a number of Connecticut relatives and friends followed in succeeding years. Judge White was a man of ability and much physical strength. He attained considerable influence with the Oneida, who adopted him into their tribe. Dying in 1812, he left many descendants. Originally known as Whitestown, the village surrendered that title to the township, and was incorporated (1811) as Whitehall Landing, a name changed two years later to Whitesborough. The Oneida Historical Society in 1884 celebrated the centennial of the founding of this place by erecting a granite shaft upon the village green. Whitesborough at one time bid fair to rival Rome and Utica, but has now a population of only two thousand.—ED.

[209] The village of New York Mills, the site of the first cotton factory in the state, was founded in 1808 by Walcott and Company. In 1825 a partnership was formed with Benjamin Marshall, of New York City, who retired in 1847. The mills are still owned and managed by the Walcott family.—ED.

[210] Skenandoah (Skenando) died in 1816, reputed to be a hundred and ten years old. He favored the Americans in the Revolutionary War, and was long known as the white man's friend, an eloquent advocate for peace, and a Christian of strong character. His grave is at Clinton, Oneida County, near that of his friend, the missionary Samuel Kirkland.

The incident in relation to White's granddaughter (not daughter) is well authenticated. See D. E. Wager, *History of Oneida County*, New York (Boston, 1896), p. 618.—ED.

[211] At the close of the American Revolution a grant of 300,000 acres upon Grand River, Ontario, was secured from the British government, and the entire tribe of Mohawk removed thither, accompanied by British sympathizers from the other Iroquois tribes. The reservation is now reduced to about 60,000 acres. Mohawk also live at St. Regis, Caughnawaga, and Bay of Quinte, Quebec. A descendant of Joseph Brant, the great Mohawk chief, recently stated that there were still 30,000 Iroquois in Canadian boundaries. See F. W. Halsey, *Old New York Frontier* (New York, 1901), p. 320.—ED.

[212] At Utica, originally a ford on Mohawk River, a small fort was erected during the French and Indian War, named Fort Schuyler, but it was abandoned before the Revolution. The first two houses were built upon the

site in 1786; the early prospect for growth was not bright, and the increase was slow. The village was incorporated in 1798, when the new name was selected by lot. The city charter was received in 1832.—ED.

[213] German Flats was the original seat of the Palatines who emigrated to New York in large numbers in 1710, and began to settle as early as 1712 on land patented to them by the Mohawk. The settlement was for many years the outpost of the Mohawk Valley, and thus was sadly harassed in Indian wars. In November, 1757, French and Indians led by Belestre fell upon the village, carried away captive many of its inhabitants, and burned the entire settlement. A similar fate befell the place in 1778, when the Mohawk chief Brant advanced against this valley, and continued attacks were maintained by his people until the close of the war. The Germans were loyal to the American cause, and under General Nicholas Herkimer formed the bulk of the army that won the day at Oriskany. About 1784 there was a large influx of new settlers of American stock. The chief town of the settlement is now known as Herkimer, with a population of about six thousand.—ED.

[214] Canajoharie, in Montgomery County, was the site of a Mohawk village where Joseph Brant had his early home. In 1750 Philip Van Alstine built the first house upon the site, and ten years later erected thereon a mill. The early settlers were chiefly Germans, and the place suffered severely during the Revolutionary War, being raided successively in 1780 and 1781. By 1790 the settlement had taken on new life, and by 1829 was incorporated as a town.

Near Rotterdam, an early Dutch settlement, is located the oldest house of that region now extant, thought to have been built in 1680, and known as the Jan Mabie house.

Schenectady (also called Corlaer in early days) was laid out in 1662 by Arent Van Curler and fourteen associates. As a frontier settlement in King William's War, it suffered an attack and massacre by French and Indians (1690). In 1705, Queen's Fort was built therein, and it was garrisoned until the Revolution. The first town charter was obtained in 1763, and the city incorporated in 1798.—ED.

[215] The Mohawk and Albany Railway was projected by George W. Featherstonehaugh, an Englishman of some eminence, who had married an American and settled near Albany. A friend of George Stephenson of England, Featherstonehaugh conceived the idea, as early as 1825, of uniting Albany and Schenectady by a railway. The next year a company was incorporated, whose president was Stephen Van Rensselaer. Delay was incident upon construction, and the line was not opened until August, 1831, when the locomotive "Detroit Clinton" drew a train of carriages from Albany to Schenectady. The Mohawk and Albany Railway was the progenitor

of the present New York Central and Hudson River Railway. See G. S. Roberts, *Old Schenectady* (Schenectady, 1904), pp. 143-152.—ED.

[216] For a biographical account of Dr. Edwin James, see our volume xiv, preface, pp. 13-25.—ED.

[217] For sketches of these scientists, see our volume xxii, p. 29, note 3, and p. 64, note 27.—ED.

[218] Samuel George Morton (1799-1851) was educated in medicine at the Universities of Pennsylvania and Edinburgh. In 1823, he settled in practice in Philadelphia, and interested himself in the development of natural science, being a member for many years and finally president (1850) of the Philadelphia Academy of Natural Sciences. To this institution he bequeathed his collection of skulls, which he began in 1830, and which is the largest museum of comparative craniology in the United States, containing over fifteen hundred specimens, nearly two-thirds of which are human. For the origin of Peale's Museum, see our volume ix, p. 55, note 22. Titian Peale is noted in our volume xiv, p. 40, note 1.—ED.

[219] For brief notice of John Jacob Astor, see Franchère's *Narrative*, in our volume vi, p. 186, note 8.—ED.

[220] For Dr. Julius, see *ante*, p. 179, note 198. The riots of July 9-11, 1834, were occasioned by popular opposition to the abolition movement. The American Anti-Slavery Society held a meeting in New York on the fourth of July; immediately excitement arose, and the leaders were threatened. On the night of the ninth, the attempt to hold a meeting of the society resulted in an attack on the Chatham Street chapel—the place of meeting—and the house of Lewis Tappan, one of its prominent members. See *Niles' Register*, xlvi, pp. 332, 346, 357-360.—ED.

[221] See p. 169, for illustration of harpoon for dolphins.—ED.

APPENDIX

I. VOCABULARIES OF SOME OF THE TRIBES OF NORTHWESTERN AMERICA, WITH AN ACCOUNT OF THE INDIAN SIGN LANGUAGE

INTRODUCTION

Much has been written by scholars in recent times on the Asiatic extraction of the American peoples; and the attempt has been made, particularly in the United States, to prove such a relationship. This exceedingly interesting subject opens to the investigator a boundless field; but one whose paths are dark and difficult to make clear. Many good reasons can be given for an Asiatic descent of the Americans; on the other hand, objections can be made which cannot easily be set aside. In either case strikingly similar traits have been found in the peoples of the two continents, as may be seen from Delafield's new work, where everything that can be said on the subject has been brought together.[222]

As the traveller stands in front of the long lines of the old Indian burial mound near St. Louis, he can easily believe that he has before him one of the south Russian kurgans. Moreover, surprising correspondences are found from a comparison of the works of art, as well as the intellectual and moral characteristics, of the peoples of Mexico and Peru with those of India and Egypt. But we search in vain for Mongols in North America. When one has seen the Hindoos, Kalmucks, Bashkirs, and Chinese, he will find that the features and complexion of the type of man now inhabiting North America are very different from those of the Asiatic peoples; and will feel justified in regarding the Americans as a distinct race.

The most firmly-grounded objections to the theory of the Asiatic extraction of the Americans seems to lie in the difference in the color of the skin and in the slight relationship of the languages; for the few words related to American, which have so far been sought out with great difficulty in the Asiatic languages, do not appear to have much weight.

D'Orbigny[223] assumes that there are different races among the peoples of America. But even if it is necessary, for the sake of clearness, to make various subdivisions in such an extended and varied population, on the basis of distinguishing characteristics, nevertheless such a division is difficult and arbitrary. If representatives of all these peoples could be brought together, a classification would present fewer difficulties; but great distances often separate related tribes, and memory rarely suffices for making these exact comparisons. I cannot render a decision on D'Orbigny's supposition that in the American branch of humanity the North Americans form a different race from the South Americans, since I have become acquainted with only a small number of the South American nations.

One claim, which seems to me to have decided probability, is that the ancient Mexicans migrated from the more northern parts of the continent of America. There are many indications of this. The hieroglyphic painting of the migration of the people, which later rose to a higher culture in Mexico, which was discovered by Boturini and brought out by Delafield, is, from this standpoint, a highly interesting document.[224] The drawings of the present North American Indians still show many similarities to those of old Mexican pictures, although it must be said that they are much rougher, cruder, and more childish.[225] Therein, also, foot prints are represented when it is desired to show a continued movement of the figures; and other correspondences have already been pointed out. In various places in the account of my travels, I have sought to call attention to them and to the conjectured southward migration of the Americans. The skulls, however, which have been taken from the old burial grounds on the Wabash, do not show that flattening of the heads that is portrayed on Delafield's first plate; but their crowns are rounded just as nature formed them.

All conjectures over the origin and relationship of these peoples must await the more trustworthy conclusions which it will be justifiable to draw from the relationship of their languages; only through more exact knowledge of them can we hope to make progress in this broad and obscure field. Several of the North American dialects are already fairly well known to philologists; for a majority of the rest there are, at least, vocabularies which allow a superficial classification according to relationship. Distinguished American philologists, Duponceau, Pickering,[226] Edwin James, Gallatin, and several others have accumulated much material, but there has been no comprehensive work on the subject. This lack has in part been filled by Mr. Albert Gallatin, whose learned work is in the hands of the publishers.[227] Since at the present time the attention of travellers is being directed more and more to this highly interesting subject, these materials are likely to be largely increased in the near future, and to give American scholars the chance of constantly perfecting their work. Some authors, among them McKenney, in his *History of the Indian Tribes of North America*,[228] do not seem to attach much value to vocabularies collected by travellers. To be sure, these often are handled in a thoughtless and superficial manner; but it must be remembered that in the interior of North America excellent interpreters of the Indian languages may now be found, and that the Indians themselves often fluently speak several languages. Through these agencies interesting contributions to our knowledge of the dialects referred to may always be expected.

In an examination of the tribes of America, the multiplicity of their languages is very striking. These languages are often confined to quite small tribes; their origin is quite correctly explained by Mr. Gallatin.[229] From the interesting work of this scholar it appears, however, that a certain similarity of character belongs to this multitude of tongues—a circumstance that testifies to their common origin as well as to the antiquity of the American population.[230] All this material thus gains value in the eyes of the philologist; and in this connection it is with pleasure to be noticed, that with the extension of these investigations the interest in them in America constantly brings forward diligent co-operators.

Such work would be far easier and much more useful if all the vocabularies were compiled and copied on the same principles. Most of those in existence have been written down by Englishmen, or Anglo-Americans; and as a rule they, like the French, cannot, as Gallatin admits, correctly reproduce the Indian gutturals;[231] yet it is characteristic of all these languages that they abound in gutturals. Another defect in the usual vocabularies, lies in the omission of accents; for these, also, are peculiarly characteristic of the American languages. One of the dialects which I investigated is so difficult to write, that even after the greatest effort I could reproduce but a few words—I refer to that of the Grosventres of the prairies, sometimes called by the English Fall Indians.[232] For this tongue, even the fur trade company had not been able to find an interpreter; and was compelled to carry on all business with those Indians in the Blackfoot language. Most of the other languages of the Missouri Valley can more easily be reproduced by the Germans and Dutch than by other nations; because, as has already been explained, their own speech abounds in gutturals and regularly has hard endings. Consequently the English vocabularies for these tribes are always more or less defective. Pickering felt this very decidedly, and has consequently proposed for his countrymen a notation of tones which is analogous to the German, and which, if it comes into use, will produce most beneficial results. Pickering's scheme requires that the vowels be pronounced in America as follows:

- *a* as in the word *father*,
- *e* as in *there*,
- *i* as in *machine*,
- *o* as in *note*,
- *u* as in *rule*,
- *y* as in *you* (or as *ee* in English).

In short, he adopts the German system, completely. In place of the German *æ* and *œ*, or *ä* and *ö*, he proposes to write in English *a^e* and *o^e*; in place of *c* to use *k*, a change that will avoid many misunderstandings; and when the pronunciation is hard, to use *ᴣ*, etc. If this system had been used earlier, a smaller number of errors would have crept into the works on this subject, and into the translations from one language to another. For instance, my vocabularies of the Brazilian peoples have in places been very incorrectly reproduced by French translators.

Another defect in the usual English system, for such vocabularies, arises from the division of all words into syllables, a method which Duponceau very rightly censured; for in this way the correct pronunciation of the words is generally lost. When the word with its accents has been written as a whole, the division into syllables is the next task, in order thus to reach conclusions regarding its inflection and derivation—something quite indispensable for the philologist. A word divided in the English style into its component parts, could be correctly pronounced neither by a German nor by a Frenchman; besides, every language has its own intonation, not common to others. I have, therefore, held it to be the surest way of making the Indian words intelligible to all my readers, to call to my aid the pronunciation of several nations. For instance, *on* and *an*, in the Indian languages are spoken, sometimes as in German, sometimes as in French; in such cases I have noted in a parenthesis the system according to which the word or syllable is to be pronounced. Other notes of this character have seemed necessary, and these require the following explanations:—

(1) Sharp *c* is designated as in French by *ç*.

(2) Guttur. denotes guttural, *i.e.*, the German or Dutch pronunciation.

(3) *a^o* or *o^a* denotes full *a* or *o*, somewhat like *aw* in English. Here I might have written *o͡a*; but by using *a^o* and *o^a*, I also indicate that the sound of the lower letter predominates.

(4) d. d. N. (durch die Nase) denotes through the nose: *i.e.*, a nasal sound.

(5) When the sign ½ follows a letter, it means that it is to be only half pronounced, somewhat as the first *e* in the German word *gegangen*, or the second *e* in the English word *achievement*.

(6) I have tried to indicate the length of a syllable by adding an *h*, a plan which I preferred to the ordinary signs ⌣ or ⌣, since these might easily be confused in printing.

(7) A *g* is often heard at the end of the syllables *on* and *an*; consequently I have written them *ong* and *ang*. This is the German system, as I have indicated by the word "German." It is assumed that the philologist will be familiar, at

least in general, with German as well as with French and English pronunciation.

(8) As the French acute accent seemed to me entirely adequate for indicating the correct intonation of the Indian words, I have chosen it to show on what letter or syllable the emphasis is to be placed. Occasionally, owing to haste or lack of time, it may have been forgotten or omitted.

(9) In the case of the letter *j*, I have not followed Mr. Pickering's scheme, for everyone knows how it is pronounced in French and in German. When it has the former value—as very often in the American languages—I have noted "French:" *i.e.*, pronounce as in French. In no other way, it seems to me, can the soft French *j* be clearly indicated.

(10) The German guttural sound *ch*, as in the syllables *ach*, *och*, or *uch*, is, as Gallatin observes, difficult for Englishmen and Frenchmen;[233] but it occurs everywhere in the American languages, and the reader must learn it if he wishes to pronounce such words correctly.

(11) The *r* is never pronounced by these peoples as a guttural, but always with the point of the tongue against the roof of the mouth; *d* and *r*, as well as *r*, *l*, and *n*,[234] are quite often interchanged, or indistinctly pronounced.

(12) On the syllable *in*, I have often noted that *n* is to be pronounced as in French: *i.e.*, the syllable *in* does not sound like *ain* in French, but merely the *n* is pronounced as in French; the whole sound is, therefore, almost *i* nasal, and only a little at the end sinks to *n*.

It is the duty of every traveller in distant, little-known lands to make contributions, according to his ability, to the knowledge of their languages; hence I have brought together in the following pages my own notes, however insignificant and incomplete they may be, under the difficulties which stand in the way of such work. The ignorance of the interpreters, their lack of sympathy with any kind of scientific investigation, the frequent unwillingness of the Indians to assist, superstitious and unintelligible ideas, and lack of time and leisure—these usually combine to make such examinations difficult. When, here and there, I detected some deviations from Mr. Gallatin's vocabularies, it was my duty to record them in order to aid investigation and come nearer the truth. The fault-finding spirit would certainly never prompt me to this, since we are concerned here, not with the use of the material, but with the former method of collecting it.

I have written these vocabularies, in part from the pronunciation of the Indians themselves; in part, from that of interpreters, who are usually half-breeds, and therefore thoroughly acquainted with the Indian as well as with the French or English languages—they have, at least, lived for a long time with those nations; finally, in part from the pronunciation and with the kind assistance of the Indian agent, Major Dougherty,[235] who speaks several of these languages fluently. From some tribes, owing to lack of time or interpreters, I have obtained but few words; from others, more; the most complete vocabularies are in the Mandan and Minnitarri languages, because I passed the winter among them. While I was living with the Mandans I undertook something of a grammatical study of their language; but unfortunately its continuation and completion were interrupted by illness.

Since but a moment was sometimes at my disposal for collecting a few words, I chose a list of twenty of those that frequently occur, and asked for them first, in order to make a comparison and draw conclusions regarding the relationship of the tribes. These words were as follows:

- sun

- moon

- star

- god

- fire

- water

- earth

- man

- woman

- child

- head

- arm

- hand

- hair

- eye

- mouth

- bow

- arrow

- tobacco pipe

- tomahawk

In each of the vocabularies I have noted the source from which it was obtained. The order in which the tribes are arranged is not according to linguistic relationship, but alphabetical for the sake of easier reference.

From an examination of the following examples of the languages of twenty-three peoples it appears, as is observed by the Rev. Dr. Reck, a philologist,[236] that the Sauki, Musquake, Kickapuh, Ojibua, and Krih tribes belong together—a circumstance that has long been known. The speech of the Wasaji [Osage], Konsa, Oto, Omaha, Punca, Dacota, Assiniboin, and Mandan tribes appear to be only dialects of the Dacota (Sioux) linguistic group, of which the last, which I can give most completely, has been but little known. The ten remaining tribes seem to be more foreign to one another—only between the Blackfoot and Snake (Shoshone) dialects, do we find word relationships. There are likewise many similarities between the Mandan and Minnitarri languages; but these, as I was repeatedly assured, arose only after the two peoples had lived near each other, as I have already related elsewhere in the account of my travels. The name of the deity is "manito" among the Musquake [Fox], Sauki, Kickapuh, Ojibua, and Krih tribes, all of which belong to the Algonkin, or Algic linguistic group; among the seven tribes of the Dacota group, it is "wakonda," or "wakanda," which has the same or a similar meaning in half of the tribes mentioned. The word for water is very similar among most of these people, and the name of the tobacco pipe is the same or similar in half of the dialects.

First and last, various corrections have been made in these lists; yet they remain incomplete, and further observation will add many new corrections. I must, therefore, as always, request consideration from learned critics. Finally, I must note that if in the body of my narrative some words are not written as in the vocabularies, the spelling of the latter is to be preferred.[237]

FOOTNOTES:

[222] S. Delafield, *Inquiry into the origin of the antiquities of America.* Cincinnati, 1836.—MAXIMILIAN.

Comment by Ed. The author is John Delafield, Jr., and the work bears the imprint of New York, London, and Paris, 1839. A few copies are also marked Cincinnati, 1839.

[223] For d'Orbigny, see our volume xxiii, p. 300, note 273.—ED.

[224] Chevalier Lorenzo Boturini Beneduci was an Italian scholar who came to Mexico in 1736 on a mission for a descendant of Montezuma. Becoming interested in Mexican antiquities, Boturini spent eight years in making a valuable collection of aboriginal manuscripts; but having incurred the suspicion of the government, he was imprisoned and his collection confiscated (1745). On his return voyage to Spain, whither he was sent for

trial, the galley was captured by the English, and the last vestiges of his antiquities disappeared. In Spain he sought redress, which was granted him, but this of course did not restore his collection. While in Spain he published *Idea de una nueva historia general de la America septentrionale* (Madrid, 1746), in which appears a catalogue of this collection. A portion was recovered, and is now in the museum in the City of Mexico. The manuscript seen by Delafield was the property of William Bullock (for whom see our volume xix, preface), who was also a specialist in Mexican antiquities.—ED.

[225] Consult Plate 55, in the accompanying atlas, our volume xxv; also the authorities quoted in note 53, p. 184, of Brackenridge's *Journal*, in our volume vi.—ED.

[226] For Duponceau, see our volume xxii, p. 29, note 3.

John, eldest son of Timothy Pickering, the Massachusetts statesman, was born at Salem in 1777; being graduated from Harvard (1796), he began the study of law at Philadelphia, where his father was in residence as a member of the federal cabinet. The following year, however, John went to Portugal as legation secretary, being transferred to the embassy at London, where he remained until 1801. Returning to Salem, he again devoted himself to the legal profession, also to linguistic studies which he had diligently pursued abroad, making contributions to Greek philology, and publishing a lexicon of that language. He was offered chairs of both Hebrew and Greek at Harvard, but declined, preferring to live in Boston, whither he removed in 1829. His interest in North American linguistics was awakened (1819) by Duponceau's work, and the following year he published an "Essay on a Uniform Orthography for the Indian Languages of North America," in the American Academy of Arts and Sciences *Transactions*, iv. He also edited, with copious notes, John Eliot's *Indian Grammar*, Jonathan Edwards's *Observations on the Mohegan Language*, and Father Sebastian Rasle's *Dictionary of the Abnaki Tongue*; and prepared the article on North American languages for the *Encyclopædia Americana*. Pickering was a member of many learned societies, at one time being president of the American Academy of Arts and Sciences, and was granted the degree of LL. D. by both Bowdoin (1822) and Harvard (1835). His death occurred at Boston in 1846.—ED.

[227] See *Archaeologia Americana*, vol. 2. Cambridge, 1836. In this volume is Mr. Gallatin's *Synopsis of the Indian tribes within the United States east of the Rocky mountains.*—MAXIMILIAN.

[228] See our volume xxii, p. 29, note 3.—ED.

[229] Mr. Gallatin (p. 151) expresses himself on this subject as follows:—"on the other hand, the great extent of ground necessary to sustain game sufficient for the subsistence of a very moderate population, compels them

(the Indians) to separate and to form a number of small independent communities. It may easily be perceived that the perpetual state of warfare, in which neighboring tribes are engaged, had its origin in the same cause which has produced the great diversity of American languages or dialects. We may also understand how the affections of the Indian became so exclusively concentrated in his own tribe, the intensity of that natural feeling, how it degenerated into deadly hatred of hostile nations, and the excesses of more than savage ferocity, in which he indulged under the influence of his unrestrained vindictive passions."—MAXIMILIAN.

[230] Gallatin, *Ibid.*, p. 142.—MAXIMILIAN.

[231] *Ibid.*, p. 4.—MAXIMILIAN.

[232] See on these Indians, Franchère's *Narrative*, in our volume vi, p. 371, note 183.—ED.

[233] Gallatin, *Ibid.*, p. 4.—MAXIMILIAN.

[234] *Ibid.*, p. 45.—MAXIMILIAN.

[235] For Dougherty, see our volume xiv, p. 126, note 92.—ED.

[236] Johann Friedrich von Recke, born at Mitau, in Livonia, in 1764, early turned his attention to historical and linguistic pursuits. Educated under a brother of Emanuel Kant, he studied at Göttingen with Professor Johann Friedrich Blumenbach, who later gave an impetus to Maximilian's investigations. About 1785 Recke retired to Mitau where for over forty years he was state archivist, with leisure to pursue his special investigations. As a philologist his fame rests on his *Allgemeinen Schriftsteller und gelehrten Lexikons der provinzen Livland, Esthland, und Kurland* (Mitau, 1827-32). It would appear that Maximilian consulted Dr. Recke upon the analogies of his Indian vocabularies.—ED.

[237] In transcribing the Indian words of these vocabularies, the word divisions and diacritical marks of the German edition have been copied exactly as they stand, save when the division of a word at the end of a line has necessitated an additional hyphen. Most of the diacritical marks are explained by the author in his introduction. The vertical accent seems to be used to indicate secondary, or less emphatic stress; the horizontal superior ° appears, likewise, to be used to show that the sound is less prominent than when the usual superior ° is used.

Exact translation of the German words has been very difficult in some cases, owing to the entire absence of context. The parentheses following the English contain alternative or explanatory words. Some of these are given by Maximilian himself, some lie in the form of the German word, and some are supplied by the translator.—TRANSLATOR.

ARIKKARAS (Rikkaras; French, Ris)[238]

American (an), Nehsikuss (Long Knife, the name which the Americans have among all Indian nations).

Arm, uïhnu (*uih* very long; *nu* very short and low).

Arrow, nïh-schu (*nih* with strong accent; *sch* very short and falling in tone).

Autumn, niskútsch.

Beans (the fruit), a'ttika-hunáhn.

Beard, hakaráhnuch (*uch* guttural).

Bird, nix.

Black, tecatïh.

Blind, tschirikarúch (*uch* guttural).

Blood, páhtu (*u* barely audible).

Blue, tischidanáhuisch.

Bone, djeïh-schu (*schu* short and low; *je* French).

Bow, náhtsch (*sch* hissed softly at the end; German throughout).

Bow-lance, na'hts-saha'hn.

Brave, uïhta-nakóh.

Brave (n), uïhta-ti.

Bridle (horse), hah-karachkóhku (*ach* guttural; *koh* with strong emphasis).

Brook, taháhneni-kakïrihu.

Brother, ináhn (*i* barely audible).

Chief (leader), däscháhn.

Child, pïhrau (German throughout; *r* with the point of the tongue).

Cold, tipsïh.

Come here, schi-schá (both short); or, schi-schá-pisch, come here quickly.

Dance (v), tiráhnauïsch-uischu (very short; run together).

Day, tiuëne-sáhkaritsch (second *e* ½; the last word low and short).

Deaf, kaketschiesch (first *e* ½; otherwise German throughout).

Devil (evil spirit), szirïtsch (same word as for wolf).

Die (v), necksáhn.

Door, hihuattóhnin (*nin* short and low; *hih* together).

Dream (v), itcháhn (*it* barely audible; *ch* guttural).

Drink, metetschïhka.

Dumb, wakárru (*u* barely audible).

Ear, atkahaḣn (*at* barely audible).

Earth, honáhnin (*n* barely audible; *nah* very long; German pronunciation throughout).

Enemy, páh-tu (like word for blood).

Englishman, Sáhnisch-takapsia (*a* low and short; *i* and *a* separated).

Evening, hinách (*ach* guttural).

Eye, tschirïhko (*ko* short and low).

Father, hiáchti (*ti* low and short; *ach* guttural).

Feather, hïh-tu (*u* barely audible; the whole run together).

Fire, ha-nïh-tu (*ha* short; *tu* barely audible; the whole run together).

Fish, tschiuátsch (*t* indistinct; *ua* like *wa*).

Flesh, sászsch.

Fog, uettetaraṅsa (*e* full value).

Forehead, nikakinn.

Forest, waráhkt (*t* barely audible; *r* with the point of the tongue).

Frenchman, Sáhnisch-táhka.

Friend, sih-nánn (German, run together).

Go (v), tiuáhwanuck.

God, pachkátsch (*ach* German guttural).

Good, tunahä.

Great, teüitschähs.

Green, same word as for blue.

Gun, tnáhku (*t* and *u* barely audible), or nahku.

Hair, ůhchu (*ch* guttural; *uh* guttural sound; final *u* very short).

Hand, éschu (*u* barely audible).

Head, pá-chu (*ch* guttural; the whole run together).

Heart, uïssu (*u* indistinct).

Heat, tah-werïstu (*u* short; the whole run together).

Horns (of stag), warikaráhn.

House (hut), akáhn.

Hunger, tiriuatä.

Hunt (v), tiráhuisch-kaëhsch (*a* and *e* separated; *e* and *h* together).

I, náh-tu (*tu* short; run together).

Ice, nachéhtu (*ch* guttural; *u* short and low).

Island, auáhk (*a* and *u* separated).

Jar (pot), kószsch.

Knife, nisïtsch.

Laugh (v), täwachko (*ko* short and low).

Lead (ball), nischtiúidu.

Leg, káhchu (*u* barely audible).

Life, tïhko (*ko* short and low).

Lightning, hunachtschipsch.

Maize, nähschü (*schu* very low and short).

Man, uït-h (*h* prolonged as an aspiration).

Meal (to eat?), teuah (*e* and *u* separated).

Medicine, tiuahruchi (*i* and *u* separated; *ti* short; *ah* with strong accent; *uch* guttural).

Medicine drum, akadéhwuchnahch (*ch* guttural; *wuch* and *ahch* very indistinct).

Medicine pipe, napàhruchti (*uch* guttural).

Moon, pa.

Morning, hinȧchtit.

Mother, schȧchti (German; *i* indistinct).

Mountain, wáo-tirïhuh.

Mouth, hah-kȧu (*kau* together, with the accent).

Much, tiráhnehun (*e* full value; *un* like *oun* in French).

Negro, sȧhnisch-kahtitt.

Night, uettekattïh-sïha (*e* full value; final *a* short and low).

Nose, sinïht.

One-eyed, tschirikak-cho (*ch* like a guttural breath).

Partizan (leader of a war party), däschtschïta (German throughout).

People (folk), sȧhnisch.

Pipe (tobacco), nauschkatsch (German throughout).

Pouch (for ammunition), ischtachkóhku (*ach* guttural).

Powder (gun-powder), it-kȧhn (*it* barely audible; otherwise German).

Pumpkin (the fruit), nekȧhse (first *e* full value; final *e* ½).

Quick, pïsch.

Quiver, uachtáss (*ach* low; *uach* very low, in the throat).

Rain, uettasuhe (*e* ½).

Rattle (sysyquoy, or gourd-rattle), atschihikúchtsch (*uch* guttural).

Red (color), tippahȧht (*t* barely audible).

Red (to paint red), tippahȧhnu (*u* barely audible).

Revenge (v), uëuittetut-kauïht (*aui* separated; likewise *ue*).

River, sahá-nin (German throughout).

Saddle, anarïtschi-tauï (the whole low; *ta* together; *a*, *u*, and *i* separated).

Scalp, uittirah-hunnu (*nu* very short and barely audible; *u* and *it* separated).

Sick, tenáhchehu (*ch* guttural; *e* full value).

Small (short), kakirihuh.

Smoke, tirȧh-uchschkȧ (*uch* very short guttural; *schka* very strong emphasis).

Snow, hunaho (*o* short and low).

Speak, tihuáhwachtéhku (*u* short and low; *ach* guttural).

Spirits (distilled), séh-sannach (*ach* guttural as in German).

Star, sakkah.

Stingy, tähuïss-ch (*ch* guttural prolonged).

Stirrup, achkatatáu (*ach* merely a guttural sound, nearly *ch*).

Stone, kanéh-tsch (*tsch* merely hissed at end).

Strong, tetárach-tschisch (last word loud with emphasis; *ach* guttural).

Sun, schakúhn (German).

Sunflower (helianthus), stschüpünáh-núhchu (*ch* guttural).

Sweet, uettáh.

Teeth, ahna (*a* barely audible, thus nearly *ahn*).

Thunder, uaruchte-teuachnáho (*e* distinctly pronounced).

Tobacco, nahuischkáhn (*nah* together; *uisch* like *wisch*, merely a hiss).

Tobacco-pouch, nanochkóhku (*och* guttural; *koh* rather indistinct).

Tomahawk (with the pipe), katarátsch-nauschkatsch (German throughout).

Tomahawk (without the pipe), katarátsch.

Tongue, háhtu (*u* barely audible).

Toothache, tikuchkaráhnu (*uch* guttural; *nu* short and low).

Trail, hatúhn.

Ugly, kakúchne (*ch* rather indistinct; *e* ½).

Village, etúhn.

War, naminakohn, i.e., to fight.

War-club (with the iron head), akachtáhka (*ach* guttural).

Wash, tanïh-karúhku (final *u* short and low).

Water, stóh-cho (*st* with the point of the tongue; *ch* guttural).

Weep (v), titschïck.

White (the color), tetschéh-schauatá (together).

White-man, sáhnisch-thaka.

Wind, tihútt.

Winter, hunáhka (*a* merely a guttural aspirate).

Wood, náh-ku (*u* low and short; run together).

Wood (piece of), natsch (German throughout; same word as for bow, but pronounced shorter).

Yellow, tirachkatáh (*ach* German guttural).

Yes, haa (nasal).

Names of Animals

Antelope (general term), nanonatsch; the buck, arikatoch (*och* guttural); doe, achkahuahtaesch.

Bat, wáhch.

Bear (black), mató.

Bear (grizzly), kúhnuch (*uch* guttural).

Beaver, tschíttuch (*uch* guttural).

Bighorn, arikússu; usually arikúss.

Buffalo (bull), hoh-kúss; the cow, watahésch.

Deer (black-tailed), tahkatítt.

Deer (common), nochnunáhts (*noch* barely audible).

Dog, chahtsch (*ch* guttural, German throughout).

Duck, kúh-ha (*ha* merely a breathing).

Eagle (bald-headed), aríchta (*ich* German, with the point of the tongue).

Eagle (war), dáhtach-káss (*ach* guttural).

Elk (general term), uá; the stag, uá-nukúss; the doe, uauátaesch.

Fox (gray), tschiwakóh-kussohtaráhuisch (*rah* together; *u* and *i* separated).

Fox (prairie), tschiuáhk (*ua* separated, accent on *uahk*, abruptly ended).

Fox (red), tschiwakúh-kuss.

Horse, chawáhruchtä (*ch* and *uch* guttural).

Moose, wah-suchárut (*ch* guttural).

Mule, chawaka̓du (*du* barely audible; *ch* guttural).

Otter, tschita̓hpat, or tschittahpatte (*e* ½).

Skunk, nimbïtt.

Swan, scha̓htu (*tu* very short).

Turtle, tschïu-ha̓hn (*i* and *u* separated: *i* accented; *hah* very strong emphasis; the whole run together).

Wolf (gray), szirïtsch-tehunéhnoch (*e* full value).

Wolf (prairie), pachka̓tsch (*ach* guttural; same word as for god).

Wolf (white), szirïtsch-sta̓hka.

Articles of Dress and Implements

Breechcloth, mischa̓ch-kaëhtu (*ach* guttural; *ka* and *eh* separated; *tu* short).

Buffalo-robe, sahóhtsch (German throughout).

Hair-ornament (the crow), nachkúch-katóch (*ch* guttural).

Head-dress (the long hood of feathers), pachta̓hruka-wüe (*ach* guttural; *wu* and *e* separated; *e* ½).

Leggings, gógutsch (*go* guttural; *o* full; German throughout).

Moccasins, chútsch (*ch* guttural).

Necklace (of bear's claws), kunúch-chwütu (*ch* guttural).

Powder-horn, pah-rïh-ku (*ku* short).

Sledge, ta̓ruch-ta̓hsch (*uch* guttural).

Whip, pïnnuch (*uch* a strongly hissed, low guttural sound).

Wolf-tail (ornament for heel), ha̓chtit-kutawö (*hach* merely a guttural sound like *ch*).

Numerals

One, a̓chku (*u* barely audible; *ku* merely a guttural aspirate).

Two, pïttcho (*o* barely audible; *cho* merely a guttural aspirate).

Three, ta̓h-uitt (*uitt* very short and low; *tt* barely audible).

Four, tschetéhsch (*e* full value).

Five, sï-huch (*huch* low and short; an aspirate).

Six, tschaʼhpis (*pis* short and low).

Seven, taui-schaʼhpis-uahn (the last two words run together; *a* and *u* separated).

Eight, tauischaʼhpis (*a* and *u* separated).

Nine, nochenéh-uahn (*ch* guttural; first *e* ½).

Ten, nochén (*ch* guttural).

Eleven, pitkóche-nëuahn (first *e* ½; *ne* and *u* separated; *ch* guttural).

Twelve, pitchóchin (*ch* guttural; *in* German).

Twenty, uïtaʼ.

Thirty, sauï (*a* and *u* separated).

Forty, pitkonane-nonchen (*on* French; *chen* as above).

Fifty, here they begin again with ten and count to one hundred by tens; fifty is thus five times ten.

Hundred, schucktahn; i.e., all the tens.

Names of Rivers

Bighorn, Arikúss-okaháhn.

Cannonball, Natschïo-háu (*i* accented; *i* and *o* separated; *hau* pronounced together as in German).

Grand, Sáchkau-waháhn (*ach* guttural; *au* together as in German, but barely audible).

Heart, Tostschïta.

Knife, Ésitsch-kaháhn.

Little Bighorn, Ariksúh (really Arikússu)-kaháh-schiripáss.

Little Missouri (upper), Okaháh-tschiripáss.

Missouri, Swarúchti (*uch* guttural); or Hokaháh-ninn (*nin* German), i.e., Medicine-water.

Muddy (upper), Hohrutschítt (*r* with the point of the tongue; German throughout).

Musselshell, Skápedoch-saháhn (*och* guttural; *e* ½).

Powder, Kanáchtu-suhukaháhn (*ach* guttural; German throughout).

Rivière à Moreau, Kadïh-kahïtt.

Rivière au castor, Zitech-saháhn (*zi* German; *ech* guttural; *e* nearly the same as ü, and barely audible).

Rivière au rempart, Laráh-páhwi.

Rocky Mountains, Wagátti-stáhga (*ga* German; *sta* with point of the tongue).

Square Butte creek (Butte-carrée) Tschïh-issu (emphasis on the first word; the second word low; German throughout).

Teton, Sih-sawïh-tii; i.e., the stagnant water.

Tongue, Hatúhu-kaháhn (German, run together).

White (lower), Hokahach-kúss (*ach* guttural).

White-earth, Horúss-tuhusscháhn (German throughout; *ch* guttural).

Yellowstone, Wáh-hukaháhn.

Names of Neighboring Tribes

Arrapahos, Schahä'.

Assiniboins, Pa'hoak-sa'.

Blackfeet, Chochkátit (*ch* guttural; last *t* barely audible).

Crows, Tuch-káh-ka (*uch* guttural; *ka* low and short).

Dacotas, Schaónn.

Minnitarris, Uïtatt-saháhn.

Pahnis, Tschïhrim (*ri* very short).

FOOTNOTES:

[238] Written from the pronunciation of the Arikkara Indians themselves. The words are pronounced exactly as in German; *ch* has almost always a guttural sound; *r* is spoken with the point of the tongue. Mr. Gallatin remarks (*ibid.*, p. 129) that up to this time there has been no vocabulary of this tribe; it is, therefore, gratifying to me to be able to fill this gap, at least to some extent.—MAXIMILIAN.

American (an), Mïna-haske (*e* ½; run together); i.e., Long Knife.

Arm, nistó.

Arrow, uahïntepä (*pa* short; *e* ½).

Bird, sittekanne (*e* only ½ in both cases).

Black, sáhpa.

Blind, chóncha (*ch* guttural; *on* French).

Blood, uä̈.

Blue, schunktóh (*o* full).

Bone, hóh.

Bow, ntásipa (*n* barely audible).

Brave (adj), uïuktschasch (German).

Brook, kachä̈ (*ch* guttural).

Brother, mitschïnna.

Child, hokschinn.

Cold (adj), osnïh.

Dance (v), uatschïwe.

Day, ampa (*am* French).

Deaf, nóge-wanintsche (*ge* guttural; second word low).

Devil (evil spirit), uakan-schïdja (*an* and *dj* French and soft).

Die (v), tïnktä (*t* separated from *i*, and barely indicated).

Door, tióhpa.

Dream (v), uï-hamana (*hamana* short and low).

Drink (v), menat-kïnte (first *e* ½; *te* short and low).

Dumb, non-chäk-kpah (*on* French; *ch* guttural).

Ear, nóhge (*g* guttural).

Earth, manká.

Enemy, tóge (*o* between *a* and *o*; *e* ½).

Englishman, Uasiáh-maschidju (*j* French; second word low and without emphasis).

Evening, chtaiétu (*ch* guttural).

Eye, nischtá.

Father, atä.

Feather, hen (*n* French; the whole nasal).

Fire, pähte (*e* barely audible).

Fish, hogan (*an* French; *g* guttural).

Flesh, tanó (*o* short).

Forest, tschon-tanke (*on* French; *tanke* German; *e* ½).

Frenchman, Uaschïdju (*j* French and soft; final *u* short).

Friend, koná (*a* short).

Go (v), honktáu (*au* pronounced together).

God (the creator), uakán-tang-e (*an* French; *e* ½; the whole pronounced together; *tange* lower than the first word).

Good, uaschtä (*ta* cut short with emphasis).

Great (tall), hanska (*an* French).

Green, tóh (*o* full).

Gun, tschótange (German throughout; *e* ½).

Hair, pahá.

Hand, nampä.

Head, páh.

Healthy, tähdja (*dj* French; *a* short).

Heart, tschantä.

Heat, onïnitta.

Horns, tahä; the name of the animal is added, e.g., tatánka-tahä, buffalo horns.

House (of the white-man), uaschï-dutti (*dutti* without emphasis).

Hunger, oah-tink-täch (*ach* guttural; the whole pronounced together).

Hunt (v), eiámeia (*ia* together; the whole short).

I, meiä (*ia* together).

Ice, tscháh.

Island, uïta (*ta* short).

Jar (pot), wóhan-pe-ä (*an* French; the whole pronounced together).

Knife, mïhna (*na* short).

Laugh (v), ncháh (*ch* guttural).

Lead (ball), mandassú (*an* French).

Leg, hussänn.

Life (n), uintschone (German throughout; *e* ½).

Lightning, uakïän-tuámpi (*n* and *am* French; *pi* short).

Man, uïtschá (*ui* separated).

Meal (to eat?), wótinkä (*o* full; *ta* short and low).

Moon, hayétu-hiáye (*e* ½).

Morning, háhkena (*kena* even and rather low).

Mother, iná (*a* short).

Mountain, chä (guttural).

Mouth, ih.

Much, ohta (*oh* full).

Negro, hatsáhpa.

Night, kpása.

Nose, póhge (*o* full; *g* guttural; *e* ½).

One-eyed, schtakeba (*e* ½).

Pipe (tobacco), tschanú-hupa (*hupa* low).

Powder (gun-powder), tschachnï.

Quick, kontschüe (*on* French; *schue* short and rapid).

Red, scháh.

Revenge (v), aóin-tsïa (*in* German; *i* and *a* separated).

River, sih-uatpáh-tanga (*tanga* low; the whole pronounced rapidly together).

Sick, uaiasa.

Small (short?), tschihk-at.

Smoke (n), schóhta.

Snow, uáh.

Speak (v), i-á.

Spirits (distilled; i.e., literally fire-water), menïh-päht (run together).

Star, uitschachpe (*ch* guttural; *e* ½).

Stingy, uatéchina (*ch* guttural; *china* short).

Stone, ïng-a (run together and nasal).

Strong, menih-han (*an* French).

Sun, hanuï (*an* French; *u* and *i* separated).

Teeth, hïh.

Thunder, uakïan (*i* and *a* separated; *n* French).

Tobacco, tschandï.

Tomahawk, tschanúpa-tschachpä (*ach* guttural).

Tongue, tschä-jï (*ji* short and French).

Trail, tskankú.

Ugly, schïdjä (*j* French; *e* short).

Village (camp), uïntschóti (*ti* short).

War, ketschïsawe (*awe* short and low).

Warmth, tschäkï.

Wash (v), jujaje (*jaje* French; *e* ½).

Water, menïh (*e* ½).

Weep (v), tschäa (*tscha* together).

White (the color), skala (*sk* with the point of the tongue).

Widow, uïtaschnau (nasal; *nau* pronounced together).

Wind, katä.

Winter, uaniäto.

Woman, huïna (*hui* nasal; *na* short).

Wood, tschán (*an* French).

Yellow, sïh (soft).

Yes, hán (French).

One, uántscha (*an* French).

Two, nompa (*om* French).

Three, jámene (*ne* short).

Four, tópa (*o* full).

Five, sáhpta.

Six, schahkpe (*e* ½).

Seven, schagoë.

Eight, schaknóga (*a* short).

Nine, namptschúnak (*n* French).

Ten, uïktschemane (final *e* ½).

Eleven, akéhuaji (*ji* French; short).

Twelve, akéh-nómpa (*om* French).

Twenty, tschimna-nómpa.

Twenty-one, tschimna-nómpa akéh-uaji: and so on in the same way.

Hundred, opan-uache (*an* French; *e* full value; *opan* with emphasis and loud; the whole indistinct and rapid).

I eat, woáht-atsch (*woa* almost like *uoa*).

You eat, uaiáta.

He eats, juht-atsch.

We eat, wóh-untáhpi (*untahpi* without emphasis).

You eat, uitáta-hetsch (together).

They eat, wóht-atsch (together).

I shall eat, héianko-toh-uauat-atsch (the whole pronounced together).

I would eat, jenk-uaua-tschinkte.

I have eaten, uauáht-atsch.

Eating, uanóh-uóhmantucke (*e* ½).

Eat (imperative) uóhtam (*o* full).

Names of Animals

Antelope, tatógana.

Bear (black), uïnketschenna (*ke* barely audible; *na* likewise).

Bear (grizzly), mató.

Beaver, tsápe (*e* ½).

Bighorn, häïhktschischka.

Buffalo, tatánga.

Dog, schónka (*on* French).

Elk, choiá (*ch* guttural).

Fox (gray), tohk-hanne (*e* short).

Fox (red), schonga-schanne (*e* ½).

Horse, schón-atanga (*schon* with emphasis; *n* French; *atanga* low).

Mountain goat (white), schunkä-ukänne (*e* ½).

Otter, petán (*an* French; *e* short and ½).

Skunk, mankáh.

Wolf, schunk-tógitsche (*e* ½).

FOOTNOTES:

[239] Written from the pronunciation of the half-breed interpreter, Halcro.—MAXIMILIAN.

BLACKFOOT[240]

American (an), Omakstoä; i.e., Long Knife.

Arm, ot-tiss.

Arrow, ápse (*e* distinctly pronounced).

Bird, pehkseü (final *u* barely audible).

Black, sicksinámm.

Blind, náh-pesti (*e* ½; *pesti* short).

Blood, ahah-pane (*pane* short; *e* ½).

Bone, ochkinn (*och* guttural).

Bow, spikenn-áhmai (*mai* German and together; *sp* with the point of the tongue).

Boy (small boy), sa-kú-man-pö (*an* French; *o* distinctly pronounced); usually pronounced sachkó-ma-pö (*ach* guttural).

Brave (a trusty man), iehkitappeh (*ie* German).

Brook, asséh-tachtay (*tach* guttural and very short).

Brother (elder), nehs.

Brother (younger), niskánn.

Chief (n), nachkóhzis (*ach* guttural; *zis* low); or ninau (*au* together, and German).

Child, póh-ka.

Dance (n), paskáhn.

Day, kristikui (*kui* together).

Deaf, sanastóke (*e* distinctly pronounced).

Die (v), änih (accent on *a*); i.e., he is dead.

Door, kitsïmm.

Dream (v), papokahn.

Drink (v), simih.

Drink (imperative), simiïtt.

Dumb, katäh-puie; i.e., one who does not speak.

Ear, ochtóhkiss (*och* guttural).

Earth, ksáchkum (*ach* guttural; the whole German).

Eat this, auáttoht (*au* together).

Enemy, kachtumm.

Englishman, Suiápä.

Evening (towards evening), attakui (*ui* together).

Eye, o-abs-pih (*oabs* together; German).

Father, ninnah.

Feather, mamïnn.

Fire, stïh (*st* with the point of the tongue).

Fish, mamïh.

Flesh, ehksakuy (German; *uy* together).

Forehead, oh-niss.

Forest, atsoahskoi (*koi* German and together).

Frenchman, Náhpi-kuäcks.

Friend, this word is wanting; my kinsman, nézichkáoah (*zich* guttural; *kaoah* short).

Girl (small girl), ah-ké-kuann (German).

Go, ätapoh; i.e., he has gone; the infinitive is wanting.

Go (imperative), estapóht (*e* barely audible).

God, their god is the sun.

Good, achséh (*ach* guttural).

Great (tall, used of men), espitáh.

Green, kómonä.

Gun, náhmay (German).

Hair, same word as for head.

Hand, oh-ke-tïss (*i* almost like *u* umlaut).

Head, oh-tu-kuáhn (*kua* together).

Healthy, katäkiuaht; i.e., he has no sickness.

Heart, uskitsi-pachpé (second *i* barely audible; *ach* guttural).

Heat (it is hot), kristotisséh (*tis* very short).

Horn, ohtsihkinnah; the name of the animal is always added.

House (their lodges), moiéhs.

Hunger, nitóh-nontsi (*on* French).

Hunt (v), sáhme (*e* distinctly pronounced).

I, nistó.

Ice, sahkukotoh.

Kettle (iron), äski.

Knife, stoánn (*st* with the point of the tongue).

Laugh (v), ajimih (*ji* German).

Lead (musket ball), uaksopánn (*uak* together).

Leg, ohchkatt (*ohch* guttural).

Live (he still lives), sakeh-tapéh; i.e., he is still in the world.

Man, nahpe (*e* distinctly pronounced).

Meal (to eat?), oyé-ü (final *u* barely audible).

Moon, kokui-éta-úawakah (*ui* pronounced together).

Morning, skonnah-tonnih.

Mother, nikrist.

Mountain, messtäck.

Mouth, ma-å-ih (pronounced together).

Much, akajimm (German).

Negro, siksahpä-kuänn; i.e., a black Frenchman.

Night, kohkui (*ui* together).

Nose, ohkrississ.

Old (an old man), náhpe, or nahpi (final *e* or *i* short).

One-eyed, apáu (*au* together as in German).

People (two young people in love), netakka.

Pipe (tobacco), akuï-nimahn (German).

Powder (gun-powder), satsóhpats (German).

Quick (go quickly; hasten), kipanétsit.

Red, ahsahn.

Revenge (I have taken revenge), nitäht-skitáh.

River, omachkéh-táchtay (German throughout; *ach* guttural); i.e., a large river.

Sick, pastimmähsi, or aiochtokúh (*och* guttural).

Small, enakutsi (*kutsi* very short, almost *tsi*).

Smoke (n), sahtsïh.

Snow, kóhn.

Speak (v), äpuiéh (*ieh* pronounced together).

Spirits (distilled), stïoch-keh (*och* guttural; *st* with the point of the tongue).

Star, kakatóhs (German throughout).

Stingy, sickimisïh.

Stone (rock, or cliff), ohkotock.

Strong, miskapéh; i.e., a strong man; miss, a strong horse.

Sun, nantóhs (*an* French; otherwise German).

Sweet, the word does not occur; they say, good to eat, achséh (*ach* guttural).

Teeth, ochpéhkinn (*och* guttural).

Thunder, kristikúmm.

Tobacco, pistáchkan (*ach* together).

Tomahawk, kaksáhkin (German).

Tongue, matsinnih.

Track (trail), ochsokui (*och* guttural; *ui* together); a word is added to tell whether of men or a certain animal.

Trail, ochsokui (*och* guttural; *ui* together).

Ugly (not good), pachkápe (*ach* guttural; *e* full value).

War (to go out to war), sohóh.

Wash (v), siskiochsatis (German; *och* guttural).

Water, ochkéh (*och* German guttural).

Weep, auáhsann.

Widow, this word is wanting; they say in general, a woman who has no husband, náhmakeü (final *u* barely audible).

Wind, suppúy (*sup* almost like *sep*; the whole German).

Winter, this word is wanting; they say, the cold, stuyäh (German; *st* with the point of the tongue).

Woman, ah-ké.

Wood, mehstïss.

Yellow, otachkui (*ach* guttural; *ui* together).

Yes, aʹh.

Numerals

One, séh.

Two, náhtoka.

Three, nohóka.

Four, nehsohúi (*ui* together).

Five, nehsitó.

Six, nau (*u* and *a* separated; *u* indistinct).

Seven, äkitsikkům.

Eight, nahnisujïm (German throughout).

Nine, pehksúh.

Ten, kehpúh.

Twenty, náhtsipo.

Thirty, nehépu (*e* distinctly pronounced).

Forty, nehsïppu.

Fifty, nehsitsïppu.

Sixty, näʹhpu.

Seventy, äkitsikkïppu.

Eighty, nahnisïppu.

Ninety, pähksïppu.

Hundred, käpippu.

Thousand, kipipïppi.

Names of Animals

Antelope, auokáhs (*au* short and together).

Bear (black), sïku-kiäyu (German throughout).

Bear (grizzly), a'poch-kiäyu (*och* guttural).

Beaver, kéhstake (*e* pronounced distinctly).

Bighorn, ämach-kïkinägs; plural, ämach-kïkinä; from ämach, meaning large horns.

Buffalo (bull), stomïck.

Dog, emitá.

Elk, purnokähstomick.

Horse, purnaköimitä (*mita* short).

Moose, sikitisuh.

Mountain goat (white), apumachkikiná (*mach* German guttural).

Otter, emonähs.

Skunk, a'hpikaieh (*ah* accented; *pi* short).

Wolf (common gray), sikkapéhs.

Wolf (prairie), sehnipa'h.[241]

FOOTNOTES:

[240] Written from the pronunciation of the interpreter Berger, and several Blackfoot Indians.—MAXIMILIAN.

Comment by Ed. For Berger, see our volume xxiii, p. 23, note 11.

[241] The words from the Blackfoot language given by Gallatin (*ibid.*, p. 373), are for the most part, incorrectly written. We find, for instance, that in the word *pistachkan* the copyist avoided the guttural sound and wrote *pistarkan.* I must also remark here that Townsend in his *Narrative of a Journey across the Rocky Mountains to the Columbia River,* speaks in very exaggerated terms of the Blackfoot Indians. This is due to the fact that his information came from trappers and fur hunters who usually have the greatest respect for those Indians who are their bitterest enemies. On the other hand, what Townsend says of the injustice of the fur hunters towards these Indians is thoroughly justified.—MAXIMILIAN.

Comment by Ed. Townsend's Narrative is published in our volume xxi.

CHAYENNE (Shyenne of the Anglo-Americans)[242]

Arrow, mah-hóss.

Axe, jóh-ie-wúch (German throughout; *uch* guttural).

Bad, iháwa-süwa (very short).

Bow, máh-tachk (run together; *ch* guttural).

Bullet, wihóh-imáh-husch (the last three syllables are run together).

Cherries, máhmenuss.

Chief (leader), wǐh-hu (*hu* short; *u* between *o* umlaut and *u*).

Child, kaichkúnn (*ich* guttural).

Day, wawóhn.

Far (distant), háh-iss.

Father, nǐho-äh.

Fire, hoïsta.

Fire (to kindle a fire), dächo-ihäs (*ch* guttural).

God, okúhme (*e* ½).

Good, ipáua (*a* and *u* separated; final *e* very short).

Great (of bodies), hiáh-est (*hi* together; *ah* together; *est* distinctly pronounced).

Gun, mah-ah-tán (run together; *ma* short).

Head, mǐhk (*k* with a peculiar breathing).

Kettle (of metal), máï-taï-tó.

Knife, wó-tach-ke (*ach* guttural; *ke* very short).

Left-handed person, náhbuchs (*uch* guttural; *s* audible).

Little, o'ch-kumm (*och* guttural).

Man, itán.

Man (old), waháhkis (*kis* low).

Man (young), cassuáhä.

Mother, nachkuä (*ach* guttural).

Much, iháhstuch (*uch* guttural).

Near, kách-kiss (German; *ach* guttural).

On that side (of the river), ȯhhä-hohúmm.

On this side (of the river), ȯhhä-hastó.

One-eyed (a one-eyed man), ȯkinn.

Pipe (tobacco), hióchko (*och* guttural; *ko* almost like *ke*, *e* ½).

Poor (to be poor), staminóhha (*st* with the point of the tongue; *ha* very short; the whole run together).

Powder (gun-powder), páï.

River, ȯh-hä (pronounced as if *oh-o-ä*).

Rocky Mountains, Húh-hunáu (*nau* together).

Small (of bodies), ïkokesta (all syllables equal).

Sun, ischä̈.

Water, má-pe (*ma* nasal; *pe* short; *e* full value; the two syllables run together).

Weep (v), ïh-acháh (*ih* with emphasis; *ch* guttural).

Wife, hi-ïh-u (run together).

Woman (old), machta-máh-hä (*ach* guttural; the whole run together).

Comrade, I am going to sleep, húa-manna-aus (German throughout; *u* and *a* separated; accent on *u*; *aus* together).

Comrade, let us smoke, húa-hïhputt.

Comrade, take care of the kettle, hóa-niomüst-nomostetúnn.

Give to me, nïsta (*ta* short).

I have finished, ihïhs (with strong emphasis; abruptly ended).

Names of Animals

Antelope, wóh-ka (run together; *ka* lower).

Bear (grizzly), náchku (*ach* guttural).

Buffalo (bull), hottúe (*u* and *e* separated).

Buffalo (calf), wohksá (*sa* short).

Buffalo (cow), issiwóhn.

Dog, chotónn (*ch* guttural).

Elk, mo-úi (*ui* together).

Hedge-hog, ichtú-messïmm (*ich* German with the point of the tongue; *e* ½).

Horse, woindohámm (*oi* separated).

Mule, akéhm.

Wolf, hoh-nï (*ni* short).

Names of Indian Tribes

Arikkaras, Oḥnunnu (short).

Awatichay (village) [Minnitarri], Amatsichá.

Crows, Hóh-otann.

Dacotas, Oḥohma.

Mandans, Wïhwatann.

Minnitarris, Honúhn.

Minnitarris (the small village) [Ahwahnaway], Hahpeiu (*e* full value; *peiu* short and separated into two syllables).

Pahnis, Hóh-ni-tánn.

Ruhptare [Mandan village], Wóh-ah (run together).

FOOTNOTES:

[242] Written from the pronunciation of a Mandan Indian. The Chayennes call their nation Istayú (German pronunciation). Gallatin says (*ibid.*, p. 124) that they formerly lived on the Red River near Lake Winipik [Winnipeg]. They were driven out by the Sioux, according to Mc Kenzie, and now live at the sources of Chayenne River, a branch of the Missouri. What Gallatin states regarding the signatures of the treaty in the Dacóta language is something which repeatedly occurs, since there are frequently no interpreters for little-known nations, and recourse must be had to the translation of other Indians. I shall instance a similar case in connection with the Mandan language, where the signatures of a treaty were translated into the Minnitarri language by Charbonneau.—MAXIMILIAN.

CROW (Corbeau)[243]

Arm, aʹhdä.

Arrow, annúhtä.

Bow, mannáchi-iahsä (the last word even and lowered in tone).

Child, wah-káh-tä (run together).

Eye, ischtä.

Fire, biddä (short).

God (the ruler of life), búattä (*u* and *a* separated; *ta* short).

Hair, ichsïe (*ich* German with the point of the tongue; *si* and *e* separated; *e* ½ and short; *i* with strong accent).

Hand, ischsä.

Head, aʹnschua (*an* French; *sch* and *u* separated; *a* short).[244]

Man, matsä.

Moon, minitásia (*sia* short and low; *i* and *a* a little separated).

Mouth, ïh-a (*a* very short and ½; pronounced together).

Pipe (tobacco), ïimpsä (accent on the first *i*; separated from the second *i*).

Star, ichkä.

Sun, achá-se (run together; *se* distinctly pronounced but short).

Tomahawk, manïhtsip-ihpse (*an* French; *e* distinctly pronounced).

Water, minä.

White-man, máeste-schïhrä; literally yellow-eye.

Woman (wife), mïa (*mi* run together; *a* separated; the whole short).

FOOTNOTES:

[243] Written from the pronunciation of a Crow Indian. They pronounce the words in the manner of the Minnitarri; *ch* is guttural, *r* is spoken with the point of the tongue unless there is an exception noted. According to Donald Mc Kenzie who lived among the Crows (Gallatin, *ibid.*, p. 125), they number some three hundred lodges and three thousand souls. This seems to me to be a correct estimate.—MAXIMILIAN.

Comment by Ed. Gallatin doubtless intends Kenneth (not Donald) Mc Kenzie, for whom see our volume xxi, p. 45, note 25.

[244] According to Captain Bonneville, it is called *popo* in the Crow language; this does not agree with my experience.—MAXIMILIAN.

Comment by Ed. This refers to Washington Irving, *Rocky Mountains; or Scenes, Incidents and Adventures in the Far West* (Philadelphia, 1837).

DACOTA (Sioux) of the band of the Yanktonans[245]

American, Mïna-haska (*haska* nasal); i.e., Long Knife.

Arm, istó.

Arrow, uahïtpe (*ua* nasal).

Beard, putä-hin (*n* French; *hin* nasal).

Bird, sitká (*s* soft).

Black, sáhpa.

Blind, ischtá-chon-gä (*ch* guttural; *on* French; *g* in the roof of the mouth; *chonga* nasal and without emphasis).

Blood, uäh.

Blue (also green), tóh.

Bone, huh-huh.

Bow, itáh-sipa (*itah* with emphasis; *si* very short; *pa* without emphasis).

Brave (adj), uadïtake (*uadi* with emphasis; *e* ½ or a little more; *take* lower and without emphasis).

Brook, uathpanne (*e* short).

Brother, tschï-ä (emphasis on the first syllable).

Child, okschiókapa.

Cold, snïh.

Dance (v), uatschï.

Day, hanposka (*an* French).

Deaf, nóchät-pá.

Die (dead), táh.

Door, thiópa (*i* and *o* somewhat separated).

Dumb (v), ihéschni (*ni* short).

Dream (v), uihamana (*ui* together; *hamana* short and rapid).

Drink (v), uatkan (*an* French).

Ear, nónchä (*on* French; emphasis on *non*; *ch* guttural; low and short).

Earth, manká (*an* French).

Enemy, tohk-ha.

Englishman, Sakedaschi (*e* short; *i* barely audible).

Evening, chta-ié-tu (*chta* guttural; *ie* together; *tu* short).

Eye, ischtá; one-eyed, pschtat-pä.

Father, atä; i.e., my father.

Feather, uï-iak-ha (*ha* guttural; *iakha* low and short).

Fight (n), ketschehsap (first *e* short).

Fire, pähta.

Fish, rochan (very guttural; *an* French).

Flesh, tadó.

Fog, pó (*o* full).

Forest, tchán (*an* French).

Frenchman, Uaschïdjo (*jo* French and very short).

Friend (comrade), kotdá (great friend); or ketschïuah (friend).

Go (v), máhni (*ni* short).

God (the creator), uakán-tanka (*an* French nasal); i.e., great spirit.[246]

Good, uaschtä (*ua* almost like *wa*; run together).

Great, hánska (*an* French).

Green, tóh (*o* rather full).

Gun, mansak-han (*an* French; the whole run together).

Hair, pihï.

Hand, napä.

Head, páh.

Healthy, uaschtä; or uaiá-saschni (last word short and low); i.e., not sick.

Heart, tschåtä.

Heat, didïtach (*ach* German guttural).

Horns (antlers; and horns of all animals in general), hä; the name of the animal is added.

House (lodge), tihpi.

Hunger, wóta-wacheda (all syllables of second word even).

Hunt (v), uïheni (*e* short; the whole indistinct, short, nasal, and run together).

I, miä.

Ice, tschága (*g* in the roof of the mouth).

Island, uïhta (*u* and *i* separated; *ta* short).

Jar (pot), tschäga (*g* guttural; *ga* short).

Knife, mïhna (*na* short).

Laugh (v), icháh (*ch* guttural).

Lead (metal), mansassuh (*an* French).

Leg, húh.

Lightning, uakán-hädï(*an* French; *hadi* short).

Live (life?), uanickt.

Lodge or tent (of leather), wakäa.

Man, uïtscha.[247]

Meal(to eat?), wóhta (*ta* short).

Moccasin, hánpa (French).

Moon, hahépi-uïh (first word rather nasal).

Morning, hïh-hanna (emphasis on *hih*; *hanna* low and short).

Mother, inan (*an* French).

Mountain, chä (*ch* guttural).

Mouth, ih.

Much, öhta (*o* full; *ta* short).

Negro, uaschïtschu-sáhpa (run together).

Night, hanhöp (*an* French).

Nose, póhchä (*ch* guttural; *a* short).

Pipe (tobacco), schandúh-hupa (*hupa* short and low, without emphasis).

Powder, tschachedï (*ch* guttural).

Quick, kohán (*an* French).

Red, duhta.

Revenge (v), itoh-kidjuh (emphasis on first word; *j* French; second word lower).

River, uathpá; the Missouri, Uathpá-mnischoschá; i.e., the river with muddy water.

Sick, uaiasa (short).

Small, tihstina.

Smoke (n), schóhta (*o* full; *ta* short).

Snow, uáh.

Speak (v), jáh (*i* and *a* separated).

Spirits (distilled), menïh-uakán (*an* French); i.e. divine, or medicine water.

Star, tscháchpi (*ach* guttural).

Stingy, ochań-schitscha (*ochan* with emphasis; second word without emphasis; the whole short and run together).

Stone, ihia (emphasis on *i*; nasal).

Strong, waschahke (*e* ½; *ke* short).

Sun, uïh.

Sweet, skúia (*sk* with the point of the tongue).

Teeth, ïh.

Thunder, uakïn-a (*n* French, nasal; *a* short).

Tobacco, tschandïh (*an* French).

Tomahawk, onspä-tschanupa (final word without emphasis and lower).

Toothache, ih-asan (*asan* French).

Trader, wópäton-uïtschásta (*o* full; *on* French; last word short).

Trail, tschankuh.

Ugly, schïdja (*ja* French).

Village, otón-a (*on* French; *a* short; the whole nasal).

War, suiá (*s* soft).

Warmth, pätïschka.

Wash (v), waiújaja (*jaja* French, without emphasis, and low; *iu* German).

Water, menïh.

Weep (v), tschäa (final *a* short).

White, skáh.

Widow, juá-sitscha (*j* and *u* separated).

Wind, tatäh.

Winter, uanïete (*u* and *a* separated; *e* very short in both cases).

Woman, uïïa (*ui* nasal).

Wood, tschan (*an* French).

Yellow, sïh (softly pronounced).

Yes, haṅn (French nasal).

Numerals

One, wántscha (*an* French).

Two, nómpa (*om* French).

Three, jámen (*men* German and low).

Four, tópa (*o* full).

Five, sáhptan (*s* very soft; *an* French).

Six, scháhkpe (*pe* short; *e* ½).

Seven, schakoï (*o* and *i* separated).

Eight, schákedoch (German).

Nine, nahptschï-uanká (*uan* nasal; *n* French; last word without emphasis, nasal, and low; the whole run together and short).

Ten, uïktschémna (*u* and *i* separated; *na* short).

Twenty, numm.

Twenty-one, uïktschemna-nom-sommuaji (the whole run together and short; *ji* French).

Thirty, jamen.

Forty, toop; or toom.

Fifty, sáhpta.

Sixty, scháhkpe.

Seventy, schakoï.

Eighty, schakedoch.

Ninety, nahptschiuanká.

Hundred, opánuachä (*an* French; *u* and *a* separated; *ch* guttural; the whole run together and short; *uacha* nasal).

Thousand, iktó-panuachä (*an* French; the whole run together and short).

I eat, uauáhta (*u* and *a* separated).

You eat, uayáta (German).

He eats, uóhtä (*u* and *o* like *w*; *o* full; *ta* short).

We eat, óntape (in pronouncing *tape* the voice falls; *pe* distinctly pronounced).

They eat, uóhtapä (*o* full).

I shall eat, uauáhtäkta (*u* and *a* separated; *takta* low and without emphasis).

I have eaten, uauáhta.

I had eaten, hähan-uauáhta (*an* French).

I would eat, hähan-uauáhta-net-schetscha (last word short and rapid).

Eat (imperative), uóhta-io (together; *o* full).

Eating, uóh-tä-sa (*sa* short).

Names of Animals

Antelope, tatóhka; or tatókana (*na* rather inaudible).

Bear, (black), uachánk-sitscha (emphasis on *chank*; *sitscha* low).

Bear (grizzly), mantó (*an* French).

Beaver, tscháhpa (*pa* short).

Bighorn, kihská.

Buffalo (bull), tatánka; cow, ptäh; calf, ptäh-sidja (*j* French); the general word is that for cow.

Dog, schónka (*on* French).

Elk, upán (*pan* nasal; *an* French); this is the general word.

Elk (stag), acháhka (*ch* guttural).

Horse, schónka-uakán (*on* and *an* French): erratum says read ïhia.

Otter, ptán (*an* French).

Skunk, mankáh (*an* French, very short, and barely audible; *kah* loud and with emphasis).

Turkey (wild), sisitscha-kanka (*s* soft; *kan* in the throat).

Wolf, schuk-tóketscha-tanka.

Wolf (prairie), mïhtschak-sïh.

FOOTNOTES:

[245] Gallatin writes "Dahcota;" but I think that it is more correct to write Dacóta. He divides the Sioux into a northern and a southern group; and includes in the latter division eight tribes, the Quappas, or Arkansas at the mouth of the Arkansa river, the Osages, the Kansas, the Ayowäs (Jowas), the Missouris, Otos, Omáhas, and Puncas, since they speak dialects of the Dacóta language (Gallatin, *ibid.*, p. 127).—MAXIMILIAN.

[246] Not *wakatunka*, as Vail says. This name is composed of two words; and, therefore, is not to be written as one. The first word, *uakan*, less correctly *wakan*, is the expression for god, divine, supernatural; the second, *tanka*, not *tunka*, means great. Vail and others also very often write *uakan*, incorrectly *wah-kon*. The Dacóta words which I give here are written from the pronunciation of the half-breed interpreter, Ortubize.—MAXIMILIAN.

Comment by Ed. This reference is to Eugene A. Vail, *Notice sur les Indiens de l'Amerique du Nord* (Paris, 1840).

[247] Mr. Gallatin (*ibid.*, p. 195) thinks that the word *uitschá* is an abbreviation of *uitschasta*. I cannot decide the question with certainty. The singular number, man, was always given to me as *uitscha*; *uitschasta* seems to me to be the plural, or a general term, as for instance, in the word *uitschasta-iuta*, man eater.—MAXIMILIAN.

DACOTA of the Teton Tribe

Antelope, tatóhkana.

Bear (black), wåchánk-sitscha (the first word with emphasis).

Bear (grizzly), matóh.

Comb, ipáhks.

Day (the day breaks), àm-pa-inam-pä (*am* French; *pa* short).

Elk, upán (*an* French and rather long); the stag, hächáhka.

Fish-hook, hoïtzua (*o* and *i* separated).

Fish-line, hachóhta (*ch* guttural).

Hoop (of wood), sankodeska.

Hoop (game of), sankodeska-kutépi.

Moccasins, hán-pa (*an* French).

Morning (early), àm-pa (*am* French).

Prairie dog, pispïsa.

Rattle (sysyquoy, gourd rattle), tascháhka.

Shield, oahát-sanka (first word with emphasis; last word low and without emphasis).

Water, menïh.[248]

FOOTNOTES:

[248] The variations in the different tribes of the Dacótas seem to be very insignificant.—MAXIMILIAN.

FALL INDIANS, or Grosventres of the Prairies[249]

Antelope, hottewianinay (*ay* German).

Arm, nah-köth (the syllables separated).

Arrow, nennitch (*ch* with the point of the tongue and not guttural).

Bear (black), uatániss.

Bear (grizzly), uosse (*uo* like *wo*; *e* very short).

Beaver, hábass (*a* almost like *a* umlaut, but ½ and short).

Bighorn, hottéh.

Black, wå-atåh-nits (*wa* short; *atah-nits* a little lisped).

Blood, mah-ahtz.

Bow, nemáth (*e* ½).

Buffalo (bull), enáhkiä (*e* barely audible; *kia* like *kie*, short and ½).

Buffalo (cow), büh.

Child, täyalle (all syllables cut rather short and separated; *e* ½).

Day, ehse (*eh* long; *se* very short).

Deer (black-tailed), bühe-i (*e* ½; *i* short).

Deer (common), låsikge (*ge* German; *e* ½).

Dog, hótewi.

Ear, nenottónnü (*ton* with emphasis; *e* ½).

Earth, meth-auuch (*au* together; *auuch* very short).

Elk, uósseh.

Eye, ne-séh-seh (*ne* short and ½; accent on the first *seh*).

Fire, esittah (*e* very short).

Foot, nesse-estan (*se* short and ½; *tan* French and distinct).

God, mehåa (*e* short; the two *a*'s separated).

Hair, näwi-táss (*tass* with emphasis).

Hand, nah-kettinach (rather indistinct).

Head, nöth-ah (indistinct; *ah* separated).

Heart, nöttah.

Hot, be-ke-néh-se (*be* rather longer; *ke* short; *neh* very long; *se* short).

Ice, wå-awuh.

Leg, na-áhtz (*na* short and ½; *ahtz* long).

Man, nenïtta (*e* and *a* short).

Moon, kahå-hássa (together).

Mountain goat (white), otteh-nozïbi (*zibi* short).

Mouth, nöt-ti (*ti* rather lower).

Night, taiké-ee (*ee* separated and distinctly pronounced).

Nose, nä-es (*es* ½ and low).

Pipe (tobacco), eht-tsá.

Rain, a-sá-nitz (lisped).

Snow, ïh-i (*ih* very long; *i* short).

Star, áto (*o* almost like *o* umlaut).

Sun, ehsïss.

Tomahawk, aha-loss.

Water, netse (*e* very short).

Wolf, kïatïssa (indistinct).

Woman, ésta (*es* lisped).

FOOTNOTES:

[249] Written from their pronunciation. They call their tribe, Ähni-ninn. Gallatin (*ibid.*, p. 125) speaks of them in connection with the Minnitarris. He calls them the Rapid, Fall, or Paunch Indians; and remarks quite correctly, that from the latest information their language is wholly different from those of the Minnitarris and Blackfeet (*ibid.*, p. 132).—MAXIMILIAN.

FLATHEADS of the Rocky Mountains[250]

Arrow, tah-pu-minn.

Bear, semachann (*ch* guttural).

Beaver, skaló.

Bow, soh-nónn; same word as for gun.

Buffalo, zotúnn (soft low, and indistinct; *o* full).

Child, skochkússa (*ch* guttural; *sa* low and indistinct).

Deer, zinechkóhch (*ch* guttural; the whole indistinct and low).

Dog, nachketsä (*e* short).

Ear, tchäh-säuonn.

Earth, sopúth.

Elk, chton-skutsiss (*ch* guttural; the whole indistinct and low).

Eye, ehsuetst.

Fire, stehchke (*st* with the point of the tongue; *ch* guttural; final *e* ½).

Foot, tah-essïnn (*e* ½).

God, inuméhcho (*i* like *e*; *ch* guttural).

Head, estáchk (*es* soft; *ch* guttural).

Man, taiskáltomo (little emphasis and low).

Moon, ehs-pach-kann (low and in the roof of the mouth).

Mouth, onuchuaye (*ch* guttural; final *e* ½).

Pipe (tobacco), simäh-noch (*simah* short; *noch* guttural; little emphasis).

Star, skoch-koiomm (low and run together; *och* guttural).

Sun, ehs-pach-kann (low and in the roof of the mouth).

Tomahawk, soh-nónn.

Water, saotuch (low; *ch* guttural).

Woman, semääm (*e* ½; *a* and *a* separated).

FOOTNOTES:

[250] Written from the pronunciation of the Blackfoot chief, Ninoch-Kiäïu. The Flatheads live in the Rocky mountains; and according to the missionary, Parker, number only eight hundred souls. They are said to speak the same language as the Ponderas [Pend d'Oreille] and Spokein [Spokan] Indians. The custom of flattening the head by pressure is not found among them, at least at present (Townsend, *op. cit.*, p. 175); but this is done by several tribes on the Columbia as is stated also in *Astoria*. All travellers who have visited this people bear witness to their upright and noble conduct, as well as to their piety. Like the Nez-Percés, of whom the same is said, they have borrowed a number of Christian usages and beliefs, among them the conscientious observance of Sunday (see *Adventures of Captain Bonneville*, p. 248; and Ross Cox). They are reputed to be brave warriors; of this I was assured by the Blackfoot Indians themselves, who are often at war with them and are their bitterest enemies, and who also showed me many trophies taken from them.—MAXIMILIAN.

Comment by Ed. Samuel Parker, *Journal of an Exploring Tour beyond the Rocky Mountains* (Ithaca, N. Y., 1838). See also our volume xxi, p. 335, note 112; Washington Irving, *Astoria* (Philadelphia, 1836); Ross Cox, *Adventures upon the Columbia River* (London, 1831); and our volume vi, p. 276, note 84.

Arm, nenächkonn (*ach* guttural).

Arrow, pequikihi.

Belly, näjäck (*j* French).

Bow, måstahá (*a* between *a* umlaut and *o* umlaut; *ha* often barely audible).

Breast (the whole) ne-kå̊-kä (*ka* short).

Ear, nettouakaian (*ua* nasal; *kaian* likewise).

Eye, neskescheck.

Foot, nekåtan (*n* distinctly pronounced).

Hair, ninessónn.

Hand, nenächkonn (*ach* in the roof of the mouth).

Head, nehch (German).

Knife, peskoatéska (*ka* without emphasis).

Knife (long), måtatä.

Leg, nemóttata (*a* somewhat as if with umlaut).

Leggings, nekóchkuahan (*och* German guttural).

Mouth, netohn.

Nail (on the hand), näskóssähk.

Nose, näkiuónn.

Pipe (tobacco), póakan (emphasis on *poa*).

Skunk, schekakw (*w* barely audible).

Sun, kischess.

Teeth, nepitonn.

Thunder, kä̊hschko (*kahsch* slightly drawled).

Tobacco, nessåman (*an* French).

Tomahawk, popokiä.

Tongue, ninónni.

Water, neppé (final *e* somewhat like *a* umlaut).

<h2 style="text-align:center">*Numerals*</h2>

One, näkút.

Two, nïhsw (*w* barely audible).

Three, nássue (*sue* like *we*).

Four, niäua (nasal).

Five, nianan (nasal).

Six, noiká.

Seven, nohiká (nasal; *ka* short).

Eight, nessua-siká (*ka* short).

Nine, schohaká (*schoha* indistinct; *ka* short).

Ten, metaa-tue (*e* short).

FOOTNOTES:

[251] Written from the pronunciation of a Kïckapu. These Indians speak the same language as the Saukis and Foxes. According to Gallatin (*ibid.*, p. 62), they do not now number over five hundred souls. They all live at present west of the Mississippi.—MAXIMILIAN.

<h2 style="text-align:center">KONSA[252]</h2>

Arrow, måh.

Bear (black), uåssóbä.

Child, schïnga-schïnga.

Earth, móhnika (*n* nearly like *h*).

Eye, ischtá.

Fire, pähdjé (*j* French).

God, wahkóhdagä.

Hair, på-hï.

Hand, nom-pö́ (*om* French).

Head, påh.

Island, rumätschï.

Man, niká.

Mountain, påhü.

Mouth, hüh.

Pipe (tobacco), nåh-hi-ba.

River, wâtïschka (*t* often like *h*).

Sun, pih.

Tomahawk, må-sospä-jingá (*j* French).

Water, nih.

Woman (wife), wåh-ko.

FOOTNOTES:

[252] The Konsas, or Kansas Indians have always lived on the river of that name (Gallatin, *ibid.*, p. 127). For the past thirty years they have lived at peace with the Osages; and the two tribes have intermarried. They still number fifteen hundred souls, and possess a tract of three thousand acres. They speak the Osage dialect, which belongs to the Dacota linguistic group.—·MAXIMILIAN.

KRIH, or Knistenau[253]

American (an), Ketsemohkoman (*e* short and ½; otherwise German).

Arm, ospetonn.

Arrow, atúss.

Autumn, taquáhkinn.

Bird, piesiss (*i* and *e* separated; *e* full value).

Black (the color), kaskitähsu (*su* short).

Blind, nanon-skïssiko (*on* French).

Blood, mich-kó (*mich* short, like *mi*).

Blue, kaskitähuakinn.

Bone, oskánn; plural is oskanná.

Bow, adsabï (*adsa* soft).

Brave (adj), sohketäheu (*e* ½; *eu* short; *u* barely audible).

Brook, sihpi-siss.

Brother (elder), nistååhs.

Brother (younger), nissim.

Child, auáhsis (*sis* short and low).

Cold (adj), kesinnau (*e* ½; *au* German and together).

Dance (v), neméhetu (second *e* ½; *tu* short).

Day, uapánn.

Deaf, kakehpi-teu (*pi* like *pich*, guttural; *e* and *u* separated).

Devil (evil spirit), matsimann-tuh (short and run together).

Die (v), nepúh.

Dog, atïmm.

Drink (v), menih-kuä (final syllable short).

Dumb, namanich-tauéu (*manich* short and guttural; *e* and *u* separated).

Ear, ochtauakay (*ch* guttural; *aua* separated; *kay* German, with the rest of the word).

Earth, askï.

Enemy, ayachzïnuack (German; *a* barely audible).

Englishman, Hakaiahsu.

Evening, otahgusinn (*gu* German).

Eye, oskïhsick.

Father, nochtauï (*noch* nasal; *ch* German, but barely audible).

Feather, meh-koánn (*koann* very short and run together).

Fire, skuttéhu (*u* barely audible).

Fish, kinussäu (*au* separated and short).

Flesh, wuïäs (*wui* almost like *wi* or *ui*).

Forest, sakao (*a* and *o* separated).

Frenchman, Wemstegosó (German; second *e* short).

Go (v), pümontä.

God, keseh-mann-tóh (first *e* short).

Good, mioassih.

Great, kïnussuh.

Green, zipätákassu.

Gun, pasksigan (soft).

Hair, uästöchaiah (rather indistinct).

Hand, otsä-tschih.

Head, ustekuáhn (*us* very short).

Healthy, namoyáhkussu (*kussu* low and short).

Heart, otä.

Heat, ksasteo (*eo* short and half pronounced).

Horns (of a stag), hähskann.

Horse, mesatimm (*e* ½).

House (lodge), uaskaëgan; i.e., house of the white man; matsehkin, a leather tent.

Hunger, notä-keteu (*keteu* short; *u* barely audible).

Hunt (v), máhtsíu (*u* barely audible).

I, neia' (emphasis on *ia*, which is very short).

Ice, miskuami.

Knife, mohchkumann (*ch* barely audible, guttural).

Laugh (v), páh-piu (*i* barely audible).

Lead (ball), mosasinnï.

Leg, oskáht.

Lightning, uauase-skutä-paiú (*e* ½; emphasis on second word; last word lower).

Live (v; life?), pemah-tesuh (second *e* ½).

Man, hiyenú.

Meal (to eat?), meh-tsú (*tsu* very short).

Moon, tepiskao-pissïmm (*o* barely audible).

Morning, kichsäpah.

Mother, enkauï (*e* barely audible).

Mountain, uatsih.

Mouth, otóhn.

Much, meh-zett.

Negro, keskiteuias (*e* short and ½; *e* and *u* separated).

Night, tipskao (*a* and *o* separated).

Nose, uskiuánn.

One-eyed, páskahpu (*pu* short).

Pipe (tobacco), spoagánn (soft).

Powder (gun-powder), kaskitéu (*e* and *u* separated).

Quick, kiépa (*e* ½; *pa* short; *i* and *e* separated).

Red (the color), mechkossúh (*ch* barely audible and with the point of the tongue).

Relate (v), ah-tsimo (last word short).

River, kistsissibi.

Sick, ahkussú.

Small, apsáhsinn (*sin* very short and without emphasis).

Smoke, (n), kaskaba-teu (*e* and *u* separated).

Snow, kóhna (*na* short).

Spirits (distilled), skutä-uapui (*pui* run together).

Spring (the season), meiuskamin (short; *n* French; *in* almost like *i* nasal).

Star, atsah-kossack (short and run together).

Stingy, sasahkiu (*i* and *u* separated).

Stone, assiniack (*i* and *a* separated).

Summer, nehpïnn.

Sun, pisïmm.

Teeth, uïpitt.

Thunder, piéh-su (pronounced together; *su* without emphasis).

Tobacco (smoking), tstäman (*an* French).

Tomahawk, tschïga-hïka-spoagánn.

Tongue, uttäh-enï (*e* ½).

Trail, mäskanó.

Tub (barrel?), machkaak (*ch* guttural).

Tub (small), mach-kach-kuss (*ch* guttural).

Ugly, mayahtan.

War, notintuock (*u* and *o* separated and barely audible).

Water, nipï.

White (color), wahpiskesu (*e* ½).

Wind, jeotïnn (*ie* German; run together).

Winter, pöpúnn or pipúhn.

Woman (wife), iskwäu (*au* separated; *u* barely audible).

Wood, mistick.

Yellow, ussáussu (*a* and *u* separated).

Yes, ähä.

I eat, nemitsonn.

You eat, kimitsonn.

He eats, meh-dsú (*ds* soft).

We eat, nemitsunann.

They eat, mit-sú.

Eat (imperative), mihtissú.

Months of the Year

They reckon the months from one full moon to the next. [The order here given is that of the original.—ED.]

November, Kaskattinoh-pisimm; i.e., the ice moon.

December, Kaie-iequatä-pisimm.

January, Kesäh-pisimm (*e* ½); i.e., the big moon.

February, Paua-zakenassis-pisimm (*a* and *u* separated; *za* short and like *a*); i.e., the moon which shakes the trees.

March, Mekssiuh-pisimm (*e* short and ½; *siuh* almost like *suh*); i.e., the moon when the eagle comes.

----, Niski-pisimm; i.e., the moon of the wild geese.

----, Ayiki-pisimm; i.e., the moon of the frogs.

May, Opineya-uäu-pisimm (*uau* separated), i.e., moon when the birds lay their eggs.

June, Opaskoh-pisimm; i.e., the moon when the geese shed their feathers.

July, Oochpahoh-pisimm (*ooch* guttural); i.e., moon when the birds fly.

----, Onont-chicheto (*on* French; *tch* with the point of the tongue; *e* ½); i.e., moon when the buffalo is in heat.

October, Opinna-skoh-pisimm; i.e., the moon when the leaves fall.

Numerals

One, pähek (*e* ½).

Two, nehsu.

Three, nistó.

Four, neó (*e* and *o* separated).

Five, neanann (*e* full value and separated from *a*).

Six, nguttuahsick (*n* barely audible).

Seven, tähpakup (*up* like *uffp*).

Eight, aehnaneu (*a* and *e* separated; *ne* and *u* separated and short).

Nine, kähkametatatt (*e* ½).

Ten, mitahtat.

Twenty, nehsittano.

Hundred, mitahtat-tamittanoh.

Thousand, kich-tche-mta-tach-tommetano (*ich*, *tch*, and *ch* with the point of the tongue; *e* ½).

Names of Animals

Antelope, apestat-jéhkus (*e* ½; *j* French; *jeh* with emphasis; *kus* low and without emphasis).

Bear (black), kaskitäh-maskuá (*kua* German).

Bear (grizzly), uapïh-maskuá.

Beaver, amïsk.

Buffalo, mostúss; the general term.

Buffalo (bull), japöh-mostúss.

Buffalo (cow), onintcháh-oniuack.

Elk, uauasskéhsu (*su* short and barely audible).

Elk (stag), eyapeu-uauasskéhsu.

Fox, machkéhsiss (*ach* guttural).

Otter, nikïtt.

Skunk, sikáhk.

A Few Phrases

Sit down, a-péh.

Sit down and smoke, a-péh-pih-tuá.

Sit down and smoke and relate to us, a-péh-pit-tuá-ah-tsimo.

Whence do you come? tan-täh-kotuch-tann (*ch* guttural).

FOOTNOTES:

[253] Written from the pronunciation of a Krih Indian.—MAXIMILIAN.

KUTANÄ, or Kutnehä[254]

Arm, achkusóttis (indistinct; *ach* guttural).

Arrow, a'hk (*k* prolonged as a guttural).

Black, kamokoch-kukossni (*ch* guttural; the whole very short and indistinct).

Blood, uann-muh (short and run together).

Blue, confused by most tribes with green and given the same name.

Bow, züpil (*i* very short, indistinct, and almost like *e*).

Child, skámmu (low and soft, guttural).

Cold (adj), uanéht.

Day, kiukiet (indistinct).

Dead, epinih.

Ear, akochkuates (*ch* guttural).

Earth, ám-ma.

Eye, akaksisches (*es* distinctly pronounced).

Fire, akingkóko (indistinct).

Foot, achksikkis (*ch* guttural; *k* clicked with the tongue; final *i* like *e*).

God, núma.

Green, kekochmacha (*ch* guttural; *e* ½).

Hair, akuksammus (*k* lisped with the tongue).

Hand, achkehs (low and guttural).

Head, achksemnis (*k* lisped; indistinct, short).

Heart, achkissuehs (*ch* guttural).

Hot, jaehsukket.

Ice, áchkuitt.

Leg, akesokkes (*e* barely audible).

Man, aks-macki (a slight pause after *aks*).

Moon, same word as for sun.

Mouth, achkesmaës (*ach* guttural; *s* lisped).

Night, zesmuiet (indistinct; *iet* like *et*, distinctly pronounced but short).

Nose, achkúnes (*es* distinct; *ch* guttural).

Pipe (tobacco), achkússa (*ch* and the whole guttural and low).

Rain, esuch-kukuttunn (very short and indistinct; guttural).

Red, kanóhs (*a* almost like *e*; short and low).

Snow, achksoh (*ks* like *sch* with a clicking of the tongue).

Star, akisnohs (*s* with a peculiar clicking sound).

Sun, natánnik (*k* barely audible, only a slight guttural sound).

Tomahawk, achkensä (*ks* with a clicking of the tongue, like *sch*).

Water, woh (short and abruptly ended).

White, kamonuckso (*so* with a clicking of the tongue).

Woman, páski (*ki* low and short).

Yellow, kemacktze (first *e* ½; final *e* distinctly pronounced).

Names of Animals

Antelope, nestukp.

Bear (black), népke.

Bear (grizzly), ksaus (German; *s* with a clicking of the tongue, like *sch*).

Beaver, sïnna.

Bighorn, kuisskussä (*kus* short and indistinct).

Buffalo, jiámmo (first *i* barely audible).

Deer, zupka (*u* between *u* and *o*).

Deer (black-tailed), aknesnïnk (*s* like *schw*).

Dog, cháhtsin (*ch* guttural; *a* almost as if with umlaut).

Elk, keskásse (*sk* with a clicking of the tongue).

Mountain goat (white), zenúchcho (*ch* guttural; the whole run together).

Wolf, kachki, or kachkin (*ch* guttural).[255]

FOOTNOTES:

[254] Written from the pronunciation of the old Kutanä Indian, Hómach-Ksáchkum, the Great Earth, of whom a most excellent likeness is given on Plate 79 of my Atlas. I have spoken of this people in several places in the first volume of this work. Parker (*ibid.*, p. 304) says of the Kutonäs, Kutnehäs, or Kutanihs: "The Cootanies inhabit a section of country to the north of the Ponderas along M'Gillivray's river, and they are represented as an uncommonly interesting people. They speak a language distinct from all the tribes about them, open and sonorous, and free from gutturals, which are common in the language of the surrounding tribes. They are neat in their persons and lodges, candid and honest, and kind to each other. I could not ascertain their numbers, but probably they are not over a thousand." In Ross Cox, (p. 242), there is also information regarding them; but the missionary Parker (*ibid.*, p. 286) seems to call this traveller's truthfulness in question. From my carefully copied words of the Kutanä language, it is evident that it is not easy to pronounce on account of its lingual clicking; and that it has a large number of guttural tones.—MAXIMILIAN.

[255] The Kutanäs, or Kutunäs, also Kutnehäs, dwell in the Rocky mountains beyond the sources of Maria river; and on their mountains lives

the white mountain goat. They are said to call themselves Kutonachä; the French know them as Coutonais; and the Blackfeet call them Kutanä. They are few in number, having only some forty lodges. Among their ornaments they highly prize cylinders cut from mussel-shells, especially those cut from the shell of the dentalium, which they obtain from the western seacoast. The Blackfeet, especially the Blood Indians, are their declared enemies. They do not live on the flesh of the buffalo, which is not found in their mountains; but in their country many beaver are obtained, excellent fish (trout), and several other species of animals, especially the orignal (*cervus alces amer.*), the white mountain goat, and the bighorn; also many kinds of roots and berries serve them as food. They raise large numbers of strong and handsome horses; they are well clothed; and are expert beaver hunters. They are skilful in making bows and arrows. Their language is difficult to learn. The words are spoken softly and indistinctly; in addition there are many clicking tones and hollow gutturals; and they also lisp.—MAXIMILIAN.

MANDAN, or Númangkake[256]

Abode (dwelling place), iwakschúntusch.

Above, a'hkitta.

Abyss (precipice), pähúsch.

Ahead, untihäddisch (*un* French, like *oun*).

Aim (v; take aim), mitáhrusch.

All (everything), ekúnhä (*n* French, like *oun*); all men, or people, a'mbä (*m* French).

Alone, ji'cha (*ch* guttural).

Always, amánkahu-sch (*an* French; *husch* run together as a final syllable).

American (n), Mánhichtä (*an* French; *ch* guttural); i.e., Long Knife.

Animal (quadruped), wáhockschukkä.

Another, táhonsch (*on* French; *honsch* lower and shorter than *ta*).

Anxiety (fear), wohkarachka (*ch* guttural).

Approach stealthily (v), cherúhradéhusch (*che* guttural; *r* with the point of the tongue).

Arm, a'hdä.

- 190 -

Arrow, manna-máh-hä (the whole pronounced together).

Ashes, uáraschuntä.

Ask (v), kiimáhche-sch (*ch* guttural).

Awake (v, intr), ïwakschuntusch (*un* German).

Awake (v, tr), kittáhrusch.

Axe, oʻhmanatä.

Back (n), (v; to move with a jerk?), nápp-chä (*ch* guttural).

Back (adv), kirïje (*je* French); i.e., he is back, (*il est deretour*).

Backward, naschïtta (*ta* short).

Bad, warákä-ächkasch (*e* full value).

Bald, pah-e-sérroko-sch (*e* ½ and barely audible).

Ball (for playing), mihp-toht-kisch (pronounce together); the game is called by the same name.

Ball (same word as for lead), uáhtöschemáhhä (*o* almost like *e*; *e* only ½).

Ball-game of the women, miʻhptott-käʻ; ball, miʻhptodäʻ.

Basket (leather; used by women for carrying), chäʻhank (*ch* guttural).

Bear (v; give birth), éhtu-sch (*eh* long).

Beard, hïh.

Beautiful, schïnaschusch.

Behind, náschitero (*e* distinctly pronounced).

Belly, äʻhchi (*ah* long and accented; *ch* guttural).

Below (beneath), mánpeta (*an* French; *e* ½; *ta* short).

Bend (v), kihskóppohärrisch (*arrisch* barely audible).

Berdash, miʻhdäckä.

Beside (near), mipächtihsch (*ach* guttural).

Best (man), koschïsch (final *sch* slightly hissed).

Between, nastá.

Big with young, same word as for pregnant.

Bile (the yellow water on the stomach), wáh-sih-dä (*da* low and short).

Bill (bill or beak of a bird), same word as for nose.

Billiard game (Billard-spiel), skóhpe (*e* ½).

Bird, mándeck-sukkä (*an* French); wild-fowl, menickä.

Bite (v), naschä-sch (run together; *ch* slightly hissed).

Bitter, páhrusch.

Black, psïh.

Bladder, ïhdächä (*ch* guttural).

Blind (adj), istá-chädetosch (*ch* guttural; *chade* short; the whole run together).

Blond, pahïn-sïhdusch (*n* French; *hin* like *hi* nasal).

Blood, ïhdä (*da* short).

Bloody, ïh-kerréje (*je* French).

Bloom (v), hóh-säddähosch (*hoh* accented; second word short; *sch* sometimes slightly hissed).

Blue, tohä.

Blush (v), stassähärreh (*st* with the point of the tongue).

Boil (v), umpäsch (*sch* sometimes slightly hissed).

Bone, wahúhdä.

Bough, does not occur in the singular; boughs, ohchancha (*ch* guttural).

Bow, woraërúhpa (*e* full, distinct, and short), or waraërúhpa; this is the bow of elm.

Bow (strengthened with elk or sheep horn), wahú-erúhpa.

Bow-lance, erúhpa-hichtä (*ich* guttural).

Box on the ear, rotkäsch (*r* with the point of the tongue).

Braid (v), kaschkä-sch (*sch* slightly hissed).

Brain, nathenu (*e* distinctly pronounced).

Break (v; shatter), pährusch.

Breast, táchärächä (*ch* guttural; *r* with the point of the tongue).

Breath, ohnnihä.

Bridge (tree-bridge), mánna-achkinïhnde (second word without emphasis; *ach* guttural).

Bridle (of a horse), manïssikaskä.

Brilliant (splendid), éduchtukosch.

Broad, pchïhrusch (*ch* guttural).

Brook, passán-kschuck (*an* French); kschuck, narrow.

Broom, ïngka-gischka (*ing* German; second word low).

Brother (eldest), mong-ká.

Brother (youngest), pschong-ká.

Brown, tkópp: that is brown, anttkopposch (*an* French); it is brown, tkópposch.

Bud (n), aschïngkohsch.

Burn (v), ratsiposch: the prairie burns, máh-ódisch; i.e., the prairie is colored black.

Burn (v, tr or intr; destroy by fire), náchuhdusch (*ch* guttural).

Buttock, ïh-ta (*ta* very short).

Buy (v), wikáhrusch.

Call (v; shout), ruhärrisch (short).

Calm (n), ïhpatta-häschkasch.

Canoe (of leather), minnánke (*an* French; *ke* short and low).

Carrion (a dead animal), kómmahä.

Catch (v; capture), owáschakosch.

Caught (taken prisoner), ïhnissä.

Cave (house in the rock), mïhsánnakeh-kúhsta-auti-túhsch.

Chew (v), rapsáhkosch.

Child, suck-chámahä.

Chin, ïhku.

Circle (n), ohkamischkakusch.

Clear, karáschäkosch (*sch* but slightly audible).

Clouds (masses of cloud), háhdä.

Coal, bächchä (*ch* guttural).

Cold (adj), schïnnihusch.

Collar, warapening-gä (*e* ½; the whole run together).

Colt, ünpa-manisinïhka-sch (*n* French).

Comb, païwachunkä (*ch* guttural; *ai* together; *ka* short).

Come (v), kuhóhsch, or kuhosch.

Come here (imperative), hú-ta (first syllable long; last syllable very short).

Console (v), kehápp-herrisch (*e* distinctly pronounced; *herrisch* short; the whole run together).

Convenient (comfortable), ohmannaka-schïhsch (second word spoken lower).

Corpse, uattäh-hädde (*e* distinctly pronounced; the whole run together).

Cough (v), hokäruka.

Count (v), pakkirïhdusch.

Cover (v; ornament), ah-kuposch (*osch* barely audible).

Cowardly, wakarrachkáhsch (*rr* with the point of the tongue; *ach* guttural).

Crack (v; crack a whip), karaparaschusch (*r* full, with the point of the tongue).

Crooked, skóposch.

Crow (way of wearing the hair), pahïn-okaskäsch (*sch* slightly hissed).

Cure (v), kimikóh-sch.

Curly, minnïmenihsch (*e* ½).

Curry (v), ruhïntu-sch (*ruhintusch*).

Cut (v), pauä-schusch (run together; *paua* short; *a* and *u* separated).

Cut down (v), pauïschosch (short).

Cut down (a tree), mánna-kassähherrisch (*herrisch* very short and run together; the last two words pronounced together).

Dance (n), uáhnapä.

Dark, hapähreschka (*pah* long; *ka* half short).

Daughter, suck-mïh-husch; i.e., maiden.

Day, kaschäkosch.

Day after to-morrow, mahtke-óhmaestá (*e* barely articulated, heard only as a light sound).

Dead, ottährusch.

Deaf, nakóckä-sidikosch (*ch* guttural; the whole run together).

Dear (costly), ïscha-hähónsch (*on* French).

Dearest (i.e., "the most beautiful"), suck-mïhä-koschïnaschämïhkasch.

Death, tährusch.

Deceive (they say "he has not paid his debts"), ïhscha-häuahma-kuï-néhchusch (*ch* guttural; *e* distinctly pronounced).

Decoy (v; an animal), wattáchakhuhrosch (*ch* guttural); i.e., because I imitate their call, I make them come.

Delay (v; make late), ohhi-kahunuahärrisch (*hun* run together, like French *oun*; the whole short and pronounced together).

Demolish (v; e.g., take down a lodge), ohséhrusch (*rusch* low).

Destroy (v; ruin, spoil), tellepóhsch.

Devil (evil spirit), omahank-chikä (*an* French; *ch* guttural).

Dew, béddädä (*e* distinctly pronounced; the whole short).

Die (v), tährusch.

Dirty (v), tkappoahärrisch (pronounced very short).

Dirty, warát-keddisch (run together; *keddisch* short; *e* full value).

Dish (of wood), mánna-pachä (*ch* guttural).

Dive (v), kschïppo-sch.

Divide (v), ïhkappähdusch.

Do (v), isäkosch; do not do it, káhdä-isäckta.

Door, béddähä (*da* and *a* short).

Double, náhta-sch (*natusch*; *sch* slightly hissed).

Drag (v), paschïh-husch (run together).

Draw (v; draw water), ïnnisusch (run together; short).

Dream (n), same word as for verb.

Dream (v), chïckhäddähsch (*ch* guttural).

Drink (v), hïhndosch (*n* French).

Drive (v), kochährutosch.

Drop (n; e.g., of water), sähhusch.

Drown (v; to be drowned), numangkáke-kámahä.

Drum (n), mánna-berächä (*e* distinctly pronounced; *ch* guttural).

Dry (adj), sáhkosch.

Dung, ähde (*e* distinctly pronounced).

Dumb, uáhronächa (*ch* guttural).

Dust, uaratä; it is dusty, uaratädachingkosch.

Ear, nakóchä (*ch* guttural and short).

Ear-ornament, uóhkaske (*e* distinctly pronounced and short).

Early (of time), koskäch-chámahä (*ch* guttural).

Earth, máhhankä (*an* French; *ka* short and low).

Egg (bird's), mándeck-suck-nïïtka (*an* French).

Elbow, akschïsche-náhde (first *e* ½; final *e* distinctly pronounced).

Embroider (v), nïhhä-ohwaptäsch.

Empty (adj), okikóhhä.

Enemy, uïhratandä (*an* French).

Englishman, Uaschï, or Waschïmihsiháhkta; i.e., a Frenchman from the north.

Enough, ántechksach (*e* ½; *ech* guttural).

Entangle (v; involve), ïhki-ruhmenisch.

Even (flat), kahósta; really a level prairie or plain.

Evening, istúnhä-dähus (*n* French).

Everywhere, äkunhä-ahkskä-üahärrisch (the two last words short and run together).

Expectorate (v; vomit), oksóhkusch.

Eye, istá; both eyes, istómmi.

Eyelid, istá-rupchä (*ch* guttural; the whole run together).

Face (sight), istá.

Fade (v; grow pale), sterruckäschäh.

Fade (v; wither), dachïhdusch (*ch* guttural).

Fail (v; miss), kakáhon-sch (*kakahonsch*; *on* French; *honsch* short and low).

Fall (v), dóhbchösch (*chosch* short and guttural).

Fall (v; of the leaves), haráhrusch (*r* with the point of the tongue): mánna-ahpöharáhrusch, the leaves are falling; mánna-ahpó, the leaves.

Fan, ïhkärä-häditta (*ka* short).

Far (distant), téhhan-sch (*tehhansch*; *an* French).

Far (remote), ruhchäddäta (*ta* short).

Fat (melted), ihkirï.

Fat (stout), sïhndä.

Father, kóhtä (*o* full; *ta* short).

---- (his), kóhtosch.

---- (my), wáhtosch.

---- (your), ráhtosch (*r* with the point of the tongue); the plural is never used, they say instead "the father."

Feather, sïh.

Feel (v), paschkáttusch.

Female (of animals), mïhkasch.

Fin, póssi.

Find (v), onóppohsch.

Finger, ungkáh-hä (*ha* very short and lower).

Finger (fore), ungkóh-mihä (*mi* short).

Finger (fourth), unghnátsä-mingkä.

Finger (little), ungknï-ingka (run together).

Finger (middle), ungknátka-kánachkah (*ach* guttural).

Fire, uáradä (*ua* nearly like *wa*; *da* distinctly pronounced and short).

Fire-brand uára-rakschä.

Fish, pó.

Fish (v; catch fish), póhru-pschikóhsch (first *e* with the point of the tongue).

Fish (v), póhrup-schïkohsch.

Fish-hook, poïkinnih (short).

Fist, ongkirrussa-nakä (*russa-naka* very short).

Flame, uára-kapïdihä.

Flat, pschïhdä (*da* short).

Flatter (v), ïhkiri-áhkawaschusch (*ch* guttural).

Flea (insect), péschki.

Flee (v; escape), ptähó-sch (*ptahosch*; *sch* slightly hissed).

Flesh, mánskapö (*an* French).

Flint, máhkick-schukä.

Flood (v; overflow), mönnih-suckhäddisch.

Flute (with holes for fingering), ïh-wochka (*och* guttural).

Flute (without holes), ïh-koschka.

Fly (v), kikárehdusch (*r* with the point of the tongue).

Foam, puchtä (*ch* guttural; *ta* short).

Fog, masihsch.

Food (something to eat), wóhruté.

Foot, schïh.

Foot-path, nánko (*n* French).

Force (v; compel), sïn-hin-kehde (*e* distinctly pronounced; *in* in both cases like *i* nasal; the whole run together).

Forehead, ithakä (*ka* short and low).

Forest, mánna-rucktá.

Forget (v), ikihanchikusch (*an* French; *ch* guttural).

Free (he is no slave), waïnihsïhnichosch (*ch* guttural).

Freeze (v), ktáhohsch.

Frenchman, Waschï, or Uaschï.

Friend, manuká (*a* ½).

Frost (hoar-frost), istúnhä-uáhätúhsch (*n* French; *ua* together).

Full, ohïhsch.

Full moon, mïhnangkä-okahï (short and run together); it may also be written, mihnang-ga.

Fully, ráttacosch.

Game (play), kïhni.

Gay-colored, puhsä; it is gay-colored, or spotted, puhsähsch.

Go (v), déh-husch.

Go hunting (v; go on a hunt), schánterähusch (*an* French; *e* ½; *ra* short).

God, ohmahank-numákschi (*an* French); literally the lord or chief of the earth.

Good, schihsch (*sch* often slightly hissed; but not regularly).

Grandchild, tauïhangka-sch (*hankasch*; *sch* slightly hissed), or tauïh-hangkasch.

Grape-vine, hasch-huhdä (*a* short).

Grass, chahä (*ch* guttural).

Grave, there is no such word; burial scaffold, maschóttä; see below, under "inter."

Gray, chóttä (*ch* guttural).

Gray-haired, pahïn-chóttä (*ch* guttural).

Great (tall), haschkasch (*sch* slightly hissed).

Green, wïïratohä.

Ground, mánpeterroh (*an* French; *e* ½; *terroh* short and low).

Grow (v), inïhndusch (first *i* rather long).

Gums, hiddó-sä (very short and run together).

Gun, wáhta-schirúhpa, or erúhpa (*e* sometimes pronounced like *i*); rifle, ehrúhp-achtä (the whole run together).

Gut (intestines), sihpä.

Gut (v; gut an animal), pokkanáhhusch.

Hail (n), rakánnandeh (*kannan* short; *an* French).

Hair, pahïn (*n* French; somewhat like a nasal *pahi*).

Half, ïhschanhä (*an* French).

Hand, ung-kä.

Hard, kahsäsch (*sch* sometimes slightly hissed).

Hate (v), woráttehusch (*r* with the point of the tongue).

Haul (v; fetch), kittáhhusch, or kichkararusch (*ich* guttural).

Head, pá (short).

Headache, panáhrusch (*r* with the point of the tongue).

Hear (v), ä-sch (run together; but *sch* is sometimes prolonged).

Heart, nátka.

Hearty (stout-hearted), kakáhhonsch (*on* French; *sch* often a little prolonged).

Heat (n), dádeschusch (*e* distinctly pronounced).

Heat (v; inflame), manassinko-sch (*manassingkosch*; *sch* slightly hissed); i.e., I am warm.

Heaven (sky), cháre-toho-sch (*ch* guttural; *e* ½; the whole run together).

Heavy, tkähsch.

Heel, schirúttä; plural, schirutosch.

Help (v), oʹhta-iuássakusch (pronounced together).

Hem (v; clear one's throat), háuikissekusch (the whole run together).

Hide (v), achawéhsch (*ch* guttural).

High, wáh-kohrusch.

Hoarse, hoh-chikóhsch.

Hole, oʹhoh-pusch (*o* full; the whole run together).

Hollow (adj), chówokosch (*ch* guttural).

Hoof, scháh-hä (*ha* short).

Hoop (of a barrel), mánna-bihduckä-ïh-kamenihnde (first *e* ½).

Hope (v), iwatéhrusch.

Horns, ansä́ (*an* French).

Horse, úmpa-menïssä (*m* French; *e* ½).

Hot, dádähschusch.

House (lodge), otḯ.

Hunger, warúhtä-sch.

Hungry, wawarútä-sch; i.e., I am hungry.

Hunt (n), schántä (*an* French).

Hunt (v), wáhnin-déhusch (*a* full; *nin* German).

Hunter, kaschánteka (*an* French; *e* distinctly pronounced).

Hurricane, schächtä-sch (*ach* guttural), or schächtäsch.

I, mïh.

Ice, chóhde (*ch* guttural; *de* distinctly pronounced), or chóhdä.

In (come in), dóbcheta (*ch* guttural; *e* ½; *ta* short).

Incurable, o'hkemick-härrächïhkusch (*ch* guttural).

Indistinct, ihïnnikosch.

Inter (v; place on the scaffold), omáhchä-dähhereje (*ch* guttural; *hereje* barely audible; *je* French; *e* barely pronounced); ohmáhchä, or maschótta, the burial scaffold.

Interior, kúhschta.

Intoxicate, russidïhrusch (*r* with the point of the tongue).

Iron, uáhtasche (*e* distinctly pronounced).

Island, uittká (*ka* short).

Itch (n), schirúhha (*ha* short).

Jar (of clay), berächä (*ch* guttural).

Jaw, dóhhupa.

Joy, nettkaschï-sch (*sch* slightly hissed).

Kernel (of a fruit or seed), tsúhnta (*n* French; *ta* short; *uhn* somewhat nasal).

Kidneys, pïcksukkäh.

Kindle, raptähärri-sch (*harrisch* very short and indistinct).

Knee, súhpachä.

Kneel (v), súhpachä-natannakosch.

Knife, man-hï (*man* French; often nearly *ma* with superior *o*).

Know (v), ïhua-hähkohsch (*ih* together; *ua* separated).

Know (v; be acquainted with), ïhwahäkosch.

Knuckle, assóh-keninde (first *e* ½; *in* German; final *e* distinctly pronounced; the whole run together).

Lame (limping), onnï-ndächïkosch (*ch* guttural).

Lament (v; they say "he has pain, he weeps"), náhdä-irratahusch (*ch* guttural; *r* with the point of the tongue).

Lance, mánna-hiteruck-schukkä.

Land, same word as for earth.

Laugh (v), ihkchanhosch (*ch* guttural).

Lay (v), makhärrähsch.

Lead, same word as for ball.

Leader (chief), numákschi.

Leaf, ahpä.

Leap (v; spring), skä-sch.

Leave (imperative; go out of the way), húh-ketá.

Left (adverb), nusúskasch.

Leg, otïh.

Lick (v), pédeh-sch (first *e* distinctly pronounced but short).

Lie (v; deceive), schähäkóhsch.

Life, nán-kesch (*an* French; *kesch* moderated; the whole run together).

Lift (v), ruhchóhku-sch.

Light (n), ïddä-ächä (*ch* guttural).

Light (v), ïhdä-chäwaharisch.

Lightning, chä-kúhnde (*ch* guttural; *e* ½).

Like (v), watïhkidasusch.

Lip, ïhchdobchi (*ch* guttural).

Little, sánkasch (*an* French).

Liver, pïh.

Long, hánschka (*an* French; *ka* short; usually pronounced *haschka*).

Loose (of clothes), pchïhdä (*pchi* guttural; *da* short).

Lungs, koppähk (*o* between *a* and *o*).

Maiden, suck-mïh-husch (the whole run together).

Maize, kóhchantä (*ch* guttural; *an* French).

Man, númangkohsch, or númangkosch.

Man, (human being), numangkáhkesch.

Marry (v), they say "he has taken a wife," or "she has taken a husband."

Meal (to eat?), warrutó-sch, (*warrutosch*; *sch* slightly hissed).

Medicine, chóppeni (*ch* guttural).

Medicine-feast, machóppenihuahäddisch.

Medicine-lodge, ti-chóppenisch (*ch* guttural; pronounced together).

Medicine-man, numánk-chóppenisch (*ch* guttural; *e* ½).

Melt (v), raschedähsch.

Merchant, kauïkahka (*aui* separated; *u* short).

Messenger, kasäddähsch; i.e., I employ him in order to send him.

Mirror, ih-mïngkiäsch (run together).

Mistake (v; lose one's way), chïqua-härrisch (*ch* guttural).

Money, matáschä-schóttä; i.e., the white metal: or okihkikidasusoch; i.e., that which the white men love very much.

Moon, istú-menahke (first *e* ½; final *e* distinctly pronounced; the whole run together).

Moon (which is full), mïhnangkäokahïsch.

Moonshine, istú-menahke-iddäechosch (*e* ½; *ch* guttural; the last two words short and run together).

Morning, mámpsita (*amp* French; *ta* short).

Mother, kohúhndä (*n* French; *da* short).

---- my, mihúhndä.

---- your, nihúhndä.

---- his, ih-kohúhndä.

---- (plural), kohúhnka (*n* French).

Mountain, maháhk-chtäsch (*ch* guttural; *sch* slightly hissed).

Mouth, ïh-hä.

Much, hunsch (*un* like French *oun*).

Murder (v; same word as for kill), tährusch.

Music, there is no such word; they say "song."

My, uawakáhrusch, or uáwaka-s.

Nails (on the feet), ung-ka-hä.

Nails (on the hands), ung-ka-hä.

Naked, ikara-súh-ninakosch (*r* with the point of the tongue; the whole run together).

Name, dássä.

Nape (of the neck), náhkuttä.

Narrow, kschukó-sch (*sch* slightly hissed).

Navel, dähp-ta-súh.

Neck (throat), itaïnú.

Needle (for sewing), mihstuheräóhhopä-túhsch (short).

Negro, waschïpsi; i.e., the black man who has everything.

Nest (of birds), tachánde (*an* French; *ch* guttural; *e* distinctly pronounced and short).

Net (fish-net), pó-ïkuhndä (*n* French; *da* very short).

New, nánkasch (*an* French).

New moon, mi̇́hnangkä-nangkanakóhsch.

Night, istú-hunsch (*istu* very short; *hun* like *houn* in French).

Noon, hapánnatosch.

Northern lights, wauawáschirutä.

Nose, páhchu (*pah* a nasal tone between French *ah* and *an*, the same in *mahchsi*, eagle; *chu* guttural).

Nostril, páhchu-suh.

Not (nothing, none), mikóhsch; chosch (*ch* guttural) is the French *pas*, or not.

Old, chihósch (*ch* guttural).

Old man, wáratohka-chihósch (*chi* guttural).

Old woman, rokánka-chihénn (*an* French; *ch* guttural).

Oldest (the), koráttorusch.

On the other side, kutá.

Once, máchana-i̇̈cha (*ch* guttural).

Over, ȧ́hkita.

Oversleep (v; neglect by sleeping), ȯ́wakinate-kahun-husch (first *a* distinctly pronounced; *n* French like *oun*; the whole short and run together).

Pain (n), wahúhde-náhdusch (*e* distinctly pronounced).

Paint (v), uȧ́hkapusosch (*a* somewhat like å, or full).

Pair, nupschá.

Palate (roof of the mouth), nuti̇́ske-okissángka (*e* distinctly pronounced).

Partizan (leader of a war party), karókkanakah.

Peace, herróhka-härri-sch (run together; lisped).

People (lowest people), wáhchikanaschä (*ch* guttural); this is the most abusive word used by the Mandans.

Pinch (v; to carouse?), rúschkapusch.

Pipe (big medicine pipe), i̇́h-hinkchóppenih (*ch* guttural; *ihhink* run together).

Pipe (tobacco), i̇́h-hink-ossúhä (run together); usually ih-hingkä (the whole run together).

Pitch (rosin), ohruschkop.

Plant (v), uåhkihäddäisch (*haddaisch* short).

Play (v), menïcheni (*ch* guttural).

Pluck (v; feathers), pachkä' (*ch* guttural).

Point (v; with the finger), hähmeni-häddisch.

Pointed, schïh-husch.

Poison, there is no word for it.

Polish (v), ihkich-kánusch (*ch* guttural; *an* French).

Pond (or pool), mönnih-chädochä (*ch* guttural).

Pouch (of leather), ïhdukä.

Pouch (painted, of leather), ïhwatarrackä.

Powder (gun-powder), waráschuntä.

Prairie, oʻh-karachtah (*ach* guttural).

Pregnant, ähchichtä' (*ah* rather long; *ch* guttural; *ta* short).

Press out (v; to express?), ïhkastatusch.

Pretty, schïhnaschusch.

Prick (v; or sting), rápäsch.

Prisoner, iniss-häddisch.

Proud, tahuichtä-schïhkerisch (*u* and *i* separated; *ch* guttural; *ta* short; final *e* ½).

Pulse, katink-tink-kanáhgisch (run together).

Push (v; thrust), patkäh-sch.

Quarrel (v; fight), ráhpusch.

Quarter (of the moon), mïhnangkä-kaschúra-déhusch.

Quick, kattuscho-sch (*scho-sch* like a subdued *schosch*).

Quiver (for arrows), schuntháschk-ichtïckä (*ch* guttural).

Race (contest in running), ptïhhing-kikéhrusch.

Rain (n), chäh-husch (*ch* guttural; the whole run together).

Rainbow, chäh-ikuhndä (*ch* guttural; *da* short).

Rattle (sysyquoy, gourd rattle), ïnahdä (*nah* occasionally like *nan* in French, nasal).

Ready (completed), wakingkosch; it is not ready, wáuakin-kïnichosch (*n* French; *ch* guttural).

Reconcile (v), härróhka-härrisch (run together).

Red, sähsch, or sä-sch.

Refuse (v; deny), rúhkahusch.

Revenge (v), taüïhscha-hätúhsch.

Rib, dút-huh-dä (*da* short; the whole run together).

Ring (v), nïhhä.

Ripe (of fruit), ráttakosch.

River, passan-hächtä (*an* French; *ch* guttural; usually run together, then pronounced *passachta*, *ach* guttural).

Roast (v, or n), rokïnni.

Rock (cliff), ïhschanschekeh (*an* French; first *e* distinctly pronounced).

Rocky Mountains, Mïhndämánkä (*an* French).

Root, mánna-hissä.

Rot (v), tärräpo-sch (*sch* slightly hissed).

Rotten (lazy?), natkachïhpo-sch (*ch* guttural; *sch* slightly hissed).

Round (adj), sánnakohsch.

Row (v; paddle), ihuachákasch (*ih* together).

Run (v), ptä-husch (run together).

Saddle (for a horse), mannissáhganakä (run together).

Salt (v; or sweeten), skuhóhsch.

Sand, mapúschakohsch (*sch* slightly hissed).

Scalp, padóbchi (*ch* guttural).

Scalp-dance, uïhskäkä-náhpisch (*uihs* long; *kaka* short).

Scar, ocha-túhsch (*ch* guttural).

Scratch (v), ungkáh-härrisch (*harrisch* low; the whole run together).

Scream (v), saráhrusch.

Sea, mönnïh-kerre, or monnïh-kärrä (*kerre* low, even, and without emphasis; *e* distinctly pronounced but short; *r* with the point of the tongue).

Secret (adj), achawä̈hsch (first *ch* guttural).

See (v), hä-sch.

Servant (marmiton, kettle-tender), kapä̈chka (*ach* guttural).

Shade (shadow), ä̈hkunchä (*n* like French *oun*; *ch* guttural).

Shake (v; rock), katïdirischusch.

Shallow (water), mönnïh-psïhkasch.

Sharp (keen), schïh-husch (run together).

Shave (v), hïhkirukess.

Shed tears (v; or n, tears?), istámönni-húhrusch (the whole run together).

Shield (pare flèche), wakïhdä.

Shin (shin-bone), dobkáhgä (*g* guttural; *ga* short).

Shiver (v; with cold), kachóhkahárra-wáhankisch (*an* French).

Shoot (v; with a bow), mánnamahnïhndusch.

Shoot (v; with a gun), eruhpákahtä (run together).

Shooting-star, chkäkä-rohhankadéhhusch (the whole run together).

Shore (bank), mönnih-wakáchta (*kach* a strong nasal sound).

Short, sánnakosch.

Shoulder, ahkïttä.

Show (v; instruct in a matter), ïkikuhntäsch.

Sick, ahgännadusch (also with *rusch* instead of *dusch*).

Side (of the body), dóh-ïschanhä (*an* French; the whole run together).

Sigh (v), ïnihä.

Sing (v), wakanáhrusch.

Sister (youngest), ptánka (*an* French); eldest sister, menúkä (*e* ½).

Sit (v), kïkanakä.

Skin (hide of animal), dohbchïh (*ch* guttural).

Sledge (dog-sledge, travail), man-ïssischan (*an* French, but often like *a*).

Sledge (sled), mánna-üïratahne.

Sleep (v), hánnarusch.

Sleepy, hannaruck; I am going to sleep, wahánna-edúck-sanhúsch (*an* French; the whole short and run together).

Slow, chährusch (*ch* guttural; *rusch* low and short).

Small (short), chámahä (*ch* guttural).

Smell (v; sniff, scent), uïhhä.

Smoke (n), pïh-husch.

Smoke (v; tobacco), manóschhïhndusch (short and run together).

Smooth, sánhisch (*an* French).

Snarl (v; growl), channah-hahosch (*ch* guttural; the whole run together).

Snow, wáh-hä.

Sole (of the foot), schirokä.

Son, konickä.

Song, wakánnarusch.

Sore-throat, itäï-nunahrusch.

Spark, uaranïhka (*ua* almost like *wa* in the word for fire).

Speak (v), róhdä.

Spirits (distilled), mönni-páhre (*e* short).

Spittle, óksohkä.

Spoon, mansä' (*an* French); if it is of the horn of the buffalo or bighorn the name of the animal is added.

Spot (v), ähksehusch (*e* distinctly pronounced).

Spring (the season), bäh-hinundä (*n* French; the whole run together).

Spring (source), mannahinnïh.

Spy (v), mïnnakochä-uakärup-schä-sch (*sch* slightly hissed).

Squint (v), istáck-chäkohsch (*ch* guttural; *a* short).

Star, chkäkä (*ch* begins as a guttural).

Start (v; to start an animal), kachärutosch (*ch* guttural).

Steep (adj), kascháppähschkasch.

Step-father, called father; likewise step-mother is called mother.

Sterile, ohro-mikohsch.

Stick (n), mánna-kschúkä.

Stifle (v; choke, repress), russïng-ko-sch (*russingkosch*; *sch* slightly hissed).

Still, happoähärohn-nkúnihusch (*r* with the point of the tongue).

Stinginess, schïrukohsch.

Stirrup, maniss-iwachungkä.

Stomach, tachárachä (*ch* guttural).

Stop (v; stop up), pattarókosch (*r* with the point of the tongue; *o* accented).

Stone (n), mïsannakä.

Storm (they say "a bad day," or "bad weather"), hapäh-chikóhsch (*ch* guttural).

Straight, schóhrusch (*sch* often slightly hissed).

Strike (v), dótkihsch.

Strong (of drink or other things), páhrusch.

Strong (physical strength), sinhusch (*in* nasal like *i*).

Stump, sónkohsch.

Stupid, ochka-sch (*ochkasch*; *och* guttural; *sch* slightly hissed).

Summer, ráskikä.

Sun, maháp-mïh-nangkä (the whole run together).

Sunrise, mïhnangkä-tïhsch.

Sunset, mïhnangkä-opókkohusch.

Surround (v; enemies), ikisánpasch (*an* French).

Swallow (v; choke), oschárroposch.

Swamp (or lake), manichtä; a dirty place, tuntukosch.

Sweat (v), dássing-kohsch (run together).

Sweet, skunhó-sch (*hosch* abruptly ended; *un* like *oun* in French).

Swim (v), paschún (*n* French; *un* like French *oun*).

Swollen, páh-hosch (run together; *sch* slightly hissed).

Tail (of bird), ïhpä (*pa* short).

Tail (of animal), schunntä (*ta* short).

Teach (v), ikkikúhntä (*ta* short).

Tear (v; tear or break to pieces), ruchángkosch (*ruchangkosch*).

Tear out (v), pachkä; same as to pluck.

Tears, istá-mönni-húhrusch (the whole run together).

Teeth, hïh.

Testicle, asútka.

There (yonder), etta.

Thick (stout), chtä-sch (*ch* guttural; *sch* slightly hissed).

Thin, pampïh-sch (*pampisch*; *sch* slightly hissed; *am* or *an* French).

Throat, nutiskä.

Thumb, umká.

Thumb, umpkä.

Thunder, chä-i-nihä (*ch* guttural; the whole run together).

Tickle (v), ruksicksikusch (*r* with the point of the tongue).

Tie (v; fasten), kaskéhje (final *e* barely audible; *j* French).

Tinder-box, mïhka-de (low and short).

Tobacco, mannaschä.

Tobacco (mixed with red willow), mánna-séka.

Tobacco (mixed with sakkakomi or bear-berry), mannaschot-kuschä.

Tobacco-pouch, mánnaschä-dockä.

Toe, schï-nihka.

To-morrow, máhtke (*e* distinctly pronounced, but short).

Tongue, dähsike (*e* ½).

Toothache, hïh-náhrusch.

Top (summit), mahakáhgitta.

Toughness, käddährusch.

Track (of an animal), onïhnde (*de* short; *e* nearly full value).

Trade (n), uïh-karusch.

Trap (for animals), aͨhchkatachka (*ka* short; *ch* guttural).

Tree, mannáh, or mánna.

Tremble (v), katïderischusch.

True, tkuschósch.

Turn (v, twist), mïh-nuptakohsch (run together).

Turn back (v, return), kiptáhanni-kuhosch (the whole run together).

Ugly, chikósch (*ch* guttural), or chikóhsch.

Unhealthy, uáhschi-chïhsch (run together; *ch* guttural).

Unripe, schánhohsch (*an* French).

Until (unto), oͨhdähä.

Urine, dächä (*ch* guttural).

Valley, oͨwako-pä.

Vein (artery), jïdukkä, or hissä (German throughout).

Void (adj; stale; or cool, moderate), nahnka-wawarut-tenech-osch (first *e* French and so somewhat nasal; *e* distinctly pronounced; *ch* guttural).

Wait (v, await), kiháhnakosch.

War, there is no such word; to fight, kïddack-sahndusch.

War-club (of stone), mïh-kaské.

War-club (of wood), mánna-pauïschä.

War-club (small iron tomahawk), oͨhmanat-tchámahä (*ch* guttural).

War-club (with iron point), mono-pschïhdä, or mánna-ókatanhä (*an* French).

Warm, dadéschusch (*e* distinctly pronounced).

Warmth, same word as for warm.

Warrior (a brave fighter), kirak-san-charakusch (*an* French; *ch* guttural; *r* with the point of the tongue).

War-whoop, scheddekóhsch.

Wash (v), kirúskikusch.

Water, mönnïh; occasionally, mennïh.

Water-jar, mönni-mïhnda (*da* short).

Wax, o̍hkerusche-schïpka-o̍hdä-chä (*e* in *sche* ½).

Weary, ïua-hatésch (*iua* separated; *h* barely audible; *e* distinctly pronounced; the whole run together).

Weather (fair), happe-schiéhsch (*e* ½; run together without break); i.e., it is fair weather.

Weep (v), rattachósch (*ch* guttural).

Wet, skapposch.

What (or how), taschká-tl (*tl* lisped as in Mexico).

Whip (for horses), ïh-kaparaschä.

Whirlpool, mönnih-ruhmenischka (*e* ½)

Whistle (v; or pipe), ïhkoschä.

White, schóttä.

White-man, waschï, or uaschï; i.e., he who has everything, or everything good.

Whole, ekún-ha (*n* French; *ha* short).

Widow, they say "the husband is dead."

Wind (n), schä.

Wind (v; of game), ïhkamenihn-dusch (*e* ½).

Wing (n), ahpcha (*ch* guttural; final *a* almost as if with umlaut, short and low).

Winter, máhna.

Wither (v), ráhsakosch.

Woman (wife), mïh-hä; this is a woman, mïïh-husch.

Wood, mánna.

Work (v), waïsakosch (*wai* pronounced together).

Wound (v), u̍hsch.

Wound (v), o̍hcha-tu-kärähusch (*ch* guttural); i.e., he went away wounded.

Wrap up (v), ikikáhmenisch (*e* ½).

Wrinkle (n), sïhpo-sch (*sihpohsch*).

Yawn (v), ichbedährusch (*ch* guttural; *sch* slightly hissed).

Year, máhna: there is really no word for year; they say "winter,"—"I am so many winters old."

Yellow, sïhdä (*da* short).

Yellowish, chïhdä (*ch* guttural).

Yes, hon (*on* French), or hau (pronounced as in German).

Yolk (the yellow in the egg), mándeck-suck-nïïka-kuhschta-ossiidä.

Young, suck-chámahusch.

Young animal, konïhnka (second *n* French; *ihn* somewhat nasal).

Animals

Antelope (general term), kokä; the buck, kockberockä.

Antelope (with horns), kokástu.

Badger, mahtäckä.

Bat, háhchurahdä (*ch* guttural).

Bear (black), ischiïdda (*da* short).

Bear (grizzly), mató.

Beaver, uárapä, or wárapä.

Bighorn, ansechtä (*an* French; *e* barely audible; *ch* guttural; *ta* very short; the whole therefore almost *anschta*).

Buffalo (bull), berockä.

Buffalo (calf), nïhka.

Buffalo (cow), ptïhndä, orptïhnde.

Crane, tähräcke (*e* distinctly pronounced).

Crane, (white), tähräck-schóttä.

Crow, chóhchichanka (*ch* Dutch guttural throughout).

Deer (black-tailed), schumpsi.

Deer (common), máhmanakuh.

Duck, pattóhä.

Eagle (bald-headed), pattáckä.

Eagle (old war-eagle), kichká (*ch* guttural).

Eagle (war-eagle), máhchsi (*mah* almost like *man*, French nasal; *ch* guttural).

Eagle (young bald-headed), chtachtáha (*ch* and *ach* guttural).

Elk, ómpa, or úmpa (*om* French, *um* like *oum* in French).

Elk (doe), ómpa-míhkasch.

Elk (stag), ómpa-berockä.

Fisher (mustela pennantii), ichtíck-psíh (*ch* guttural).

Fox (black), hirútt-psíh.

Fox (cross-fox), hirútt-chack-chäh (*ch* guttural).

Fox (grey), hirútt-chóttä (*ch* guttural).

Fox (prairie), óhcha (*ch* guttural).

Fox (red), hirútt-sä.

Frog, psánka (*an* French).

Goose (white), míhhan-schóttä.

Goose (wild), míhhan-kschukkä (*an* French).

Gopher (arctomys hoodii, striped prairie squirrel), maschirónika.

Hare (white), máhchtikä (*ch* guttural; *ti* short).

Horse, úmpa-meníssä (*um* like *oum* in French; *e* ½).

Horse, (young), úmpa-meníssiníhkasch (*sch* sometimes slightly hissed).

Humming-bird, manasch-chóhpkocháchka (*ch* guttural; the whole run together).

Lizard, míhkanatka.

Lynx, schontä-pussä.

Magpie, uihkchák-chäkä (*ch* guttural).

Mink, mönnika-súnntackä.

Mole (gopher), machtóhpka (*ach* guttural; *o* full).

- 215 -

Moose, páhchub-ptaptá (*ch* guttural).

Mouse, mïhtickä.

Mule, schúmpsi-manïsseh.

Nighthawk (goatsucker), pïhska.

Otter, pähchtekeh (*ch* guttural; *e* ½; *keh* somewhat prolonged).

Owl (German uhu, strix bubo; western horned owl?), ichkïhä (*ch* guttural).

Panther, schuntä-háschka; literally the long tail.

Pelican (great, or "scheteck"), nuthkuchtä (*uch* guttural); i.e., the thick throat.

Pigeon (passenger-pigeon), uárawit-chtä.

Pigeon (turtle-dove, columba carolinensis), uárawit-kschukä.

Rabbit (lepus americanus), máhchtikä (*ch* guttural; *ti* short).

Rat, mïhtick-chtä (*ch* guttural).

Raven, kähka.

Skunk, schóchtä (*och* German guttural).

Snake, wahchkeruchká (*ch* guttural; *e* distinctly pronounced and short).

Snake, (rattle-snake), matáh-chóppenih (*ch* guttural; *e* ½).

Swan, mandéh-chóppenih (*an* French; *ch* guttural); i.e., the medicine bird.

Swine, waschïta-mató; i.e., the white man's bear.

Titmouse, patáhpsi.

Toad, chatká (*ch* guttural).

Troupial (red shouldered), ahpcha-sä (*ch* guttural).

Turkey (wild), máhnu (*a* rather full, almost as if with superior *o*).

Turkey buzzard, ruh-hah-deh.

Turtle, kïpsandä (*an* French; *da* short).

Waxwing, ohpa-kótika (*oh* and *o* full).

Weasel (stoat), máhchpach-pïrakä (only slightly separated; *ch* guttural).

Weasel (the small weasel), machschipka (*ach* guttural).

Wolf (black), cháhratä-psïh.

Wolf (gray), cháhratä-chóttä.

Wolf (prairie), schähäckä, or schähäcke (*e* short).

Wolf (white), cháhratä-schóttä.

Wolverene (gulo borealis), matóka (*ka* abruptly ended; run together).

Woodpecker, tóschka.

Plants

Ash, tapsá.

Birch, wáhchochä (*ch* guttural).

Negundo maple, mïhnchka-tah-manaka, (*n* French, barely audible; last word short and run together).

Oak, itá-huhdä.

Poplar, wáhchä (*ch* guttural).

Prairie turnip (pomme blanche), mahä (short).

Reed, wïh-puhdä (*puhda* lower; *da* short).

Willow (salix), háchsä-huhdä (*hach* with emphasis and nasal; *sa* and *huhda* low; *ach* guttural).

Clothing and Implements

Bracelets of metal, ünki-tanhä (*n* and an French; *un* like *oun*).

Breechcloth, nókkä.

Buffalo robe, mahïtu, or mïh-ihä.

Cache (hiding place), mochä (*ch* guttural).

Girdle (belt), ïchparakä (*ich* guttural).

Gloves (or mittens), ogïchtikä (*gich* guttural).

Hair-ornament (for the front part of head), itáhua-schúngkä (*ua* separated).

Head-dress (the long feather hood), máhchsi-akub-háschka (German throughout).

Leather shirt, wapánpi-ïmaschottä (*an* French).

Leggings, wapánpi-húnschi (*an* and *n* French, like *oun*).

Moccasins, humpä (*um* like French *oum*).

Necklace of bear's claws, matóunknappi-nihudä (the last two words run together).

Place in a cache (v), mochdaráhkosch (*och* guttural).

Pouch (for ammunition), mánhä-íhdukä, or assóh-kacherúkkä (*ch* guttural).

Scraper (for cleaning hides), íhwachipka (*ch* guttural).

Snow-shoes, mánna-humpä.

War-whistle, íhkoschka.

Kinship

Cousin, same words as for brother and sister.

Daughter-in-law, ptauíh-hangkasch (*au* together; *ih* with emphasis).

Father-in-law, ptútt.

Father's brother, same word as for father.

Father's sister (aunt), kotóminikohsch.

Grandfather, táttä-chihä' (*ch* guttural).

Grandmother, nan-chihä' (*an* French; *ch* guttural).

Mother-in-law, ptó-hinix (run together).

Mother's brother (uncle), ratodé.

Mother's sister, same word as for mother.

Son-in-law, roh-hángkasch.

Names of Rivers

Cannonball, Passáchtä.

Chayenne (Great Chayenne), Passáchtä.

Grand, Wáraschunt-pássahä.

Heart, Nátka-pássahä.

Knife, Mánhi-pássahä.

Little Missouri, Máhtach-schukä'.

Missouri, Mántahä (*an* French, rather nasal, like *ah*).

Muddy, Mattúhntu-pássahä.

Muscleshell, Tóhki-pássahä.

Rivière à Moreau, Pássahä-ïhtahi.

Rivière au castor, Mattúhntu-pássahä.

Rivière du rempart, Manáhmeni-pássahä.

Teton (Little Missouri), Mönnichäh-pássahä.

Upper White earth, Matáck-pássahä.

White, Mönnïh-schott-pássahä; literally Water-white river.

Yellowstone, Mïhsi-pássahä.

Names of Tribes

Assiniboins, Hósika.

Blackfeet, Schipsï.

Chayennes (Chats of the French), Tamáh-ónruschkahpe (*on* French; *e* distinctly pronounced; last word low and short; the whole run together).

Crows, Hähderuka (*e* ½).

Dacota, Hahä-numangkosch (run together).

Grosventres of the prairies, Arrapahó, or Ächichtä-numangkake (*ich* guttural).

Kayaüas, Káy-ua (the whole run together; *u* and *a* separated): the French call them Gens des ptat-côtés [*sic*].

Krihs, Schahï.

Omahas, Oʾhmaha.

Otos, Oʾhto.

Pánis, Chárätä-numangkä; i.e., the People of the Wolf, or of the Wolves.

Snakes, or Shoshonés, Wáhkiruchka-númangkä (*uch* guttural).

FOOTNOTES:

[256] I am indebted to the untiring patience of Mr. Kipp, who is thoroughly familiar with this language, for this extensive vocabulary which I wrote down with the help of several Mandans. My attempt at a grammar, as I have already said, was interrupted by illness. Mr. Gallatin (*ibid.*, p. 125) includes the Mandans with the Minnitarris; but he had no vocabulary of their language and could, therefore, in no wise form a correct judgment. The signatures to the treaty which he mentions (pp. 125 and 379) were translated into the

Minnitarri language because of the lack of a Mandan interpreter. This is shown clearly from the words *matsa* (man) and *lahpeetzee*, or *lachpitzi* (bear), both of which are pure Minnitarri words. I hope by means of the following examples of the Mandan language to refute many of the errors regarding this people which were formerly spread abroad.—MAXIMILIAN.

Comment by Ed. For a brief biography of James Kipp, see our volume xxii, p. 345, note 319.

Notes on the Grammar of the Mandan Language[257]

Prepositions

From (German, von; French, de), tá.

Near (German, unweit; French, proche, près de), askásch.

To (German, nach; French, à), óh.

Examples:

I come from Ruhptare: Ruhptáre äta wa huh-rusch; i.e., Ruhptare from I come.

I go to Ruhptare: Ruhptáre hiddä wa dähhusch; i.e., Ruhptare to I go.

For "close to" or "hard by," they say also "on the margin of." On the margin of Ruhptare: Ruhptáre ïwakachta (*ach* guttural); from ïwakachta, on the margin of the water, a pond, etc.

Interjections

There are nearly as many interjections as in our language.

Äh-hä-hä! (run together), an expression of surprise.

Jïa (nasal), used in case of exertion which is not wholly successful.

Héi! héi! héi! (German, shrill, pronounced with the tongue), thank you, thank you.

Wáh i sack chárackä! (*ch* guttural), oh, my God (German, mein Gott)!

Schá! oh (German ach).

Wáh-ah! or **ohsch!** ho there!

Conjunctions

And, káni.

Or, does not occur in our form; at least, it is difficult to discover.

Examples:

A man and a dog, numánk kani manissuérutä.

The one or the other, kotäwäcktosch; kitosch signifies that the event is yet to happen.

Kotäwa, which is it? in this expression it is difficult to find our word "or."

The Definite Article

Singular	Plural
Nom., **the man**, numangkä.	*Nom.*, **the men**, númank-keréhsch.
Gen., **of the man**, numangkä-óh.	*Gen.*, **of the men**, numangkáke.
Dat., **to the man**, numangkä.	*Dat.*, **to the men**, numank-keréhsch
Accus., **the man**, numangkä.	
Voc., **O! thou man**, numangkä.	
Abl., **from the man**, numank-däta.	

Examples:

Gen. The knife of the man whom I have seen: numank uahässiro óh támanhisch; i.e., the man whom I have seen, this is his knife.

Dat. I will give this to a man and not to a woman: numangkä wáh kuhk tusch mïhhä wah wach kuhnichtusch; i.e., to a man I will give it woman I will not give.

Accus. I saw a man do this: numangkä áhska uáhissache uahähsch; i.e., a man this do I have seen.

Abl. The knife comes from the man to whom you have given it: numank däta mánhi sakuh-rusch-idäta waruschesch.

The Indefinite Article

Nom., **a man**, numánk.

Gen., **of a man**, numánk.

Dat., **to a man**, numánk-ä, or numankä.

Accus., **a man**, numank.

Example:

Gen. The head of a man, numank-pa.

Remark. No difference in form is made for sex; and in the case of human beings, appears to be only occasionally indicated by an ending. They say: a man, numánk-máchana; and in exactly the same way, a woman, mïhha-máchana; an egg, máh-nïhka-máchana. The case where the sexes are indicated is when, for instance, some one addresses a person and tells him he should do something; if it is a man the syllable *tá* is affixed, if a woman the syllable *na*.

Auxiliary Verbs

To be, kitóhsch. This word does not occur frequently.

Examples:

To be rich: wá kah dä hun; i.e., much wealth.

To be tall is good: háschka kä schihsch; i.e., tall that is good.

I am tall: máh káschkasch; máh, I.

You are tall: nïh káschkasch.

He is tall: ih káschkasch.

We are tall: núh däta háschkasch.

You are tall: nïh däta haschkasch.

They are tall: ïh däta háschkasch.

To do, isäkosch:

I shall do it: waë wasácktosch.

You will do it: wa idá sácktosch.

He will do it: ih wah esácktosch.

We shall do it: nuh däta esácktosch.

You will do it: nih däta ïhda säcktosch.

They will do it: ih däta ih säcktosch.

Däta always signifies the plural in this use.

Do not do it: (imperative): káhdä isäckta.

To do: isäckosch.

Done: kúhrusch.

Doing: isäkka-mánkahusch (*an* French).

To have, wakáhtosch.

I shall have him (or it): wa káhktosch.

He will have him (or it): ih wa káhktosch; or, in káhktosch (*n* French; *in* nasal).

We shall have him (or it): núh káhktosch.

You will have him (or it): wa ra káhktosch.

They will have him (or it): ih onn na káhktosch.

I shall not have him (or it): wa wa kánechosch (*ch* guttural).

I shall have: wa káhktosch.

Nouns

Singular

The old man: waratóhka-chihosch (*ch* guttural).

The old woman: rokánka-chihénn (*ch* guttural).

The fish-hook: poïkinïh (*o* and *i* separated).

The arm: a'hdä.

The branch: o'hchancha (*ch* guttural; *an* French).

The eye: istá.

The eyelid: istá-rupchä.

The axe: óhmanatä.

Plural

The old men: waratóhka-kerïsch; really keréhsch.

The old women: rokánke-kerïsh.

The fish-hooks: poïkinïh-keréhsch.

The arms: a'hdä-keréhsch.

The branches: o'hchancha-keréhsch.

The eyelids: istá-rupchi-keréhsch.

The axes: o'hmanat-keréhsch.

A great forest: mánna-keréhsch; i.e., many trees, from mánna, tree.

Remark. From these instances it is easy to derive the rule that to form the plural of nouns the word keréhsch is affixed. It is occasionally pronounced kerisch, and denotes plurality.

Exceptions:

Máhna, the year; the plural is not mána-keréhsch, but manáhna, the years, or better, the winters.

Both arms, i.e., the arms, are called in the plural, a'hdä-náhta; the legs, dóhke-náhta. This exception is due to the fact that the number of arms on the body is definitely known; they are never more than two, so the plural is "both."

The word keréhsch also signifies in some few cases that objects of only one kind are included, yet always in the plural. Thus, when one enters a lodge where old men or women are assembled, he would say waratóhka-keréhsch, only old men; or rokánka-keréhsch, only or merely old women; waschï-keréhsch, merely white men; waschipsi(*waschi-psih*)-keréhsch, merely negroes, etc.

Declension of the Noun

Singular	Plural
Nom., **the man**, númang-kä.	*Nom.*, **the men**, numang-kärrä.
Gen., **of the man**, numank-äda.	*Gen.*, **of the men**, o'h-numang-kä.
Dat., **to the man**, o'h-numank.	*Dat.*, **to the men**, númang-kärrä-tá.
Accus., **the man**, númank-kä.	*Accus.*, **the men**, numang-kärrä.
Voc., **O man!** numánk.	*Voc.*, **O men!** numang-káke.
Abl., **from the man**, númang-kä.	

Singular	Plural
Nom., **the bow**, woraërúhpa.	*Nom.*, **the bows**, woraërúhpa-keréhsch.

Gen., **of the bow**, woraërúhpa-dä.

Gen., **of the bows**, woraërúhpa-kärrä-tá.

Dat., **to the bow**, woraërúhpa-äta.

Dat., **to the bows**, woraërúhpa-kärrä-ätá.

Accus., **the bow**, woraërúhpa.

Accus., **the bows**, oh-woraërúhpa-keréhsch.

Voc., **O bow!** woraërúhpa.

Voc., **O bows!** woraërúhpa-keréhsch.

Abl., **from the bow**, woraërúhpa-tá.

Abl., **from the bows**, woraërúhpa-kärrä-tá.

The word "from," motion towards the speaker, is expressed by tá; as in hutá, come here. The word "to," motion from the speaker, is expressed by the word äta.

Exception:

Idäta-keréhsch, the others; in this expression keréhsch is usually omitted, and only idäta used.

Proper Names

The names of these Indians always have a meaning, and often include a whole phrase. All familiar objects and their different states are drawn upon for the names of persons, and these are often very vulgar. I have given some of them above.

Adjectives

Adjectives are placed after the nouns; e.g., menïss-schóttä, horse white, not as in German and English, the white horse.

Examples:

Mandeck suck-sä (*an* French), the red bird; i.e., bird the red.

Numank-chárakä (*ch* guttural), the brave man.

Passán-schïhsch (*an* French), the beautiful river.

Manïssuarut-psïhsch, the black dog.

Comparison

The comparative degree is formed by affixing the word opáchadehsch, or opáchádähsch (*ch* guttural), i.e., more. The superlative degree is formed by affixing the word mïhkasch, i.e., the most.

Good, schihsch: better, schïh-opáchadehsch: best, schïh-mïhkasch.

Bad, chïcosch: worse, chikä-opáchadehsch: worst, chïk-ä-mïhkasch.

Near, askahá: nearer, aská-opáchadähsch: nearest (next), aská-mihkasch.

Much, hunsch: more, hun (*un* like French *oun*)-opáchadähsch: most, hun-mïhkasch.

Old, chihósch (*ch* guttural): older, chihä-opáchadähsch: oldest, chihä-mïhkasch.

Sure (certain), does not occur: they say instead, true, tkúschosch; truer, tkschä-opáchadäsch: truest, tkuscha-mihkasch.

Great (tall), háschka: greater, háschka-opáchadähsch: greatest, haschka-mïhkasch.

Wise, schïrukosch: wiser, schïruko-páchadähsch: wisest, schïruko-mïhkasch.

Remark. Occasionally the comparative and superlative are used together in order to give greater emphasis.

Example:

The most beautiful river: pa'ssanhä(or pássahä)-koschï-opachadäh-mïhkasch.

Use of Adjectives as Nouns

The rich man, ko-wakáhdä-hunsch; ko, the.

The poor, ko-áhchkereh-kerïsch (*ch* guttural; second *e* ½).

The divine (godlike), máh-choppenih-tá.

The beautiful, they say "the good," ko-schïhsch.

The colors are expressed in the plural just as in German and English.

Example:

The greens (the various greens), wïhra-tohä-tatá-keréhsch; i.e., wïhra-tohä, green; tatá, the various.

Indefinite Numerals

These answer the question, how many times? or; how often?

Once, schanáhre-máchanasch.

A single one, máchana-ïncha (in the second word, *in* almost like *i* nasal).

Twice, schanáhre-numpóhsch; and so on to and including ten. First, second, third, etc. are expressed in like manner.

Stosch (with the point of the tongue), a single one.

The Positive Degree

That is large (great): äth-háschkasch.

That is good: äth-schïhsch.

That is bad: äth-chikósch (*ch* guttural).

That is much: äth-hunsch (*un* like French *oun*).

It is long: háschkasch.

It is thick: chtähsch; from the word chtä, thick.

It is beautiful: schïhsch; from schïh, beautiful.

In these instances, therefore, *sch* is added [to form the positive].

Numerals

Cardinals

There are as many expressions for them as in the language of civilized peoples, from one to 1,000,000, etc.

One, máchana (*ch* guttural).

Two, numpä (*m* French, *um* like French *oum*).

Three, náhmeni (*e* ½).

Four, tóhpe (*e* ½); often shortened to tóhp; tóhposch, there are four.

Five, kächón (*ch* guttural; *on* French).

Six, kïhma.

Seven, kúhpa.

Eight, tättake (*e* or *a* umlaut).

Nine, máchpe (*ach* guttural; *e* about ½).

Ten, pitágh (*gh* guttural); really pïrakosch, but it is very much shortened.

Eleven, a'hga-ma'chana (*ga* guttural).

Twelve, a'hga-numpä.

Thirteen, a'hga-náhmeni.

Fourteen, a'hk-tóhp.

Sixteen, a'h-kïhma.

Seventeen, a'h-kúhpa.

Eighteen, ahk-tättake.

Nineteen, a'hga-ma'chpe (*ch* guttural).

Twenty, nompá-piráhg (*om* French).

Twenty-one, nompá-pirákä-roh-máchana.

Thirty, na'hmeni-ampïrakosch.

Forty, tóhpa-pïrakosch.

Fifty, kächón-ampïrakosch.

Sixty, kïhma-ampïrakosch.

Seventy, kúhpa-ampïrakosch.

Eighty, ta'ttake-ampïrakosch.

Ninety, máchpe-ampïrakosch.

One hundred, éhsuck-máchana.

One hundred and one, éhsuck-máchana-roh-máchanasch.

One hundred and two, éhsuck-máchana-roh-numpóhsch.

Two hundred, éhsuck-numpá.

Three hundred, éhsuck-náhmeni.

One thousand, isúkki-kákohi.

One thousand and one, isúkki-kákohi-roh-máchanasch.

One thousand one hundred, isúck-áhga-máchanasch; i.e., eleven hundred.

Two thousand, isúck-ikákohi-numpóhsch.

Ten thousand, isúck-ikákohi-pïrakosch.

One hundred thousand, isúck-ikákohi-isuck-mácha-pïrakosch; i.e., one thousand ten times one hundred.

Ordinals

The first, ko-ónti (*on* French).

The second, ko-númpä-hank.

The third, ko-náhmeni-hank.

The fourth, ko-tóhp-hank.

They continue in like manner, Ko, the, is always prefixed; and hank is always affixed; it is equivalent to German "te," or French ième.

The thousandth, ko-sukkikáhkohi-hank.

The last, ko-ïhkaháhschä.

Fractions

One half, ïhschanhä (*an* French).

There is a word for half; the other fractions are expressed by saying "a part."

Pronouns

[No attempt has been made by the translator to rearrange these confused forms.]

I, you, he, we, you, they; she and it are lacking.

Singular	Plural
I, mïh.	**We**, nuh.
You, ïh.	**You**, nïh-ätta.
He, ïh.	**They**, ïh-ätta.

First Person Singular	First Person Plural
Nom., **I**, mïh.	*Nom.*, **we**, núh.
Gen., **of me**, man-nan (*an* French, nasal like *ah*).	*Gen.*, **of us**, nuétta.

Dat., **to me**, mó (rather full).

Dat., **to me**, róh-dätá.

Accus., **me**, uáck.

Accus., (or dative; German, uns), **us**, nuétta.

Abl., **from me**, roh-ätá.

Second Person Singular

Nom., **you**, ïh.

Gen., **of you**, nittá.

Dat., **to you**, nïh.

Accus., **you**, nïh.

Example:

Mïh nïh rotkä, I shall strike you; i.e., I you shall strike.

Example of the first person:

You are ashamed of me: man-nan ïhnkidichihsch (*n* French; *ch* guttural); i.e., of me you are ashamed (German, shame yourself).

Third Person Singular   Third Person Plural

Nom., **he**, ïh.

Nom., **we**, núh.

Gen., **of him** (his), ïhta.

Gen., **of us**, nuthá.

Dat., **to him**, ïhta.

Dat., **to us**, róh.

Accus., **him**, ïh.

Accus., **us**, róh.

Example:

His eye has served him ill: ïhta istá ïh kirúchikosch; i.e., his eye him has served ill; ïhta istá, his eye.

These notes were interrupted by sickness.

Addenda

I eat, wawarutóhsch.

You eat, wararustosch.

He eats, ïhwarutohsch.

We eat, wanurutohsch.

You eat, ïhwarutochedesch.

They eat, roh-waruta-mankahusch.

I have eaten, wawarut-makibchasch (*ch* guttural).

I shall eat, wawarustosch.

I would eat, ihua-haraposch (run together).

Eat (imper sing), warustá (*ta* short).

Eat (imper plur), wárutenistá.

Eating, warútta-mánkahusch.

FOOTNOTES:

[257] These were discontinued owing to illness, and are, therefore, incomplete.—MAXIMILIAN.

Mandan Village Dialects

[The two villages are Mih-tutta-hángkusch and Ruhptáre; the variants are distinguished by prefixing thereto (M) and (R) respectively.—TRANS.]

Blanket (white woolen): (M) manhïchtä-schóttä; (R) waráchschóttä (*ach* guttural).

Board (plank): (M) mánnaopschïhdä; (R) mánna-gapschïhdä.

Boat: (M) minnanke (*an* French; *ke* short); (R) mánna-kinihnde (*de* distinct and short).

Bow: (M) woraërúhpa, waraërúhpa, or baraëruhpa; (R) warauïruhpa-gapschihde (*e* distinctly pronounced).

Child: (M) suck-chámahä (*ch* guttural); (R) sucke-hïnnichä (*e* ½).

A child who cries constantly: (M) suck-chámahä-nattach-sinhusch (*ach* guttural; *n* French): (R) suckchinick-saráh-sinhusch (*e* ½; in the second word *n* is French).

Cloth (blue or black) (M): manhïchtä-psïh; (R) warách-psïh.

Cloth (green): (M) wïratohä; (R) warách-tohä.

Cloth (scarlet): (M) manhïchtä-sä; (R) warách-sä.

Clothes (article of dress): (M) ïhmaschuntä (*un* like French *oun*); (R) ihmakotä.

Cotton cloth (Indian): (M) maächtepáhpe; (R) marachpáhpina (*ach* guttural).

Cover the fire: (M) uáradä-wakatachta; (R) uaráhdä-wáchkuhárata (the two last words run together).

Covering of a lodge: (M) tïhähnachtah (*ach* guttural; *ta* long); (R) tihäh-karastáh.

Cut meat for drying (v): (M) wahgap-chïhda (*ach* guttural); (R) wahgap-schïhdä.

Dress yourself (imperative): (M) ïnni-maschuntä-okáwaschacktá; (R) onnïwakottä-okawakostá.

Dried meat: (M) móh-ihp-ka; (R) wah-ïh-hip-kä.

Ear of corn (maize): (M) húhpatka; (R) húhpan.

Entrance to a lodge (tambour): (M) berrä-páhchu (*r* with the point of the tongue; *ch* guttural); (R) berrä-óschiduhdä.

Fort (of the white men): (M) mannach-kinihnde (*ach* guttural; *e* distinctly pronounced); (R) mannách-kinïhnde (*e* distinctly pronounced).

Four inner posts of a lodge: (M) tidock-húhdä; (R) mahun-kih-häddä (*un* like French *oun*; the last three syllables run together.)

Give me water: (M) mönnih-mámakutta; (R) mönnïh-mam-makúhta.

Go and tell this: (M) náhha-kïnahta; (R) náhha-kikïnihta.

He beats the drum: (M) bäräch-dot-kisch (*ach* guttural; *r* with the point of the tongue); (R) bärächt-kïh-osch (*ach* guttural; *r* with the point of the tongue).

He dances: (M): wánapisch; (R) wáh-ana-pohsch.

He has arrived: (M) kirihsch; (R) kiri-osch.

He is dead: (M) tährusch; (R) täh-isch.

He is here: (M) mánkahusch (*an* French); (R) ahkamehusch (*e* distinctly pronounced).

He is victorious: (M) wachkaná-hrusch; (R) wachkanná-asch (*ach* guttural).

He rises (stands up): (M) nán-teh-isch (*an* French); (R) náh-etosch (*e* barely audible).

He seeks (tries): kichkárarusch (*ich* German); (R) kikáraasch.

Hoe: (M) chúnapa; (R) ahhudäne (*e* ½).

I have found the bones: (M) wahuh-kärrewa-huhsch; (R) húh-kärräwáni-isch (the two last words run together).

I have given (rejeté): (M) kahärre-isch; (R) kahärre-usch.

I have said it (said so): (M) äh-pisch; (R) wahänni-waäh-äs (run together).

I have scraped it (a hide): (M) warrúh-hintuhsch; (R) wapácho-husch (*ch* guttural).

I have seen: wahähsch; (R) waháusch (German).

I sell: (M) wĭh-káhrusch: (R)wĭh-tusch.

I sew: (M) ïwa-tarakosch; (R) kikáh-akosch (*a* barely audible).

I shall tell him (say to him): (M) wakinnahktusch (run together); (R) wakĭkinihktusch.

I sleep: (M) wahánarusch; (R) wahána-asch.

I talk with you: (M) waháh-dohrusch; (R) wáhko-haráhrusch.

I think it is so: (M) on-usch-ka-iwa-paschidéhhusch (*n* French); (R) o'nschka-ewadehusch.

I throw out the dirt: (M) wapattikosch; (R) wacktóhsch (*wack* short).

I sit: (M) wakich-kanakosch (*ich* guttural); (R) kikánakosch.

It is sold (the meat): (M) dá-cherä-pusch (*ch* guttural; *r* with the point of the tongue); (R) dáhktun-wehdusch (*un* like French *oun*).

Lower part of a hill: (M) káh-werisch-kat (*e* ½);(R) mahäh-kar-astá (*r* with the point of the tongue).

Medicine: (M) chóppenih (*ch* guttural); (R) chóppenih-hosch (*ch* guttural).

This is medicine: (M) chóppenisch (ch guttural); (R) chóppeni-osch (*e* short and ½).

One year old buffalo cow: (M) ninkï-patú (*in* like *i* nasal; *ï* separated); (R) ninkï-páhtune (*e* barely audible).

Otter: (M) pähchtekeh, or pächtackä (*ach* guttural); (R) chóhpäckä (*o* full).

Pray go there! (M) dahhini-äĥäta; (R) hänni-ääta.

Pretty: (M) schïh-óchadisch (run together); (R) schïdo-óchorusch (*r* with the point of the tongue).

Put on your leggings and moccasins: énni-kïhtata; (R) onnïh-kihtata.

Robe: (M) mïh-ihä (run together); (R) má-i-hä.

Scaffold (frame): (M) maschóttä; (R) waschtähn (*w* like *ua*; occasionally an *e* is heard at the end).

Seat yourself: (M) kichkánackta (*ich* German); (R) nunschiman-hihárata. (*n* and *an* French).

Shield: (M) wakïh; (R) wakïhdä, or wähkachkopä (*ach* guttural).

Small brook: (M) passách-kschukkä (*ach* guttural); (R) passá-ihïnikän.

Sow (v): (M) wahih-häddisch; (R) bóhwachtosch (*ach* guttural).

Thank (jemand zum danke streichen): (M) wáhki-ähsch; (R) owáh-kuhunsch (*un* like French *oun*).

The water is high (or deep): (M) mönnïh-päʰhosch; (R) monnih-kuwuhosch.

They come: (M) hóhrusch (*r* with the point of the tongue); (R) hóh-usch.

They have shot: (M) erúhpa-ka-tähsch (*r* with the point of the tongue); (R) erúhpa-ka-tamm-unusch (*un* like French *oun*).

They strike one another violently: (M) oʰhki-sa-charakosch (*ch* guttural; *r* with the point of the tongue); (R) kïhkawo-sin-hosch (*in* like *i* nasal).

Thread (n): (M) wäi-wattarakänn; (R) wïhkikankähne (*n* French; *e* ½).

We have arrived: (M) núhtisch; (R) wäh-te-usch (*e* distinctly pronounced; the whole run together).

You have said (singular): ähtisch; (R) ähto-sch.

You tell the truth: (M) on-usch-kasch; (R) unsch-kusch (*un* like French *oun*).

Young cow: (M) ptin-chámahä (*in* like *i* nasal; *ch* guttural); (R) ptin-ihïnikä (*n* as before).

MINNITARRIS, or Grosventres[258]

Abode (dwelling place; shooting stand), uaköh-schähs.

Above, aʰh-kuka (*ah* strongly emphasized).

Abyss (precipice), awaräta-dach-apïhsäs.

Ahead (forward), wĭh-akuwatáhs.

All (the whole, all together), ähsa (*sa* short).

Alone (single), ïchsaki (*saki* short).

Always, tĭh-achkuss.

American, Mahtschi-ichtïä.

Another, iháh-s (*s* slightly hissed).

Answer (v), wih-a-kákiwähs (the whole short and run together).

Antelope park (the), oʻh-chidäi (*dai* run together).

Anxiety (fear), wah-ereïchu-pascháhsis (*sis* distinctly pronounced).

Approach stealthily (v), uïtadähs (*ui* somewhat separated).

Arm, aʻhra (*r* with the point of the tongue).

Arrow, bïdda-arúhtischa (*scha* short).

Ashes, wirásipa (the whole short).

Ask (v), kiwáschusch (*wa* very short; *chusch* low).

Awake (v, intr), mah-käï-sähs. (*kai* shrill, with the point of the tongue).

Axe, waïpsá.

Back (adverb), kiïss (*ii* separated); i.e., he is back.

Back (n, or v; to move with a jerk?), äschitá.

Backward, epéhtïqua (*e* ½; *qua* run together and short).

Bad (angry), natatähs.

Bald, aʻhchtu-rukotis (*ahch* long).

Ball (bullet), oʻhwassa-werúchaarúhtischa; or simply arúhtischa.

Ball (for playing), maóh-tape (run together; *e* distinctly pronounced).

Ball-game of the women, ma-úhtape (*e* distinctly pronounced; the whole run together).

Bathe (v), wirichpï (*pi* short).

Bear (v; give birth), eïmattúhäs (indistinct and short).

Beard, ih-ih-tass (pronounced together).

Beautiful, sakïchtiss (*ich* with the point of the tongue).

Behind (back of us), wapí-tikua.

Belly, ïhchi.

Below (beneath), mechtáhchqua (*e* ½; *qua* together).

Bend (v), rúhskupiss.

Berdash, biattï (*ti* short; *bi* separated from *a*).

Beside (near), watáh-óhtiruch.

Best (all genders), akussakïss.

Between, nu-uáh-taru (the whole run together; *taru* low and without emphasis).

Big with young, same word as for pregnant.

Bile, wáh-aruschïde (*schi* long; *de* short and low).

Billiard game (Billard-spiel), máh-kache (*e* ½; the whole short).

Bird, sakkanka.

Bitter, arauiss.

Black, schüpïscha (*scha* short).

Bladder, arachi.

Blind, ischtá-läjiss (*ji* French); i.e., no eyes.

Blond (of hair), arrasïhdiss.

Blood, ïhdi; bloody, ïhdi-sakïss.

Bloom, (v), ohrakapakiss.

Blow out (v; blow), kah-sahs.

Blue, tóhhiss.

Blush (v), ehtu-wihähs.

Boil (v), birruáss (very short; *ass* soft).

Bone (n), hädú (*du* very short and explosive; *ha* almost like German *hai*).

Bough, birá-arukaká(*kaka* short).

Bow, berúcha-paruiï.

Bow-lance, bidúcha-háski.

Box on the ear, jïh-tarrickï (*ii* separated; second word short).

Braid (v), naksútti.

Break (v; shatter), irúchupiss.

Breast (female), aʰsi (*si* short).

Breast (the whole breast), ïhwaki (*ki* short, almost like *ke*).

Breath, idïachis (*i* with emphasis).

Brilliant (splendid), hopháh-hischötts (second word low and short).

Broad, schúchkass.

Brook, ahji-karischtá (*ji* French).

Broom (for sweeping), mahchschïa-ïhcha.

Brother (eldest), ih-akáss.

Brother (youngest), hähderusch (*r* with the point of the tongue, as always).

Brown, takápiäs (*i* and *a* somewhat separated).

Bud (n), bïdda-ächpú (the whole short).

Burn (v, reflexive), aʰotiss (*ah* and *o* separated).

Burn (v, tr or intr; destroy by fire), arach-púpiss (run together).

Buttock, ischïttarucka (*tarucka* short).

Buy (v), mah-éh-ho.

Call (v; call anyone), haähdaha (*a* and *ah* separated; *daha* short).

Calm (n), há-hei-hischess (*hei* German, together; *ha* with emphasis; the whole pronounced together).

Candle (light), biddá-i-awacháhtä (the whole run together).

Canoe, máhn-ti (*mahn* nasal; *n* French; *ti* short).

Carrion (a dead animal), wah-puhäs (*s* barely audible).

Catch (v; capture), dúhchsiss.

Caught (taken prïsoner), náhchke (*nahch* long and with emphasis; *e* ½ and short).

Chew (v), marúchtuas (*as* moderated).

Child, máh-karischtá.

Chill (v; be cold, freeze), mih-áhkapahts (run together).

Chin, wïhchka.

Circle (n), kakïchis (short).

Clap (v; with the hands), lacksútti.

Clasp (v; enclose), kidachpáhs.

Claws (of an animal), isächpo.

Clear, kischïss.

Clear (bright), awacháhtis.

Clouds (masses of cloud), achpáhchä (*cha* short).

Coal, bïdda-apuckschá (*scha* short and explosive).

Coals (glowing), bïdda-arra-áracha (the whole run together, short explosive).

Cold (adj), siddïh-as (first word with emphasis; *as* moderated).

Color (n), oʰhdä.

Comb (n), máh-ara-ächkidochokä.

Come (v), húhs; come here, hú.

Console (v), dïddä-ätá (the whole short).

Corpse, täes (*a* and *e* separated).

Cough (v), máh-hoáss (last word short).

Count (v), kirruwïss.

Cover (v; cover up), ïruchupiss.

Cowardly, maäh-sa-kiáss.

Crooked, schakupï (*pi* very short).

Crop (maw), ahpichtïa (*ich* German, not guttural; final *a* ½).

Cure (v), kiraïschachkais (*rai* and *kais* run together; the whole short).

Curly (of hair), araschikïäs (emphasis on *i*).

Curry (v; tan), mánpachu (*an* French; *pachu* low and short).

Cut (v), pá-sakiss (run together).

Cut down (v), wahk-ksakkes (run together; *kes* short).

Cut down (v; fell), bidda-rachkoáss.

Dance (n), mahdischï (*schi* short, explosive).

Dark, haphähischäs.

Daughter, same word as for maiden.

Dawn (daybreak), lackscháhwaräs (run together; *ras* not very short).

Day, áhtas.

Dead, arrutähs.

Deaf, ach-ko-chi-táh-us (the whole run together).

Dear (costly), eïhwassi-akuss (*e* short; *ih* with strong emphasis; the whole run together).

Death, täes (*a* and *e* separated).

Death's head (totenkopf), dokaráhcha-atú (*atu* short and explosive).

Decoy (v; an animal), watáhchiwahuhs.

Delay (v; make late), arrukühdak-schüpïss.

Dependent, awahährichka (*ka* short).

Devastate (v), háh-wihähs.

Devil (evil spirit), ïhsichka-wahäddisch.

Dew, bïddi-bitáss (*tass* with strong emphasis).

Die, (v), täes (*a* and *e* separated; *e* ½).

Dirty, awach-sákiss (words pronounced in quick succession).

Dirty (v), awachsákkis.

Dive (v), sippïss.

Divide (v), ïhwakisshähs (most of the word without emphasis).

Door, biddä.

Double, rúhpassakua (*kua* together, German, short).

Drag (v), rúh-sirruä (*ru* and *a* separated; *a* very short).

Draw (v; draw a load), dúh-särruäs (*u* separated from *as*).

Draw (v; draw water), aúschähs (*au* almost like full *o*; *s* indistinct).

Dream (n), same word as for verb.

Dream (v), mah-schïhrähs.

Dress (clothing), wa-ich-kikschiss (the whole pronounced together), or wikit-schïwiss (*schïwiss* short).

Drink (v), hä-ihs (*ha* loud cry; *ihs* lower).

Drive (v), nak-hïas (*hi* and *as* separated; *i* with strong emphasis).

Drop (of water; or v), chähs.

Drown (v; be drowned), nachpáhka-nacksá.

Drum (n), biddá-charriki (the whole very short).

Dry (adj), uhsiss (*siss* short).

Dumb, idähtas.

Dung, pähri (*ri* very short).

Dust, abá.

Ear, achpá (*pa* very short).

Ear-ornament, wa-achpóhksche (*o* very full; *e* ½).

Early, antarähts (*an* French; *tarahts* low, especially *rahts*).

Earth, auá (strong emphasis on *a*; *a* and *u* separated, almost like *awa*).

Egg (of a bird), sakkáh-karáhka; or sakkáh-kanáhka.

Elbow, ischpachä.

Empty (adj), wa-aúscha-rähschïs (*au* together).

Enemy, mah-ehá (*e* almost like *i*).

Englishman, Waschï-pachsïttako (*sittako* very short).

Enough, kochk-kats (*k* half modulated; *kats* low; the whole run together).

Entangle, (v; involve), chachaodïss.

Entertain (v), sakkiïuahs.

Even (flat), arusuchka.

Evening, ohksies (*o* full; *sies* distinctly pronounced; *e* ½).

Everywhere, chakáhäta.

Exchange (v; or mistake), koatóhk-madiäsisch-eschiwáhwarähs (*o* full; *i* and *a* separated; *i* with emphasis; *a* ½).

Expectorate (v; vomit), aruschúha (final *a* short).

Eye, ischtá.

Eye-ball, ischtárusche-pischa (*e* ½).

Eye-lash, ischách-pi.

Eyelid, ischtarach-pé.

Face (sight), jïtá.

Fade (v; wither), chéhdis (*cheh* with strong emphasis; *dis* short and low).

Fail (v; miss a shot), dachkisïss.

Fall (v), patthiss.

Fall (v; of the leaves), beréhpehahsïss (second *e* ½).

Fan (of feathers), o'hhiddi-ächkidda-kóhdi (*iddi* and *idda* very short).

Far (distant), téh-i-schiss (run together).

Far (distant), téh-schiss.

Fat (stout), schuwï (*wi* very short and with strong emphasis).

Father, a'htuch (*ah* nasal).

Feather, maïs-chóhki (the whole pronounced together).

Female (of animals), wuüchka.

Festival (corn festival), wah-ruïkohke (*u* and *i* separated; *e* distinctly pronounced; the whole run together).

Fin, wóa-éschu (*schu* short).

Find (v), óhrapiss (*o* full; *piss* indistinct and low).

Finger, maschákke-arussáwi (*e* ½).

Finger (fore), matï-wa-óhwi (*waohwi* together).

Finger (little), maschákke-káhscha (*a* only ½, almost like *e*).

Finger (middle), maschákke-eruhaski (the whole very short and run together).

Finger (third), maschákke-náhschidasche (*e* ½); i.e., the finger without a name.

Fire, bidá-a (*da-a* short and explosive).

Fire-brand, bida-assá (*assa* short and explosive).

Fish (n), buá (*a* with strong emphasis and rather full, like *o*).

Fish (v), wóhrak-schïass (*ass* like *att* and indistinct).

Fish (v; catch fish), wóhrak-schïes (*es* together; and distinctly pronounced).

Fish-hook, woh-ich-tikúhe (pronounced together).

Fist, scháhki-waóhpa-kichkähs (*ich* German, with the point of the tongue; the whole run together).

Flame, bïda-adaäëchi (*e* ½).

Flat, súhchkas.

Flatter (v), saráhki-páhchus (*ki* and *us* lower in tone).

Flee (v; escape), karáhs (*s* barely audible).

Flesh, erúkschitti (short; *schitti* short and low).

Flint, o'wassa-widuchá.

Flood (v; overflow), biddi-uhahahs.

Foam, biddi-puchä' (*biddi* short).

Fog, nakahotä'.

Force (v; compel), issïh-achkehs (the whole short, indistinct, and run together).

Forehead, ih-chï'.

Forest, bïdda-wahukáh.

Forget (v), uichkaráhchischess.

Foot, ittsï' (*si* very short).

Foot-path, adïïh (*a* short).

Free, arrudïtass (*di* accented; *tass* sinks in tone).

Freeze (v), maruchán-kapan (*an* French; *kapan* indistinct and lower).

Frenchman, Uaschï, or Waschï'.

Friend, marakoá (*koa* short).

Frost (hoar frost), macháurakiss (*au* together).

Full, ma-ássiss.

Full-moon, wáhch-kubbedïh-áhchkakóhri (*ri* pronounced lower).

Fully, aotti (*a* and *o* separated; *ti* low and short).

Gay-colored (variegated), pohjïss (*j* French).

Go (v), dähts (indistinct and low at the end).

God (lord of life), ehsich-kawáh-hiddisch (*hiddisch* without accent or emphasis and low; *ich* German and not guttural).[259]

Good, sakkïss (*kiss* very short; *ss* barely audible).

Grandson, matauapïscha.

Grape-vine, bïdda-páheri (*pah* together; *e* ½; *ri* short).

Grass, miká (*mi* very short; *ka* strong explosive).

Gray, sáotta.

Gray-haired, arrahascheháh-attakits (*e* ½; *its* low; the whole short).

Great, hatskits (low).

Green, maëilöüichka (*ich* with the point of the tongue).

Ground, same word as for earth.

Gums, ihch-schá-arúh-idú (last four syllables run together; *idu* very short).

Gun, ohwa-tsawirúcha (second word short and low); rifle, arruhappissúa (*u* and *a* separated).

Gut (intestines), schïhpa (*pa* short).

Gut (v; gut an animal), ehri-hatáhs.

Hail (n), múhkach-pittauï (run together).

Hair, ará (nasal).

Half, súhta (*ta* short and low).

Hand, waschakï.

Hard, sa-su-kïss (*sa* short; the whole short and run together).

Hate (v), arre-ä-wahs (*arre* short; *e* ½; the whole pronounced together).

Haul (v; fetch), kikïhriss.

Head, ah-tú (*ah* nasal; *tu* very short explosive).

Headache, ah-tú-areä (*e* ½; last word short and indistinct).

Hear (v), uïhkikess.

Heart, waratá.

Hearty (stout-hearted), uútahs (*uu* separated; *s* somewhat like *t*).

Heat (n), sauähs (*a* and *u* separated).

Heat (v; inflame), mïh-sa-uähs.

Heaven (sky), achpáhchi-tóhä.

Heavy, taksïäs (*as* short; *i* and *as* separated; *i* with emphasis).

Heel, issähki (*ki* short).

Help (v), ah-pewahais (second word pronounced softly and short; *hais* German, together; *e* distinctly pronounced).

Hem (v; clear one's throat), áhpatsekickschiss (strong emphasis on *ah*; *e* ½).

Hide (v), a-áchoass (*ass* low; the whole run together).

High, wáhkuss.

Hill of the children, Máh-karistáhti.

Hoarse, erúhschiäs (short and run together; final *s* distinct).

Hole, máh-arhoppe (*e* has almost full value).

Hollow (adj), cháhkupiss.

Hoof (cloven), esïchpu (*e* like *i*).

Hoop (of wood), wirrawáh-apé (*ape* very short; *e* ½).

Hope (v), ihwatïss.

Horn, aaschï (*aa* separated); or aanschï; (*a* and *an* French and separated).

Horns, máhroka-ánschi (*an* French; second *a* barely audible).

Hot, sawáis (German; the whole short and run together).

House (lodge), attï, (*i* short).

Hunger, wah-ahrïtis; i.e., they are all hungry; marïhtis, I am hungry.

Hunt (v), wáhri-iwaráhs (second *i* barely audible).

Hunter, wáhri-irakurähs (second *i* barely audible).

Hurl (v; or overthrow), mih-patïss.

Hurricane, hóhsi-ichtïas (*ich* German and not guttural; *i* with strong accent; *i* and *a* separated).

I, mïh.

Ice, warúchi.

In (come in), bidäht.

Incurable, arrukischidähset (*dah* prolonged with emphasis; *arru* short).

Indistinct (of seeing), i-äss.

Interior, awahuká (*awa* short).

Intoxicate, waráchapahs.

Iron, uhwassa (*sa* short).

Island, wiritáhä.

Itch (n), chediäss (*e* distinctly pronounced).

Jar (vessel), biddachá.

Jaw, mara-oróhpa (*o* full; the whole run together).

Joy, naatássakiss (*aa* separated).

Kernel, súhwa (*wa* short).

Kindle (v), arachahähs.

Knee, wachóh-acha (*choh* together; the whole pronounced together).

Kneel (v), äschuwissä.

Knife, máhtsi.

Know (v), ahchkähs (first *a* ½, almost like *a* umlaut).

Know (v; be acquainted with), awachkähs (*kahs* low and moderated).

Knuckle (n), watsï-orussáh (short and run together).

Lame (limping), ashkáus (*kaus* almost like *kohs*).

Lament (v), arra-akïwiät; i.e., he weeps from pain.

Lance, bïdda-tirutä (last word short).

Land, same word as for earth.

Laugh (v), káhs (German throughout).

Lay (v; lay down), rúhscha (*scha* short).

Leader (chief), uassä-issis.

Leaf, a'hpa.

Lean (v), ihtáhkachta (*ta* short).

Leap (v; spring), sich-chïss (*sich* short; *chiss* likewise).

Left (adverb), ïrach-kïscha (the whole short; *scha* short).

Lick (v), náhsipiss.

Lie (v; deceive), wittapáss.

Life, nachkúss.

Lift (v), dóhkiss (rather indistinct).

Light (v), awachath-hähs (run together).

Light (nimble), dagóchtiss (*go* German guttural).

Lightning, karichkáhs (*ich* hissed as in German and not guttural).

Like (v), kiráschiss.

Lip, ïhdä-ätá (*ta* short).

Little, kohsch-táss (*o* full).

Long, háski; this word was undoubtedly borrowed from the Mandans.

Loose (of clothes), ichtïass (*ich* German, with the point of the tongue; *i* with emphasis and separated from *ass*).

Maiden, bïh-akáhsa (final *a* ½); they also use akáhscha for akáhsa.

Maize, kóhchatä (*o* full); this word was certainly borrowed from the Mandans.

Man, matséh, or matsäh.

Man (human being), massä, or matsäh.

Meal (eat?), babutïss.

Medicine, chupáhs (*ch* guttural).

Medicine-feast, mah-chupáh-ääs.

Medicine-feast (the Okippe of the Mandans), akupéhri (*ku* very short; *ri* short and with the point of the tongue).

Medicine-lodge, atechupáhs.

Medicine-man, madséh-akuchupáhs.

Medicine-stone, wïhdä-katachï (*da* and *chi* very short).

Melt (v), sukïss.

Messenger, dáchkahts (*a* peculiarly modulated).

Milk (n), ma-áhtsi-biddï (short and run together; *biddi* very short).

Mirror, ma-ich-kïh-ka (*ich* with the point of the tongue; *ka* short).

Mistake (v; lose one's way), wachkaráhchisschess (*schess* low and soft).

Moon, wáhch-kubbedïh (the whole short and run togeher; *e* ½).

Moonshine, wáhch-kubbedïh-sihsah (*sah* lowered).

Morning, kirahkutá (*ta* short).

Mother, ächká (*ach* not guttural, but *ch* hissed).

Mountain, awacháüi (the whole together).

Mouth, bïh.

Much, ahúss.

Murder (v; kill), tawahs (*wa* like *ua*).

Music (beat the drum), wïrrachárriki (the whole short).

My, watawá.

Nail (on the hand), wascháckächpú.

Nail (on the foot), wassïchpu.

Naked, widdi-bikkikoáejes (*e* ½; *a* and *e* separated; *je* French; *s* ½).

Name, náhji (*nah* with emphasis; *ji* French, low and short).

Nape (of the neck), machpóh-ottä (together; *otta* short).

Narrow, karïschtass (*ss* indistinct).

Navel, watarächpá.

Neck (throat), ahperu (*peru* very short).

Negro, waschïh (or uaschih)-ischüpïscha.

Nest (of bird), ichkïschi (*schi* short).

Nettle (n), wáh-ächáhke (*e* ½).

New, hiddáhs (short, *s* low).

New-moon, wáhch-kubbedïh-kiddahïss.

Night, aúk-sïe (*auk* together, with emphasis; *u* somewhat like *i*; *si* together; *e* ½, separated and somewhat like *a*).

Noon, widdiwáh-péirapi (*pei* together and shrill; the whole short and rapid); i.e., the sun is in the middle.

Nose, apá (short).

Nostril, apáre-hopö (*e* ½; the whole short).

Not (no), dähsches (*e* ½; *s* soft).

Old, chiäs (*as* soft and low).

Old man, itháka-chiäs.

Old woman, káhru-chiäs.

Oldest (the oldest), akouáh-ichtïäs (*o* and *u* separated; *ch* guttural; *ti* together; *as* together).

On the other side, tsóo-ka (*ka* lowers in tone, short; *oo* somewhat separated).

On the other side of the hill, awa-itá-sohqua (*qua* together).

Outside (without), atáhjikua (*ji* French; *kua* together).

Over, máh-kuka (run together).

Oversleep (v; neglect by sleeping), häddauittïäs (*ti* and *as* separated, *ti* with emphasis).

Pain (n), hädú-ade-äss (*e* ½; strong emphasis on *ass*; the whole run together).

Paint (v), warahk-hiriss.

Pair, rúhpassa (*passa* low and short).

Palate (roof of the mouth), nóotisch-karuscháscha (*oo* separated and full; *karuschascha* short; *scha* sinks in tone).

Pardon (v; forgive), kiräh-schachkähs (run together).

Partizan (leader of a war party), akurïhdi (*di* short).

Past (over; go past), eischiss (*ei* very shrill, with the point of the tongue, with strong emphasis).

Peace, make-itteruchpahk-hatsch (*e* ½; *hatsch* low and indistinct, like *hahts*).

People (men, folk), ruchpáhga (*ga* German guttural).

Pinch (v; to carouse?), wirúskapis (*pis* distinctly pronounced).

Pipe (tobacco-pipe), éikipi (*ei* very shrill, almost like *i* and with strong accent; *kipi* low and short).

Plant (v), awa-áuschess (*au* together).

Play (v), bidáchatichke (*ich* German, with the point of the tongue; *e* ½).

Pluck (v; feathers), ïhruketiss (*e* ½).

Pointed, apsáss.

Polish (v; adorn), ächkikschïss.

Pond (or pool), bïddicha-kúp-hä.

Pouch (for ammunition), beädse-ïschi (*e* distinctly pronounced).

Pouch (painted, of leather), wákiischi (run together).

Pouch (of leather), wassitó-üschi.

Powder (gun-powder), birá-sipa.

Prairie, ama-awesuchka (*e* distinctly pronounced).

Pregnant, äcdichtïäs (*i* with emphasis; *i* and *as* separated).

Press (v), sasuck-hähs (run together).

Press out (v; express?), núhbiris.

Pretty, sackïchtiss (*ich* with the point of the tongue).

Prick (v; or sting), mah-aráchpüwiss.

Prisoner, náhkehäs (*e* ½).

Proud, ichóa-ischi-sakïssas (*o* and *a* separated; *ischi* short).

Pulse, dúschi-schïäs (*i* with strong accent; *i* and *as* separated).

Push (v; thrust), páki-dïäs (*di* and *as* separated; the whole run together).

Quarrel (v; fight), aúk-schass-hähs (*auk* with strong emphasis; the whole run together).

Quarter (of the moon), wáhchkubbedïh-erúschkapiss.

- 249 -

Quick, hih-itats (run together; *tats* low; the whole short).

Quiver, arúhtischa-ïschi.

Rain (v), charähs.

Rainbow, bïddi-apóka; i.e., the cap of the water.

Rattle (sysyquoy, gourd rattle), éi-poh-chä (*ei* like *ai*, together; a loud, shrill fore-tone).

Reconcile (v), make-ikáh-as (*e* ½; the whole pronounced together).

Red, heischïss (*hei* together and pronounced very shrilly with the point of the tongue).

Refuse (v; deny), e-ischï-arähs (the whole run together); i.e., I will not.

Rib, wirrúh-tirrú (the whole very short).

Ring (v), tawóes (*o* and *e* separated; *es* together and ½).

Ripe (of fruit), aotiss (*ao* separated; the whole short and run together).

River, anji-ischtiäss (first *i* often silent; *j* French).

Roast (v; or n), wahwerití (*e* ½).

Rock (cliff), bi-hách-pa (*hach* guttural, yet almost like *ha*).

Root, äscháhwichkä (*wich* German, with the point of the tongue).

Rot (v), karähs.

Rotten (lazy), nah-ta-chéh-piss.

Row (v; paddle), wáh-tirachóhke (*e* distinctly pronounced).

Run (v), tiriäs (*s* very low and barely audible).

Saddle (for a horse), matanáh-chukchä-rubidá.

Sand, póhcha-ka (*ka* short).

Scaffold (for the dead), mánsachti (*man* French, long; *ti* very short).

Scalp (n), biddarú (*ru* with the point of the tongue, short, and soft).

Scalp (v), addadúhs.

Scar, oh-áttass.

Scratch (v), rúchkapiss.

Scream (v), saskïss.

Sea, bïddi-akichtïa (*biddi* very short; first *a* barely audible; *ti* and *a* separated).

Secret (adj), a-achóas (together; *as* ½ and low).

See (v), ïkahs.

Seize (v; attack), wapach-tïsiss.

Shade (shadow), arru-óhkse (*e* ½; *o* between *a* and *o*).

Shake (v; rock), chakáhrachkuss.

Shallow (water), biddi-chähpis.

Sharp (keen), apsáss (second *a* modulated).

Shield (pare-flèche), widáhki (*ki* short).

Shin (shin-bone), wassóhpa (*pa* short).

Shiver (v; with cold), wïhtarichtiss (*ich* German, with the point of the tongue).

Shoot (with a bow), bïdda-arúhschischa-iwáhre-ïss (*e* ½).

Shoot (with a gun), óhwassabérucha-ihwáhre-ïss (*e* ½).

Shooting-star, ichkaró-han-kar-ähs (*ich* German, with the point of the tongue; *an* French; the whole run together).

Shore (bank), biddi-däh-tadu; (first and last words very short).

Short, párruwi (short and rapidly pronounced).

Shoulder, ah-tirú (*tiru* very short).

Show (v; instruct in a matter), kikúhs-kïss (short and run together).

Sick, ächurähs (*u* and *a* separated).

Side, itá-sú (*su* very short).

Sigh (v), idïahiss (*di* and *a* separated; emphasis on *i*).

Sing (v), mah-páh-hiss.

Sister, ittawïa (first *i* barely audible; *i* and *a* separated, emphasis on *i* not very strong).

Sit (v), amáhgis (*mah* very long; *gis* German guttural).

Skin (hide of animal), dachpï.

Sledge, bïdda-wa-ádussadua (the whole run together; the last word indistinct and short).

Sleep (v), hïddawiss, or heidabïss (*hei* shrill, with the point of the tongue).

Slow, hóp-ha (*ha* short).

Small, karïschta.

Smell (v; sniff, scent), wúhpiss.

Smoke (n), pi-ähs.

Smoke (v; tobacco), aúpe-hihs (*ua* together; *e* ½).

Smooth, ah-atats (run together).

Snarl (v; growl), eháhte (final *e* distinctly pronounced; first *e* short).

Sneeze (v), mahhachpïss.

Snore (v), appatáhchis.

Snow (n), máh-a (short and run together).

Sole (of the foot), ittsï-wahú (*wahu* very short).

Son, idischá.

Sore-throat, ahperu-arreäss (first *e* distinctly pronounced; last word very short).

Spark (n), bïdda-alánka (*bidda* very short; *an* French; *lan* prolonged).

Speak (v), ïddähs.

Speech (language), máh-arúhdä (run together).

Spirits (distilled), widïh-araüi.

Spittle, arukschuá (strong accent on *a*).

Split (v; wood), bïdda-kiriki.

Spring (the season), ama-arähs (run together).

Spring (source), mahá.

Spy (v; listen), achkochä-ruktahs.

Squint (v), ischtärruchtahs.

Star, ichká (*ich* German, with the point of the tongue; *ka* short).

Start (v; start game), kárahäs.

Steep, nacháppäischass (*a* and *i* somewhat separated).

Step-father, same word as for father.

Step-mother, same word as for mother.

Stick (n), bidda-káhscha (*scha* short).

Stifle (v; choke, repress), dút-hapiss.

Still, há-chä-hi-schïss (pronounced together).

Stinginess, márachzats (*zats* low and indistinct; the whole nasal).

Stomach, bïhwaki (*bi* with stronger accent; *i* short; *waki* sinks in tone).

Stone (n), bih-ï (*i* very short and explosive).

Stop (v; stop up), kipáhtakiss.

Storm (n), maapischïa (*aa* separated; final *a* short and low).

Straight, zawóchtsitz (*tsitz* low).

Strike (v), nikïss.

Strong, iss-hïh-äs (run together; strong emphasis on *hih*; *as* very short and low).

Stump, schohkiss (*o* full and long).

Stupid, wahruchtahs.

Summer, abba-adähs (*abba* very short).

Sun, maápi-widdï (*aa* separated).

Sunrise, widdï-atähs (*widdi* very short).

Sunset, widdï-eihwachpiss (*ei* shrill; pronounced together as in German).

Swallow (v; choke), dáh-aschúhtis.

Swamp, biddichtïa-karähs (*i* with strong emphasis; *ti* and *a* separated).

Sweat (v), sabähs.

Sweat-medicine, bih-óh-aku-es (the whole short and run together; *oh* with strong accent; *akues* sinks in tone; *es* short and low).

Sweep (v; clean), maschï-arachahs.

Sweet, si-kóh-as (*si* and *as* short).

Swim (v), biddi-dïhris (*biddi* very short; the whole run together).

Swollen (swell), póh-ats (*ats* very soft and low).

Tail (of a bird), ïhpi.

Tail (of a quadruped), sïhta (second *i* barely audible; *ta* short; *sih* long).

Tattooing (n), arukpï (*pi* with strong emphasis and very short).

Teach (v), kikúhs-kï (*ki* very short, explosive).

Tear (v; tear or break to pieces), duuchähschis (*uu* separated; *schis* low).

Tear out (v), rúhkitiss.

Tears, istá-biddi-huhs (short and run together).

Teeth, ihch-schá (*ihch* German, with the point of the tongue; *scha* short and explosive).

Testicle, ähschuka (*ka* short).

There, hidóhs.

Thick (stout), ichtïhäs (*tih* together).

Thin, chahpis.

Thorn, wah-apsáh.

Throat, nóhtischka (*ka* short).

Thumb, scháhkitta, or mascháktá (*ta* very short).

Thunder, tachúrakiss.

Tickle (v), wihscheschúkhäs (*e* ½; *has* soft and modulated).

Tie (v; fasten), warut-hiss (run together).

Tinder-box, bïdischa (*scha* short).

Tobacco, aópi (*ao* somewhat separated; *pi* short).

Tobacco-pouch, áopischi.

Toe, ittsikansa (*an* French, and prolonged; *sa* short).

To-morrow, ähtaruck.

Tongue, däh-eschi (*dah* with strong emphasis, *e* ½; and short; *eschi* short; the whole run together).

Toothache, ihch-schá-adähs.

Top (summit), awa-áhguka (*awa* nasal; *gu* guttural; *guka* short).

Toughness, erúhpupiss.

Track (of an animal), etsittï.

Trade (n), maschakï (*i* short).

Trader, akuwa-éh-hu (*kuwa* and *hu* short).

Tree, widá (*da* short and with emphasis), or bida.

Tremble (v), tadichtïss (*ich* German, with the point of the tongue).

True, káh-tähs.

Ugly, i-schï-äs (run together).

Unmarried, uh-arähschis; i.e., he has no wife.

Unripe, sáhs (nasal).

Until (unto), arudähs.

Urine, wä-äh-chiss (*chiss* guttural, short, and low).

Valley, arúcha-kupï (*pi* short).

Vein (artery), akáhscha.

Village, awatï (*ti* short).

Void (adj; stale; or cool, moderate), wïhtau-auschirähsches (*wih* with emphasis; *au* together).

Wait (v; await), áh-kuch-takahs (*ah* nasal, with strong emphasis).

War, matauáh-ehá (*e* ½; *aua* has each vowel separated); i.e., they are my enemies.

War-club (casse-tête; with the iron point), bïdda-ïhktärrä (*tarra* very short; *bidda* likewise), or bïdda-aspapsá.

War-club (of stone covered with leather), bïï-dakútse (*bii* very short; *e* ½), or wa-óh-upake (*e* distinctly pronounced; the whole run together).

War-club (of wood with knots), bïdda-pahuachi (the whole short).

War-whistle, ïh-akóhschi (short).

War-whoop, ïh-kirikïss.

Warmth, same word as for warm.

Warrior, wassaréhrickschack.

Wash (v), kiruskïschis.

Water, biddï, or bidï.

Weary, wahr-häkatis (the whole run together).

Weather (it is good weather), wáhpe-sakïss (*e* ½, almost like *i*).

Weep (v), éhwüass (*eh* with strong emphasis).

Wet, scharähs.

What? how? toháhsi (nasal).

Whip, mata-ïhki.

Whirlpool, bïddi-arúhwiddi (*widdi* very short; likewise *biddi*).

Whirlwind, hoh-si-paruwï (*wi* short).

Whistle (or flute), bïdda-kóhotse (*o* full; *ot* short; *e* ½).

Whistle, (v; or pipe), ïh-akóhsche (*a* barely audible; *e* ½).

White, ächóhtakiss (*o* full; *takiss* short).

Whole, chákahä-tan (*an* French).

Widow, there is no corresponding word.

Wind (n), hoh-sï (*si* short).

Wind (v; of game), mah-wóh-piss.

Wing (n), ächpá (*pa* very short).

Winter, má-arahts.

Woman (wife), bïa (*a* subdued).

Wood, biddá, bidá, or widá.

Work (v), wah-hid-ähch-kuss (German).

Wound (n), oh-átta (*ta* short).

Wound (v), uh-uss.

Wrap up (v), wah-ipúh-wiss.

Wrinkle (n, or adj; wrinkled), chïhpiss.

Turn (v; twist), wipatáh-üiss (run together).

Turn back (v; return), kiwi-achkúhs (run together).

Yawn (v), büidahts (*u* and *i* separated; the whole indistinct).

Year, máh-ara (the whole run together; *ara* very short).

Yellow, zïhdits (*dits* very low).

Yes, äï (together; a shrill sound).

Young, they say small.

Clothing and Ornaments

Bracelets of metal, itråuwassa (*sa* short; the whole short).

Breechcloth, edde-ipschake (*edde* very short; *e* distinctly pronounced).

Buffalo robe, waschï.

Buffalo robe (painted), waschï-ïrutsicki.

Girdle (belt), ma-i-páschagih (*gih* guttural).

Gloves (or mittens), chu-tï (*ti* short and explosive).

Hair-ornament (flat ornament for the back of the head), arraúhwassa (*arra* with the point of the tongue; in last word *a* is only ½).

Hair-ornament (on the temples), ächidúhwassa.

Head-dress (feather crown), wahaschu-lakukárahä.

Leather-shirt, wacháhpi-wa-itóhchi.

Leggings, wacháhpi-hu-psïh.

Moccasins, huupá (*uu* somewhat separated).

Necklace of bear's claws, lachpitzï-sichpo-ahpöä (run together).

Plants

Ash, wüschpá.

Poplar, máhchku.

Prairie turnip (pomme blanche, psoralea esculenta), ahï.

Reed (arundo), wüskapa-ah.

Willow (salix), bïdda-hahsï (*si* very short).

Animals

Antelope (cabri), uhchi; or ohchikïhdapi (*dapi* short).

Badger, amakáh.

Bat, äschuattischïa (short).

Bear (black), haschidá.

Bear (grizzly), lachpitzï.

Beaver, wïrapa.

Bighorn, ansichtïa (*ti* and *a* separated; strong emphasis on *ti*; first *i* barely audible).

Buffalo, witä.

Buffalo (bull), kïhrapi (*pi* short).

Buffalo (calf), nahksïhdi.

Buffalo (cow), üichtïa (*ich* with the point of the tongue, German; *i* and *a* separated).

Crane (gray), apïssa.

Crane, (white), apïssa-tocki (*tocki* lower and short).

Crow, ahrischa (*scha* short).

Deer (black-tailed), sïh-tschüpischa.

Deer (common; general term), sïh-tatacke (*e* distinctly pronounced).

Deer (stag or buck), sïh-tatacke-kïhrape (*e* distinctly pronounced); the doe, sïh-tatackte-mïchka (*ich* German, with the point of the tongue).

Dog, maschúkka.

Duck, mïhchahka.

Eagle (war eagle), mah-eschó (*e* short).

Fox (black), éhchokuschi-süpischa.

Fox (cross-fox), éhchokuschi-cháchi.

Fox (gray), éhchokuschi-sáotta.

Fox (prairie), éhchochka.

Fox (red), éhchokuschi.

Gopher (arctomys hoodii), dáhksassi (*sassi* even and without accent).

Hare (white), ïhtaki.

Hedge-hog, apäh-dii (run together; *dii* slightly separated, almost like *di*).

Horse, eisóh-waschukka (*ei* very shrill, with the tongue; second word very short).

Horse (young), éhsu-wassucka-náhnka (some pronounced first word *ehsu*, others *eisoh*).

Lizard, wahkachpa.

Lynx (wildcat), sïh-ta-chahe (*sih* with strong accent; *e* ½; the whole run together).

Magpie (pica), ïh-pe (*ih* with strong emphasis; *e* ½).

Mink, dacksúa (*u* with strong emphasis; *u* and *a* separated).

Mole, appa-apsá.

Mole (gopher), kippapúhdi.

Moose (orignal), apatapá.

Mouse, éhtaho (*taho* low and short; *eh* with strong emphasis).

Mule, achichtia (*ich* German, with the point of the tongue).

Muskrat, zïh-zirúkka (strong accent on *zih*).

Nighthawk (goatsucker, caprimulgidae), péhriska, or päʹhriska.

Otter, bïdda-póhkä.

Owl, etáh-kupäʹ.

Owl (German uhu, strix bubo; western horned owl?), itáhkupä.

Panther, itupáh-ächtïa (*ach* with the point of the tongue; *i* and *a* separated; *i* with strong emphasis).

Pigeon (great), máh-adach-kakichtïa.

Prairie-dog, sihchpá.

Prairie-hen, sihská.

Rabbit, ïhtach-schüpïscha.

Raccoon, sïh-tachächä (*sih* with strong emphasis).

Rat (common, or house rat), ähta-hichtïa (*ti* with strong accent, and separated from *a*).

Rat (wood rat), aïhta-hitïa (*ti* and *a* separated; *i* with emphasis).

Skunk, chúchkä.

Snake, mapúckscha (*scha* short).

Snake (rattle-snake), arrussidïawattú (the whole very short; *i* and *a* separated; *i* with strong accent).

Swan, dúhwisch-scha (the whole run together; *duh* long and with emphasis; *sch* very short).

Toad, schánke-káhru (*an* French; *e* ½; likewise *u*).

Troupial (red-shouldered), ichpáhka-hischï.

Turkey (wild), sihs-kichtïa (run together; *ich* with the point of the tongue; *ti* and *a* separated).

Turtle, wattáchä.

Waxwing (bombycilla), máhsi-pïschakurúhti.

Weasel (stoat), o̊hsisa (*oh* with special emphasis and force).

Wolf (black), säh-tschüpischá.

Wolf (gray), sähscha (*scha* short).

Wolf (prairie), bóh-sa (*boh* long and full; *sa* very short).

Wolf (white), sähsch-attácki.

Wolverene (gulo), eh-tupáh.

Woodpecker, toschká.

Names of Tribes

Arrapahos, Ïta-ïddi.

Arrikkaras, Arakárahu.

Assiniboins, Haduschïh-idi (run together; *idi* short).

Blackfeet, Issi-schüpïscha.

Chayennes, Itáh-ischipáhji (first *i* very short; the whole short and low).

Crows (general term), Haideróhka.

Crows (the one band), Gïhchaitsá; i.e., the fighters for the stomach.

Crows (the other band), Haideróhke; i.e., those who dwell in the middle.

Dacota, Schaónni.

Grosventres of the Prairie, Eirichti-aruchpáhga (*ei* together; *tih* with emphasis; the whole short).

Krihs, Schahï.

Mandans (inhabitants of Mihtutta-hangkusch), Awatirátácka (*tacka* short).

Mandans (inhabitants of Ruhptare), Awa-ichpawati (*awa* very short; *ich* with the point of the tongue; *pawati* short; *ti* very short).

Pahnis, Säjeruchpaga (*j* French; *ga* guttural).

Names of Rivers

Grand, Birridsipáhji (*ji* French).

Heart, Nah-táh-schi (*schi* short).

Knife, Maëttseruáhji (*e* ½; *ji* French).

Missouri, Amáhti (*ti* short).

Muscleshell, Mató-káhsi (*o* full; *si* low and short).

Teton, Biddi-schu-wah-áhji.

Upper Little Missouri, Amáhtikasche (*mah* nasal; *e* ½; *sche* short).

White, Biddi-attakáhsi, or Aúkatakáhsch.

White earth, Oh-katakáhsi (*si* barely audible).

Yellowstone, Wïsih-dáschi.

Numerals

One, nowassá (low).

Two, dúupa (*uu* separated); usually pronounced rúhpa.

Three, náhwi (*wi* very short).

Four, tohpá (*o* full; *pa* short and explosive).

Five, kechú (*e* distinctly pronounced; *u* short and explosive).

Six, akahuá (*kah* long; *wa* together and short).

Seven, scháchpu.

Eight, dúhpachpi (*pi* short).

Nine, nowássachpi (*pi* short).

Ten, piraká.

Twenty, dúchpa-pirakas (*as* low).

Thirty, dá-wïa-pïraka.

Forty, tochpáh-pïraka.

Fifty, kechóa-pïraka.

Hundred, pirikchtïa (*ti* together and with strong accent; *ti* and *a* separated).

Two-hundred, pirikichtia-rúhpa.

Thousand, pirakichtïa-achkakóhri.

I eat, mah-woh-tüwiss (*tuwiss* very short).

You eat, máh-raruti.

He eats, mah-arutïss.

We eat, máh-woh-tüwihas (final word short).

They eat, máh-ruta-áss (*ruta-ass* pronounced together).

FOOTNOTES:

[258] Written from the pronunciation of the Indians themselves, especially that of the old chief, Addïh-Hïddisch, and with the help of the Mandans who best understood the language. Where no exception is noted, *ch* always has the guttural sound; *r* is always spoken with the point of the tongue. Gallatin says that the Minnitarris consist of three tribes, of which two are the Mandans and Annahaways. I have already refuted this statement; besides, the Mandans themselves say that they had nothing in common with the Minnitarris, and that their language was utterly different when they came together; in the case of the Annahaways the statement is equally unfounded, for I could not even find this term, which no one recognized. I have already said that the Minnitarris are a branch of the Crows. These Indians, as well as the Mandans, have not moved their village for many years; they are, moreover, quite safe in them, for Indians do not usually attack fortified places, especially since the two tribes together can at any time put six hundred warriors into the field. Neither did I find among these Indians unusually light complexions nor blue eyes; they do not differ in this respect from the other Indians of the Missouri valley. The legend, likewise, that the Minnitarris are a white race, descended from the Welsh, has just as little foundation, as Gallatin has already shown (*ibid.*, p. 125). Gallatin's words from the Minnitarri language are not correctly written, doubtless through the fault of incompetent interpreters.—MAXIMILIAN.

Comment by Ed. See, for the Ahnahaway, our volume xxii, p. 350, note 326.

[259] God is said by some to be called *manhopa* in this language; but this term was never mentioned to me, and is, therefore, without doubt, incorrect.—MAXIMILIAN.

MUSQUAKE, or Fox[260]

Arm, neneck.

Arrow, onué.

Beard, nemisstóllakan.

Beaver, amachkuá (*kua* short; *ach* guttural).

Bell, katúchtåoal (*uch* guttural).

Black, machkettauaw (*a* and *u* separated).

Blanket (woolen), makunaan.

Bow, matáck.

Buffalo, moskutáck-nallusuá (final *a* short): i.e., prairie cattle; for they call the domesticated ox, nallusuá.

Child, apannó.

Cool (of weather), kesüa.

Day, kischek.

Devil (evil spirit), matsché-mánito; often shortened to mallato.

Dog, honémua (*mua* short and indistinct).

Elk, maschauáwe (*e* short).

Eyes, naskissako; i.e., my eyes.

Fire (n), ascutä.

Foot, nassöt.

God (good spirit), kasché-manité.

Green, askipokáhk.

Hair, minásse; the red hair-ornament or deer's-tail, kateüikúnn.

Hand, nalake (*e* very short).

Head, uësche (*e* somewhat short).

Heart, netä.

Horse, nákoto-kaschá.

Lance (spear), achtauáll (*ach* guttural; *a* and *u* separated).

Leader (chief), hokimaw (*w* audible, but soft).

Leg (entire), nakátsch.

Man, ninï.

Mouth, nattóle (*e* barely audible).

Night, pachkuttáwe.

Nose, nakiuólle (*e* very short).

Otter, kattatawe (*w* between *u* umlaut and *w*; *e* short).

Red, meschkuáwe.

Red-head (General Clark), Maskata-pate (*e* short).

Sun, kischés.

Sword-lance (lance with a sword blade), táüan (short).

Teeth, nettóne.

Tongue, ninonï (indistinct).

Turkey (wild), mässesá (*a* short); or messesá.

War-club (with the iron point), pakakachkó (*ach* guttural).

Warm, nihŏs.

Water, nápch (*pch* almost like German *pich*).

White, wapé; wapé-mallato, the white devil; this was the name of the Indian who gave me the words of this vocabulary.

Woman (wife), ikuá; hence the word "squaw."

Wood, mattäque (*que* pronounced separately; *e* short).

Yellow, assåuake (*e* short).

Yes, hehä.

FOOTNOTES:

[260] These words were written down from the pronunciation of a Musquake Indian.—MAXIMILIAN.

OJIBUAS, OJIBEUAS, CHIPEWAS, or Algonkins[261]

American (an), Tschimoh-kuman (*an* French).

Arm, unïck.

Arrow, uïbmah (*u* and *i* separated).

Autumn, tagoagick (*gick* German).

Black, machkattäh-uah (*ach* guttural).

Blind, kagipin-inquá (*n* French; *qua* together).

Blood, miskuï (*ui* separated; the whole short; emphasis on *kui*).

Blue, machkattä-uah.

Bone (bones), ochkánn (*och* guttural).

Bow, mitïguap.

Brave (adj), sungedä (*su* with the point of the tongue); a brave man, mangodas.

Brook, sibins (*n* French; *s* soft but audible).

Brother, nitschkoé-esin (*esin* low, short, and indistinct).

Child (boy), kuiuisän (short and run together; second *ui* somewhat separated; the whole short; *an* like French *ain*).

Child (small girl), squasän (*an* like French *in*).

Cloud (n), anakuätt.

Cold (n), kissïnna.

Die (v), nipú (*u* between *o* and *u*).

Dog, animúss.

Drink (v), mönnikué.

Ear, otauack (*o* rather inaudible, short).

Earth, achkï.

Enemy, boanack, or poanack; i.e., the Sioux, or Dacota.

Englishman, Ságanasch (German throughout).

Evening, onáhkuschink.

Eye, oschkïnjick (*n* French).

Father, ohsann.

Feather, mikuánn, or miguánn.

Fire (n), schkuttäh.

Fish (n), kikon (*on* French).

Flesh, uiiahs, (*ui* separated; *iahs* German).

Forehead, oskattick.

Frenchman, Uämestihóhsch.

Friend (my friend), nsaag-itimih (short and run together); i.e., they love each other.

Go (v), pimussäh.

God, kijäh-mannittá.

Good, onischisching.

Great (tall), ischpigáboë.

Green, squáh.

Gun, pahskejigann (*e* ½ and short).

Hail (n), sassähgan.

Hair, uïnisiss.

Hand, uninjinn (*j* French; otherwise German).

Head, uschteguán.

Healthy, nimino-aïá; i.e., I am well.

Heart, otäh.

Heat, kijachtä' (*j* French; *ch* barely audible).

Heaven (clear sky), mischáhkuätt.

Horns (of deer), otäsch-kanann.

Horse, päbäjiko-cajï.

House (lodge), uïkiuámm.

Hunger, nuiuissinn (*ui* separated); i.e., I am hungry.

Hunt (v), giussä (*g* palatal).

I, nin (*in* soft).

Ice, michkuamm.

Knife, mohkuman (*an* French).

Laugh, paach-pï.

Lead (n), annoin-abick (run together).

Leg, ochkaht.

Life, pühmáhtiss.

Lightning, oahstigann.

Man, hinnini.

Meal (or to eat?), uistinnetá (*e* ½ and short); i.e., let us all eat.

Milky-way (le chemin de St. Jacques), michkanank (*ich* as in German); i.e., the trail.

Moon, tibïck-kïhsis.

Morning, pïht-áhbann (*ah* somewhat lengthened).

Mother, ning (*g* like French *gue*).

Mountain, uattschiu (*u* and *a* somewhat separated; *i* and *u* likewise).

Mouth, otóhn.

Negro, machkatä-üiahs (*ch* guttural).

Night, tibichkatt (*ich* German).

Nose, oschung-guann.

Otter, nikick.

Pipe, poagánn.

Powder (gun-powder), machkatä (*ach* guttural).

Quick, uïha.

Rain (n), kimïhuann; it rains, papángi-pïssa.

Red (color), miskuáh.

River, ktschissïhpi.

River (a very large river), missisïhpi.

Sea, kitsikamïn (*n* French).

Sick, ndahgkuss.

Small, agaschin (*in* like *i* nasal; *ga* German).

Smoke (n), kaschkáhbattä.

Snow, kóhn; it snows, soh-kipunn.

Speak (v), kïh-kitó.

Spirits (distilled), skutéo-apó.

Spring (the season), minóchkaming.

Star, anánk: otschïganank (i.e., the Star of the Pekan, or Fisher), the Wain, or Great Bear; otáhua-moh (les trois rois), "the Three Kings" of the Canadians; makúsch-teguann (run together) the Seven Stars, or the Pleiades; uåh-banank (l'étoile du jour), Venus.

Stingy, sasáhgissi (*si* short); or shortened to sasáhgiss.

Stone, assïnn.

Strong, maschkåh-uissih (run together).

Summer, nibïnn.

Sun, kïhsis.

Thunder, (n), nimekïh (*e* ½).

Tobacco, assäman (*an* almost like *ah*).

Tomahawk, uagachkuatons-poagann (*ach* guttural, *ons* French, but *s* audible; *ann* German).

Trail, mihkannah.

Ugly, manah-tïss.

War, mikahtink.

Water, nipï.

White, uahpisch-kah (somewhat nasal).

Wind (n), notïnk.

Winter, pibúhnk.

Woman (wife), ichkuá (*ich* German).

Wood, mistïck.

Yellow, ossáuah (*uah* shortened).

Yes, häa (like a prolonged *hae*).

Numerals

One, päʰhjick (*j* French).

Two, nïhsch.

Three, nissúe (*e* distinctly pronounced).

Four, neh-uinn (short and run together).

Five, nóhnonn (first *o* full).

Six, nkótto-uåssoe (*soe* short; *e* rather distinctly pronounced).

Seven, nijoåssoe (*j* French; *e* rather distinctly pronounced).

Eight, schoåssoe.

Nine, jank (*j* French).

Ten, mitassoe (*e* distinctly pronounced, but short).

Twenty, nischtanna.

Thirty, nissoe-mitannáh.

Forty, neh-mitannáh.

Fifty, náhno-mitannáh.

Sixty, nkotoásse-mitannáh.

Seventy, nijóasso-mitannáh.

Eighty, schwásso-mitannáh.

Ninety, jangasso-mitannáh.

Hundred, ngottóack.

Thousand, ktschï-ngottóack.

Animals

Antelope, apïsti-tigosch.

Badger, mitánnask.

Bear (female), machkuáh-nojäahkuann.

Bear (male), machkuáh-ayáhbä.

Bear (black), machkadéh-machkuáh (*ach* guttural).

Bear (grizzly), ktschǐ-ayáh: when whitish he is called, wâbachquah (*ach* German and guttural).

Caribou (cervus tarandus), atǐck.

Deer (black-tailed deer, cervus macrotis), machkadéh-uanósch: machkadeh, black; uanosch, tail.

Deer (common deer, cervus virginianus), uauáschkess.

Elk (cervus major), omaschkóhs.

Elk (the doe), onidjánn-omaschkohs.

Elk (the stag), ayábä-omaschkóhs.

Fox (general term), uagóhsch; the name of the color is added.

Hare, uabóhs.

Hedge-hog, káhk.

Lynx (loup cervier), pischúh.

Lynx (red; felix rufa, le chat sauvage), äh-säbban (*sabban* short).

Marten, uahbischänsch (*an* like French *ain*).

Mink, tschang-goäsch (run together).

Moose (cervus alces), mons (French, but *s* audible).

Muskrat, uaschásk.

Pekan (stone marten, or fisher), otschǐhk.

Skunk, schikáhk.

Weazel (stoat), sching-gohs (run together).

Wolf, maǐhngann (*ihn* like *i* nasal).

Wolverene, kuing-gua-agä (run together).

FOOTNOTES:

[261] Written from the pronunciation of an Ojibua Indian. The letter *l* is said to be wanting in this language, and the words given here seem to confirm this view. These Indians received the name Sauteurs from the French, because they lived at the falls (sauts) of St. Anthony. They are commonly called Chipeways (Tschipewäs); but pronounce this name, themselves, Ojibua.—MAXIMILIAN.

Comment by Ed. The name "Saulteurs" was derived from the residence of these Indians at Sault Ste. Marie.

OMAHA[262]

Ahead (in front), påhanga.

All (the whole), så-ni, or wå-så-nï.

Alone, snog-djé (*j* French; *g* almost like German *ch*).

Always, schon-schon (*on* French).

American (an), Måhi-tánga; i.e., Long Knife.

Anxiety (fear), no-pä̈.

Arm, ah-schih.

Arrow, måh.

Ashes, må-chu-dä̈ (*ch* guttural).

Ask (question), j-uá-cha-ga (*ch* palatal; *ga* short).

Awake (v, intr), wåtómbe-najeh (*j* French; *e* distinctly pronounced).

Awake (v, tr), ih-ki-räh (the whole even); same word as in the Oto language.

Axe, måsöppä.

Back (n), nokkån (*n* French).

Back (backwards), chára (*ch* guttural).

Backward (back), charah (*ch* guttural); charah-monni, go back, return.

Bad (malicious), båskidä.

Ball (bullet), måh-seh-man (*an* French).

Beard, ndähï.

Beautiful, oh-campé (*campe* French; the whole pronounced together).

Belly, nïcha (*ch* guttural).

Below (beneath), mottata (all syllables even).

Beside (near), ohanga.

Between, ohrisa.

Bird, uåjïnga (*j* French).

Bite (v), wåråchta (*ch* guttural; *ta* short).

Bitter, ski-da-jä (*j* French); i.e., not sweet.

Black, såh-bä' (*ba* short).

Bladder, nächä (*ch* guttural).

Blind (adj), ischtá-uäraje (*je* French; final *e* distinct).

Blond, på-hïssong.

Blood, uåh-mï.

Bloody, uåh-mï-ogippi.

Blow (v; blowout), abichä (*ch* guttural).

Blue, túh.

Bone (bones), uaï-hih.

Bough, jån-jinga (French).

Bow, mondähï.

Break open (v), grabä.

Breast, mong-gä'.

Breast (female), månsä' (*an* French), i.e., iron.

Bridge, ohäata.

Broad, bróska.

Brook, wåtischka-jinga (*j* French).

Brother, sónga.

Brown, chudä' (*ch* guttural).

Burn (v), nåh-ning-gä.

Burn (v; consume by burning), nåh-chu-dä' (*ch* guttural).

Bury(v; inter), oh-chä (*ch* guttural).

Buy (v), uåh-ri-mäh.

Calm (n), obrágä (*ga* short).

Call (v), hah-gä.

Canoe, mondäh.

Cave, mon-schont-djé (*on* French, likewise *j*; *e* audible).

Caught (taken prisoner), uåhnihih.

Child, schĭnga-schĭnga.

Circle, uah-nasseh (run together).

Clear (bright), kéhra (*ra* with the point of the tongue).

Cloud (masses of cloud), mååchpĭh.

Cold, snĭh.

Come (v), gih-ga.

Conquer (v; be victorious), uåhuang.

Convenient (comfortable), same word as for good.

Count (v; number), råh-uä (*a* short).

Cure (v), ginĭh.

Cut (v), måh-chån (*ch* guttural; *an* French).

Cut (v; cut down, fell), gå-säh.

Cut down (v; fell), gåhsä̇.

Cry (v; scream, shout), pån (French).

Dark, hogan-nåpasseh.

Daughter, ih-jang-gä (*j* French).

Day, ombá; to-day, ombara.

Dance (n), uatschĭ-góchä (*cha* guttural).

Dead, tsäh.

Deaf, nåh-chiddä-ning-gä (*ch* guttural; the whole run together).

Dear (costly; of goods), uåhrimitächä (*ch* guttural).

Death, tsäh.

Deceive (v; cheat), siesch-tánka.

Devil (evil spirit), wåhkonda-pehjhé (*j* French).

Die (v), gih-tsäh.

Dirty, mån-chri-chri (*n* French; *ch* guttural).

Dirty (v; or adj), må-cherihcherih (*ch* guttural; *e* very short; the whole short).

Door, tih-ombah (*om* French).

Double, nombá (French).

Drag (v; pull along), påhï-gåh-chä (*ch* guttural).

Draw (v; draw water), nih-isé.

Dream (n), ombrä (*om* French).

Dream (v), ihra-ombrä (*om* French).

Drink (v), ratan (*an* French).

Dry (adj), bihsä (*sa* short).

Dust, måh-åh-schudä.

Dwelling place (hunting stand), goss-sin (*in* like *i* nasal).

Ear, nittá.

Ear-ornament, uh-uïn (*in* nasal, like *i*).

Early, chossonn (*ch* guttural).

Earth, moniká.

Egg, uësa.

Enemy, okïthä.

Englishman, Ságanasch (German throughout).

Enough, schéhna (*na* short).

Entertain (v; eat), wåratä-gih-i.

Evening, påh-séh.

Everywhere, mánschon-brughä (*on* French).

Eye, ischtá.

Eyelid, ischtá-hï.

Face (sight), indjäh (*i* barely audible; *j* French).

Fall (v) gochhiára (*ch* guttural; the whole short).

Far (distant), uä-ahiddä (the whole run together).

Far (distant), uäh-ahiddäh.

Fat, uägri.

Father, dah-däh.

Feather, måh-schung.

Female (of animals), ming-gá.

Finger, nombä; same word as for hand.

Fire, pädé.

Fish, hŭh.

Fish (v), hu-issä.

Fish-hook, hu-uä-gossä.

Fist, nombä-sóngä (*om* French).

Flee (v; escape), onhä (*on* French, and nasal).

Flesh, tah-núka; i.e., fresh meat.

Flesh (dried), táh.

Flint, manhissï (*an* French).

Flow (v), kahirá.

Fog, schuschudä.

Foot, sihá.

Forehead, päh.

Forest, chråbä (*ch* guttural; *ba* short).

Forget (v), gih-sirajäh (*j* French; the whole run together).

Freeze (v), osnih.

Frenchman, Uåchä (*ch* guttural).

Friend, kågä.

Full, ogipi.

Go (v), monnïh.

God (creator, good spirit), wåhkonda.

Good, udá; the best, eh-jna-udá (*j* French).

Gray, són (French).

Gray-haired, påhï-son (French).

Great (tall), tangá.

Green, tuch-tsche (*e* short); i.e., literally, very blue.

Ground (earth), moniká.

Grow (v), granräh-tigräh (*an* French; *gr* with the point of the tongue).

Gun, uahutan (*ua* like *wa*; *an* French).

Hair, påhï.

Hand, nombä' (*om* French).

Hard, sågäh.

Head, nasch-kéh.

Healthy, uåh-kägajäh (*j* French).

Hear (v), nåhk-on (*on* French; the whole run together).

Heart, nondä'.

Heavy (difficult), sking-gä.

Hide (v), na-che-ran (*ch* guttural; *an* French; *e* short).

High, manschih (*an* French).

Hope (v), bräh-gan (*an* French).

Horn, häh.

Horns, häh.

Horse (a young horse), schantón-schïnga (*an* and *on* French; first word with emphasis; second without).

Hot, manschtä (*an* French).

House (lodge), tïh.

Hunger, nånpähi (*an* French).

Hunt (v), åh-baäh.

Hurricane, taddäh-soggäh-noppewårre (*e* always distinctly pronounced).

I, uïh.

Ice, nuchä' (*ch* guttural).

Incurable, ginitächä.

Intoxicate (v; intoxicated), tåhni.

Iron, månsä' (*an* French).

Jar (vessel), dähchä (*ch* guttural).

Knife, må-nïh, or mahï.

Know (v), ihpahan (*an* French).

Know (v; be acquainted with), ih-pahán (*pa* short; *an* French).

Lance (spear), måndähï (*an* French).

Land, manschon (*an* and *on* French).

Laugh (v, or n), måndehï (*an* French).

Leader (chief), kahigä.

Leaf, jån-hich-pä (*jan* French; final *e* distinct).

Leg, jägá (*j* French).

Lie (v; deceive), i-uh-sisch-tan (*an* French; the whole run together).

Lip, ih-há.

Little (in quantity), diuba.

Loose (of clothes), gran-deh (*an* French).

Maiden, mïh-jinga (*mih* with emphasis; *ji* French; *jinga* without emphasis).

Maize, uå-tån-säh (*an* French).

Man, núh.

Man (human being), núh.

Marry (v), ming-grán (*gran* French).

Meal (or to eat?), uårateh.

Messenger, ikih-monnäh.

Milk (n), påsé-nih.

Mirror, nïo-kigrásse (*a* audible; *i* and *o* separated).

Moon, mih-om-ba (*mih* with emphasis; the whole run together).

Morning, kåsïn (*in* French).

Mother, nåh-håh.

Mountain, påhï-moschä.

Mouth, hïh.

Much, ah-hïgä.

Music, uåhuan (*an* French).

My, uïh-uïh-tá.

Nail (on hand, foot, hoof, claw), schagä.

Naked, juh-núka (*j* French).

Name, jajä (French).

Neck (throat), táh-hi.

Necklace, uåh-nompï (last word French).

Needle, uåkóh.

Negro, nikka-schinga-sóbbä; or wåchä-sóbbä (*ch* guttural).

New, tähga.

Night, hán (*an* French).

Noon, mih-oh-kan-ska (*an* French).

Nose, påh.

Old, isch-ágä.

Old man, isch-ágä.

Old woman, uåu-schïnge (*uau* somewhat separated).

Oldest, jinï (*j* French); my oldest brother, vijinï.

Over (above), manschiata (*an* French).

Pain (n), nih-ä (run together).

Paint (v), gih-kon-sä (*on* French; *sa* short).

Peace, manchon-úda (*an* and *on* French); i.e., not war.

Pipe (tobacco), ninibåh.

Play (v), skådä.

Pluck (v; feathers), hi-snú-djä (*j* French).

Pray (v), wåkonda-berihs-tubä (*e* short; otherwise German throughout).

Prisoner, uåh-nihih.

Point (n), påhï.

Pouch (sack), uh-jï.

Powder (gun-powder), måh-chudä (*ch* guttural; the whole run together).

Pull (v; draw), gih-snuh.

Punish (v; whip), uh-tih.

Quarrel (v; fight), kihkinna.

Quick, hocherä (*ch* German).

Rain (n), nah-jé (*j* French).

Red, jidä (*ji* French).

Rib, rittih.

Ripe, (of fruit), nidä.

River, uåtïschka.

Roast (v, or n), djä-gran (French).

Rock (cliff), in-in (French nasal).

Round, buut-ton (*on* French).

Run (v), toh-neh.

Sack (leather), uh-jï-hå.

Sand, bih-saak.

Sea, nïh-tánga; i.e., big water.

See (v), tom-bä.

Sharp (pointed), på-hï.

Shave (v), båhs-kébbä.

Shoot (v; with a bow), måh-wåkiddäh.

Shoot (v; with a gun), wåhutonwåkiddäh (*on* French).

Shore (bank), nih-cåhan (*an* French).

Show (v), ahbasuh.

Sick, uåh-ká-ga.

Sister, tangä.

Sit (v), gerin (*e* short; *r* with the point of the tongue; *in* like *i* nasal).

Skin (hide), håh.

Sleep (v), ajan (French).

Sleepy, ján-gonda (*jan* French).

Small, jingá (*j* French).

Smell (v; sniff at, scent), amberan (French).

Smoke (n), schudä, or schudé.

Smoke (v; tobacco), ninihï.

Snow (n), måh.

Son, ji-ingä (*j* French; the whole run together).

Speak (v), ïh-ä.

Spirits (distilled), pädji-nïh (*j* French).

Spring (source), nïh-hónga.

Spring (the season), mäh.

Spring (v; leap, jump), o-uis-seh (run together).

Squint (v), tåguscheh.

Star, pikä.

Stomach, mång-gäh.

Stone, ih-in (*n* French; *in* like *i* nasal).

Storm (thunder storm), tadähsoggäh.

Strong, uååsch-kán-tanga (*an* French).

Stump, buhtan (*an* French).

Stupid, uåje-ningé (*j* French).

Summer, núgä.

Sun, mïh.

Sunrise, mïh-hïh.

Sunset, mïh-núschä.

Sweet, skidä.

Swim (v), nïhuan (*an* French); same word as in the Oto language.

Tail (of an animal), sindä (German throughout).

Tear (v; tear, or break to pieces), ih-bråh-sä (*ah* French; *sa* short).

Tear out (v; pull out), schuúdä.

Tears, ischtá-nih; i.e., eye water.

Teeth, ihí.

Thick, tångá.

Thin, bräkä.

Tobacco, niníh.

Toe, sih-schogä.

Tomahawk, máse-päjiīnga (*se* short; *j* French; last word rapidly pronounced).

To-morrow, kåsonn.

Tongue, rähse (*e* distinctly pronounced); téh-rähs, buffalo tongue.

Toothache, ihí-nidä.

Top (summit), måschiadä.

Trace (track of an animal), sihgerä.

Trader, uåh-ri-mäh.

Tree, chråbä (*ch* guttural).

True, mikkä.

Turn (v; twist), ohma-terischan (*an* French).

Unhealthy (sickly), wåh-kägaschtån (the whole even and run together).

Unripe, nihd-aije (*ai* together; *j* French; *e* low but distinct).

Wait (v), ihra-pä.

War, noh-dan (*an* French).

Warm, moschtä.

Warmth, tåhbrä (*bra* short).

Warrior, uå-schu-schäh.

Wash (v), niīh-ja-hä (*j* French).

Water, niīh.

Water-jar (water cask), niīh-ujé (*j* French).

Wax, kegranchä-uägrä (*an* French; *ch* guttural; *g* with the point of the tongue).

Weep (v), hahgä.

Wet, núka.

What? how? dah-dan (*an* French).

Whirlpool, nih-berih-berin (short and run together; *e* short; *in* like *i* nasal).

Whistle (v; pipe), suhdä.

White, ská.

White man, nika-schinga-hïchaskah (*ch* guttural).

Widow, igrangä-tsäh (run together).

Wind (n), tahdä.

Wind (v; wind game), obrán (*an* French).

Wing, ahï.

Winter, måhrä (*ra* short).

Woman (wife), wåh-úh.

Wood, ján (French).

Work (v), monnï.

Wound (v; shoot), oh.

Wrap up (v), ih-kónta.

Yellow, sïh.

Yes, anhán (indistinct, nasal).

Young, jingáh (*ji* French; *g* guttural).

Numerals

One, miachtscheh (*ach* guttural).

Two, nombáh.

Three, råh-beneh (*be* short).

Four, túba.

Five, såtoh (*n* French).

Six, schåh-peh.

Seven, péh-nombáh.

Eight, péh-råbene (first *e* short; second *e* audible).

Nine, schónka.

Ten, chräbene (*bene* short).

Animals

Bear (black), wåssóbbä.

Bear (grizzly), mån-tchú (*an* French; *tchu* German).

Beaver, jåbä (*j* French; *ba* short).

Buffalo, téh, or täh.

Deer (common), tahg-tchä (German).

Dog, schinúda (*da* short).

Elk, onpåh (*on* French).

Horse, schóngä-tónga.

Lynx, igrong-gá (pronounced together).

Otter, tuhsch-nongä.

Ox (European), täh-ská (run together).

Panther, igronga-sindä-snaddäh; sindä-snaddäh, with long tail.

Skunk, móng-ga.

Snake, ueh-sá.

Swine, kokosch.

Turkey, (wild), sihsikah.

Turtle, kehtan (*an* French).

Wolf, (black), schánton-sóbbä (*a* short).

Wolf, (gray), schánton-son (*an* and *on* French).

Wolf (prairie), mikkasseh.

FOOTNOTES:

[262] Written from the pronunciation of Major Dougherty, who understood this language perfectly. The Omáhas belong to the Dacóta linguistic group, and form with the Osages, Konzas, Ayowäs (Joways), Missouris, Otos, and Puncas, Mr. Gallatin's southern Sioux. Among the nations named there are several different dialects, of which the Osages and Konzas speak one; the Otos, Ayowäs, and Missouris another; and the Omahas and Puncas a third. On these peoples, see Gallatin (*ibid.*, pp. 126-28). There it is noted that a vocabulary of the Ayowäs (Jówäs) is lacking; a gap which I can claim to have

filled, since I was assured by Major Dougherty that the Ayowäs speak the Oto language, whose words are given below.—MAXIMILIAN.

OTO[263]

Abyss, moksché; iro-moksché, steep cliff.

Air, ta-djä (*j* French).

All (all together), brogä; the whole mass (or multitude), akiwoasan (*woa* like *voi* in French; *an* French).

Alone, asch-nå (*sch* like *j* French).

- I myself alone, mij-nå (*j* French here and below).

- You (thou) alone, dij-nå.

- He alone, ij-nå.

- We alone, guj-nå.

- You alone, dij-nå.

Always, eiiåhma (*ei* together).

American (an), Måhi-hónn-ie (*ie* short; *e* audible); i.e., Long Knife.

Another, i-tan-dö (*an* French).

Answer (v), i-hä.

Anxiety (fear), nongguä (*gua* short).

Approach stealthily (v; stalk), sridje-monnä (*j* French).

Arm, asché.

Arrow, mïto.

Ashes, må-chudjé (*ch* guttural).

Awake (v, intr), uatá-nayé (run together).

Awake (v, tr), ih-ki-reh.

Axe, ïsuä (*sua* short).

Back (adverb), hatá.

Back (n), nåh-kan (*an* French).

Bad (malicious), tsichogä (*ch* guttural).

Bald, nantó-rusch-ra (*an* French).

Ball (bullet), måh-seh-måh; same word as for lead.

Bathe (v), ni-uah (*uah* nasal).

Beard, ndä-hi (*n* only a fore-tone).

Beautiful, ocompih (French).

Before (ahead), på-gran (*an* French).

Behind (behind us), a-rúcha-gä (*ch* guttural).

Belly, ni-cha (*ch* guttural).

Beside (near), oh-kang-äh.

Best, pi-tånra, (*an* French).

Bird, wåe-ing-ä (*e* barely audible; the whole together).

Bite (v), rochtagä.

Bitter, sehko-schkunä; i.e., not sweet, they do not have a direct expression.

Black, seuä (*e* and *u* separated).

Bladder, nächä (*ch* guttural).

Blind, ich-tåch-hidje (*j* French; final *e* short).

Blood, wåpågä-oyú.

Bloom (v), pahüson (*on* French).

Blow (v; blow out), a-bi-chä (*ch* guttural).

Blue, tóh.

Blush (v), schudjö (*j* French).

Boil (v; cook), oh-hon (*on* French).

Bone (bones), uah-hï (*uah* nasal).

Bough, nå-ing-ä (run together).

Bow, måndehï (*an* French).

Break (v), to-ié.

Break open (v; force open), wå-gre-ue.

Breast (female), påsä (*sa* short).

Breast (the whole breast), mong-ä.

Breath, hï; same word as for mouth and tooth.

Bridge, ohä.

Broad, brå-ské (final syllable short).

Brook, nischna-ing-ä (run together).

Brother, song-ä; my brother, mi-song-ä.

Brown, chudje (*ch* guttural; *e* distinctly pronounced); i.e., dark, smoky, they have no word for brown.

Burn (v), todjé (*j* French).

Bury (v; inter), ochä (*ch* guttural).

Buy (v), wå-ru-mäh; same word means to trade.

Calm (n), oh-bra-gä.

Canoe, på-djé (*j* French).

Carrion (a dead animal), uå-hu-mä (*ua* short and together).

Catch (v; capture), rusä.

Caught (v; captured), ua-ni-hih (*u* and *a* separated).

Cave, ïro-chrogä; i.e., a hollow rock.

Chew (v), same word as for meal, or to eat.

Child, tchitching-ä (*ch* like *tgi*, with the point of the tongue).

Choke (v; press to death, smother), o-nong-ä.

Clear (bright), o-haun-uäh (*n* French; *uah* nasal).

Clear (water), ni-bréjé (French); they give this name to the Mississippi.

Cloud (masses of cloud), moch-pih (*ch* guttural).

Coal, åchudjeh (*ach* guttural).

Coals (glowing), pedjé-sih (*j* French).

Cold (adj), snïh.

Comb (n), härusäh, i.e., louse-catcher; from hä, louse, and rusäh, catch.

Community (company, many men), manksché-gerohan (*an* French; *ge* German).

Compel (v; force), a-u-scheh-geh (run together).

Convenient (comfortable), pï; same word as for good.

Cough (v), hogh-pä.

Count (v; number), uårauä (*au* together).

Cowardly, same word as for lazy, or rotten.

Crooked, rutan-schkunäh (*an* French).

Crow (way of dressing hair), nantó (*an* French).

Cure (v; heal), ginih.

Curly (hair), påhï-riberin (*in* nasal, like ï).

Cut (v), gron-tschéh (*on* French).

Cut down (v; fell), gron-tsché (*on* French).

Cut down (v; fell), grontsché (*on* French).

Cut into (v; incise, carve), grontsché (*on* French).

Dance (n), wotschí.

Dark, ohånsä (*an* French).

Daughter, ih-wung-ä.

Day, han-uä (*an* French, the whole short and run together).

Dead, tsäh.

Deaf, nå-cho-dje-ning-e (*j* French; *ch* guttural; *e* short).

Dear (costly), tschä-chäh (*ch* guttural).

Deceive (v; cheat), gistoncha (*ch* guttural).

Decoy (v; decoy an animal), tah-sching-ä-on (*sching* and *a* pronounced together; *on* French).

Devastate (v), schéh-na.

Devil (evil spirit), wåhkondapisch-kunnäh.

Die (v), tsäh.

Dirty, måh-chrih (*ch* with the point of the tongue).

Dirty (v), måchré (*ch* guttural).

Dive(v), nïh-rotata. [MS. note in Library of Congress copy by J. O. Dorsey, says that this is not a verb but ni, water, and rótata, under.—TRANS.]

Divide (v; share), ikirutan (*an* French).

Door, tschi-okä (run together).

Double, nouä; same word as for two.

Drag (v; drag a load), påhï-on-reh (*on* French).

Draw (v; draw water), nih-ru-seh.

Dream (v), ombrä; ira-ombrá, you dreamed (plural).

Drink (v), ratan (*an* French).

Dry (adj), buh-sä.

Dumb, i-tiä-ru-scha-gä.

Dung, ming-grä.

Dust, månschuh-schudje (*an* French; likewise *j*; *e* short).

Dwelling place (hunting stand), irappä (final *a* between *e* and *a* umlaut).

Ear, nan-toa (French).

Ear-ornament, uåhnon-pin (*non* French; *pin* nasal, like *pï*).

Early, heruh-tach-tsché (*ach* guttural); early in the day.

Empty (adj), chroschkä (*ch* guttural).

Enclose (v; shut up), uå-nåssé.

Enemy, okitsché.

Englishman, Sanganasch.

Enough, kahäna (*na* short).

Entertain (v), nontutan (*on* and *an* French).

Even (equal, flat), bra-ské, or bras-ké; same word as for broad, or great.

Evening, pï-kuiä, or pïkuiä; from pi, sun, and kuiä, low.

Everywhere, mayon-brughä (*on* French); i.e., over the whole land.

Expectorate(v), grä-uä.

Eye, ichtá (*ich* German and not guttural; nearly the same as with the Dacota, Omahas, Osages, and Puncas).

Eyelid, ichtá-hi.

Face (sight), indéh.

Fall (v), o-chua-nä (*ch* guttural).

Far (distant), ha-rä.

Far (distant), hah-reh.

Fat, uå-schi.

Father, ing-koh.

Feast, same as meal, or eat; they say, give to eat; also gi-ko.

Feather, manschon (*on* French).

Female (of animals), ming-eh.

Festival, så-gä.

Fever, okisché-gétachran (*ch* guttural; *an* French).

Find (v), ikiré.

Finger, nau-ue (*ue* short).

Fire, pedjé (first *e* distinctly pronounced; *j* French).

Fish (n), hó.

Fish (v), ho-rusä.

Fish (v; catch fish), same word as for fish-hook.

Fish-hook, horusé.

Fist, nauä-sogä.

Flame (n), pedjé-takan (*j* and *an* French).

Flat (level), braskä.

Flee (v; escape), hå-sä.

Flesh, tåh.

Flint, ju-tsché-ogran (*an* French).

Flood (v; overflow), nih-ton (*on* French).

Flow (v), kahïra (*ra* short).

Fog, schuschudjä (*j* French).

Foot, sï.

Foot-path, nong-ä.

Forehead, päh.

Forest, chrå-uäh (*ch* guttural).

Forget (v), giksuh-schkúnnä.

Freeze (v; chill), o-snih.

Freeze (v; congeal), nih-tåh.

Frenchman, Måsongkä-okannä (*a* umlaut, also pronounced like *e*).

Friend, ntará.

Full, oh-yuh.

Fully (of cooking, done), ni-djä (*j* French).

Gall (bile), grä-ue-sih.

Gay-colored (variegated), gréjé (*j* French).

Go (v), monnih.

God (creator), wåhkonda.

Good, pïh.

Grandson, intaqúa.

Grape-vine, hå-seh-hih.

Grave, óh-chä (*ch* guttural).

Gray, cho-djé (*j* French; *ch* guttural).

Gray-haired, pahi-son (French).

Great (tall), grón-rä (*n* French).

Green, tohch-djä (*ch* guttural; *j* French).

Ground (earth), måhå.

Gun, jútschä (*tscha* short); rifle, jútschä-kïh-berúh-berúh (the whole short, and run together).

Gut (intestines), schiuä.

Gut (v; gut an animal), nicha-gi-na-sché (*ch* guttural).

Hair, på-hï.

Half, oskisserä (*e* short); så-ning-ä, the second part.

Hand, nau-uä.

Hard, sågeh.

Hate (v), hasch-ing-äh.

Head, på.

Headache, nan-soh-nih-djä (*an* French; *dja* likewise).

Healthy, ogischegä-schkúnnä (*e* short).

Hear (v), nåkon (*on* French).

Heart, mon-tchä (*on* French; *ch* with the point of the tongue).

Heat (v; inflame), tåcherang (*ch* guttural); i.e., warm; they also say monschtiö (*on* French).

Heavy (difficult), tscháh-tan (*an* French).

Hide (v), nåh-chron (*ch* guttural; *on* French).

High, mock-scheh.

Hole, chro-gä (*ch* guttural).

Hollow (adj), chro-gä (*ch* with the point of the tongue).

Horn, häh.

Horns (antlers), häh.

Horse (young horse), schangtóing-ä.

Hot, moschtä.

House (lodge), tschĭh.

Hunger, chrånĭ (*ch* guttural).

Hunt (n), kinángra.

Hunt (v), kinángra.

Hunter, kinángra-uarupeh.

Hurricane (storm), tåh-såggä-uayhäh-häh (the whole run together).

I, mĭh.

Ice, nóchä (*ch* guttural; *a* short).

Incurable, ginih-schkúnnä.

Indistinct, tahĭ-schkúnnä.

Internal (within), róhtata.

Intoxicate (v), tå-ningé (*ninge* nasal).

Iron, må-sä (first syllable longer; first *a* almost like *an* French).

Island, rú-mi-tschï (*rumitschi*, or *rumaetschi*).

Jar (vessel), däh-chä (*ch* guttural).

Joy (enjoyment, mirth), gïro (German throughout).

Knife, måh-hi.

Know (v), ju̇a-hamg-äh.

Know (v; be acquainted with), hah-pang-äh.

Lame, uåh-hïragä.

Lance (spear; sword-lance), uåh-yaueh (letters in *yaueh* are separated).

Land, mayón (French).

Laugh (v, or n), ick-scháh.

Lay (v; lay down), jan (*an* French).

Leader (chief), uong-gé-gi-hi (first syllable almost like *wong*; *g* guttural).

Leaf (of a tree), nåchpä (*nach* long).

Left (direction), aratscheh.

Leg, rägä.

Lie (v; deceive), tohshäh.

Light (v; illuminate), hån-ue-on-re (*an* and *on* French; *ue* nasal, likewise *han*).

Light (v; kindle), ohan-ue (*an* French; *u* and *e* separated).

Lightning, wáhkonda-gron (*gron* French).

Like (v; be fond of), ooch-thá (*ch* guttural).

Lip, ih-hå.

Little, tscho-kerá.

Long, sreh-djeh (*j* French).

Loose (of clothes), grån-reh (*an* French).

Maiden, tschichmi-ing-ä (*ich* guttural).

Maize, wå-dud-djé (*j* French).

Man, uong-gä, or uong-äh; same word as for human being.

Man (human being), uong-äh.

Marry (v; of a man), grong-äh.

Marry (v; of a woman), uåruchä.

Meal (or to eat?), uåårudjé (*j* French).

Messenger, ikomónne (*ne* short).

Milk (n), teh-på-seh-nih (run together).

Mirror, måse-angitan (*e* short; *an* French).

Money, må-ses-kå (all syllables even); i.e., white metal.

Moon, pïh: they add a limiting word; the words for sun and moon are the same, but they believe the two to be distinct.

Morning, hån-uä.

Mother, ináh.

Mountain, hämokschä.

Mouth, hï.

Much (many), roh-han (*an* French).

Murder (v; kill), tsäh.

Music, uå-yanuäh (*yan* French).

My, mih-te-uäh.

Nail (on the feet), sïha-schágä.

Nail (on fingers), naue-ue-schágä.

Nail (on the hands), nombä-schágä (*nom* French).

Naked, tåh-huh.

Name (n), rahjä (*j* German).

Narrow, broskäsch-schkúnä (*na* short).

Necklace (neck ornament), wånon-peh (*on* French).

Needle, måh-sickan (*an* French).

Negro, mååk-schi-säuäh.

Night, haáñ-hä.

Noon, pïoh-cons-ská (*cons* French).

Nose, påso.

Not (no), niäkóh.

Old, isch-ágä.

Old man, uánscha (*an* French).

Old woman, inahak-schingä (German throughout).

Oldest, inó.

On the other side (of a river), nïagreck.

Once, jóng-kä.

Over, mok-schüátta (*atta* short).

Over (above), mååk-schäh.

Pain (n), nih-djé (*j* French).

Paint (v), okompé (French throughout).

Palate, räsä.

Pale (v; grow pale, fade), indéhska; i.e., white or pale face.

Peace, mayon-pïh (*on* French).

Pipe (tobacco), rå-no-uä.

Plant (v), o-yú (together); i.e., put something in the earth.

Play (v). schkåh-djé (*j* French).

Pluck (v; feathers), hi-snudjä (*j* French).

Pointed, påh-hi.

Pond (pool), same word as for swamp.

Pouch (sack), osché (*e* somewhat like *a* umlaut).

Powder (gun-powder), åh-chudjäh (*ch* guttural; *j* French).

Pray (v; to the lord of life), wahkonda-åchagä (*ch* guttural).

Pregnant, nichta-chontjä (*ch* guttural; *j* French).

Press (v), brïchä-onongä.

Press out (v; express?), sagéonang-ä (the whole run together; *ge* German, as in *geben*).

Pretty, oh-com-pih (French).

Prick (v; sting), wå-yah-uä (*ua* short).

Prisoner, same word as for caught, or captured.

Proud (haughty), tan-ra-gon-da (*an* and *on* French).

Pulse, ahk-kan (first *a* barely audible; *an* French).

Punish (v; whip), utschï.

Push (v; thrust), nih-djé (*j* French).

Quick, ho-che-rä (*ch* guttural).

Rain (n), ni-o-iu (run together).

Reconcile (v; appease), mayonpih (*on* French).

Red, schu-djä (*j* French).

Resistance (self-defence), ankirragä (*an* French).

Rib, roh-toh.

Ripe (of fruits), sïh-da (*da* short).

River, nisch-nong-ä.

Rock (cliff), ïro.

Rot (v), obrån-pesch-kunä (*an* French).

Rotten (lazy?), chritagä (*ch* guttural).

Round, schnåh-schnåh.

Run (v), nong-ä.

Salt down (v; pickle, corn), nischko-oiú.

Scalp, nantó (*an* French).

Sea, nih-chonn-djé (*dje* French); the Ayowas say, nih-chon-je (*je* German).

Secret, nå-chron (*ch* palatal; *on* French).

See (v), uatah (*u* and *a* follow closely).

Sexual organs (female), uieh (*u* separated).

Sexual organs (male), reh.

Shade (shadow), oh-uan-seh (*an* French).

Shallow (water), nichä-uäh (*ch* guttural).

Sharp (pointed), på-hih.

Shave (v), chru-scherá (*ch* guttural).

Shoot (v; with an arrow), måhkudjeh.

Shoot (v; with a gun), jutjehkudjeh (*j* French).

Shore (bank), nih-må-åh.

Short, süít-tscheh.

Shout (v; call), sih-uan (*uan* short, like *wan* nasal; *an* French).

Shout (v; give the warhoop), graah (*r* with the point of the tongue).

Sick, okischegä.

Side, såh-ning-ä.

Sing (v), yan-uah (*an* French).

Sister, tång-äh.

Sit (v), ah-mi-nåh.

Skin (hide), hå.

Sleep (v), iyán (*i* and *y* slightly separated; *an* French).

Sleepy, yon-gondah (*on* French).

Slowly, srih-djeh (*j* French).

Small, ing-äh.

Smell (v; sniff at, scent), obran (*an* French); smell (something), obranré.

Smoke (n), scho-djä (*j* French).

Smoke (v; tobacco), rah-nehi.

Snow (n), påh; same word as for head and nose.

Sole (of the foot), si-ro-ta-tá (*sirotata*).

Son, hih-ing-äh.

Speak (v), id-djé (*j* French).

Spirits (distilled), pedjé-ni (*j* French); i.e., fire-water.

Spot (v; stain), måchré (*ch* guttural).

Spring (source), nih-hong-ä.

Spring (the season), päh-käh.

Spring (v; leap, jump), attåunuah (nasal; *aun* nasal; *n* French).

Spy (v; listen), ånoch-ron-no-kron (*on* French).

Star, piká.

Start (v; start an animal), hå-sé.

Stick, nan-ing-ä (*an* French).

Still (silent), echan-schkunäh (*ch* guttural; *an* French).

Stinginess, (greediness), gi-tschächä (*cha* palatal).

Stomach, mong-ä (*a* short).

Stone, ïro, or ïh-roh.

Stop (v; hold fast, arrest), o-nongä (run together).

Storm (thunder-storm), tájä-soggä (*j* French).

Straight (direct), ruh-tan (*an* French).

Strangle (v), gi-to-dje (*j* French).

Strike (v; beat), uh-tschin (*tschin* nasal; *in* like *i*).

Strong, brih-chäh (*r* with the point of the tongue; *ch* guttural).

Stump, påhï-schkunäh.

Stupid, bréjé-schkunä' (*j* French).

Summer, tohk-äh.

Sun, pïh.

Sunrise, pïh-grïh.

Sunset, pïh-hïh.

Swamp, tschérauä (*ua* short).

Sweet, skóh.

Swelling (boil), ouä' (short and together).

Swim (v), nih-uan (*an* French).

Tail (of an animal), sinn-djä (*j* French).

Teach (v), wå-kon-seh (*on* French).

Tear out (v; pull out), gi-na-sché.

Tears (n), ischtá-nïh; i.e. eye-water.

Teeth, ihï.

There (of place), tschekä, or köta.

Thick (large), chonje chonje (*j* French).

Thin, brékä.

Thumb, nau-uä-chonje (*ch* short); i.e., thick, or big finger.

Thunder (n), gron-gron (*on* French); wahkonda-gron-gron.

Tie (v; bind, fasten), ru-ski-djä (*j* French).

Tinder-box, pedjé-on (*j* and *on* French).

Tobacco, rah-nih.

Toe, sihasch-schángä.

Tomahawk, i-sua-ing-ä (run together).

To-morrow, härúh-tata.

Tongue, redseh.

Toothache, ihï-nidjeh (*j* French).

Trace (track of an animal), sih-grä (last syllable short).

Trade, uå-ru-ma.

Trader, same word as for buy.

Trap (snare), månse-råch-tagä (*ach* guttural).

Tree, grå-uéh (*gr* guttural).

True, mikä.

Ugly, püsch-schkunnä.

Undress (v; strip), unaie-gistrüdje (*j* French).

Unmarried, ming-grong-äschkunnä; of a woman, uåruch-äschkunnä.

Unripe, sidah-schkúnnä.

Until (unto), ätchån (*ch* guttural; *an* French).

Urine, däjä (*j* French).

Vein (artery), kán (French).

War, mayón-peschkunïh (*on* French); literally, bad land.

War-club (with the iron point), uehrutschin (*tschin* nasal; *n* French).

Warm, mosch-tschä.

Warmth (of weather, or water), tåh-chran (*ch* guttural).

Warrior (brave man), wå-schúscheh.

Wash (v), uå-ruh-jäh.

Water, nïh.

Wax, uagriska-minggräh.

Weep (v), cha-gä (*ch* guttural; *ga* short).

Wet (adj), tohkä.

What? how? tå-ku-rä.

Whistle (v; pipe), suh-dä.

White, skáh.

White man, må-song-kä; i.e., he works in iron.

Whole (very), brughä (*gh* guttural).

Widow, aegran-ning-ä (*an* French).

Wind (n), tad-djé (*j* French).

Wing, ahú.

Winter, påh-nih.

Within (come in), gúh.

Woman (wife), ina-hakä (final *a* barely audible).

Wood, näh.

Work (v), uå-on (*on* French).

Wound (v), òh.

Wound (v; shoot), òh.

Wrap up (v), ruberin (*in* like *i* nasal).

Year (winter), páhni (*ni* short).

Yellow, sïh.

Yes, hontiö' (*an* French).

Young (not old or little), schiniä' (*nia* nasal).

Numerals

One, jon-kä.

Two, noh-uä.

Three, tåh-ni.

Four, toh-uä.

Five, såh-tan (*an* French).

Six, schåh-kuä (*kua* short).

Seven, schåh-cheman (second *ch* guttural; *e* short; *an* French).

Eight, kräh-råbbeneh (first *e* short).

Nine, schonkä.

Ten, kräh-bran (*an* French).

Twenty, krän-bran-noh-uä.

Thirty, kräh-bran-tåh-ni.

Forty, kräh-bran-toh-uä.

Animals

Bear (black), montchä (*cha* almost like *tia*).

Bear (grizzly), måntó (*an* French).

Beaver, rauä (*a* and *u* somewhat separated).

Buffalo, tjä (*j* French).

Deer (common, or Virginian), tahg-tsche, or simply thá.

Dog, schonk-okännäh.

Duck, michä-iniä (*ch* guttural).

Elk (great deer), hóma (*ma* short).

Fox (black), mischnäkä-sä-uä.

Fox (gray), mischnäkä.

Fox (red), mischnäkä-schudjä (*j* French).

Hare, misch-tsching-gä (run together).

Horse, schong-äh.

Mule, noñ-tua-chonjä (*ch* guttural).

Opossum, ik-scha-mina (run together); i.e., the one which lies down, or sleeps with laughter.

Otter, tohsch-nong-ä (all syllables even).

Ox, tschehs-kah.

Skunk, mong-äh.

Snake, wå-kån (*an* French).

Turkey (wild), wåe-ink-chontjeh (first *e* barely audible; *ch* guttural; *j* French).

Turtle, keth-han (*an* French).

Wolf (black), schanton-sä-uä.

Wolf (gray), schanton-schkáh (*anton* French).

Wolf (prairie), schah-monnikassïh.

FOOTNOTES:

[263] Written from the pronunciation of Major Dougherty, Indian agent for this nation, who understands the language thoroughly. This language, with only slight variations, is spoken by the Otos, Ayowäs, and Missouris.— MAXIMILIAN.

PAHNI[264]

All (the whole), tsche-túh (*e* short).

Bad, hå-ku-na-heh.

Buffalo, taraháh.

Child, pïh-rau (*rau* together and German).

Cold (adj), te-pe-tseh.

Come (v), ueh-ta.

Father, attiasch (*i* and *a* separated).

Gone (gone away), ueh-tiet.

Good, tunaheh.

Goods (wares), låh-pion (*pion* French).

Great (tall), ti-réh-hu.

His, ku-tá.

Horse, arúhsch.

Kill (v), uetekut (*ue* separated).

Love (v; prize), tiråh-pire-huh (*e* audible).

Maize, lå-khé-schu.

Man, såhnisch.

Meal (or to eat?), tih-uáh-uah (run together).

Mule, kit-kehåh-keh (first *e* short).

My, ku-ta-tih.

Not (no), kåh-kih.

Pipe (tobacco), lah-uisch.

Quick, uisch-ke-tiuh (*ke* short).

Sleep (v), titkah.

Slow, påhith.

Small, kakiréhhu.

Sun, sok-kóh-ro (*ro* half short).

Trade (n), tiråh-poh.

What? tire-kéhro (first *e* distinctly pronounced but somewhat short).

White, tå' h-kåh.

White man, sáhnisch-tåh-kåh.

Woman (wife), tsoppat.

Your (plural), ku-ta-schih.

FOOTNOTES:

[264] Written from the pronunciation of an American; I, therefore, cannot guarantee the correctness of these words.—MAXIMILIAN.

PUNCA, Pons of the Canadians

Arm, adn (*d* and *n* barely audible).

Arrow, mán (French).

Bow, mandéh (*an* French).

Child, schĭnga-schĭnga.

Earth, tån-dä.

Eye, ischtá.

Fire, pähd.

God (creator), wåhkonda.

Hair, nanschiha (*an* French; *ha* short).

Hand, nombä̈ (*om* French).

Head, nanschti (*an* French).

Man, nŭ́h (*u* between *o* and *u*).

Moon, mĭh-om-báh (*om* French), or mih-ombáh.

Mouth, hĭh.

Pipe (tobacco), nĭnibá.

Star, mĭhka.

Sun, mĭh.

Tomahawk, manse-päschingá (*an* French; *se* short).

Water, nĭh.

Woman, wáh-uh.[265]

FOOTNOTES:

[265] From the words given above it appears that the Puncas are descended from the Omáhas; for their language is the same with only very slight variations, a fact which they, themselves, admit.—MAXIMILIAN.

SAUKIS, SAKIS; Sacs of the French[266]

Arrow, annó.

Beautiful, uatchitá.

Beaver, améhk.

Black, makåtä.

Bow, matä.

Buffalo, nannosó.

Child, nänitschonés (es with emphasis).

Devil (evil spirit), mdjï-mnitó (j French), or motschi-manito.

Elk (great deer), mäschauáh.

Eye, skïschick.

Fire, skotäw (aw short; w barely audible).

Foot, nasset.

God (good spirit), bakéhmánito.

Green, skepok-kuaiuah, or spe pokiä.

Hair, minesai (ai together).

Hand, nanätsch (second a between a and a umlaut; ch soft).

Head, utab.

Horse, naketóhsh-kescháh (first e and ke short).

House (lodge), uïkiahb (ui short).

Leader (chief), tapáne-táke (e barely audible).

Leg (whole leg), nekáht.

Maiden, schaskesé (first e short).

Man, nännï.

Mirror, woapamúhn.

Morning, uapåk.

Mouth, tätóhn.

Night, anaquick.

Nose, machkiuonn.

One-eyed, po-ke-kua.

Otter, kittäh.

Pipe (tobacco), poakan.

Red, máschkue-wiauáh.

Tobacco, saëmon (*on* French).

Tomahawk (battle axe), papake-hüit (*huit* short); the real tomahawk is, popokiä.

Turkey (wild), pänáh (first *a* umlaut).

Ugly, mianåt.

War, nitscheschkuá.

Warrior, uätåsä̊ (final *a* between *a* umlaut and *o* umlaut).

Water, näpe (short; *e* barely audible, almost like *i*).

White (the color), uapeschekann.

Woman (wife), ïkua.

Wood, massahan (*h* barely audible).

Yellow, ůssuah, or assáuah (*aua* separated).

FOOTNOTES:

[266] Written from the pronunciation of a Sauki Indian.—MAXIMILIAN.

SNAKE INDIANS; Shoshones, in the Rocky Mountains[267]

Arrow, tóhietsitta (*iet* together; *sitta* distinctly pronounced).

Bow, náhmeack.

Earth, ähsche (*ah* long; *e* ½).

Far (distant), máhnarko.

Fire, kohn-ne (*e* ½).

God, tiwitsim-pohhacante (*e* distinctly pronounced); i.e., the lord of life.

Hair (hair of head), uchkannea (second *a* barely audible).

Head, ochkanneh (*ch* guttural).

Horse, punko.

Horse (race horse), punko-emáhhi-mia (*mi* separated from *a*; *a* distinctly pronounced).

Love (I love), tiwitsin-kamahk.

- 305 -

Love (I love all white men), oyette-tabebo-kamangkä.[268]

Man, han-aht-se (*an* French; *e* ½ and short).

Meal (or to eat?), máhrichkia (*ich* with the point of the tongue).

Moon, ohtse-táhbe (*e* ½); i.e., the night sun.

Pity (have pity, ayez pitié), tiwitsch-naschuntita.

Sun, táhbe (*e* distinctly pronounced).

Water, ohksche (*e* ½).

Woman (wife), uáh-ai-pe (*ai* together; *e* ½).

FOOTNOTES:

[267] Written from the pronunciation of the Spanish interpreter, Isidor Sandoval. On the Snake Indians, or Shoshonés, see the reports of the missionary Parker (*ibid.*, p. 300), *Astoria*, p. 163, and Captain Bonneville, p. 159, etc.—MAXIMILIAN.

Comment by Ed. For Sandoval, see our volume xxiii, p. 132, note 109.

[268] The Snake Indians (les Serpens) call themselves Shoshonés. They are allies of the Flatheads, and enemies of the Blackfeet and Crows. They dwell in the Rocky mountains and beyond, on the Columbia; they fall into two divisions—the true Shoshonés, and the so-called Gens de Pitié, or Radiqeurs (Root-diggers)—the Maradiços of the Spaniards. The former keep a great number of dogs, which they do not use as pack animals, but for food. They do not have as many horses as the Blackfeet; but employ them for carrying burdens. They live in leather tents. They are generally not so well formed as the Blackfeet; still there are many tall, well developed men among them. Their tribe is said to be very numerous, more so than the Dacotas. They carry on trade with the Spaniards, who exchange beaver and other furs for leather shirts and similar articles. They are not hostile to the whites. The Root-diggers, on the other hand, are a wretched people. They do not have leather tents; but merely set poles together which they cover with boughs, hay, and grass. Their physiognomy is said to be distinguished by rather flat noses. They are very poor and barbarous, go nearly naked, live chiefly on roots, and possess no weapons. They eat ants in quantities; scooping up a whole hill of these, they wash them, knead them into balls, bake these between coals, pulverize them, and then make a soup. Mr. Campbell of Fort William, who has often visited them, gave me the following account of them. They were so barbarous and so indifferent to their environment, that everything about him seemed new and ridiculous to them. At that time they did not know the value of the beaver skins, which they singed. Some of their huts, which he visited, had remained for a long time in the same place

without their ever having looked about for a better region. He found a large number of mountain goat skins among them; and, as they were so little acquainted with the whites, it was possible to carry on a very profitable trade with them. The Comanches, who call themselves Jamparicka, are said to speak practically the same language as the Snake Indians. They live at the sources of the Rio Colorado (Rivière rouge). They decorate one arm of their shirts with tufts of hair, the other with feathers.—MAXIMILIAN.

Comment by Ed. For Robert Campbell and Fort William, see our volume xxiii, p. 198, notes 154, 155, respectively.

WASAJI, or Osage[269]

American (an), Manhï-tánga (*an* French).

Arm, ischtó.

Arrow, uan (*an* French).

Autumn, tandje (*an* and *j* French).

Avenge (v), gráschupä.

Beard, putain (*tain* French), or indjähin (*j* French; *in* nasal, like *i*).

Bird, uaschïnga.

Black, sábä.

Blind, ischtá-uärabaje (*j* French; *e* distinctly pronounced).

Blood, uahpïh.

Blue, tóh.

Bone (bones), uah-huh.

Bow, minn-djä (*j* French).

Brave, uanompasche (*sche* German; distinctly pronounced).

Brave man, uassissigä (guttural).

Brook, uatschïska.

Brother (older), uischiniäh.

Brother (younger), uissonga.

Child, schïnga-schinga.

Cold (adj), snïh; very cold, snïh-uatschä.

Copper (metal), mansä-sih.

Dance (v), uatschï.

Day, hambá (French).

Deaf, nihütsche-ning-kä (*e* ½; the whole run together).

Devil (evil spirit), uakán-pïhschä (*a* short and ½).

Die (v), ts-äh (*ts* is merely a fore tone).

Dish (of wood), ïntschipä (German throughout).

Dog, schong-gä (German).

Door, tischúpä.

Dream (v), hombra (German throughout).

Drink (v), latan (French).

Dumb, ïha-baje (*j* French; *e* distinctly pronounced).

Ear, natáh: hence mule, natáh-tánga; i.e., big ears.

Earth, makáh, or maniga (guttural, indistinct).

Enemy, okitsche (*e* ½).

Englishman, Sanganásch.

Evening, pah-set-tan (*an* French).

Eye, ischtá.

Father, indadjä (*j* French).

Feather, manschon (*on* French).

Fire, pedje (*j* French; *e* distinctly pronounced).

Flesh, táh-tóhka.

Forest, schán.

Frenchman, Ischtáchä (*ch* German, guttural).

Friend, korá.

Go (v), grih-grah (German throughout; *r* with the point of the tongue).

God, uakán-tánga (first *an* French) or uakónda.

Good, tanhä (*an* French); it tastes good, láhgenih.

Great (tall), tánga (German, guttural).

Gun, uahóta; rifle, minh-gïng-graha.

Hair, pah-hah.

Hand, nompé (*om* French).

Head, páh.

Healthy, ansïri.

Heart, nonn-je (*j* French; *e* distinctly pronounced).

Heat, (n), man-schtä (*an* French; *schta* German).

Horse, kawa; plural is the same.

House (lodge), tïh.

Hunger, nompä-anhin (*om* French likewise *an* and final *in.* nasal, like *i*).

Hunt (v), tábreh.

I, uïe (*e* ½).

Ice, tschácha (*ch* guttural).

Iron, mansä̈ (*an* French); yellow iron.

Kettle (iron), tschäckä̈.

Knife, manhi (*an* French).

Lame, ih-rá-ha.

Lance, uä̈h-schap-schäh (the whole run together).

Lead (n), mansä-man (*an* French).

Leader (chief), kahigä̈.

Leg, schäga (German throughout).

Life, anïh.

Lightning, uakin-ala (*in* nasal, almost like *i*; the whole run together).

Man, niká; nika-schiga, several men, people.

Meal (or to eat?), uanúmbra (German throughout).

Medicine-feast, opä̈han-uakan (*an* French); or medicine-day, hámba-uakan (*am* and *an* French).

Medicine-lodge, kih-uakándagä.

Medicine-man, uakándagä (German throughout; *g* guttural).

Medicine-pouch, uahhóbä.

Moon, mïh, or mïh-ómba (*om* French).

Morning, han-bach-tschä (*han* French; *bach* German guttural).

Mother, nïh-tánga.

Mountain, pahha.

Mountain (great), pahha-tánga.

Mountain (small), pahha-schïnga.

Mourning (n), nanschischon.

Mouth, i-há.

Much (many), hühe (*e* ½).

Negro, nïka-sabä.

Night, hán-dje (*an* and *j* French; *e* short).

Nose, pah-schu.

Pipe (tobacco), naniómba.

Powder (gun-powder), nichotsche (*ch* guttural; *e* distinct).

Quick, uasch-kan (*kan* French).

Quiver, uáh-onju (*n* and *j* French); this, as well as bow and arrow, no longer occurs among them.

Red, schúdja (*j* French).

Red (to paint red), schudja-gáhcha (*ch* guttural).

River, uatschïska-tánga; i.e., great brook, or river; they call the Missouri, Nih-schodje (*j* French; *e* ½), i.e., the muddy water.

Sand, tschansemon (French).

Scalp (n), pahá.

Scalp (v; scalp an enemy), pahá-rüsá.

Scalp-dance (war-dance), tután-uatschi.

Shield (n), uágrä (short; *r* with the point of the tongue); to carry a shield, tschehá-uágrä.

Sick, itüh-häga (run together).

Silver, mansaskan (*an* French); i.e., white iron.

Small, uah-hohstia, or uah-hohta.

Smoke (n), schódiä.

Snow (n), wáh.

Speak (v), ïhha-uaska.

Spirits (distilled), pädjinïh.

Spring (the season), päädje (*aa* separated; *j* French).

Star, uïtscháchpe (*ch* German, guttural).

Stingy (greedy), uah-chrih (*ch* with the point of the tongue).

Stone, in (*in* somewhat nasal, like *i*).

Strong, uaschkan-gran-rä (*an* and *gran* French).

Summer, bellokellan (*an* French).

Sun, uin (*u* and *i* separated; *in* nasal, like *i*).

Teeth, hïh.

Thunder (n), gronhóta.

Tobacco (smoking tobacco), nanähü.

Tomahawk (with the pipe), manhispä-nanïomba (*an* French).

Tongue, lähja (*j* French).

Toothache, hïh-hïh.

Trail, ohscháng ä (German).

Ugly, pih-sche (*e* ½).

Village, taman (*an* French).

War, tu-tan (*an* French).

War-club (casse tête, tomahawk), manhispä-schïnga.

Warmth, manschtä (*an* French).

Wash (v), gruschá.

Water, nïh.

Weep (v), hagä.

White (color), skáh.

Widow, nïhka-tombaschä (*om* French).

Wind (n), tadjä (*j* French).

Winter, páhletan (*e* short; *an* French).

Woman (wife), uakó (*ua* separated).

Wood, tschán (*an* French).

Yellow, sïh.

Yes, hóh-uä.

Articles of Dress

Blanket (woolen), hahïn (*in* nasal, like *i*).

Deer's-tail (hair ornament), táhsinnja (*j* French).

Leggings, hühninggä (German).

Moccasins, hómpä (*om* French).

Shirt, o'ch-kiüera (*ch* guttural; *e* ½); i.e., white man's shirt, for they wear none, not even of leather.

Numerals

One, uïnchtschä (*uinch* nasal; *u* and *i* separated; *n* French; *ch* guttural).

Two, nombá (*om* French).

Three, lahbeni (*e* ½; *ni* short).

Four, toh-bá.

Five, sah-tá (*s* soft; *ta* short).

Six, schah-pé.

Seven, peh-umbá (German).

Eight, kih-atóba.

Nine, gräbena-tscheh-uïningkä' (the whole run together); i.e., ten less one; they also say, schangká.

Ten, gräbena (*e* ½; *na* short).

Eleven, gräbena-ahgenä-uächze (*uach* nasal; *ach* guttural; *ze* short).

Twelve, gräbena-agenih-nombá.

Thirteen, gräbena-lahbeni.

Twenty, gräbena-nombá; and so on.

Hundred, gräbena-hütanga.

Thousand, gräbena-itó-grabëna-hütanga.

I eat, uaranombra-tatsch, or uanumbra-minktsch.

You (thou) **eat**, uaranumbra.

He eats, same as I eat.

We eat, there is no plural form, the plural is expressed by using "many."

Eat (imper singular and plural), uanumbra.

I shall eat, nomp-eh-anhin-uaranumbra-tatsch (*an* and *n* French); i.e., I am hungry and shall eat.

Names of Other Tribes

Ayowas, Páhodjä.

Comanches, Baschtá.

Crows, Kahchä (*ch* guttural).

Dacotas, Schauánn (*a* and *u* separated).

Foxes, given same name as Sahkis.

Konzas, Kansä (*an* French).

Missouris, Waschóra.

Omáhas, Omahá.

Otos, Wadochtáta (*och* guttural).

Pahnis, Panï.

Sakis, Sáhki.

Animals

Antelope, tatóhka.

Badger, hogá (*ga* German, guttural).

Bear (black), uassábä.

Bear (grizzly), mantó (*an* French).

Beaver, tscháhbä.

Buffalo (bull), tschetoga.

Buffalo (calf), tschéh-schínga.

Buffalo (cow), tschéh.

Cat, mïhka.

Cat (European), ing-grong-gräscha (German).

Elk (general name), opán (*an* French).

Elk (calf), opán-schinga.

Elk (doe), opán-mïnga (second word German).

Elk (stag), opán-tánga, or hächága (*ch* guttural).

Fox, schongréscha (German).

Fox (prairie), schongréscha-schïnga.

Hare (white), manschtin-skah.

Lynx (felix rufa), mih-ká.

Muskrat, táh-si.

Opossum, sindiäschtá.

Otter, tochenángä (*ch* German, guttural).

Panther, ingróng-ga (German throughout; run together).

Panther-skin, ingrónggaha.

Rabbit (hare), manschtin-schïnga (*an* French; *in* nasal, like *i*).

Skunk, mang-gá.

Snake, uets-ah (*u* and *e* separated; the whole run together).

Snake (rattle snake), sin-diä-chala (*ch* guttural).

Spider, tschäbüka.

Turkey (wild), súhka.

Wolf, schomikásse (*e* distinct).

The Months

July and August, tschetoga-kĭrucha; i.e., the moon when the buffalo is in heat.

September, October and November, tah-kiruchä, i.e., the time when the deer is in heat.

December, tah-habrähka; i.e., moon of the thin hides.

January and February, mĭhka-kiruchä; i.e., the time when the lynx is in heat.

March and April, oh-uä-gachä (*ch* guttural); i.e., the time of the maize.

FOOTNOTES:

[269] Written from the pronunciation of Mr. Chardon, who had lived a long time among the Osages and understood the language perfectly. They call their people Wasaji. Formerly they were a powerful tribe, and were always at war with the neighboring Indians, even with the Konsas who speak the same dialect. They were originally divided into the Great and Little Osages; but about forty years ago a part of them, known under the name of the Chaneer's, or Clermont's band, separated from the rest and moved to the Arkansa. On the present dwelling place of the Osages, see Gallatin (*ibid.*, p. 126). They regard themselves as autochthonous.—MAXIMILIAN.

Comment by Ed. For F. A. Chardon, see our volume xxiii, p. 188, note 144. For Clermont's band and its separation from the Osage, consult our volume v, pp. 191, 192.

INDIAN SIGN LANGUAGE[270]

This sign language has been treated in various works. Say has given noteworthy vocabularies in Edward James's *Account of the Expedition of Major Long to the Rocky Mountains*. The Arikkaras, Mandans, Minnitarris, Crows, Chayennes, Snakes, and Blackfeet all understand a system of signs, which, as we were told, are unintelligible to the Dacotas, Assiniboins, Ojibuas, Krihs, and other nations. The following vocabulary is taken from the first group.[271]

[From Colonel Garrick Mallery's "Sign Language of the Indians of the Upper Missouri in 1832."]

Although nearly every book of travels among the Indians found between the Alleghenies and the western slope of the Rocky Mountains, refers to their frequent and convenient use of sign language, there are only three useful collections of described signs of any early date, either printed, or, so far as ascertained, in manuscript. These are as follows:[272]

- 315 -

The one collected by Prince Maximilian von Wied-Neu-Wied, in 1832-34, from the Cheyenne, Shoshoni, Arikara, Satsika, and the Absaroki, the Mandans, Hidatsa, and other Northern Dakotas.[273] This list is not published in the English edition, but appears in the German, Coblenz, 1839, and in the French, Paris, 1840. Bibliographic reference is often made to this distinguished explorer as "Prince Maximilian," as if there were but one possessor of that christian name among princely families. No translation of this list into English appears to have been printed in any shape, while the German and French editions are costly and difficult of access, so the collection cannot readily be compared by observers with the signs now made by the same tribes. The translation now presented is intended to facilitate such comparison. It is based upon the German original, but in a few cases where the language was so curt as not to give a clear idea, was collated with the French edition of the succeeding year, which, from some internal evidence, appears to have been published with the assistance or supervision of the author. Many of the descriptions are, however, so brief and indefinite in both their German and French forms, that they necessarily remain so in the present translation. The princely explorer, with the keen discrimination shown in all his work, doubtless observed what has escaped many recent reporters of aboriginal signs, that the latter depend much more upon motion than mere position—and are generally large and free—seldom minute. His object was to express the general effect of the motion, rather than to describe it so as to allow of its accurate reproduction by a reader who had never seen it. For the latter purpose, now very desirable, a more elaborate description would have been necessary, and even that would not in all cases have been sufficient without pictorial illustration. In a few instances the present writer has added explanations preceded by a dash—. Remarks on the signs might be indefinitely extended, but the present object is to assist present observers in making their own comparisons and suggestions, which, it is hoped, they will contribute to the final work on Sign Language, now in preparation by the Bureau of Ethnology of the Smithsonian Institution, of which notice has been given in a preliminary pamphlet lately issued.

It is worthy of note that the distinguished explorer, who was the earliest to publish a comprehensive and scientific account of the tribes of the upper Missouri, is the only printed authority agreeing with the present writer in denying the existence of a universal sign language among the several tribes, in the sense of a common code, the report of which has generally been accepted without question. He states that the signs described, gathered by him from the tribes above mentioned, are unintelligible to the Dakotas (probably Sioux), Assiniboins, Ojibwas, Krees, and other nations. He undoubtedly means, however, that different signs prevailed among the two bodies of Indians, so divided by himself, and that the individuals who had only learned by rote one set of those signs, would not understand the other set which they had never seen, unless they were accomplished in the gesture speech as an art, and not as a mere memorized list of arbitrary motions. It has been clearly ascertained that two Indians of different tribes who have neither oral language nor previously adopted signs in common, can, after a short trial, communicate through familiarity with the principles of gesture speech, signs being mutually invented and accepted.

The philosophic prince also was one of the first to correct another common error, in attributing the use of signs to the poverty of the aboriginal tongues.

List of the Prince of Wied-Neu-Wied

1. Good: Place the right hand horizontally in front of the breast, and move it forward.—This gesture is more fully described by a recent observer, as follows: "Place the right hand horizontally in front of the breast, and touching it, fingers and thumbs closed and extended, back of hand up, move rather sharply to the front until the forearm is nearly extended." It may convey the suggestion of "level," "no difficulty," and resembles some signs for "content." Many Indians and deaf mutes use gestures to express a pleasant taste in the mouth, for "good" even in a moral sense. (G. S. 124; S. L. 25.)

2. Bad: Close the hand and open it whilst passing it downwards.—This sign is still frequent, the idea of dropping out the supposed contents of the hand as not worth keeping, being obvious. (G. S. 27; S. L. 26.)

3. See: Pass the extended index-finger forward from the eye. (G. S. 229.)

4. Come: Elevate the index-finger near the face, extend the hand and return it with a number of gentle jerks.—In the prevalent sign noticed now for "come," in the sense of "come here," the index, after the forearm (not hand alone) is extended, is crooked slightly as if hooking on to an object, and drawn sharply toward the person. The degree of motion is, however, proportioned to the occasion, and the successive "gentle jerks" of the author indicate less urgency than one sharp redrawal. (G. S. 68.)

5. Arrive: Clap the hands, elevating the index-finger of the right hand.—To express arrival at a place indicated by previous gestures, some of the upper Missouri tribes now hold the left hand fingers extended and closed, well out in front of the body, palm toward it, forearm horizontal, right hand between left and body, index extended vertically, other fingers and thumb closed, nails outward, then the right hand is carried sharply out until it strikes the left. The same sign is used in a direction to go to a place indicated, and that for returning from a place is the same with reversed position of hands. It is conjectured that the clapping of the hands mentioned by the author as commencing the sign refers to the accomplishment of the motion, as southern negroes say "done come." (G. S. 70.)

6. Go, depart: Like *come*; but begin near the face and extend the hand with a number of gentle jerks. (G. S. 120.)

7. Speak: Place the flat hand back downward before the mouth and move it forward two or three times. (G. S. 245.)

8. Another speaks: Place the hand in the same position, beginning farther from the mouth, drawing it nearer and nearer. (G. S. 246.)

9. Man: Elevate the index-finger and turn the hand hither and thither.—The "turning of the hand hither and thither" probably signifies more than the simple idea of man, and is used for "only one man" or "a man who is alone." The finger represents the male organ of generation, and among some tribes the finger is held erect or crooked downward, to indicate mature or declining age. (G. S. 176.)

10. Woman: Pass the palm of the extended hand downward over the hair on the side of the head, or downward over the cheeks. (G. S. 287.)

11. Child: Push the index-finger rapidly into the air then draw the hand back downward.—The distance of the hand from the ground when the motion ceases, indicates the height of the child referred to. Indians often indicate the height of human beings by the hand placed at the proper elevation, back downward, and that of inanimate objects or animals not human by the hand held back upward. (G. S. 54.)

12. Kill: Clinch the hand and strike from above downward.—This motion, which may be more clearly expressed as the downward thrust of a knife held in the clinched hand, is still used by many tribes for the general idea of "kill," and illustrates the antiquity of the knife as a weapon. The actual employment of arrow, gun, or club in taking life, is, however, often specified by appropriate gesture. (G. S. 158.)

13. Arrow, To shoot an: Place the tips of the fingers downward upon the thumb, then snap them forward. (G. S. 25.)

14. Gun, Discharge of a: Place both hands as in No. 13, extend the left arm, contract the right before the face, then snap the ends of the fingers forward. (G. S. 130.)

15. Arrow, To hit with an: After the fingers have been snapped, strike the hands together and elevate the index-finger of the right hand. (G. S. 24.)

16. Gunshot, To hit with a: After the fingers have been snapped, strike the hands together as in No. 15. (G. S. 131.)

17. God, great spirit: Blow upon the open hand, point upward with the extended index-finger whilst turning the closed hand hither and thither, then sweep it above the earth and allow it to drop. (G. S. 89.)

18. Medicine: Stir with the right hand into the left, and afterwards blow into the latter.—All persons familiar with Indians will understand that the term "medicine" foolishly enough adopted by both the French and English to express the aboriginal magic arts, has no therapeutic significance. Very few even pretended remedies were administered to the natives, and probably never by the professional shaman, who worked by incantation, often pulverizing and mixing the substances mystically used, to prevent their detection. The same mixtures were employed in divination. The author particularly mentions Mandan ceremonies, in which a white "medicine" stone, as hard as pyrites, was produced by rubbing in the hand snow, or the white feathers of a bird. The blowing away of the disease, considered to be a malign power foreign to the body, was a common part of the juggling performance. (G. S. 179.)

19. Gun: Close the fingers against the thumb, elevate the hand and open the fingers with a quick snap. (G. S. 129.)

20. Bow: Draw the right arm back completely, as if drawing the bowstring, whilst the left arm is extended with clinched hand. (G. S. 43.)

21. Arrow: Pass the index-finger of the right hand several times across the left arm. (G. S. 23.)

22. Arrowhead, Iron: With the index-finger of the right hand, touch the tip of the extended forefinger of the left hand several times. (G. S. 25.)

23. Gunflint: With the index-finger of the right hand cut off a piece of the extended thumb, so that the finger is laid across the thumbnail. (G. S. 131.)

24. Gun-screw: Elevate the hand to indicate a gun, and twist the fingers spirally around the thumb. (G. S. 131.)

25. Question: Extend the open hand perpendicularly with the palm outward, and move it from side to side several times. (G. S. 210.)

26. Gunpowder: Rub the thumb and index-finger together repeatedly. (G. S. 131.)

27. Coat: Separate the thumb and index-finger of each hand and pass them downward over the sides of the body. (G. S. 61.)

28. Leggings: Open the fingers as before and draw them upward along both legs. (G. S. 166.)

29. Moccasins, shoes: Raise the foot and stroke it from front to back with the index-finger of the hand on the same side. (G. S. 232.)

30. Breechcloth: Pass the flat hand from between the legs upward toward the belly. (G. S. 48.) **31. Hat**: Pass the parted thumb and index-finger about both sides of the head where the hat rests upon it. (G. S. 135.)

32. True, It is: Lower the hand in front of the breast, then extend the index-finger, raise and move it straight forward before the person. (G. S. 273.)

33. Lie: Pass the second and third finger of the right hand toward the left side in front of the mouth.—By the expression "second and third" finger the author means, as appears in other connections, the index and middle finger. The idea of double tongued, two kinds of talk, prevails now among all Indian tribes, though it is sometimes made by one finger, the index, moved successively from the mouth in two different directions. (G. S. 166.)

34. Know: Spread the thumb and index-finger of the right hand, sweep toward the breast, moving them forward and outward so that the palm turns up. (G. S. 161.)

35. Do not know: First place the fingers in the preceding position, then turn the right hand upward with spread fingers so that they point outward toward the right side. (G. S. 162.)

36. Much: Move both hands toward one another and slightly upward.—This is the formation of a "heap." (G. S. 208; S. L. 24.) **37. Little**: Pass the nearly closed hands several times by jerks over one another, the right hand above. (G. S. 238.)

38. Trade: Strike the extended index-finger of the right hand several times upon that of the left. (G. S. 268.)

39. Exchange: Pass both hands with extended forefingers across each other before the breast.—In the author's mind "exchange" was probably intended for one transaction, in which each of two articles took the place before occupied by the other, and "trade" was intended for a more general and systematic barter, indicated by the repetition of strokes, in which the index-fingers mutually changed positions. (G. S. 105.)

40. Horse: Place the index and third fingers of the right hand astraddle the index-finger of the left.—By the "third" the author means the middle finger. He counts the thumb as the first. (G. S. 144.)

41. Horse, To ride a: As before stated, but with this difference, that the right hand extends farther and the gesture is made quickly. (G. S. 147.)

42. Dog: Pass the flat hand from above downward, stopping at the height of a dog's back. (G. S. 96; S. L. 28.)

43. Beaver: With the back of the open right hand, strike the palm of the left several times. (G. S. 32.)

44. Otter: Draw the nose slightly upward with the first two fingers of the right hand. (G. S. 194.)

45. Bison, female: Curve the two forefingers, place them on the sides of the head, and move them several times. (G. S. 40.)

46. Bison, male: Place the tightly closed hands on both sides of the head with the fingers forward. (G. S. 40.)

47. Antelope: Pass the open right hand outward from the small of the back.—This, as explained by Indians examined by the present writer, indicates the lighter coloration upon the animal's flanks. A Ute who could speak Spanish accompanied it with the word *blanco*, as if recognizing that it required explanation. (G. S. 22.)

48. Sheep, bighorn (*Ovis montana*): Move the hands in the direction of the horns on the side of the head by passing them backward and forward in the form of a half-circle. (G. S. 231.)

49. Mule: Hold the open hands high beside the head, and move them from back to front several times like wings. (G. S. 186.)

50. Elk (*Cervus can.*): Stretch the arms above and along side of the head. (G. S. 103.)

51. Deer: Pass the uplifted hand to and fro several times in front of the face. (G. S. 86; S. L. 27.)

52. Deer, black tail: First make the preceding gesture, then indicate a tail. (G. S. 88; S. L. 27.)

53. Buffalo-robe: Pass both fists crossing in front of the breast, as if wrapping one's self up. (G. S. 59.)

54. Day: Place both hands at some distance in front of the breast, apart and back downward, elevate the index-finger and move it forward to indicate one, twice for two days, etc. When counting on the fingers begin at the left hand. (G. S. 77; S. L. 20.)

55. Night: Move both hands open and flat, that is horizontal, the backs up and in small curves in front of the breast and over one another.—The conception is *covering*, and consequently obscurity. In the foregoing sign for *day* the author probably meant that the hands, palms up, were *moved* apart, to denote openness. (G. S. 187.)

56. Sun: Form a small circle with the forefingers and hold them toward heaven. (G. S. 256.)

57. Moon: Make the same sign, after having made that for night. (G. S. 183.)

58. River: Open the right hand and pass it before the mouth from above downward. (G. S. 222.)

59. Forest: Slightly spread and raise the ten fingers bringing the hands together in front of the face, then separate them.—The numerous trees and their branches are indicated. (G. S. 112.)

60. Mountain: Raise the arm from the elbow without moving the latter, the back of the clinched hand directed toward the front. (G. S. 141.)

61. Prairie, plain: Lay the hands flat upon their backs and move them straight from one another in a horizontal line. (G. S. 198.)

62. Village: Place the opened thumb and forefinger of each hand opposite to each other, as if to make a circle, but leaving between them a small interval, afterward move them from above downward simultaneously.—The villages of the tribes with which the author was longest resident, particularly the Mandans and Arikaras, were surrounded by a strong, circular stockade, spaces or breaks in the circle being left for entrance and exit. (G. S. 277.)

63. Kettle: Same sign as for *village*, but is made closer to the earth.— Singularly enough, the configuration of a common kettle (the utensil obtained from the whites in trade being, of course, the one referred to) is the same as that of the stockaded villages, the intervals left between the hands representing in this case the interruption in the circle made by the handles. The differentiation is effected by the position closer to the earth. (G. S. 157.)

64. Lodge: The same, with the addition that the finger is elevated to indicate the number, one. (G. S. 170.)

65. Lodge, Entering a: Pass the right hand in short curves under the left, which is held a short distance forward.—The conception is of the stooping to pass through the low entrance, which is often covered by a common flap, and the subsequent rising when the entrance has been accomplished. In the same tribes now, if the intention is to speak of a person entering the gesturer's own lodge, the right hand is passed under the left and toward the body, near which the left hand is held; if of a person entering the lodge of another, the left hand is held further from the body and the right is passed under it and outward. In both cases both hands are slightly curved and compressed. (G. S. 172.)

66. Robe, Red: First indicate the wrapping about the shoulders, then rub the right cheek to indicate the red color.—The red refers to the paint habitually used on the cheeks, not to the natural skin. The Indians know better than to designate between each other their natural color as red, and have been known to give the designation *red man* to the visiting Caucasian, whose blistered skin often better deserves the epithet, which they only apply to themselves in converse with the conquering race that insisted upon it. (G. S. 59, 66.)

67. Robe, Green: Indicate the wrapping about the shoulders, and with the back of the left hand make the gesture of stroking grass upon the earth. (G. S. 59, 66.)

68. Robe, Blue: Indicate the wrapping, then with two fingers of the right hand rub the back of the left.—It is conjectured that the veins on the back of the hand are indicated. (G. S. 59, 66.)

69. Ax: Cross the arms and slide the edge of the right hand held vertically, down over the left arm. (G. S. 267.)

70. Beads, Glass: Stroke the fingers of the right hand over the upper arm of the left. (G. S. 31.)

71. Vermillion, cinnabar: Rub the right cheek with the fingers of the right hand.—The chief use of this pigment was to paint the cheeks. (G. S. 67.)

72. Knife: Cut past the mouth with the raised right hand.—This clearly refers to the general practice of cutting off food, as much being crammed into the mouth as can be managed and then separated by a stroke of a knife from the remaining mass. This is specially the case with fat entrails, the aboriginal delicacies. (G. S. 160.)

73. Fire: Hold the fingers of the right hand slightly opened and upward, and elevate the hand several times.—This portrays the forked tongues of the flames rising. (G. S. 109.)

74. Water: Same as "river."

75. Smoke: Snuffle the nose and raise the fingers of both hands several times, rubbing the fingers against each other.—The rubbing may indicate the former mode of obtaining fire by friction, accompanied with smoke, which is further indicated by the wrinkled nose. (G. S. 240.)

76. Partisan: First make the sign of the pipe, then open the thumb and index-finger of the right hand, back of the hand outward, move it forward and upward in a curve.—By the title of "partisan" the author meant, as indeed was the common expression of the Canadian voyageurs, a leader of an occasional or volunteer war party. The sign is explained by his account in a different connection, that to become recognized as a leader of such a war party, the first act among the tribes using the sign was the consecration, by fasting succeeded by feasting, of a medicine pipe without ornament, which the leader of the expedition afterward bore with him as his badge of authority, and it therefore naturally became an emblematic sign. There may be interest in noting that the "Calendar of the Dakota Nation" (Bulletin U. S. G. and G. Survey, vol. iii, No. 1) gives a figure (No. 43, A. D. 1842) showing "One Feather," a Sioux chief, who raised in that year a large war party against the Crows, which fact is simply denoted by his holding out, demonstratively, an unornamented pipe. (G. S. 53.)

77. Chief: Raise the index-finger of the right hand, holding it straight upward, then turn it in a circle, and bring it straight down a little toward the earth.—If this gesture is accurately described by the author, its conception may be "elevated in the midst of surrounding inferiors." In view, however, of the fact that Indians now make a forward curve instead of a horizontal circle, the former instead of the latter may have been intended in the curt expression. The prevailing delineation of the superior authority of the chiefs is by superior height, one form of which is reported as follows: Right forearm nearly vertical, index extended, thumb and other fingers closed, nails toward cheek and about eight inches from it. Extend right arm vertically about eight inches; turn index as an arrow turns in the air and bring down in front of face between the eyes until about opposite the chin. (G. S. 51; S. L. 19.)

78. White man, American: Place the open index-finger and thumb of the right hand toward the face, then pass it to the right in front of the forehead to indicate the hat. The fist can also be used in same way. (G. S. 283.)

79. Negro: First make the sign for white man, then rub the hair on the right side of the head with the flat hand.—The present common sign for "black" is to rub or touch the hair, which, among Indians, is almost universally of that color. (G. S. 186.)

80. Fool: Place the hand in front of the head, back outward, then turn it round in a circle several times. (G. S. 112.)

81. Scalp: Grasp the hair with the left hand, and with the right one flattened cut away over the left. (G. S. 228.)

82. Content, satisfied: With the raised right hand, pass with a serpentine movement upward from the breast and face above the head. (G. S. 119; S. L. 35.)

83. Mine, this belongs to me: With the fist, pass upward in front of the breast, then push it forward with a slight jerk. (G. S. 200.)

84. Belongs to another: Pass the hand quickly before the face as if to say, "go away," then make gesture No. 83. (G. S. 202.)

85. This does not belong to me: First make gesture No. 83, then wave the right hand quickly by and in front of the face toward the right. (G. S. 203.)

86. Perhaps I will get it: First, No. 83, then move the right hand right and left before the face, the thumb turned toward the face.

87. Brave: Close the fists, place the left near the breast, and move the right over the left toward the left side. (G. S. 45.)

88. Coward: Point forward with the index followed by the remaining fingers, each time that is done draw back the index.—Impossible to keep the coward to the front. (G. S. 106; S. L. 23.)

89. Hard: Open the hand, and strike against it several times with the right (with the backs of the fingers). (G. S. 134.)

90. Soft: Make gesture No. 89, then strike on the opposite side so as to indicate the reunion. (G. S. 242.)

91. Hard, Excessively: Sign No. 89, then place the left index-finger upon the right shoulder, at the same time extend and raise the right arm high, extending the index-finger upwards, perpendicularly. (G. S. 135.)

92. Repeat, (a thing) often: Extend the left arm, also the index-finger, and with the latter strike the arm at regular intervals from front backward several times. (G. S. 221.)

93. Heard, I have: Open wide the thumb and index-finger of the right hand, place them over the ear, and in this position move them quickly past the chin and nose. (G. S. 139.)

94. Listen: Place the open thumb and index-finger over the right ear and move them hither and thither. (G. S. 137.)

95. Run: Lay both hands flat, palm downward, and pass the right rapidly high and far over the left, so that the body is somewhat raised. (G. S. 225.)

96. Slow: Extend the left arm, curving the forefinger and holding it still. The right arm does the same but is drawn back with several short and circular movements. (G. S. 237.)

97. Fat: Raise the left arm with fist closed back outward, grasp the arm with the right hand, and rub downward thereon. (G. S. 106.)

98. Lean: Hold the flattened hands toward one another before the breast, separate them, moving all the fingers several times inward and outward toward and from the breast. (G. S. 199.)

99. Sick: Hold the hands as just stated, toward one another, bring them, held stiff, in front of the breast, and move them forward and backward from and to the same. (G. S. 233.)

100. Dead: Hold the left hand flat over the face, back outward, and pass with the similarly held right hand below the former, gently striking or touching it. (G. S. 83.)

FOOTNOTES:

[270] In the original German edition, the first paragraph and its accompanying note (270) form the only introduction to Maximilian's account of the Indian sign language. As this account had already been Englished by an expert in this field, the late Colonel Garrick Mallery, I have adopted the latter's version, found in his "Sign Language of the Indians of the Upper Missouri in 1832," in *American Antiquarian*, ii (Chicago, 1879-80), pp. 218-228. Mallery's version was also incorporated in his "Collection of Gesture-Signs and Signals of the North American Indians with some Comparisons" (Washington: Bureau of Ethnology, 1880). A few of the descriptions are also referred to in his "Introduction to the Study of Sign Language among the North American Indians, as illustrating the Gesture Speech of Mankind," published in the same year by the Bureau of Ethnology. The opinion of Maximilian's work entertained by so eminent an authority as Colonel Mallery is of course interesting and valuable, and it has seemed proper to reprint here the pertinent part of his introduction to the *American Antiquarian* article. This introduction will also be found in substance in his "Gesture-Signs" and "Sign Language," cited above. Reference to the pages in the "Gesture-Signs" (G. S.) and in the "Sign Language" (S. L.), where each description is given, are here indicated in parentheses.—TRANS.

[271] Dr. Mitchell (Warden, *American Antiquities*, p. 179) has a very incorrect conception of the Indians, if he believes that they ordinarily communicate by means of signs. The signs are used only when a person does not wish to be heard, or when he is addressing people of other nations. According to Dunbar (*ibid.*, p. 176) this sign language agrees with the Chinese letters; but I do not understand what is meant by this statement.—MAXIMILIAN.

Comment by Ed. For Warden, see our volume xxii, p. 149, note 63. Samuel L. Mitchell (1764-1831) was known as the "Nestor of American Science." His learning was encyclopædic; he belonged to many scientific societies both in America and Europe. For Sir William Dunbar, see our volume iv, p. 325, note 209.

[272] The first two lists mentioned by Mallery are: that of William Dunbar, American Philosophical Society, *Transactions*, vi; and the one, probably by T. Say, in James's *Long's Expedition*, in our volume xvii, pp. 289-308.—ED.

[273] Mallery (G. S. 11) says that from the time and attention which Maximilian gave to the Mandans and Hidatsa, it may be safe to conclude that all these signs were actually obtained from them.—ED.

II. ON THE ORIGIN OF THE OTOS, JOWAYS, AND MISSOURIS: A TRADITION COMMUNICATED BY AN OLD CHIEF TO MAJOR BEAN, THE INDIAN AGENT

Some time in the year (it was before the arrival of the Whites in America) a large band of Indians, who call themselves Fish-eaters (*Hoton-ga*), who inhabit the lakes, being discontented, concluded that they would migrate to the southwest in pursuit of the buffalo, and accordingly did so. At Lake Puant they divided, and that part which remained, still continued their original name in Indian, but from some cause or other the Whites called them Winnebagos. The rest, more enterprising, still continued on the journey, until they reached the Mississippi and the mouth of the Joway River, where they encamped on the sand-beach and again divided, one band concluding not to go farther, and those who still wished to go on called this band, which still remained encamped on the sand-beach, Pa-ho-dje, or Dust-noses; but the Whites, who first discovered them on the Joway River, called them Joways (*Ayowäs*). The rest of them continued on their direction, and struck the Missouri at the mouth of the Grand River. Having only two principal chiefs left, they here gave themselves the name of Neu-ta-che, which means "those that arrive at the mouth," but were called by the Whites the Missouris. One of their chiefs had an only son, the other chief had a beautiful daughter, and, having both a gentle blood, thought no harm to absent themselves for a night or two together, which raised the anger of the unfortunate girl's father to such a pitch, that he marshalled his band and prepared for battle. They however settled it so far as not to come to blows, but the father of the unfortunate son separated from the others, and continued still farther up the Missouri, whereupon they called themselves Wagh-toch-tat-ta, and by what means I know not they have got the name Otos. The Fish-eaters, or the Winnebagos as we call them, still continued east of the Mississippi in the State of Illinois. The Joways, having ceded to the United States all their title to the lands they first settled, have moved West of the State of Missouri, between the waters of the Missouri and the Little Platte. The Missouris, having been unfortunate at war with the Osages, here again separated, and a part of them live now with the Joways, and a part with the Otos. The Otos continued still up the Missouri until they arrived at the Big Platte, which empties into the Missouri, when they crossed and lived some time a little above its mouth, but of late years have resided about 80 miles (by water) from the Missouri, on the Platte River.

III. SALE OF LAND BY THE INDIANS—
EXTRACT FROM THE PUBLISHED CONTRACT

This Document is headed—Andrew Jackson, President of the United States of America, to all and singular to whom these presents shall come, greeting; &c. &c. Then come thirteen articles, of which the following is the preamble:

Articles of a treaty made and concluded by William Clarke, Superintendent of Indian Affaires, and Willoughby Morgan, Colonel of the United States 1st Regt. Infantry, commissioners on behalf of the United States, on the one part; and the undersigned deputations of the confederated tribes of the Sacs and Foxes; the Medawah-Kanton, Wahpacoota, Wahpeton, and Sissetong bands or tribes of Sioux; the Omahas, Joways, Otos, and Missouris, on the other part.

The said tribes being anxious to remove all causes which may hereafter create any unfriendly feeling between them, and being also anxious to provide other sources for supplying their wants besides those of hunting, which they are sensible must soon entirely fail them, agree with the United States on the following articles:

Article I. The said tribes cede and relinquish to the United States for ever all their right and title to the lands lying within the following boundaries, to wit: Beginning at the upper fork of the Demoine River, and passing the sources of the Little Sioux and Floyd's Rivers, to the fork of the first creek which falls into the Big Sioux, or Calumet, on the east side; thence down said creek, and Calumet River, to the Missouri River: thence down said Missouri River to the Missouri State line above the Kansas; thence along said line to the northwest corner of the said state; thence to the highlands between the water falling into the Missouri and Desmoines, passing to said highlands along the dividing ridge between the forks of the Grand River; thence along said highlands or ridge separating the waters of the Missouri from those of the Desmoines, to a point opposite the source of Boyer River, and thence in a direct line to the upper fork of the Desmoines, the place of beginning. But it is understood that the lands ceded and relinquished by this treaty are to be resigned and allotted under the direction of the President of the United States to the tribes now living thereon, or to such other tribes as the President may locate thereon for hunting, and other purposes, &c. &c.

The other Articles follow. Here are the names of some of the Indian chiefs who signed the contract:—

SACS

- *Mash-que-tai-paw* (Red-head).

- *Sheco-Caiawko* (Tortoise-shell).
- *Kee-o-cuck* (The Vigilant Fox).
- *Pai-o-tahit* (Heartless).
- *Os-hays-Kee* (Ridge).
- *She-she-quaninee* (The Little Gourd), &c.

FOXES

- *Wapataw* (The Prince).
- *Taweemin* (Gooseberry).
- *Pasha-sakay.*
- *Keewausettee* (Who climbs everywhere).
- *Appenioce* (The Great Child).
- *Kaw-kaw-kee* (The Crow), &c.

SIOUX

- *Wabishaw* (The Red Leaf).
- *Tchataqua mani* (The Little Crow).
- *Waumunde-tunkar* (The Great Calumet Eagle).
- *Taco-coqui-pishnee* (Dauntless).
- *Wah-coo-ta* (The Bowman).

OMAHAS

- *Opan-tanga* (The Great Elk).
- *Chonques-kaw* (The White Horse).
- *Tessan* (The White Crow).

JOWAYS

- *Wassan-nie* (The Medicine Club).
- *Mauhooskan* (The White Cloud).
- *Tah-roh-ha* (Many Stags).

OTOS

- *I-atan or Shaumanie-lassan* (Prairie-Wolf).

- *Mehah-hun-jee* (Second Daughter).
- *Kansaw-tanga* (The Great Kansa), &c.

IV. TREATY OF TRADE AND PEACE BETWEEN THE AMERICAN FUR COMPANY AND THE BLACKFEET

We send greeting to all mankind! Be it known unto all nations, that the most ancient, most illustrious, and most numerous tribes of the red skins, lords of the soil from the banks of the great waters unto the tops of the mountains, upon which the heavens rest, have entered into solemn league and covenant to make, preserve, and cherish a firm and lasting peace, that so long as the water runs, or grass grows, they may hail each other as brethren and smoke the calumet in friendship and security.

On the vigil of the feast of St. Andrew, in the year eighteen hundred and thirty-one, the powerful and distinguished nation of Blackfeet, Piëgan, and Blood Indians, by their ambassadors, appeared at Fort Union, near the spot where the Yellow Stone River unites its current with the Missouri, and in the council-chamber of the Governor Kenneth M'Kenzie met the principal chief of all the Assiniboin nation, the Man that holds the Knife, attended by his chiefs of council, le Brechu, le Borgne, the Sparrow, the Bear's Arm, la Terre qui Tremble, and l'Enfant de Medicine, when, conforming to all ancient customs and ceremonies, and observing the due mystical signs enjoined by the grand medicine-lodges, a treaty of peace and friendship was entered into between the said high contracting parties, and is testified by their hands and seals hereunto annexed, hereafter and for ever to live as brethren of one large united happy family; and may the Great Spirit, who watcheth over us all, approve our conduct and teach us to love one another.

Done, executed, ratified and confirmed at Fort Union on the day and year first within written, in the presence of Jas. Archdale Hamilton.

H. CHARDON.

- THE MAN THAT HOLDS THE KNIFE.
- THE YOUNG GAUCHER.
- LE BRECHU, OR LE FILS DU GROS FRANÇAIS.
- THE BEAR'S ARM, OR THE MAN THAT LIVES ALONE.
- LE BORGNE.
- THE SPARROW.
- LA TERRE QUI TREMBLE.
- L'ENFANT DE MEDICINE.
- K. M'KENZIE, on behalf of the Piëgans and Blackfeet.

V. METEOROLOGICAL OBSERVATIONS AT FORT UNION AND FORT CLARK, ON THE UPPER MISSOURI

[Condensed by Asa Currier Tilton]

These observations consist of those which were made by Prince Maximilian at Fort Clark in 1833-34, and of extracts from the records kept at Fort Union for the two years preceding, by Mr. Mc Kenzie. The observations were systematized by Prof. Mädler, then at Dorpat, but formerly at Berlin. His conclusions and comments are printed in his own words.

A table is given of the observations at Fort Union in 1832-33. It shows the monthly average and the daily variation of temperature. The daily and annual variations are found to be greater than in Europe, even in the interior of Russia; and are those of a typical continental climate. Some variations are manifestly unusual. The period of observation in so variable a climate is too short to reduce the figures to a formula; but a table of the differences is given, and some of the most marked variations and apparent exceptions are discussed.

The observations of the principal winds are given in another table. Here, also, the period of observation is too short for definite results; but more correspondence is found with Europe than in the case of temperature. As in Europe, the north and the south winds are rarest, the former especially.

Still another table shows the influence of the winds on temperature. This is valuable in spite of the short period covered. The south wind is found to be the warmest; and the northwest wind, followed by the northeast, the coldest. There is too little north wind to conclude that it is regularly as warm as the data indicate.

The southwest wind keeps its place throughout the year, the northwest wind only in the autumn and winter; in the spring and summer, the northeast wind takes its place as the coldest. For all the seasons, the east wind corresponds most nearly to the average temperature.

The observations at Fort Clark are given in similar tables. From November to the latter part of January the cold increased; the first part of February was decidedly warmer. The winter was very cold not alone in the Missouri valley but in the Atlantic states as well; it was, however, one of the mildest on record in Europe.

The table on the winds indicates none which corresponds to the average temperature. The northwest and west winds vary from it but little, however.

The mildest wind seems to be the southwest; while the greatest cold seems to coincide with the northeast wind.

Another table gives the cloudy and clear days, and indicates their relation to temperature. From November to the beginning of March the clear mornings are the colder; in the latter part of March there is no difference. In December, January, and February the clear middays are the colder; for the rest of the time, the cloudy or neutral days are coldest. In January, the neutral days are the warmest.

VI. BIRD CALENDAR FOR THE REGION OF THE MANDAN VILLAGES, IN THE WINTER OF 1833-34[274]

October

Beginning. *Residents:* Cathartes septentrionalis;[275] Aquila leucocephala; Falco sparverius; strix virginiana, asio; Corvus corax, americanus audub.; Pica hudsonica; Lanius septentrionalis; Alcedo alcyon; Quiscalus versicolor; Parus atricapillus; Sturnella ludoviciana; Picus villosus, pubescens; Tetrao phasianellus; Tringa; Totanus; Anas boschas fera, crecca, discors; Fulica americana.[276]

Middle. *Residents:* Same as above. Some of the following begin to migrate: Cathartes; Falcones; Corvus amer.; Alcedo; Quiscalus; Sturnella; Fringilla erythrophthalma; Fulica; Tringa; Totanus (even earlier); Pelecanus trachyrynchos lath.;[277] grus, and recurvirostra.

Migrants: Quiscalus vers.; Sturnella; Anser hyperboreus, canadensis; all species of Mergus and Anas, among them Anas sponsa;[278] likewise Pelecanus.

Birds of passage: Turdus migrat.; Grus, both species; Pelecanus.

End. *Residents:* Tetrao phasian.; Corvus corax; Pica huds.; Picus pubesc., villosus; Parus atricap.; Aquila leucoc.; Alcedo alcyon (now migrating).

Migrants: Quiscalus, solitary; Anser canad.; Ansas boschas, crecca, discors; Cygnus; Mergus; Fringilla linaria, including unfamiliar species.

November

Beginning. *Residents:* Strix virgin., asio; Corvus corax; Pica huds.; Tetrao phasian.; Lanius septentr.

Migrants: Aquila leucoc.; Anas; Mergus; Cygnus; Anser.

Middle. *Residents:* Same as in beginning of month.

Migrants: Fring. linaria; Emberiza nivalis; Bombycilla garrula.

End. *Residents:* As above.

Migrants: As in the middle of the month.

December

Beginning. *Residents:* As above.

Migrants: As in end of November; Bombycilla garrula.

Middle. Same as in beginning of month.

End. Same as in middle of month.

January

Same as in December; finches and buntings no longer occur.

February

Beginning. Same as in January; no finches or snow buntings.

Middle. *Residents:* Fring. linaria; Ember. nivalis in small finches and snow buntings often very numerous.

March

Beginning. Same as in February.

Middle. *Residents:* Same as in the winter.

Migrants: Ember. nivalis; Fring. linaria.

Birds of passage: Anas boschas. The first ducks were seen on the thirteenth of March; they were flying up the Missouri. On the fourteenth the first prairie hen (Tetrao phasian.) called. On the fifteenth a small flock of gray finches (Fring. canad.?) appeared; and on the sixteenth the first swan. Ducks now appear daily.

FOOTNOTES:

[274] Each month is divided into three parts of ten and eleven days each with the exception of February, where the divisions are shorter.—MAXIMILIAN.

Comment by Ed. For bibliographies of earlier as well as later works on American ornithology, see Elliott Coues, "List of Faunal Publications relating to North American Ornithology," being the Bibliographical Appendix to his *Birds of the Colorado Valley* (United States Geological Survey of the Territories, *Misc. Pub.* No. 11, 1878); also his "Second Instalment of American Ornithological Bibliography," U. S. Geog. and Geographical Survey *Bulletin*, v, No. 2 (1879).

[275] I describe this vulture under the term *septentrionalis*, because I now regard it as a distinct species. I am indebted to Privy Councillor Lichtenstein of Berlin for the opportunity of examining several specimens of *Urubus* from different parts of South America and from Mexico; and I am now convinced that they, together with the Brazilian, form a species which is distinct from the North American. The male of the southern red-headed *Urubu* (*C. aura*) is smaller, more uniformly dark, with stronger metallic gloss, and with less brightly-rounded wing feathers than the northern. In the Brazilian bird the iris is bright red, and in the mature bird the head is sky blue and orange. In

the North American bird the head is of a dirty violet red, occasionally violet, the base of the bill lac red the iris grayish brown with a lighter band around the pupil, and a narrow bright red band on the outer edge. The immature birds of both species have a dirty violet head, etc. I hope to deal more thoroughly with this subject in another place. I will remark in passing that the statement of Schomburgk (see *Annals of Natural History*) in a natural history of the king vulture (*Vultur papa l.*), "that the other vultures will not eat until the king vulture has satisfied himself," is most certainly a fable.—MAXIMILIAN.

Comment by Ed. For Lichtenstein, see *post*, note 276. The Schomburgk referred to is probably Sir Robert Hermann Schomburgk, the famous explorer, and the author of works on Guiana and the Barbadoes. A publication was started at Edinburgh in 1837 under the title, *Magazine of Zoology and Botany*; in 1839 the name was changed to *Annals of Natural History*, and the place of publication to London; later, the title became *Annals and Magazine of Natural History.*

[276] *Fulica americana* is different from *atra*. This is shown more clearly in Wilson's description than in that of Audubon. The latter's description of the bill of the American bird does not agree with my observation; I have always found it uniformly colored, as Wilson describes it. I found no birds of the genus *Fulica* in Brazil; consequently D'Orbigny (see De la Sagra, *Hist. Nat. de l'Isle de Cuba, ornith.*, p. 273) is in error when he says that *Fulica atra* was seen by me in Brazil. In North America I frequently found a similar bird, as has been said; but I cannot regard it as identical with the European. Regarding the *Fulica* observed by D'Orbigny in South America I can give no opinion, as I saw none myself.—MAXIMILIAN.

Comment by Ed. The references are to: Alexander Wilson, *American Ornithology* (Philadelphia, 1801-14, 9 vols.); John James Audubon, *Ornithological Biography* (Edinburgh, 1831-39, 5 vols.), forming the text to his *Birds of America* (London, 1827-38, 4 vols.); and to *Histoire physique, politique et naturelle de l'Isle de Cuba; par M. Ramon de la Sagra ... Ornithologie par Alcide d'Orbigny* (Paris, 1839, 1 vol. and atlas). Alcide Dessalines d'Orbigny was a French naturalist who spent several years in South America, collecting natural history specimens. An account of his journey is given in his *Voyages dans l'Amerique meridionale* (Paris, 1834-47, 9 vols.); he also published other works.

[277] On the pelican of the Mississippi and Missouri, which I have often mentioned under the term *Brachydactylus*, it is to be noted that Lichtenstein has rejected this word and chosen in its place for this species Latham's name, *Trachyrynchos*, and that I have followed the change. On this subject, see Lichtenstein, *Beitrag zur ornithologischen Fauna von Californien.*—MAXIMILIAN.

Comment by Ed. Martin Heinrich Karl Lichtenstein was a famous German naturalist. The work referred to by Maximilian was published in *Abhandlungen der Koeniglichen Akademie* (Berlin, 1838-39).

[278] In De la Sagra's atlas, plate xxx, there is a very good picture of this exceedingly beautiful species of duck; it is, however, to be criticised as not giving to the bill and eye the natural color, which is far more beautiful. Bodmer has painted them very accurately from life; and I hope to use this picture in another place.—MAXIMILIAN.

VII. CATALOGUS PLANTARUM IN MONTE POKONO (NORTH HAMPT., PENNSYLVANIÆ) OBSERVATARUM A. L. D. SCHWEINITZ

Callitriche *linearis* (non ead. cum autumnali).

Caulinia Canadensis, Mx non fragilis nec flexilis.

Gratiola anagalloidea, Mx non Virginica.

Utricularia macrorhiza, Le Conte.

"   gibba.

"   cornuta.

"   purpurea.

Lycopus pumilus (species vix bona).

Monarda Kalmiana.

Circæa alpina.

Lemna gibba.

" polyrrhiza.

Salix tristis.

" petiolaris.

" rosmarinifolia.

" ? indeterminata.

" ? indet.

Iris versicolor (non Virginica).

Dulichium Canadense (species non bona).

Eriophorum vaginatum.

"   Virginicum.

"   polystachium.

Polygonum racemosum.

Milium pungens.

Calamagrostis agrostoides.

Trichodium caninum.

"   laxiflorum.

"   montanum.

Panicum verrucosum.

Aira monticola, L. v. S.

Poa Canadensis.

Galium Claytoni.

Houstonia serpyllifolia.

"   tenella.

Cornus circinata.

" alternifolia.

" rubiginosa, L. v. S.

" Canadensis.

Myrica, Gale.

Ilex Canadensis.

" opæa.

Potamogeton distans, L. v. S.

Hydrophyllum Canadense (rare).

Dodecatheon Meadia.

Azalea viscosa.

" arborescens.

" hispida.

" bicolor.

" nitida.

Apocynum hypericifolium.

Campanula acuminata.

Lonicera parviflora.

Viola cordata non villosa, Ell.

" clandestina.

" rotundifolia.

Ribes trifidum.

" prostratum.

" gracile.

" resinosum.

" oxyacanthoides.

Asclepias phytolaccoides.

" viridiflora.

"   nivea?

Gentiana pneumonanthe.

"   linearis.

"   crinita.

Heuchera pubescens.

Panax quinquefolium.

Cicuta bulbifera.

Viburnum pyrifolium.

"   squamatum vix var. nudi.

"   lantanoides.

Sambucus pubens.

Parnassia Caroliniana.

Azalea racemosa.

Allium triflorum.

Pontederia angustifolia.

Convallaria borealis.

"   umbellata.

"   biflora.

"   latifolia.

Juncus conglomeratus.

Leontice thalictroides.

Prinos lævigatus.

Helonias erythrosperma.

Trillium erythrocarpum.

"   erectum.

"   pendulum.

"   cernuum.

Veratrum viride.

Menispermum Virginicum.

Æsculus Pavia (very rare).

Oxycoccos macrocarpus.

"   hispidulus, Gualth.

Vaccinium amœnum.

"   pallidum.

"   tenellum (non Pennsylv.)

"   resinosum.

Acer Pennsylvanicum (strict.)

"   montanum.

Œnothera pusilla.

"   fruticosa.

"   ambigua.

Epilobium spicatum.

"   squamatum.

Populus trepida.

Polygonum cilinode.

Gaultheria procumbens.

Epigæa repens.

Andromeda caliculata.

" racemosa.

Rhododendron maximum.

Kalmia latifolia.

" angustifolia.

Rhexia Virginica.

Ledum palustre.

Chletra alnifolia.

Pyrola uniflora.

" secunda.

Rhodora Canadensis.

Tiarella cordifolia.

Silene Pennsylvanica.

Oxalis acetosella.

Prunus Canadensis.

" Pennsylvanica.

Spiræa tomentosa.

Aronia glabra.

Sorbus Americana.

Dalibarda repens.

"   fragarioides.

Rubus strigosus.

" hispidus.

" inermis.

Potentilla hirsuta.

Saracenia purpurea.

Clematis viorna.

Ranunculus Pennsylvanicus.

"   Belvisii, Sprengel.

Coptis trifolia.

Caltha flagellifolia.

Gerardia heterophylla.

"   monticola, L. v. S.

Chelone lanceolata, Mich.

Linnæa borealis.

Geranium Carolinianum.

"   robertianum.

"   pusillum.

Taxus Canadensis.

Corydalis glauca.

" formosa.

" fungosa.

" cucullaria.

Polygala sanguinea.

" cruciata.

Lupinus perennis.

Astragalus Carolinianus.

Hypericum Canadense.

" Bartoni.

Eupatorium linearifolium.

" teucrifolium.

" verbenæfolium.

" falcatum?

" scabridum, Ell.

Liatris montana, L. v. S.

Gnaphalium obtusifolium (margaritaceum).

Erigeron purpureum.

Aster conyzoides.

" radula.

" acuminatus.

" concinnus.

" rigidus.

" thyrsiflorus.

Solidago odora.

" petiolaris.

" hispida.

" rigida.

" stricta.

" squarrosa.

" pulchella, L. v. S.

Rudbeckia digitata.

" fulgida.

Prenanthes serpentaria.

Habenaria spectabilis.

" ciliaris.

" blephariglottis.

" orbiculata.

" rotundifolia.

" grandiflora, Bigelano.

Pogonia verticillata.

Spiranthes gracilis, Bigel.

Cypripedium parviflorum.

Cypripedium spectabile.

Calla palustris.

Eriocaulon pellucidum.

Sparganium natans.

Carex disperma.

" pedunculata.

" loliacea.

" Gebhardi.

" Darlingtonii, L. v. S.

" nigromarginata, L. v. S.

" polystachia.

" xantherophyta.

" oligostachya, L. v. S.

" tarda, L. v. S.

" halsigona.

" sylvatica.

" umbellata.

Urtica procera.

Alnus glauca.

Myriophyllum ambiguum.

Betula populifera.

Pinus balsamea.

" nigra.

" inops.

" microcarpa.

Lycopodium clavatum.

" integrifolium.

Lygodium palmatum.

VIII. SYSTEMATIC VIEW OF THE PLANTS BROUGHT BACK FROM MY TOUR ON THE MISSOURI, DRAWN UP BY PRESIDENT NEES VON ESSENBECK, AT BRESLAU

RANUNCULACEÆ

Clematis cordata, Pursh. ♂—*Ranunculus* pusillus, P.—*R.* repens, L. var. laciniis foliorum acuminatis, petiolis pedunculisque hirsutis, major et minor.

Anemone Pensylvanica, L.—*Aquilegia Canadensis*, L.—*Delphinium azureum*, Mich.—*Thalictrum anemonoides*, De C.

Hydrastis Canadensis, L. (The very bitter root-stock of this plant contains a beautiful yellow dye, and is used in America as a medicine).

CRUCIFERÆ

Sisymbryum brachycarcum, Richards. An S. canescentis, Nutt. var. glabriuscula? Confer S. Sophia, Pursh.

Nasturtium sylvestre, De C. (The American plant has larger leaves than the German).—*Stannleya pinnatifida*, Nutt.

Vesicaria Ludoviciana, De C. (Alyssum Ludovicianum, Nutt.; Myagrum argenteum, Pursh.)

Erysimum asperum, De C. (Er. lanceolatum, Pursh.; Cheiranthus asper, Nutt.)

Alyssum dentatum, Nutt. Flores Nuttalio et Candollio huc usque erant ignoti.— *Dentaria laciniata*, Mich.

FUMARIACEÆ

Diclytra cucullaria, De C.—*Corydalis aurea*, Willd.—*C. flavula*, Raf.

PAPAVERACEÆ

Sanguinaria Canadensis, L. (A celebrated medicine plant.)

CAPPARIDEÆ

Peritoma serrulatum, De C. (Cleome serrulata, Pursh.)

VIOLARIACEÆ

Viola Canadensis, Pursh—*V. pubescens*, Nutt.—*V. sagittata*, Ait.—*V. villosa*, Ell.—*V. cucullata*, Ell.

POLYGALEÆ

Polygala alba, Nutt. Torrey in Ann. Lyc. Novebor II. p. 168. The root is quite the same as that of the officinal Radix senegæ.

LINEÆ

Linum rigidum, Pursh? Agrees indeed, in many particulars, but the petals are not narrow (angustissima), but obovate, longer than the calyx; the lower leaves of the stalk are opposite, very small, and linear-spatulate, 1-1½ lines long. The sepals are beautifully ciliated, with glandular teeth.

Linum (Adenoblepharum) annuum, foliolis calycinis ovato-lanceolatis acuminatis trinervibus glanduloso-ciliatis, petalis obovatis, foliis rigide erectis linearibus, inferioribus brevissimis obtusis suboppositis.

Linum Lewisii, Pursh. Vix idem ac L. sibiricum, De C. Flores sunt minores.

MALVACEÆ

Cristaria coccinea, Pursh. (Sida? coccinea, De C.; Malva coccinea, Nutt.) Seems to form a distinct genus, but I found no perfect fruit to determine the character.

RHAMNEÆ

Rhamnus alnifolius, var. foliis minoribus.

ACERINÆ

Acer saccharinum, L.

AMPELIDEÆ

Vitis cordifolia, Michx. and (probably) Vitis riparea, Michx.

OXALIDEÆ

Oxalis violacea, L. Styli hirti.

TEREBINTHACEÆ

Rhus Toxicodendron, L.—*R. aromatica*, L.—*Zanthoxylum fraxineum*, W.

LEGUMINOSEÆ

Sophora (Pseudosophora, De C.) *sericea*, Nutt. Torr. in Ann. Lyc. Novebor, p. 174, n. 65. Our specimen is entirely covered with white appressed hairs, which cover also the upper side of the leaves; the flowers are white; the calyx is gibbous below, and quinquefid; the upper teeth are broader and rather shorter. Of the 10 stamina every 2-3 are united at the bottom by the thick filaments; the two upper ones are more slender, and quite free. The ovary is covered with silky hairs; the claw of the standard is very stiff; the keel runs into a narrow point, as in Oxytropis.

Thermopsis rhombifolia, De C. (Thermea rhombifolia, Nutt.; Cytisus rhombifolius, Pursh.)

Petalostemum violaceum, Mich., var. foliis plerisque ternatis.

Petalostemum virgatum, nob. P. spicis cylindricis compactis, bracteis scariosis obovatis cuspidulatis calyce paulo brevioribus, calycibus glabris sulcatis dentibus ciliatis, foliolis subtrijugis lanceolato-oblongis glabris, caule ramoso virgato ramis monostachyis.

Intermediate, between the two divisions of this genus, the proper Petalantheræ and Kuhnisteræ. The perfectly spiked inflorescence connects it with the former; the nature of the bracteæ and the ciliæ of the shorter teeth join it to the latter. From the two white flowering Petalostemones P. candidum and macrostachyum, it is sufficiently distinguished by the two short bracteæ, quite hidden under the flowers; it cannot be more closely connected with Petalostemum corymbosum, because of the spiked inflorescence.

Psoralea incana, Nutt. (Ps. argophylla, Pursh.) Folia in nostra quinata, summa ternata.

Psoralea tenuiflora, Pursh? Foliola ternata, oblongo-lanceolata, mucronata. Legumen ovatum, in rostrum attenuatum, glandulosoexasperatum, calyce longius. Flores cœrulei. An nov. sp.? Quite the form of an amorpha, but the flowers appear like those of glycyrrhiza; unfortunately it cannot be accurately examined.

Amorpha nana, Nutt. De C. (A. microphylla, Pursh.) Calyx glaber dentibus ciliatis.—*Oxytropis Lamberti*, Pursh.

Astragalus Missurensis, Nutt. An cum A. Hypoglotti conjungendus?— *Astragalus racemosus*, Pursh. Var. foliolis foliorum inferiorum ovalibus.

Astragalus gracilis, Nutt. Torr. l. c. p. 179. This is indisputably the Dalea parviflora, Pursh, but whether really his Astragalus tenellus, I doubt.— *Astragalus Carolinianus*, L.

Lathyrus polymorphus, Nutt. De C. Torr. in Ann. Lyc. Novebor. II. p. 180, n. 99. (Lathyrus decaphyllus et Vicia stipulacea, Pursh.)—*Vicia Americana*, L.

Vicia Americana β angustifolia; foliolis oblongo-linearibus mucronatis pubescentibus. An distincta species?

FRAXINEÆ

Fraxinus platycarpa.

ROSACEÆ

Rubus trivialis, Michx. Diagnosi adde: caule primario glabro angulato aculeis sparsis rectis aut sursum falcatis (!), foliis supra pilosis subtus molliter pubescentibus, ramulis petiolis pedunculisque villosis et aculeis retrorsum curvatis armatis, corymbis in ramulis terminalibus simplicibus, sepalis ovatis brevicuspidatis. Rubus trivialis perperam ab aliis ad R. hispidum Linn. refertur. An Rubus argutus Link. Enum. hujus cenostri synonymon? (Dewberries incol.) *Potentilla supina, L.—Fragaria elatior,* Ehrh.

Rosa. A species of the division of the Cinnamomeæ, Ser., or Linkianæ, Trattin; allied to the Rosa Woodsii and Rosa Americana; it may also be compared with Rosa obovata, Raf.; but it is very probably a good new species, which may be so characterized:

Rosa Maximiliani, N. ab. E. tubo ovarii subgloboso (ante anthesin ovato), pedunculis petiolisque inermibus et glabris, foliis solitariis, aculeis stipularibus subfalcatis, stipulis subovatis planis denticulatis a foliolis inferioribus distantibus, laciniis calycinis ternis margine setis exiguis appendiculatis, foliolis glabris ovalibus obtusis basi cuneiformibus integerrimis a medio dense incurvo-serratis. The flowers are large, red, with emarginate petals; the sepals are shorter than the petals, a little broader at the apex, and downy above; the ripe fruit is conical and crowned; the peduncles are red and slender; the leaflets bi-or trijugated, small, bluish-green below, quite smooth, without prickles, the lowest pair smaller; the stalk is red, and seems to have been furrowed when alive; the prickles are nearly opposite each other.

Rosa (Cinnamomea) obovata Rafinesque? Differt specimen nostrum: floribus sub-corymbosis nec solitariis, et fructibus vix subgloboso-depressis, sed potius subglobosis. Var. floribus albis. Authors have indeed this species under R. cinnamomea, but this is certainly wrong.

Rosa Carolina? cum fructibus absque flore.—*Amelanchier sanguinea,* De C. (Pyrus sanguinea, Pursh.)

Cratægus coccinea, Lin.—*Prunus serotina,* Ehrh.—*Cerasus pygmœa,* De C.?

LOASEÆ

Bartonia ornata, Pursh.

PORTULACACEÆ

Claytonia Virginiana, Ait.

ONAGRACEÆ

Callilophis Nuttallii, Spach. in Ann. des sc. natur. 1835, Sept. p. 3. (Œnothera serrulata, Nutt. Hook exot. Fl. t. 140). In nostro specimine flores vix dimidium pollicem lati sunt.

Anogra pinnatifida, Spach. (Œnothera pinnatifida, Nutt. Oen. albicaulis, Pursh., nec Fraser.)

Pachylophis Nuttallii, Spach. (Œnothera scapigera et Œ. cæspitosa. Pursh. Suppl. Œnothera cæspitosa, Sims. Spreng.)

Œnothera pubescens, Willd. Probably a variety of Œno biennis—*Gaura coccinea*, Pursh. Gauridii est generis Spach. Fructus (immaturus) fere cylindricus, dense pubescens. Ovula 2-4, pendula, nuda.

Gaura coccinea β integrifolia. Torr. in Ann. Lyc. Novebor. II. p. 200, n. 145. Distincta species. Genus inter Gauridium Spach. et Gauram medium, illi proximum, sed differens stigmate discoideo 4-dentato. Ovula 4 in ovario uniloculari.

HALORAGEÆ

Ceratophyllum submersum, Pursh. An eadem ac species Europæa?

RIBESIACEÆ

Chrysobotrya intermedia, Spach. Ann. des Sc. natur. Juillet, 1835, p. 4, t. 1, B.

Chrysobotrya revoluta, Sp.? folia majora, magis villosa. An fructus ovalis? Secundum cl. Nuttall. omnes Chrysobotryæ species pro varietatibus Rib. aurei habendæ sunt.

Ribes Cynosbati, Michx.—*R. floridum*, L'Her.

UMBELLIFERÆ

Ziziæ species? The fruit is not sufficiently formed to be quite sure of the genus.

Chærophyllum procumbens, V. Boscii, De C.—*Pastinacca fœniculacea*, Spr. (Ferula fœniculacea, Nutt.)

Cymopterus glomeratus, De C. (Thapsia, Nutt.)—*Osmorhiza longistylis*, De C. (Urospermum, Nutt.)

ARALIACEÆ

Aralia nudicaulis, L. The root is said to be used as Radix sassaparillæ.

LORANTHACEÆ

Viscum flavescens, Pursh. De C. ♀. In nostro specimine folia ovalia, basi cuneata, distincte trinervia. An hujus loci V. verticillatum, Nutt?

CORNACEÆ

Cornus sericea, var. asperifolia, Michx.

SAMBUCACEÆ

Viburnum Lentago, L.

RUBIACEÆ

Galium dasycarpum, N. ab E. G. caule erecto ramoso ad ungulos aspero, geniculis hirtis, foliis quaternis lanceolatis obtusis trinervibus utrinque hispido-scabris, pedunculis axillaribus folio multo longioribus trichotomis in paniculam terminalem dispositis, bracteis ovalibus, fructu setis rectis densissime tecto.

In sylvis ad castellum Union aliisque in locis sylvaticis, 5 Julii.—Ser. Princ. Wied.

Differt a Galio septentrionali R. et Sch. seu Galio boreali, Pursh. caulis angulis asperis, foliis præsertim subtus et supra circa margines, setulis exiguis hispidis, fructu (immaturo saltem) densissimis setis rectis, neque apice uncinatis, candicante. Folia margine revoluta.

CAPRIFOLIACEÆ

Symphoria glomerata, Pursh. (Symphoricarpus vulgaris, De C. Michx.)

SYNANTHEREÆ

Cirsium lanceolatum, Scop.

Liatris Punctata, Hook. Fl. Bor.—Amer. I. p. 306, t. 105, De C. Prodr. V. p. 129, n. 5. Var. caule glabro. Huius loci esse videtur *Liatris resinosa*, De C. in horto Genevensi culta, semine a cl. Pourtalès ex Arcansas allato, nec. vero Nuttall.

Kuhnia Maximiliani, Sinning. (Sectio Strigia, De C.) caule herbaceo, foliis ovato-lanceolatis, inferioribus a medio grosse et inæqualiter serratis superioribus subintegerrimis sessilibusque, corymbo terminali composito ♃.

Kuhnia suaveolens, Fres. in En. Sem. horti Francofurtensis anno 1838.

Habitat in sylvis, frutetis et in collibus ad Missouri fluvium superiorem prope Fort Clark.

Differt evidenter a Kuhnia eupatorioide: foliis saltem superioribus plerisque, haud petiolatis sed basi parum angustiori sessilibus, inferioribus ovato-oblongis uno alterove dente absque ordine præditis, superioribus ovato lanceolatis lanceolatisve integerrimis, utrinque, præsertim subtus, glandulis micantibus inspersa, corymbo plurifloro magis patula, involucri foliolis inferioribus valde decrescentibus anguste linearibus laxe patulis. Corollæ albæ. Involucri foliola superiora oblongo lanceolata, nervoso striata. Antheræ inclusæ pallidæ, in plerisque syngenesicæ sed solito facilius separabiles multis etiara in tubum hinc fissum aut in binas partes divisum concretæ. Styli rami crassi, obtusi, papuloso-asperi. Pappus plumosus albus basi flavescens.

Variat foliis caulinis modo magis modo minus serratis, quandoque et subintegerrimis.

Senecio ceratophyllus, N. ab E.

S. foliis oblongis, inferioribus lyrato-pinnatipartitis superioribus pinnatipartitis petiolatis cauleque lanuginosis, laciniis acuminatis extrorsum inciso-dentatis, dentibus angustis, petiolis auriculatis amplexicaulibus, floribus umbellatis, pedunculis elongatis nudis.

On the Upper Missouri, June 13.

Nearly related to Senecio balsamitæ, but sufficiently different, as I was convinced by specimens which I received through Mr. Gray, from New York. The plant of the Missouri is much larger, 1½-2 feet high, entirely covered with loose downy hair. The lowest leaves are not entire, but lyrate and pinnatified below to the mid-rib, with a terminal lobe. The laciniæ and the terminal lobe have long, narrow, pointed teeth; the middle leaves are of the same shape; the ultimate lobe is, however, narrower, and shows the transition to the upper, entirely pinnatified leaves. The laciniæ of these upper leaves are nearly lanceolate, and have, above and below, two or three teeth, but at the middle only one or no tooth. The petiole is long, and the auricles distant from the lower laciniæ. In Senecio balsamitæ the cauline leaves are sessile; these too, have here, only blunt teeth; the receptacles are twice as large as in Senecio balsamitæ, and the scales of the involucrum are very pointed. In Senecio balsamitæ, on the contrary, they are much less pointed, and may often be designated as obtuse.

Artemisia Douglassiana, Bess. Abr. n. 39. Hook. Fl. Am. bor. p. 323. De C. Prodr. VI. p. 115, n. 118.

Erigeron sulcatus, N. ab. E. hirtus, caule sulcato corymboso-ramoso ramis foliosis unifloris, foliis lanceolato-linearibus integerrimis sessilibus, periclinii squamis hirsutissimis, ligulis angustis numerosissimis periclinio duplo longioribus (albis.) (Am. 8, Juni ♃.)

Differt ab Erigeronte pumilo, Nutt. caule fastigiatim ramoso stricto sulcato. An huius var. Pappus biserialis, seriei exterioris pilis brevibus.

Erigeron asperus, Var. caule unifloro. (Erigeron) asperum, Nutt. Gen. am. II. p. 147. De C. Prodr. VI. p. 286, n. 16.

Stenactis annua, var. obtusifolia.—Aster Novi Belgii, var. β squarrosus, N. ab E.— *Aster bellidiflorus, var. β*, N. ab E.

Aster hirsuticaulis, Lindl. in De C. Prodr. V. p. 242, n. 107. foliis conformibus lanceolato-linearibus integerrimis pericliniique foliolis ciliatis et setaceo-mucronatis pilosulis, caule pubescente recurvo a basi ramoso, ramis simplicibus patentibus, calathiis in apice ramorum confertis subspicatis (3-8), periclinii foliolis oblongo-linearibus laxiusculis apice herbaceis subrecurvis. (Aster setiger, N. ab E. in sched.)

Locus ante Asterem diffusum.

Species mucrone foliorum et squamarum periclinii setiformi (seu potius seta has partes terminante) et floribus magnitudine Bellidis in apicibus ramorum approximatis brevissime pedicellatis, spicas cylindricas in aliis autem veluti capitula exhibentibus, distincta. Radius brevis, albus.—Caulis 1-2 ped. altus, dense cano-hirtus. Folio in caule et ramis conferta, patentia, caulina 1½-2 poll. longa, 1½ lin. lata, ramea 1½ pollices longa et vix lineam lata, omnia setulis ciliata et parce pilosula, seta terminata. Rami ab infimo caule incipientes, 2½ poll. longi, apicem versus ita decrescentes, ut apex caulis racemum compositum densum angustumque exhibeat.

Aster multiflorus var. β ciliatus, N. ab E. (Gen. et sp. Ast.)

Aster rubricaulis var. β elatior, N. ab E. G. et Sp. A. Near Fort Mc Kenzie, in the prairies of the upper Missouri, 12th Sept., 1833.

Chrysopsis gossypina, De C. (Inula gossypina, Pursh.) Integumentum omnino ut in *Inula villosa*, Nutt. (Chrysopsi villosa, De C.), sed folia obtusa quandoque cum parvo mucronulo. Pappus pallide sulphureus, exteriori serie brevissima alba.

SIDERANTHUS, Fraser. (Amelli sp., *Pursh.* Starkea? *Nutt.* Aplopappi sp. *De C.*)

Calathium multiflorum, radiatum, radio uniseriali femineo, flosculis bidentulis; floribus disci 5—dentatis hermaphroditis, stigmatum cono sterili longo scabro. Clinanthii alveolæ lacero-paleaceæ. Periclinium pluriseriale, imbricatum, foliolis linearibus, setaceo-mucronatis nervo infra apicem tumente herbaceo. Achænia cuneiformi-angusta, erostria, sericeo hirta. Pappus pilosus, denticulato scaber, pluriserialis, radiolis exterioribus brevioribus. Fruticulus foliis alternis pinnatisectis, laciniis spinuloso-setigeris.

This genus is next to Aplopappus, Cass., from which it is distinguished, besides the habit, by the unequal pappus, and by the scales of the involucrum below the mucro, which are herbaceous, and marked with glandular swellings. From this last character we might be inclined to connect it with Clomenocoma, Cass.; but this genus is sufficiently distinguished by the truncated bearded branches of the style. Our genus is more nearly allied to Sommerfeltia, Less., and almost the only difference is in the fertile florets of the disk, which in the other are barren.

Sideranthus spinulosus, Fras. ex Steud. (Aplopappus? spinulosus, De C., Prodr. V., p. 347, n. 8. Starkea? pinnata, Nutt. Gen. II. p. 169. Amellus? spinulosus, Pursh. Fl. Am. septentr. II. p. 564. Torrey in Ann. Lyc. Novebor. II. p. 213, n. 223.) On the 12th of September, near Fort Mc Kenzie. Flower large, yellow.

Solidago lateriflora, var. caule simplici (Solidago fragrans, Willd.)

Achillea tomentosa, L. The North American plant differs from our European, in having a slender tall stem, shorter in florescence, and, as it seems, a pale yellow ray of the compound flower; it is perhaps a distinct species.

Brachyris Eutamiæ, Nutt., De C. Prodr. V., p. 313, n. 3. (Solidago Sarothræ, Pursh.) Radius disci altitudine; pappus radii (imperfecti) brevior. Periclinia glutinosa.

Grindelia squarrosa, R. Br. (Donia squarrosa, Pursh., Nutt.)—*Galardia bicolor v. aristata*, Nutt.

Helianthus petiolaris, Nutt. in Diar. Acad. sc. nat. Philad. a. 1821. Act. p. 115. De C. Prodr. V. p. 586, n. 6. *Var. humilis* (circiter semi-bipedalis), foliis, longe petiolatis ovatis acuminatis basi cuneatis obtuse serratis triplinerviis asperis hispidisque, pedunculo terminali solitario elongato gracili hirsuto, periclinio a folio oblongo acuto bracteato.

Obeliscaria columnaris, De C. Prodr. V., p. 559, n. 2. (Rudbeckia columnaris, Pursh., Fraser).

Iva, anthyifolia, Nutt.? Periclinium pentaphyllum, foliolis ovatis ciliatis. Flosculi feminei, 2-3, squama tenui truncata suffulti; flosculus minimus, tubulosus, truncatus; ovarium ovale, compressum, pubescens, pappo tubuloso coronatum. Flosculi ♂ plurimi, cylindrici, decem-sulcati, glandulosi, subpedicellati, pistilli nullo vestigio. Antheræ inclusæ, filamentis brevissimis. An proprii generis?—*Iva axillaris*, Pursh. Probably a new species of Lactuca or Prenanthes; but the specimen is imperfect.

Jamesia, N. ab E. (Prenanthis species dubiæ Torr. in Ann. Lyc. Noveborac. II., p. 210.)

Achænium erostre, pentagonum, sessile. Pappus uniserialis, plumosus. Clinanthium nudum, scrobiculatum. Priclinium pauciflorum, cylindricum, foliolis 5-6, majoribus subæqualibus, 3-4 minoribus inæqualibus ad basin veluti canaliculatis. Flosculi rosei 5-6.

Proximum genus Podospermo, sed differt achæniis haud stipitatis. A Scorzoneris differt habitu. Herbæ ramosæ, foliis angustis integris aut pinnatifidis, ramis uni-plurifloris.

Jamesia pauciflora, nob. (Prenanthes? pauciflora, Torrey, l. c.) Caule valde ramoso, foliis glabris lineari-lanceolatis sinuato-pinnatifidis, laciniis angustis integerrimis, ramis elongatis unifloris. Achænia glabra, pallida, longitudine pappi, obtuse pentagona, lateribus linea media notatis transversim subtorosis. Area baseos callo annulari ambitus achenii cincta.

Sonchus Ludovicianus, Nutt. (Lactuca, De C.)? Folia lanceolata, runcinata, rarissime autem denticulata.

Troximon marginatum, Nutt.

APOCYNEÆ

Apocynum hypericifolium, Pursh.

Asclepias speciosa, Torr. James in Ann. Lyc. Noveborac. II., p. 218, n. 260.

ERICACEÆ

Arbutus Uva ursi, L.

HYDROPHYLLEÆ

Ellisia Nyctelea, L.

POLEMONIACEÆ

Phlox pilosa, L.

CONVOLVULACEÆ

Calystegia Maximilianea, N. ab E. volubilis, glabra, foliis hastato-sagittatis obtusis submucronatis, pedunculis teretibus folium subæquantibus, bracteis ovali-oblongis obtusis ciliolatis calyce longioribus; calycis laciniis breviacutatis.

Species calystegiæ sepium similis, sed notis indicatis abunde diversa. Folia minora sunt, flores ejusdem fere magnitudinis (albi?) Calyx longitudine quartæ partis corollæ. Tota planta glabra, solis bracteis lanuginoso-ciliatis. Folia inferiora, ambitu ovato apice obtusissima; superiora magis triangularia, obtusiuscula cum mucronulo.

BORRAGINEÆ

Echinospermum Lappula, Lehm.

Echinospermum strictum, N. ab E. E. caule stricto superne stricte ramoso foliisque lanceolatis callosis et patenti-pilosis, corollæ tubo calyce breviori, glochidibus nucum brevibus marginalibus serie simplici dispositis. ☉ (Rochelia nov. sp., Nutt. Mscp. Torr. in Ann. Lyc. Noveborac. II., p. 226, n. 300?).

This species may be easily distinguished by the characters indicated, from E. lappula and patulum, Lehm.

Myosotis glomerata, Nutt. (Cynoglossum glomeratum, Pursh. Suppl.) Intermediate between Anchusa and Myosotis.

Lithospermum denticulatum, Lehm. (Pulmonaria Sibirica, Pursh. nec. Lin.) Stylus in nostris inclusus nec exsertus, reliqua congruunt. Limbus longitudine est tubi, qui Lithospermo pulchro est brevior.

Batschia longiflora, Pers.—*B. canescens*, Michx. (Anchuso Virginica, Lin.)

Both plants contain in the bark of their roots the same red dye as the officinal roots of the Alcanna tinctoria.

Pulmonaria Virginica, L.

RHINANTHACEÆ

Pentstemon grandiflorum, Nutt. (P. Bradburnii, Pursh.) Stamen sterile fert antheram parvam bilobam.

Pentstemon cristatum, Nutt. (P. erianthera, Pursh.)

Pentstemon viscidulum, N. ab. E. herbaceus, subtillissime subsquamuloso-pubescens, foliis lanceolatis amplexicaulibus inferioribus denticulatis, pedunculis fasciculatis, folia superiora superantibus, calycibus acuminatis corollisque glanduloso-pubescentibus fauce imberbi, filamento sterili ab apice ad medium aureo-barbato.

This plant is near to Pentstemon erianthera, but differs from that, and from the other species with which I am acquainted, by the glutinous pubescence of the flowers. These are wide, infundibuliform, and seem to have been of a dark red colour. My specimen is about a span high. This species has, perhaps, been already described among species of Pentstemon recently made known; I have not, however, been able to find any corresponding with it where I looked for it.

Pentstemon lævigatum, Nutt.

Euchroma grandiflora, Nutt. Torr. Ann. Lyc. Noveborac. II. p. 230. (Castilleja sessiliflora, Pursh.)

SCROPHULARINÆ

Scrophularia lanceolata, Pursh. A broad-leaved form, with elliptical leaves, but to be known by their acuminated base, and by the deep unequal serratures, though almost too nearly allied to Scrophularia Marylandica.

LABIATÆ

Monarda mollis, Willd.

Mentha arvensis, var. a sativa, Beth. M. sativa, Lin. Specimen nostrum omnino ad hanc speciem pertinet minimeque ad Mentham Canadensem, Lin. Pili caulis breves sunt et reversi, folia vere ovalia et ovali-oblonga, utrinque glabriuscula nec basi neque apice multum attenuata, licet acuta. This species is new in the American Flora.

Stachys palustris var. Caule prælongo simplicissimo, foliis brevioribus latiusculis. I find no mention of Stachys palustris in the American botanists.

VERBENACEÆ

Verbena Aubletia, L.?—*V. bracteosa*, Michx.

PRIMULACEÆ

Lysimachia ciliata, L.

PLANTAGINEÆ

Plantago cordata, Lam. (Pl. Kentuckensis, Michx.)—*P. pusilla*, Nutt.

OSYRIDEÆ

Comandra umbellata, Nutt. (Thesium umbellatum, Willd.) It differs from Santalum only by the parts of the flowers being quinary, whereas they are in fours or quaternary in Thesium; but the glandular scales between the stamina are the same. The ovules are erect.

LAURINÆ

Laurus Benzoin, L.—*L. Diospyros*, L. (Sassafras Diospyros, N. v. E.)

ELÆAGNEÆ

Shepherdia argentea, Nutt.

CHENOPODIACEÆ

Kochia dioica, Nutt. Flores ♂ glomerati; glomeruli pedunculati, axillares, in apice caulis nudi. Bractea infra glomerulum una, angusta. Perianthium parvum, pedicellatum, campanulatum, quinquefidum, membranaceum, laciniis ad basin extus lobulo herbaceo appendiculatis. Stamina quinque, rudimento exiguo pistilli inserta; filamenta filiformia; antheræ infra medium adfixæ, oblongæ, bilocellatæ, dehiscendo quadricornes. Femina ignota.— Planta annua, humilis, glabra. Caulis compressus, dichotomus. Folia alterna, lanceolata, obtusa, sessilia, succulenta, punctata, glauca, subpapillosa, glabra.

Variat: Simplicissima, 1-3 poll. longa, capitulo solitario terminali. An Cyclolepidi Generi Moqu. Tandon, aut Villemetiæ adscribenda?

POLYGONEÆ

Polygonum coccineum β *terrestre*, Michx. (Polygoni amphibii β terrestris Var. Meissn.)

Rumex verticillatus, Willd.—R. venosus, Pursh.

Eriogonum sericeum, Pursh. (Eriog. flavum, Fraser.)

Eriogonum *multiceps*, N. ab E. albo-tomentosum, caule suffruticoso multicipiti, pedunculo terminali simplici, involucris (florum fasciculis) capitatis, capitulo subinvolucrato, calycis laciniis ovatis ciliatis, foliis radicalibus (surculorum inferis) lanceolatis utrinque albo-tomentosis.

Distinctissima species. Differt ab Eriogono sericeo, Pursh. seu Eriog. flavo, Fras.: caule ad basin multifido, ramis dense foliosis, pedunculo 2-3 poll. longo tomentoso nudo terminatis, foliis angustioribus involucris sessilibus calycinis laciniis ovatis, ab Eriog. pauciflora: floribus multo minoribus intra involucrum pedicellatis nec sessilibus. An error in verbis Purshii, ut loco "floribus" legendum sit "involucris" aut "fasciculis?"

EUPHORBIACEÆ

Euphorbia maculata, L.—E. *marginata*, Pursh. (nec Kunth.)

URTICEÆ

SARCOBATUS. Flores amentacei. Amentum androgynum, superne masculum. Squamæ masculæ peltatæ, orbiculares, repando-lobatæ, contiguo-imbricatæ, e centro pedicellatæ, tetrandræ. Antheræ oblongæ, subtetragonæ, sessiles, bilocellatæ rima laterali dehiscentes. Squamæ feminæ subcordatæ, supra basin adfixæ. Pistillum singulum; ovarium axi amenti adpressum, ovatum, depressum, inferne strigoso-sericeum, vertice glabrum (an inferne cum calyce, seu urceolo, concretum?); stigmata duo, sessilia, divergentia, subulata, papilloso-scabra. Fructus ignotus.

Sarcobatus Maximiliani, (Pulpy Thorn, Lewis and Clarke Iter.)

Frutex pedalis et altior, ramosissimus, ramis plerisque geminis confertis subtriquetris glabris pallidis, epidermide vetusta rimosa. Cicatrices foliorum tumentes, unde rami tuberculati et vetustiores quidem hinc inde quasi annulatim diffracti. Folia ½-¾, poll., longa, ¾, lin. lata, trigono-semicylindrica, linearia, obtusa, sessilia, integerrima, carnosa, glauca glabra, siccando caduca, nervo medio (in siccis) supra et infra prominulo. Amenta in ramulis terminalia, sessilia, ½ poll, circiter longa, lutescentia, a basi ad medium feminea, superne mascula. Axis inter flosculos femineos dense tomentosus, subtrigonus et a casu squamarum infra pistillum singulum cicatrice lunata præditus, inter flores masculos glaber, tuberculatus, tuberculis quaternatim digestis sedem antherarum quaternarum, singulæ squamæ stipitem singentium, prodentibus. Limbus squamæ masculæ (membranaceæ omnino peltatatæ et indusium Aspidii cujusdam longius pedicellati referentis) repando 5-6 lobus. Squamæ femineæ diverg. ⅜ positæ sunt.

In regione Mississippi fluvii superiori tractus latos investit hic frutex.

This shrub has some similarity with Ceratiola ericoides, and may have been overlooked on that account. As we are still unacquainted with the fruit, the place of the genus in the natural system cannot be positively assigned, and it is possible that it may be connected with the Euphorbiaceæ of the tribe Hippomaneæ.

ARTOCARPEÆ

Morus rubra, W.

SALICINÆ

Salix longifolia. Torrey in Ann. Lyc. Noveborac. II., p. 248. (An Mühlenb.?) Var. sericans, foliis junioribus undique, adultioribus subtus lanuginoso-sericeis canescentibus. Flores amenti masculi inferiores triandri. Squamæ acutiusculæ. Capsulæ pedicellatæ. Fol. 1½-3 poll. longa, 1½-2 lin. lata, magis minusve denticulata quandoque fere integerrima. An distincta spec.? ♂

Salix Houstoniana, Pursh? With rose willow. (An S. longifoliæ var.?)

Salix.... Probably a new species.

Salix.... Probably the form of the male plant of Salix lucida, Willd. ♂ Tetrandrous; the stamina are very hairy at the bottom. Branches, yellow-green.

Salix lucida, Willd. ♀ Agrees with the above-mentioned male plant, and belongs to the same species.

Populus angulata, Willd.

AMENTACEÆ

Quercus imbricaria, Michx. Rather this, probably, than the cinerea, for it seems not to be evergreen.

Quercus alba, W.—*Q. castanea*, Mühl. (Fructus edules).—*Q. obtusiloba*, Michx.—*Q. coccinea*, Michx.

Carpinus Americana, L.

CONIFERÆ

Pinus flexilis, James in Ann. Lyc. Noveborac. II. p. 249, n. 428.

Juniperus barbadensis, Lin. This species probably coincides with J. Sabina of our gardens. J. Hermanni, too, probably belongs to this place.

Juniperus communis, L.

Juniperus repens, Nutt. (J. prostrata horti nostri colore intense viridi nec glauco et odore multo debiliori recidit. Fr. N. ab E).—*Juniperus Virginiana*, L.

JUNCEÆ

Juncus setaceus, Rostk.

SMILACINÆ

Smilax: caule inermi angulato, foliis cordato-ovatis acutis septemnerviis, pedunculo communi umbellæ (♂) petiolum subæquante.

An *Smilacis herbacei* varietas? Differt solummodo brevitate pedunculi, Fr. N. ab E.

Smilacina racemosa, Desf.

Uvularia grandiflora, Sm. } on the Lower
} Missouri.
Trillium recurvatum, Beck. }

LILIACEÆ

Allium reticulatum, Fraser. (All. angulosum, Pursh. Probably also Allium striatum, Torr. in Ann. Lyc. Noveborac. II. p. 251, n. 441, but not Don.)

Erythronium albidum, Nutt.

BROMELIACEÆ

Tillandsia usneoides, Lin.

COMMELINEÆ

Tradescantia Virginica, Lin.

IRIDEÆ

Sisyrinchium anceps, Lam.

CYPERACEÆ

Scirpus Duvalii, Hoppe. Scirpus acutus, Mühlenb. Involucri folium erectum in hoc convexum nec carinatum. Squamæ spiculæ emarginatæ, mucronatæ, ciliatæ. Stylus bifidus. Maculæ culmi fungi parasitici primordia sunt.

Scirpus robustus var. spiculis glomerato-capitatis.

Carex Mühlenbergii, Schkuhr.—*C. longirostris*, Torrey.—*C. pellita*, Mühlenb. Var. β (Schkuhr. t. Nun. f. 150).—*C. acuta*, Lin.

Uncinia filifolia. (Carex filifolia, Nuttall.) Rare. Torrey and Schweinitz did not see it with ripe fruit.

GRAMINEÆ

Diagraphis arundinacea, P. de B.

Hierochloa fragrans, Kunth. In nostro specimine glumæ flosculos adæquant; flosculi masculi circa apicem pubescentes.

Stipa capillata, Lin.

Sesleria dactyloides, Nutt. Deserves to form a distinct species, which belongs to the Chlorideæ, and from the habit should be placed next to Chondrosium. Two peduncles mostly come out of the upper sheath; some leaves are biennial. The unilateral spikes are hardly half an inch long, oval, and often tinged with violet on the back. The lower valve of the calyx turned to the rhachis is more than twice as small as the upper. I always found only two flowers; the upper one stalked; both similarly formed, with triple-nerved lower valve, which terminates in a short point; the upper valve is ciliated. The scales are smooth, nearly quadrate, obtusely crenated. Three stamina with yellow anthers. In many flowers the pistil is entirely wanting, and the plant is perhaps diœcious.

Our Sesleria may be compared, though only remotely, with S. disticha.

Chondrosium oligostachyum, N. ab E. spica solitaria binisve rectiusculis, spiculis subtrifloris, flosculis binis superioribus stipitatis sterilibus, inferiori sessili villoso, supremo cucullato mutico univalvi, secundo parvo bivalvi setis tribus ad basin stipato, culmo geniculato simpliciæ lævi, foliis linearibus, ore vaginarum puberulo.

Atheropogon oligostachyus, Nutt. Gen. et Spec. I. p. 78; Torr. in. Ann. Lyc. Noveborac. II. p. 254, n. 476.

Eutriana oligostachya, Kunth. En. I. p. 282, n. 12.

Cum Chondrosiis magis quam cum Eutrianis congruit, neque spicæ omnino rectæ. Rhachis dorso convexa. Spicæ circiter pollicares, vel singula adjecto mucronulo, vel duæ et tum una terminalis. Spiculæ arcte imbricatæ. Glumæ lanceolatæ, glabræ aut pilosulæ, uninerves, inferior duplo minor. Flosculi fertilis valvula inferior lanceolata ex utroque latere medio setam promit valvula paulo breviorem, non ex ipso margine provenientem sed ex nervo laterali; infra apicem bidentem valvulæ seta brevis et rigida. Pedicellus flosculorum sterilium infra flosculos barba annulari cinctus. Flosculus horum inferior parvus, ovalis, obtusus, muticus, glaber, setis ad basin una laterali et una utriusque lateris rectis æqualibus linea paulo longioribus divergentibus. Tertii flosculi valvula sursum cucullata, truncata, mutica.—Culmus 1½-1 ped. longus, teres, glaber ad genicula infractus. Vaginæ internodiis breviores. Ligula brevissima, denticulata. Folia 2-1 poll. longa, lin. 1 lata, linearia, acuminata, subtus convexa, supra concava, lævia, glauca, glabra, circa basin subtilissime puberula.

Spartina patens, Mühlenb. spicis (4-8) alternatim secundis brevibus adpressis, rhachi hispidula, glumis dorso setoso-hirsutis, superiori flosculum æquante brevi-mucronata, inferiori duplo minore setaceo-acuminata foliis culmo brevioribus patentibus in apicem fere filiformem attenuatis culmoque glabris.

Spartina patens, Mühlenb. Descr. n. 6, p. 55; Schult. Mant. Syst. Veg. II. p. 150, n. 6, a. Kunth. En. 1, p. 279, n. 12.—Dactylis patens, Act. Hort. Kew. ed. 2, p. 160; R. et Sch. S. Veg. II., p. 632, n. 19.—Trachynotia patens, Poir. Enc. meth. Suppl. II. p. 443.

Species distinctissima foliis arcu patentibus 5-7 poll, longis, ad basin 2 lin. latis, in apicem filiformem attenuatis subconvolutis, inferioribus disticho-approximatis, superioribus distantibus.—Culmus 1-1½ pedes altus, in nostris tortus. Spicæ partiales subpollicares; arcte contiguæ. Spiculæ haud pedicellatæ sed callo brevi insertæ, oblongæ, 3 lin. longæ. Gluma superior altero latere ad carinam trinervis, ex apice obtuso brevissime mucronulata, secundum carinam setis patulis mollibus densis ciliata; inferior subbinervis, apice attenuata, carina laxius ciliata, plus duplo brevior. Valvulæ obtusæ, inferior paulo brevior, carina infra apicem ciliata. Antheræ violaceæ.

Brizopyrum spicatum.

(Uniola stricta, Torr. in Ann. Lyc. Noveborac. Sept. 1824, p. 155).—Br. siculum, β Americanum LK.—Uniola spicata, Lin. Festuca distichophylla, Pursh.

Arundinaria macrosperma, Michx.

Agropyrum repens, P. de B. Var. ε Leersianum R. et Sch. Spiculis inferioribus geminis.—Specimina nostra singularia, alta, glauca. Folia radicalia angustissima, filiformia. Spiculæ 6-8 floræ, pubescentes, glaucæ. Glumarum aristæ 1-2 lin., valvularum lin. 4-5 longæ, patentes. Gluma inferior 3— superior 5-nervis.

Elymus striatus, Willd.—*Hordeum jubatum*, Ait.

FILICES

Adiantum pedatum, Willd.

EQUISETACEÆ

Equisetum arvense, L.—*E. hyemale*, L.

RHIZOSPERMÆ

Azolla Caroliniana, Willd.

MUSCI FRONDOSI

Mnium (Bryum) ciliare, Greville in Annals of the Lyc. of New York. 1825, IX. p. 273, t. 23. Our specimens are distinguished by the leaves being generally entire to the middle, in which they approximate to those of Mn. cuspidatum; but they are much narrower, cuneiform below, like those of Mn. affine. I always saw the Setæ single, much bent, and tortuous.

Dicranum purpurascens, Hedw. (Ceratodon purpureus γ purpurascens, Brid.) Most probably; but the fruit is not quite formed.

Neckera viticulosa. In some particulars approximates to Neckera minor; but the leaves are always inclined. A beautiful yellow.

Cryphæa inundata: caule pendulo laxe pinnatim-ramoso ramulis apice incurvis, foliis distantibus oblongo-lanceolatis carinatis nervo crasso excurrente, inferioribus arete complicatis obliquis, capsulis ovalibus heteromallis subsessilibus perichætio longissimo immersis, dentibus peristomii interioris longis persistentibus coloratis apice incurvis.

In ramis fruticum inundatis ad flumina Wabash, Fox and Black Rivers. Decembre cum fructu maturo.

Differs from Chryphæa heteromalla, not only by the long, slender stems, and the thick projecting nerve of the leaves, but most especially by the stiff red ciliæ of the inner peristome, which almost exceed the exterior ones in length, and are incurved inwards at the point. The lower cauline leaves are so broken that the two halves touch with their upper surface, and the leaf acquires almost an ensiform appearance. The leaves of the involucrum are quite nerveless. The capsule is yellow. I did not see the operculum and the hood.

LICHENES

Usnea hirta, Ach.—*Parmelia tiliacea*, Ach.

FUNGI

Polyporus velutinus, Fr., pileo supra sordide albo subfuligineo.—*Exidia auricula Judæ*, Fr. Syst. Myc.

Our specimen is distinguished by its size and remarkably pale colour.

IX. CATALOGUE OF BIRDS OBSERVED IN THE MONTHS OF NOVEMBER, DECEMBER, JANUARY, AND FEBRUARY AT THE MOUTH OF THE WABASH

Winter Residents:

1. Cathartes Aura septentr.
2. Aquila leucocephala.
3. "
4. " Haliaëtus amer.
5. Falco borealis.
6. " uliginosus Bon.
7. " Sparverius.
8. Strix asio.
9. " nebulosa.
10. Corvus americanus Aud.
11. Garrulus cristatus.
12. Psittacus carolinensis.
13. Picus pileatus.
14. " auratus.
15. " carolinus.
16. " varius.
17. " villosus.
18. " pubescens.
19. " erythrocephalus.
20. Sitta carolinensis.
21. Certhia familiaris amer.
22. Alcedo Alcyon.
23. Sturnella ludoviciana Bon.
24. Fringilla cardinalis.

25.   " hyemalis.

26.   Fringilla canadensis.

27.   " pennsylvanica.

28.   " melodia.

29.   " tristis.

30.   Parus bicolor.

31.   " atricapillus.

32.   Muscicapa coronata.

33.   Sialia Wilsoni Sw.

34.   Regulus cristatus.

35.   Troglod. ludovicianus.

36.   " hyemalis.

37.   Columba carolinensis.

38.   Meleagris Gallopavo.

39.   Tetrao umbellus.

40.   " Cupido.

41.   Perdix virginiana.

42.   Ardea herodias.

43.   Anser canadensis.

44.   " bernicla.

45.   Anas Boschas fera.

46.   " clangula amer.

47.   Mergus Merganser.

48.   " serrator.

49.   " cucullatus.

50.   Falco?

In November the following still occurred:

1. Quiscalus ferrugineus (a few). 2. Fulica americana (migrating). 3. Grus canadensis. 4. Podiceps carolin. (migrating). 5. Anas sponsa

(in large numbers). 6. Anas crecca, querquedula, discors, and other species. 7. Fringilla erythrophthalma.

In December a few of the following:

Fringilla erythrophthalma.

In the second half of January:

Columba migratoria. (This was due to the mildness of the winter.)

In February, returned:

Beginning:

1. Anas sponsa. 2. Anas rufitorques. 3. Anas crecca. 4. Anas acuta. 5. Icterus phöniceus.

Middle and end:

6. Falcones. 7. Fringilla erythrophthalma. 8. Scolopax. 9. Turdus migratorius. 10. Grus canadensis (flight of cranes). 11. Quiscalus versic. 12. Quiscalus ferrugineus.

In the first part of March the following appeared in the region around Harmony:

1. Anser albifrons. 2. Anser canadensis. 3. Quisc. ferrugineus. 4. Quisc. versicolor. 5. Icterus phoeniceus. 6. Larus? (fourth of March seen on the Wabash). 7. Grus canadensis (on the fifth of March Anser canadensis also appeared). 8. Fringilla purpurea (on the tenth of March). 9. Scolopax. 10. Fringa? 11. Hirundo? (on the fourteenth of March the first flight of swallows occurred).

Buy Books Online from
www.Booksophile.com

Explore our collection of books written in various languages and uncommon topics from different parts of the world, including history, art and culture, poems, autobiography and bibliographies, cooking, action & adventure, world war, fiction, science, and law.

Add to your bookshelf or gift to another lover of books - first editions of some of the most celebrated books ever published. From classic literature to bestsellers, you will find many first editions that were presumed to be out-of-print.

Free shipping globally for orders worth US$ 100.00.

Use code "Shop_10" to avail additional 10% on first order.

Visit today
www.booksophile.com

CPSIA information can be obtained
at www.ICGtesting.com
Printed in the USA
LVHW031159230323
742375LV00002B/268